The Evolution of the French Novel

1641–1782

THE EVOLUTION

OF THE

French Novel

1641-1782

ENGLISH SHOWALTER, JR.

PRINCETON UNIVERSITY
PRESS

This book has been composed in Linotype Granjon

Printed in the United States of America
by Princeton University Press
Princeton, New Jersey

Preface

Any subject as elusive as evolutionary processes in the novel is bound to be controversial. I am certain that many readers will be unconvinced by one or another of my arguments, and others will disagree with my emphases, and wonder why I have neglected their favorite author. No single work could explore fully the vast and amorphous field of French fiction in the seventeenth and eighteenth centuries, but I believe that I have covered enough to show what I wanted to show: the basic mechanism underlying the evolutionary development of realistic techniques in fiction. I will welcome the criticism of those who disagree; the study of literature will always be a matter of judgment and interpretation, not rigorous logical proof, and our understanding can be deepened as much by an intelligent debate as by a flawless demonstration. It is in this spirit that I have taken issue with some of my predecessors, while admiring their work.

The problems of critical methodology I have encountered, and the solutions I have adopted, are discussed in the Introduction. There are also a few problems of presentation. After some hesitation, I have decided not to include a formal bibliography. Full bibliographical information on most works is supplied at the first citation in a footnote; by using the index, readers can trace back any author or title that reappears later on. The exceptions are novels published in French from 1700 to 1750. Since my own bibliography is derived essentially from S. Paul Jones's *A List of French Prose Fiction 1700-1750,* it seemed wasteful to give more than the author's last name, the short title, and the date of first publication. Needless to say, I have supplied fuller information whenever I quoted from a later edition or found Jones in error. So far as I can tell, the only disadvantage of this procedure is that readers have no way of knowing what I read without quoting from it, that is, of knowing exactly how extensive my information is. That seemed to me a small price to pay for the elimination of a list that would have run to at least five hundred

Preface

items, without having any pretensions to completeness or originality.

Some readers will no doubt wish that I had modernized the spelling and punctuation in quotations, all of which are given exactly as I found them. While I admit that this method is largely a matter of personal preference, it seemed to me that several factors argued in favor of a literal transcription: many modern editions reproduce in whole or in part the archaic forms, and I would be reluctant to tamper with the text supplied by Antoine Adam or Frédéric Deloffre; a consistent style of modernization would be hard to devise and apply, with so wide a range of authors and texts; finally, the chances of error or misreading are minimized by strict fidelity to the original.

This study has taken me several years to bring to its final form, and in that time I have incurred many debts of gratitude for assistance, advice, and encouragement. I would like to take this occasion to thank particularly Princeton University and the American Council of Learned Societies for financial aid enabling me to work in Europe for a summer; my students, both graduate and undergraduate, whose ideas and questions have been extremely helpful to me over the years; and my colleagues, especially Albert Sonnenfeld and Karl Uitti, who read the manuscript and gave me useful criticism and support.

Finally, I would like to dedicate this study to Professor Georges May of Yale University. It is to him that I owe my original enthusiasm for the eighteenth-century French novel, and his continued guidance and encouragement have helped me on many occasions since then. Despite his duties as Dean of Yale College, he found time to read the manuscript of this work and make many constructive comments on it. One of my colleagues who also read it remarked that my method and style resemble Georges May's; nothing would please me more than for others to form the same opinion.

English Showalter, Jr.

Princeton, July 1971

vi

Contents

The Evolution of the French Novel

1641–1782

Introduction

Everyone seems to be agreed that the early years of the eighteenth century were crucial for the novel, but there is much debate about what happened then, and how it happened. Many literary historians contend that the novel was born at this time, the offspring of the right intellectual climate, a bourgeois social system, and individual genius, brought together by chance or by historical determinants.[1] Those who hold to this view usually read English better than other languages, and they have some difficulty explaining away the large body of French and Spanish fiction of the seventeenth century.[2] A Francophone scholar is much more disposed to see a continuous evolution in fiction, with varying rates of change.

Such is my own belief; and in denying that Defoe, or Richardson, or Fielding, was the first novelist, I do not wish to nominate anyone else for the title, which seems to me devoid of meaning. It is plain that Richardson, Fielding, Defoe, Challe, Mme de Lafayette, and Cervantes wrote within certain traditions at the same time they made great original contributions to an emerging genre, now identified as "the novel." In order to pinpoint its first appearance, others have attempted to formulate a precise definition of "novel"; I will not. Most of the works I shall discuss share elements that are undeniably novelistic with others that come from the romance tradition. As tendencies, or as critical rather than historical terms, novel and romance may be defined and contrasted with no difficulty. The novel tends to be believable, to deal with ordinary people in familiar settings, to be contemporary or nearly so, to show how things really are. The romance tends

[1] See for example Ian Watt, *The Rise of the Novel* (1957; rpt. Berkeley and Los Angeles: Univ. of California Press, 1965), p. 9; or Walter Ernest Allen, *The English Novel* (1954; rpt. New York: Dutton, 1958), p. 4.

[2] See for example Watt, *The Rise of the Novel*, p. 30; or Arnold Kettle, *An Introduction to the English Novel*, Harper Torchbooks (1951; rpt. New York: Harper and Row, 1960), Vol. I, p. 30.

Introduction

to appeal to the imagination, to deal with archetypal or allegorical or idealized characters, to show them in remote settings, to show how things might be.

Even as critical categories, however, such enumerations make the two genres seem more opposite than they are. The novel's believability depends on the imagination quite as much as the romance's appeal to fantasy or idealism. The characteristics of neither genre appear pure in most cases, of whatever date; many romance heroes have realistic ambiguity about them, while many novel heroes approach the status of type. The same can be said of the settings, and it is perhaps more the amount of detail, than the site, that distinguishes the novel from the romance. Finally, the difference between how things are and how they might be is very tenuous, when in both cases the "things" themselves are fictional. The serious romancer sought to show reality in its essence, stripped of its transient and irrelevant circumstances; the novelist came to feel that the only way to approach essential reality was by way of the circumstances. But in no single element of their respective attitudes was there a clean break between the novelist and the romancer, and during the centuries of evolution the different elements frequently progressed at different speeds, and indeed often regressed temporarily.

French scholars have seemed less interested in a general definition of the novel; for them, a more common approach has been to take some recent classic—by Zola or George Sand or Balzac—as the definitive form of the novel, and then trace its most noticeable features in a direct line all the way back to Furetière, Scarron, Sorel, Rabelais, and the tale-tellers of the Middle Ages.[3] I do not believe that this gives any truer a picture of the situation in the early eighteenth century. Evolution goes forward, not backward, and none of the early novelists had foreknowledge of what would happen

[3] See for example André Le Breton, *Le Roman au XVIIIe Siècle* (Paris: Société Française d'Imprimerie et de Librairie, 1898); or Frederick Charles Green, "Realism in the French Novel in the First Half of the XVIIIth Century," *MLN*, 38 (1923), 321-29, and "Further Evidence of Realism in the French Novel of the XVIIIth Century," *MLN*, 40 (1925), 257-70.

next. Although this method preserves the sense of continuity, which is very real in some areas, it has also led to some anachronistic misinterpretations, as I shall show in discussing comic fiction and the problems of the narrator.

It is easier to comprehend how the genre emerged if we place ourselves in the position of a writer in about 1700. He did not know, except perhaps in an intuitive sort of way, that the bourgeoisie were rising or that the European mind had just undergone a fearful crisis. What he did know was that certain works—*La Princesse de Clèves, Le Roman comique, Don Quixote*, and *Hippolyte, comte de Duglas*, for instance— had been successful. If he was more than a hack, he had something that he wanted to communicate to his readers. Often, the "message" had a conscious formulation, which modern readers find woefully inadequate to the actual achievement. For example, Cervantes evidently did more than ridicule the chivalric romances, and Richardson did something other than preach sentimental virtue. Each author then brought to the moment of composition a more or less clearly defined purpose, a literary background made up of his readings, a natural gift for observing and rendering in words the experiences chance had provided him, and a literary situation constituted in part by what he expected his public to want and in part by what they actually did want. The potential diversity of the product was enormous, and the actual product realized much of that potential. Just to list the various forms of fiction at this era gives some idea: letters, memoirs, histories, epics, chronicles, plays, poems, travel accounts, satires, folk tales—the novel tried to incorporate them all.

The evolutionary analogy describes quite well how progress emerged from such chaos. Given the literary situation, ranging from the tastes of potential readers to the mechanics of publishing, certain elements had greater fitness for survival than others. Whenever such an element occurred, it naturally seemed outstandingly successful, and was therefore imitated by subsequent writers, most of whom added nothing to it, but a few of whom perhaps advanced the genre one more evolu-

5

tionary step by some new idea or device. During these pre-
historic days, many offshoots of the original genre were
headed for extinction; the gigantic romances of the seventeenth century resemble dinosaurs in more ways than one. At
the same time, the early ancestors of the modern novel were
toiling away in obscurity, profiting from their insignificance
to adapt better and faster to new conditions.

It would be a monumental undertaking to give a full account of the evolution, even for a short period; indeed, it is
probably impossible, for many of the relevant factors seem
to be unknowable with present means of research and analysis. In trying nonetheless to respect what I consider to be the
reality of the situation, I have devised a combination of
methods, some of which, without being startlingly original,
have never been applied to the subject before. I have singled
out for intensive study the rather brief span from 1700 to
1720, generally regarded as a critical moment in European
intellectual history. Although the novel did not figure promi-
nently in this crisis, a significant redirection seems to have
begun then, evidenced in part by the first works of several
important novelists, notably Challe, Lesage, and Marivaux.
Moreover, these two decades fall in the middle of the period
I am studying, which coincides roughly with the age of
French Classicism, and this central position seemed a promising place to examine a genre actively changing and adjusting
to the various conflicting forces that characterize the period.
Finally, the early eighteenth century has the incidental advantage that a reasonably complete and reliable bibliography
exists. Thus I can say with some assurance that I have read
or examined more than three-fourths of all the fiction published in French between 1700 and 1720, thereby approximating the experience of a reader or writer of that period; and
while any analysis must organize and simplify, I have tried
never to lose sight of the complex and confused totality. Of
course, the works of those twenty years do not make sense unless they are compared to the works that preceded and followed; I have not isolated those years from the others, but

merely used them to gain knowledge of the complete situation at what I consider a critical moment.

The result of this method is to some degree a demolition. It is apparent that, despite an ample quantity of writing on the subject, no clear and useful definitions of any of the sub-genres of fiction had been widely accepted; it is equally clear that there was no significant agreement among novelists or critics about the purposes of fiction or its relation to reality. One can find almost any point of view represented, and some statements sound impressively forward-looking; but as often as not, the same author can be quoted in support of an exactly opposite argument. Sometimes this confusion can be ascribed to vagueness in terminology, but not always; in many cases, the authors of 1700 apparently perceived no inconsistency in places where we do. In any event, it seems clear that one cannot profitably trace the early evolution of the genre through self-conscious changes in the critical perceptions of its nature and functions.

Progress, slow and irregular as it was, was going on inside the novels. Second, then, a method had to be found to study the evolution of techniques within the works. Since we have hindsight, we know that in the long run fiction was becoming more realistic, that is, more and more preoccupied with elements from the world in which the writers and readers lived, presented so as to convince readers that they were real, or at least that they could very well be real. But even Ian Watt, whose *The Rise of the Novel* is the best study of the early novel's relation to reality, still does not offer much more than his own subjective impressions of what is "real" in a novel. In order to discuss the techniques by which reality is rendered in a novel, one must arrive at a useful definition of reality. I have sought a solution in taking five elements common to almost all human existence and to almost all novels, and susceptible furthermore of fairly precise measurement or definition. These elements are chronology, geography, money, names, and the narrator. Each belongs to a systematic order of existence, such that it can be tested for consistency within a work of fiction and also for compatibility with the world outside the fiction. By tracing the treatments of these five elements from the mid seventeenth to the late eighteenth century, including the very broad sample from the two decades in the middle of the period, I have been able to show in part *how* romances became novels. The same analysis also leads to significant insight into the reasons *why* the romance tended toward the novel, and why it tended toward the particular forms that it assumed in the eighteenth century.

This study of techniques must of necessity give a very partial and fragmented view of any given work; the conditions of verifiability exclude the most interesting parts of a novel, such as plot and character. I have therefore adopted yet a third, very traditional method to supplement the study of techniques and compensate for its limitations, and have devoted many pages to the analysis of one novel, Robert Challe's *Les Illustres Françoises*, first published in 1713. It offers several peculiar advantages. First, it has been undeservedly neglected for two hundred and fifty years. In the past decade, several French scholars, notably Frédéric Deloffre, have rescued it from oblivion; but it remains almost totally unknown in the English-speaking world. Second, Challe left exceptionally good clues to what his literary formation had been; in particular, his links to earlier fiction writers can be fairly easily determined. Third, his influence on later writers, or at least his anticipation of them, was significant. Prévost, Marivaux, and Richardson all appear to have borrowed from Challe, if not directly, at least in the sense that Challe prepared the public for them. In other words, it is uncommonly easy to position this work in the continuum, to see how Challe responded to the various ideas circulating in his time, and how he combined the five elements with more personal, more substantial, and ultimately more significant "real" materials.

Challe stands out among novelists of his day because of his effective combination of techniques to develop his themes. In any novel, the themes, which I am using in a broad sense, constitute the vital element. The development of new techniques is interesting only to the degree that it affects the themes in some way, permitting new ones to be treated, for example, or old ones to be treated with new depth. The fourth method I have used, again a traditional form of criticism, is to pursue one important theme through a dozen or so of the major novels of the eighteenth century. My purpose is to demonstrate the affinities between these works, and to show at the same time how the technical problems imposed certain restrictions on the genre. The theme in question, the individual in conflict with society, is especially well suited to the forms and methods available to the eighteenth-century author. As a result, an author working with that theme had a better than average chance of success, and an author sensitive to his craft would doubtless be drawn to the theme. Thus the evolutionary process works even on the subject in some measure.

The series of brief analyses of major novels does not of course give a full picture either of the individual novels or of the fictional themes of the century. Just as I selected elements of reality for purposes of my argument, I have selected a theme that facilitates what I want to show. Both the individual and society have given rise to numerous other significant themes, some of them already frequent in the eighteenth century. The study of individual psychology, for example, obviously attracted both Diderot and Rousseau, while in the other direction, a whole series of novels examined the political organization of society. These themes, however, strain the genre too much; *Emile, Le Neveu de Rameau, Les Lettres persanes,* the most successful works on these subjects, are only partly novels. The lyrical expression of passionate love, a strong current in the novel from *Les Lettres portugaises* to Mme Riccoboni, does not strain the genre enough; the first-person devices of the eighteenth century are perfectly adapted to such themes, and are still being used to treat them. The philosophical tale, a genre that includes most of Voltaire's fiction, remained aloof from most of the forces I have discussed; it always relied on wit and novelty rather than an effort to create the illusion of reality.

Introduction

For the period from 1700 to 1720, I tried to give a complete account of the French novel, including all the themes and all the forms. Coming out of this period, however, I have deliberately restricted the field of inquiry to the realistic school, which posterity showed to be the mainstream. All the works I do discuss seem to me to belong within it to a significant degree. The perspective from which I analyze them, however, does not reveal their full depth and complexity to a modern reader. I believe that in several cases the point of view is new and therefore instructive in and of itself; but in all cases, I hope primarily to show the unexpected similarities that link these diverse novels.

Finally, concentration on the theme of the individual against society makes it clear that the authors' ambitions often exceeded the means at their disposal. To go beyond the public and rather superficial aspects of the theme meant giving a wrench to the forms in vogue. By the end of the eighteenth century, it is clear, novelists were doing so more and more often, and in particular, struggling to find new modes of narration. Thus the evolution does not end where I leave off, but goes on directly to produce the third-person narrator of the nineteenth century.

— I —

Romans, Romances, *Nouvelles*, and Novels

In the introduction to his thirty-year-old but still highly regarded *List of French Prose Fiction 1700-1750,* S. Paul Jones observed: "It is noteworthy that the word *roman* which was frequently used in the titles of works of fiction of the seventeenth century has almost disappeared in the eighteenth century. Only four or five works bear the word in the title or subtitle."[1] More recent scholars echo the remark: "Le souvenir du roman baroque et de ses formes abâtardies hante si continuellement les esprits que le terme de roman n'est presque jamais employé par les romanciers pour désigner leurs œuvres. . . ."[2] Thus it would appear that in France, as in England, the emergence of a new genre led to a change in terminology, at least temporarily. This in turn implies considerable self-consciousness on the part of the novelists, and supports the argument that a sharp break occurs between the romance and the novel.

Unfortunately, Jones' remark is misleading and even inaccurate. It is true that his list of some 950 works contains only four indisputable instances of the word *roman* in a title or subtitle. There are, however, four more questionable works, and seven others in which some variant such as *romanesque* or *Romancie* occurs.[3] For the seventeenth century, R. C. Wil-

[1] S. Paul Jones, *A List of French Prose Fiction 1700-1750* (New York: The H. W. Wilson Company, 1939), p. xv. Hereafter cited as Jones.

[2] Henri Coulet, *Le Roman jusqu'à la Révolution*, tome I, Collection U (Paris: Librairie Armand Colin, 1967), p. 319; see also Georges May, *Le Dilemme du roman au XVIIIe siècle* (New Haven: Yale Univ. Press, and Paris: Presses Universitaires de France, 1963), p. 43; Philip R. Stewart, *Imitation and Illusion in the French Memoir-Novel, 1700-1750* (New Haven and London: Yale Univ. Press, 1969), p. 6.

[3] The indisputable cases are: 1718 [Thibault], *La Vie de Pedrille del Campo, roman comique*; 1725 Anon., *Le Roman tartare*; 1729 Anon., *Rhadamiste et Ozalie. Roman héroïque*; 1746, *Recueil de romans historiques*. Dubious cases are: 1741 M. de ***, *Roman*; 1745 [Mme le Prieur de Blainvillers], *Orphélie, roman traduit de l'anglais*; 1746

liams gives, in a bibliography of some six hundred novels, twenty-four titles which begin with the word *roman* or *romant*, plus nineteen in which the word is used in the subtitle. Many of these, however, are not fiction; R. W. Baldner's later revision rejects nine of the fifteen which are titled *roman*, on miscellaneous grounds. Since Baldner's work is not very reliable, it might be preferable in comparing to use Williams' figure; even so, there are just twenty-two instances per half-century between 1600 and 1700, as opposed to fifteen from 1700 to 1750.[4] This is a relatively trifling difference, at best; the term was not so frequent in the seventeenth century as Jones claimed, nor so rare in the eighteenth.

It is dangerous to rely on statistical evidence in such matters, in any event. Probably none of the bibliographies is complete, and there are numerous inaccuracies. Even if there were neither omissions nor errors, a mere count of titles equates books of vastly differing worth.

The most famous *romans* of the seventeenth century do not in fact use the term; generally, the title simply names the hero: *Cassandre*; *Cléopâtre*; *Almahide, ou l'esclave Reine*;

Beauchamps, *Imitation du roman grec de Theodore Prodomus*; 1749 Anon., *Le Roman de garnison*. Works with variant forms are: 1706 B . . . , Mr. l'abbé de, *La Fourbe découverte et le trompeur trompé, romance*; 1732 Marivaux, *Pharsamond, ou les nouvelles folies romanesques*; 1735 [Bougeant], *Voyage merveilleux du prince Fan-Férédin dans la Romancie*; 1745 [d'Arnaud], *Theresa, histoire italienne. Avec un discours sur le roman*; 1745 [Laffichard], *Caprices romanesques*; 1747 [Mouhy], *Le Masque de fer, . . . romance*; n.d. [Belin de La Faye], *Nouvelles romanesques et galantes*.

[4] Ralph Coplestone Williams' *Bibliography of the Seventeenth Century Novel in France* (London: Holland Press) was first published in 1931; Ralph W. Baldner's *Bibliography of Seventeenth-Century French Prose Fiction* (New York: for the MLA Index Committee by Columbia Univ. Press) came out in 1967. The latter purports to correct the former, and one of its objectives was "to eliminate those works which definitely did not fall into the category of novels or prose fiction in general" (p. xiii). Unfortunately, Baldner's work is even less reliable than Williams' original list; see Frédéric Deloffre's review in *Dix-septième Siècle*, no. 79 (1968), 105-107. In preferring Williams here, I am assuming that both are untrustworthy, and making my case against the one that raises the most difficulties on this point.

Romans, Romances, *Nouvelles*, and Novels

Artamène, ou le grand Cyrus, etc. La Calprenède gave *Pharamond* the alternate title *ou Histoire de France*; Mlle de Scudéry's *Clélie* bore the subtitle *histoire romaine*. On the other hand, the most famous uses of *roman* in titles are all satirical, like Furetière's *Le Roman bourgeois*, Scarron's *Le Roman comique*, and Sorel's *L'Anti-Roman*, or again, his *Le Berger extravagant, où parmi des fantaisies amoureuses on void les impertinences des Romans et de la Poësie*.

If we look beyond the titles, evidence is everywhere that *roman* remained the standard term to designate a work of prose fiction. The well informed Lenglet-Dufresnoy published an eight-volume collection under the title *Recueil de romans historiques* in 1746. Clearly he intended to attract buyers, not deter them. Furthermore, in the general preface and in the individual prefaces, the editor makes liberal use of the term: ". . . on se souviendra toujours que ce sont des Romans, et non pas des Histoires que je publie. . . ." On *La Comtesse de Montfort*: "Il n'y a peut-être à reprendre dans cet Ouvrage qu'un ton trop historique, qui l'écarte un peu du Roman."[5] To be sure, Lenglet-Dufresnoy could be accused of bias, because he had written a defense of the genre, under the title *De l'usage des romans* (1734); but he had written on the other side of the question, too, and he is not by any means the only eighteenth-century writer to use the term without apologizing.

In the early years of the eighteenth century, several collections of works by Mlle de la Roche-Guilhem appeared. She herself belonged to an earlier age, but it is the 1711 editor who begins the *Avertissement*: "Voici quelques nouveaux Romans: c'est-à-dire des Ouvrages, où la fiction est brodée

---

[5] Lenglet-Dufresnoy, ed., *Recueil de romans historiques*, 1746, Vol. 1, p. iii; Vol. 1, p. vi. Listed as anonymous by Jones. In giving references to novels published during the first half of the eighteenth century, I will supply only the author's last name, the short title, and the date; complete bibliographical information can be found in Jones's *A List of French Prose Fiction*. If, however, I have had to quote from a later edition, I will of course identify it fully.

sur un fond vrai. . . ."[6] Challe, whose preface reveals a thoughtful and innovative author, refers to *Les Illustres Françoises* (1713) as "mon roman ou mes histoires, comme on voudra les appeller. . . ."[7] Marivaux's first novel, *Les Avantures de * * **, *ou les Effets surprenans de la sympathie* (1713), appeared with a long preface which defended the *roman* and did not hesitate to name the genre: "Mais après tout, diront-ils, ce Roman n'est qu'un Roman . . . " or again, "Ainsi j'abandonne ce Roman à ses risques et fortunes . . . " or again, "Mais avant de finir, j'ai envie de dire un mot sur la maniere dont est composé ce Roman. . . ."[8] In a 1702 edition of Catherine Bédacier's *Anecdotes galans*, the preface remarks, "C'est une grande témérité, ce semble, que de choisir des Papes et des Cardinaux pour en faire les sujets de ce que l'on appelle Roman. . . ."[9] The same volume contains a *nouvelle* entitled *La Marquise d'Urfé*, which purports to be a key to d'Urfé's "inimitable Roman," *L'Astrée*; Jones himself recorded a number of reprints and continuations of the famous seventeenth-century *romans*, including *L'Astrée*, *Cassandre*, *Ibrahim*, *Polexandre*, and *Clélie*.[10] Another quotation from Catherine Bédacier shows that even though tastes and styles were changing, the prestige of the *roman* survived: "Quoique l'histoire qu'on va lire ne soit point Romanesque, elle ne laisse

[6] La Roche-Guilhem, *Œuvres Diverses*, 1711, "Avertissement."

[7] Jones's information on this work has been superseded. I am quoting from *Les Illustres Françoises* in *Œuvres Complètes de Robert Chasles*, ed. Frédéric Deloffre, Les Textes Français (Paris: Société d'Edition "Les Belles Lettres," 1967), p. lix. Hereafter I will cite this work as Challe, *Œuvres*. It is itself a reprint, with the same paging, of a 1959 edition which appeared as Fascicule 3 in the series Bibliothèque de la Faculté des Lettres de Lyon; although the earlier edition is identical, it was not titled *Œuvres Complètes*, but simply *Les Illustres Françoises*. Both editions are in two volumes, numbered consecutively. Fuller explanations of Deloffre's work and the variant spellings of Challe's name will be found in chapter 4 of this book.

[8] Marivaux, *Les Avantures de *** ou les Effets surprenans de la sympathie*, 1713, Vol. 1, "Avis au lecteur." Listed as anonymous by Jones.

[9] Bédacier, *Anecdotes galans*, 1702, "Préface," p. 11.

[10] Jones, p. xxviii.

pas d'avoir tous les agrémens du Roman le plus ingenieuse-
ment inventé. . . ."[11]

Marie Jeanne l'Héritier de Villandon, a prolific author of
about the same era, defends the genre in the preface to *La
Tour ténébreuse et les Jours lumineux, contes anglois* (1705):
"j'aime mieux qu'on me reproche de m'attacher trop scrupu-
leusement à l'Histoire dans un Ouvrage que je ne donne que
comme une espece de Roman, que de me voir accusée, ainsi
que certains Historiens, de falcifier impitoyablement l'Histoire; je croy qu'on est moins blâmable de faire des Romans
historiques, que de composer des Histoires romanesques."[12]
An enemy of the genre, Bruslé de Montpleinchamp, pays it
the homage of imitation, explaining in the preface to *Le Diable bossu* (1708): "Pour étouffer les Romans qui ne disent
agreablement que des bagatelles, et au même tems pour ne
pas effaroucher entierement les esprits qui en sont leurez, on
a pris l'air de Roman, mais on s'en est distingué en racontant
de pures veritez sous quelques voiles dessennuians."[13] The
anonymous *Histoires galantes de diverses personnes* (1709)
begins with a debate on the merits of the *roman,* to conclude
"La Philosophie et la Religion sont pour vous, l'usage du
monde est pour moi: Mais tous les trois me convainquent que
nous faisons un plus grand mal, vous et moi de disputer ensemble que nous n'en ferions à lire mon Roman."[14]

Equally convincing proofs can be found in the writings of
critics and theorists. The vogue of the old heroic romances
ended around 1660. The change in taste was evident almost
at once, and seventeenth-century commentators usually
credit Mme de Lafayette with having "killed" the old *roman;*
certainly she was the most brilliant practitioner of the shorter
genre which then came into fashion, even though Segrais or
Mme de Villedieu may have precedence chronologically.

---

[11] Bédacier, *Henry, duc des Vandales,* 1714, "Préface."

[12] L'Héritier de Villandon, *La Tour ténébreuse,* 1705, "Préface."

[13] Bruslé de Montpleinchamp, *Le Diable bossu,* 1708, "Préface," pp.
xiii-xiv.

[14] Anon., *Histoires galantes de diverses personnes,* 1709, p. 8.

Mme de Lafayette, however, saw nothing paradoxical in having the erudite Bishop Huet append to her *Zayde* a *Lettre à M. de Segrais sur l'origine des romans* (1670), nor did anyone for centuries afterwards. It is only the twentieth-century scholar, with three hundred years of tradition behind him, who might feel bound to object. Some thirteen years later, the obscure sieur du Plaisir published a perceptive "Art of the Novel" under the title *Sentimens sur les Lettres et sur L'Histoire avec des scrupules sur le stile* (1683). Like everyone at the time, Du Plaisir affirms that "Les petites Histoires ont entièrement détruit les grands Romans"; but a few lines later he remarks that "Ce qui a fait haïr les anciens Romans, est ce que l'on doit d'abord éviter dans les Romans nouveaux."[15] Fontenelle, writing in 1687 on *Eléonore d'Yvrée,* praises it as a worthy descendant of *La Princesse de Clèves*; Coulet cites the letter as showing "ce que le public attendait de la *nouvelle* psychologique . . . " but Fontenelle said " . . . je suis beaucoup plus touché de voir régner dans un Roman une certaine science du cœur, telle qu'elle est, par exemple, dans *la Princesse de Clèves*," and " . . . on voit bien que la personne qui a fait ce Roman-là a plus songé à faire un bon Ouvrage, qu'un Livre. . . ."[16] Surely if the term *roman* implied any opprobrium, Fontenelle would have used another. I have already mentioned Lenglet-Dufresnoy's defense of the *roman, De l'usage des romans* (1734). D'Argens likewise states: "Il faut peut-être autant d'esprit, d'usage du monde et de connoissance des passions pour composer un Roman, que pour écrire une Histoire."[17]

Many more quotations could be brought forward, but I have perhaps already overdone the proof. At no time in the late seventeenth or early eighteenth centuries did novelists or their friendly critics consistently find it necessary, or even

---

[15] Du Plaisir, *Sentimens sur les Lettres et sur l'Histoire*, 1683, in Henri Coulet, *Le Roman jusqu'à la Révolution*, tome 2, Collection U (Paris: Librairie Armand Colin, 1968), p. 88; hereafter cited as Coulet, *Anthologie.*

[16] Coulet, *Anthologie*, pp. 94-95.

[17] In *Les Lettres juives* (1738), in Coulet, *Anthologie*, p. 108.

desirable, to disguise the fact that works of prose fiction were *romans*. This is so obvious in the passages I have quoted that some explanation for the prevalence of the contrary opinion seems to be called for. Jones's error results from an improper use of statistics. *Roman* was never a popular word in titles or subtitles; but at the same time, it was always the most popular generic term for works of prose fiction. One reason for its rarity on title pages may well be its generality; it covered too many subgenres to be useful in attracting readers.

In fairness, though, it must be said that Jones would never have fallen into the error, had the impression not been strong anyway that the *roman* had become disreputable. Quotations to this effect are also numerous; the first line I quoted from Du Plaisir can serve as a typical example. As I have already intimated, an important change in taste did occur, and I hope in subsequent pages to shed some light on the nature and causes of it; but for the moment let me observe only that in some contexts the term *roman* has the special sense of "long, heroic romance" such as La Calprenède or the Scudérys wrote. Mlle de la Roche-Guilhem, for instance, begins the preface to *Hieron, roi de Syracuse* by saying: "Quoy que les Romans ne soient plus à la mode . . . ," and it is clear that she means the old *romans romanesques*; for elsewhere in the same collection, as in the preface to *Agripine, histoire romaine*, she calls her own work a *roman*, meaning simply a work of fiction.[18]

A second reason for believing that the *roman* had come into discredit is the appearance of explicit denials in prefaces, and even in the works themselves. Thus in Grandchamp's *La Guerre d'Italie* (1710): "A l'égard des Avantures Galantes qu'on trouvera ici, elles ne doivent rien à mon imagination; je les raporte telles qu'elles sont arrivées; et la maniére simple et naïve dont je les décris, sufit seule pour faire voir que mon dessein n'est pas d'en faire un Roman."[19] From Mlle de la Roche-Guilhem's *Histoire des Favorites* (1703): "On verra

[18] La Roche-Guilhem, *Dernières Œuvres*, 1708, pp. 248-50 and p. 103.
[19] Grandchamp, *La Guerre d'Italie*, 4e édition (Cologne: Pierre Marteau, 1710; first edition, 1702), p. 2.

dans six Histoires succintes des évenemens qui n'ont rien du merveilleux des Romains [sic] parce qu'elles tiennent toutes de la vérité, les faits y sont incontestables, et on n'y poura blâmer que la foiblesse des expressions."[20] From Olivier's *L'Infortuné Napolitain* (1704): " . . . je n'écris pas un Roman —ni ne me pique pas d'exprimer ce que l'amour fit dire de tendre, et de passionné aux deux personnes du monde les plus spirituelles et les plus amoureuses. . . ."[21] From Choisy's *Le Prince Kouchimen* (1710): "Ce ne sont point ici des Contes de Fées, ni des Avantures de Roman; on n'y verra ni Enchantemens, ni Machines, ni Enfers, ni Champs Elisées; on y suivra les regles ordinaires de la Nature. . . ."[22]

One must read these disclaimers with both eyes open, however. To deny that what follows is a *roman* is in part to promise that it will resemble a *roman*. Indeed, all the passages just cited take some pains to specify just what aspect of the *roman* will not appear in the text: the elevated style, the *merveilleux*, the epic conventions, the long amorous conversations. Lesage, in a more flippant manner, has Gil Blas use the same device: "Si j'imitais les faiseurs de romans, je ferais une pompeuse description du palais épiscopal de Grenade."[23] The architectural descriptions, like the pseudo-epic style and devices, were commonplaces of the old *romans*. Furetière satirizes them in *Le Roman bourgeois*, Bougeant in *Fan-Férédin*. The rejection of these artifices does not, however, imply any rejection of the genre as a whole. Indeed, the persistence of satires demonstrates the continuing vigor even of the poorest elements of the *roman*, while the basic concept of the novelist's art remains unchanged. The novelist wants to make the reader take

[20] La Roche-Guilhem, *Histoire des Favorites*, 1703 (enlarged edition; first edition 1697), "Préface."

[21] Olivier, *L'Infortuné Napolitain*, 1704, pp. 8-9.

[22] Choisy, *Le Prince Kouchimen*, 1710, "Avertissement."

[23] Alain-René Lesage, *Gil Blas*, Livre 7, 1724, in *Romanciers du XVIIIe siècle*, ed. Etiemble, Bibliothèque de la Pléiade (Paris: Librairie Gallimard, Vol. 1, 1960; Vol. 2, 1965), Vol. 1, p. 854. This collection of eighteenth-century novels will hereafter be cited as *Romanciers du XVIIIe siècle*.

an interest in his story, and the *roman* never lost the power to do that.

Furthermore, the denials served with many another device to invite the reader to believe. One of the changes in fashion that is most elusive is the precise relationship of the fiction to reality. The authors of the old *romans* did not set out to be incredible; quite the opposite. But as time passed—a relatively short time, in fact—the artifices they had utilized to gain acceptance marked their works as false. New devices, like the pseudo-memoir, replaced the pseudo-epic. The new novel, as it seems always to do, started off by reacting against its immediate ancestor. But the authors betray themselves in the very act of protesting. To say "This work is a true story" differs from saying "This work is not a novel," in that the latter speaker is most assuredly hoping to be mistaken for a novelist.

The third and final reason for the misunderstanding of the *roman* concerns the polemical use of the term toward the middle of the eighteenth century. Enemies of the novel, like Bruzen de la Martinière or the abbé Jaquin, go out of their way to define the *roman* in the most old-fashioned and pejorative fashion. But Denis Diderot probably has done more harm than anyone else with the opening sentence of his ecstatic *Eloge de Richardson* (1762): "Par un roman, on a entendu jusqu'à ce jour un tissu d'événements chimériques et frivoles, dont la lecture était dangereuse pour le goût et pour les mœurs. Je voudrais bien qu'on trouvât un autre nom pour les ouvrages de Richardson, qui élèvent l'esprit, qui touchent l'âme, qui respirent partout l'amour du bien, et qu'on appelle aussi des romans."[24] Thus Diderot announces his entry into the ranks of the novel's defenders, and because of his point of view, and his authority, it is easy to take his comment as definitive.

Diderot, however, wrote to persuade, and did not scruple at giving a small turn to the truth. Only a few years before,

[24] In Denis Diderot, *Œuvres esthétiques,* ed. Paul Vernière, Classiques Garnier (Paris: Editions Garnier Frères, 1959), p. 29.

he had promoted his new dramatic theories as being entirely original; their only anticipation or even inspiration came from an obscure little play called *Silvie*, which Diderot had seen in 1742 and was almost alone in remembering. Yet in the interim, Nivelle de la Chaussée, Mme de Graffigny, and even Voltaire in *Nanine* had obviously been working toward what Diderot formulated; and the critics did not fail to point it out. The situation was similar with Richardson. *Pamela* had been translated in 1742, *Clarissa* in 1751, and *Sir Charles Grandison* in 1755, the latter two by the popular Prévost. The press had reviewed them extensively, and the first two at least appear to have been among the best selling novels of the two decades. As Paul Vernière remarks in his introduction, Diderot's entry into the quarrel is belated.[25] All the more reason to make it with as much flourish as possible.

Diderot's opening lines are grossly unfair. Not only had Richardson's merit been widely recognized before Diderot, but so had the good qualities of several other novelists. In fact Diderot himself had given evidence of considerable experience and some appreciation of the works of Prévost, Crébillon *fils*, and Marivaux. He had even written a novel himself, *Les Bijoux indiscrets*, although it is true he was pushed to it by the demands of his mistress and his purse. Still, he had personal reasons for knowing that many novels before *Clarissa* were neither fanciful nor frivolous, and that very few constituted any real threat to taste or to morals. And to be sure, "On a entendu" is not "J'ai entendu." In order to emphasize the originality of Richardson and magnify his achievement to the fullest, Diderot found it expedient to begin at the farthest remove. The true import of Diderot's opening should be paraphrased, "Even if you have always considered the novel frivolous and pernicious, you will admire Richardson."

Thus the continuity of the genre in France is reflected in the name. The *roman* of today descends in an unbroken stream of conception from the *roman* of the seventeenth century, and of course beyond. But the greatest revolution in

[25] Ibid., p. 23. See also English Showalter, Jr., "Diderot and Madame de Graffigny's *Cénie*," *FR*, 39 (1965), 394-97.

meaning, that is, the greatest alterations in the thing designated by the term, take place around 1700. In England, at that moment, a new term arose to accompany the new genre, and that term has survived until today: novel. It has, of course, a cognate in French: *nouvelle*. Moreover, the early history of the *nouvelle* parallels that of the novel in certain important respects. When the vogue of the long *romans* ended around 1660, the vogue of the *nouvelle* began. Unlike the term *roman, nouvelle* did appear frequently on the title page, and Godenne lists over a hundred and fifty books titled or subtitled *nouvelle* between 1660 and 1700; before 1660 there had been only six.[26] The vogue persisted into the eighteenth century, with more than thirty occurrences during the first decade alone. It is not altogether certain that the rise in usage of the term actually signified the rise of a new genre, or even subgenre. Many of the *nouvelles* bore more than one designation, and some were reissued with different designations. For example, Godenne gives the title *Histoire des pensées, meslée de petits jeux, nouvelle galante* (1671). *Histoire* was common as the first word in the title, and also as a genre designation in the subtitle from the earliest years of the seventeenth century; in the first two decades its chief rival was *Amours*. Thus when Godenne goes on to say that the same work was published also with the title *Histoire des pensées, ou les amours de Marc-Antoine* (1673), one may well conclude that the vogue was for the term *nouvelle,* not for any new quality in fiction. The sudden sharp increase in works called *nouvelle* at the same time the long *romans* stopped appearing may be no more than coincidence. In any case, we must proceed with caution.

One of the earliest English authors to take cognizance of the novel as a new genre was Congreve. In the prefatory letter to *Incognita* (1692), he states: "Romances are generally composed of the Constant Loves and invincible Courages of

<hr />

[26] René Godenne, *Histoire de la nouvelle française aux XVIIe et XVIIIe siècles*, Publications Romanes et Françaises, no. 108 (Genève: Librairie Droz, 1970), pp. 247-298. Hereafter cited as Godenne, *Histoire de la nouvelle.*

Hero's, Heroins, Kings and Queens, Mortals of the first Rank, and so forth; where lofty Language, miraculous Contingencies and impossible Performances, elevate and surprize the Reader into a giddy Delight, which leaves him flat upon the Ground whenever he gives of . . . when he is forced to be very well convinced that 'tis all a lye." But novels "come near us, and represent to us Intrigues in practice, delight us with Accidents and odd Events, but not such as are wholly unusual or unpresidented, such which not being so distant from our Belief bring also the pleasure nearer us."[27] Congreve's distinction comes near what a modern critic would say, but for all that, Congreve's little story is not a novel in the usual sense; it is much more like a romance, or more accurately, like a *nouvelle*. The clarity which Congreve seems to bring to the question is illusory. As Ian Watt admits, the English terms romance and novel were not clearly distinguished from each other until the late eighteenth century.[28]

Congreve's contrast between novel and romance had been anticipated in France (not to mention in Spain by Cervantes, but Cervantes came too early; the romances he attacked were of a different sort from those described by Congreve, although they had much in common, and Cervantes' *novela* went long enough without emulation in France and England to seem both old and exotic, rather than familiar). Regnauld de Segrais wrote at the very beginning of the vogue of the *nouvelle* in France, for his *Nouvelles Françoises* appeared in 1656.

Segrais's work is a frame narration, with a group of French ladies telling each other stories as a diversion. They begin by discussing the value of the *roman*, meaning *L'Astrée, Polexandre, Ariane, Cassandre, Cléopâtre, L'Illustre Bassa*, and *Le Grand Cyrus*—that is, the most famous works of d'Urfé, Gomberville, Desmarets de Saint-Sorlin, La Calprenède, and

[27] William Congreve, *Incognita*, [1692] ed. H.F.B. Brett-Smith, Percy Reprints, no. 5 (Oxford: Basil Blackwell, 1922), pp. 5-6; also quoted in Allen, *The English Novel*, p. 22.

[28] Watt, *The Rise of the Novel*, p. 10.

Mlle de Scudéry (*Clélie* was still being written). The most authoritative among the ladies, the Princesse Aurélie, admits that these *romans* "ne sont pas sans instruction," but she notices even in them "des choses qui sont un peu éloignées de la raison." The princesse proposes that authors write about French society, and she is supported by one of her group who remarks that the Spanish have already done so in their *nouvelles*. One by one, the objections are met: French names and places will be acceptable to the reader; one may not invent historical events, like battles, but the incidents and secret affairs of the recent past and the present would make excellent stories; moreover, the deeds of an ordinary man would provide a more effective example for imitation than those of a king.[29]

The ladies finally agree to tell each other some such *nouvelles*, and after one of them, a debate arises regarding the propriety of an action, and the princesse says:

... nous avons entrepris de raconter les choses comme elles sont, et non pas comme elles doivent être: Qu'au reste il me semble que c'est la différence qu'il y a entre le Roman et la Nouvelle; que le Roman écrit ces choses comme la bienseance le veut, et à la maniere du Poète; mais que la Nouvelle doit un peu davantage tenir de l'Histoire, et s'attacher plûtôt à donner les images des choses comme d'ordinaire nous les voyons arriver, que comme notre imagination se les figure.[30]

The same general distinctions are made in other texts, such as the sieur du Plaisir's *Sentimens sur l'Histoire* (1683), but Segrais's statement is notable both for its succinctness and for its author's prestige. Segrais was a close friend of Mme de Lafayette, and may have taken a hand in writing some of her works. Indeed, they were originally attributed to him, so that

[29] Jean Regnauld de Segrais, *Les Nouvelles Françoises* (La Haye: chez Pierre Paupie, 1741, 2 Vols.; first edition, 1656), Vol. 1, pp. 15-24; parts of this are quoted in Coulet, *Anthologie*, pp. 74-76.

[30] Segrais, *Les Nouvelles Françoises*, 1741, Vol. 1, p. 146.

for some time he enjoyed an undeserved reputation as a novelist. Justified or no, his influence was moving the novel in the same direction as the English would take.

As I remarked before, even in England the novel did not immediately appear as an independent genre in contradistinction to the romance. As late as 1785, in *The Progress of Romance,* Clara Reeve has Euphrasia say: "No writings are more different than the ancient *Romance* and modern *Novel,* yet they are frequently confounded together and mistaken for each other."[31] Clara Reeve's own definition repeats and elaborates Congreve's, although her applications of it might mystify a modern reader. Whatever obscurity remained, however, the English novel was more and more being regarded as something separate, and the two terms were being used in contrast to each other. In France, on the other hand, the marquis d'Argens could write in 1739, on the subject "nouvelle et roman": "Leur différence, ce me semble, ne consiste que dans l'étenduë."[32]

The beginnings were similar, and ultimately, the English novel and the French *roman* would signify the same thing. Meanwhile, especially in the early eighteenth century, English writers apparently had a growing feeling that they were innovating, while the French felt that they were extending a tradition.

Around 1700, the first and most obvious difference between the French and English traditions is one of quantity. This is an area in which it is risky to seek any precision, but the apparent difference is so vast that even a large error would not alter the fundamental truth of the conclusion. In 1720, a French author had behind him a large native tradition in fiction, whereas an English author had very little. W. H. McBurney's *Check List of English Prose Fiction* lists seventy-two domestic titles for the years 1700 to 1719;[33] for the same

[31] Clara Reeve, *The Progress of Romance* (1785; rpt. New York: Facsimile Text Society, 1930), p. 7.

[32] In *Lectures amusantes* (1739), quoted in Coulet, *Anthologie,* p. 110.

[33] William Harlin McBurney, *A Check List of English Prose Fiction 1700-1739* (Cambridge: Harvard Univ. Press, 1960).

period in France, S. Paul Jones lists two hundred and sixty-three, close to four times as many.[34] Even if Jones includes many doubtful works, while McBurney is very incomplete, it hardly seems likely that such a gap could be filled. Comparisons are difficult for the seventeenth century, because Charles Mish's list of English prose fiction does not separate translations from native works and, moreover, lists reeditions along with new titles.[35] But from the French bibliographies it can be determined that the rate of novel production had been very high throughout the seventeenth century: two hundred and fifty-two titles between 1680 and 1699; two hundred titles between 1660 and 1679; seventy-nine titles between 1640 and 1659; two hundred and two titles between 1620 and 1639; and one hundred and thirty titles between 1600 and 1619.[36] The slowdown in mid-century can be attributed to two factors. On the one hand, France was torn by civil war, which disrupted trade and distracted the attentions of both novelists and readers. On the other hand, the long romances were at the peak of their popularity, and these multi-volume works occupied their authors for many years at a time. Thus La Calprenède published the ten volumes of *Cassandre* between 1642 and 1645; the next year he began the twelve-

[34] Jones, p. xiv.

[35] Charles C. Mish, *English Prose Fiction, 1600-1700: A Chronological Checklist* (Charlottesville: Bibliographical Society of the Univ. of Virginia, 1952).

[36] The figures are derived from Baldner's list; Williams gives three hundred and forty-seven titles between 1680 and 1699, two hundred and eighty-nine between 1660 and 1679, one hundred and forty-two between 1640 and 1659, two hundred and fifty-six between 1620 and 1639, and one hundred and eighty-four between 1600 and 1619. Mish gives five hundred and seventeen titles between 1680 and 1699, but one can readily identify at least one hundred and fifty-five as translations and two hundred and six as reeditions, leaving no more than one hundred and fifty-six new English novels during that period. The impropriety of the comparison can be aptly illustrated by the case of *Les Lettres portugaises*; Baldner wrongly eliminated it from his list as non-fiction, while it appears six different times in Mish's. In view of the general unreliability of the lists, I have not rechecked my counts for accuracy, but have given the exact figure from the first count.

volume *Cléopâtre*, which was not completed until 1657. Mlle de Scudéry wrote ten volumes of *Artamène* between 1649 and 1653, and ten more of *Clélie* between 1654 and 1660. One could add several less famous four-volume works of various authors. Obviously, the production of volumes did not decline nearly so sharply as the number of titles would suggest.

With so much activity over so long a period, it would be surprising if no works of merit had been written. In fact, *L'Astrée* (1607-27) had the stature of a classic, whose influence had helped to purify French taste of the excesses of the Renaissance. Such later figures as Corneille, Racine, and La Fontaine read and appreciated it. Mlle de Scudéry played a significant role in forming French taste around mid-century, for her salon was the meeting place of the *précieux*. Finally, Mme de Lafayette and her rumored collaborators, Segrais, Ménage, and La Rochefoucauld, commanded respect and attention for their learning, their non-fictional literary achievements, and for their social prominence. A later novelist could not avoid situating himself with relation to at least those important predecessors.

The reasons for the abrupt end to the vogue of long *romans* remain obscure. Although contemporary statements amply testify to their awareness of the change, the critics of the time do not offer any satisfactory reasons. The sieur du Plaisir claims that the *nouvelle* had just been invented around 1660,[37] but that is untrue; both the Spanish and the Italian forms had been translated long before, not to mention such native works as Marguerite de Navarre's *Heptaméron*. De Sacy, in the preface to his *Histoire du marquis de Clemes et du chevalier de Pervanes* (1716), reviews the history of the genre, distinguishing between "le bon goût" and "le goût du siècle"; the latter he blames for both accrediting and discrediting the *romans*.[38] Perhaps there is no better explanation.

---

[37] Du Plaisir, *Sentimens sur les Lettres et sur l'Histoire*, 1683, in Coulet, *Anthologie*, p. 88: ". . . c'est depuis peu seulement que l'on a inventé les Nouvelles."

[38] Sacy, *Histoire du marquis de Clemes et du chevalier de Pervanes*, 1716, "Epître."

Romans, Romances, *Nouvelles*, and Novels

The generation which had written and enjoyed the long *romans* was growing old; the new generation would be oriented toward the principles of classicism—concision, simplicity, purity of organization. Superficially at least, the *nouvelles* seem closer to realizing neo-classical ideals than do the *romans*.

Arnaldo Pizzorusso has demonstrated, however, that Mlle de Scudéry herself sensed that by 1660 the *roman* as a genre was in need of renewal.[39] In the 1640's the *roman* had acquired a poetics, composed mainly by the Scudérys, which bears an astonishing resemblance to the theories of Henry Fielding.[40] At the heart of the theory lay the belief that the *roman* derived from the epic; it was consequently subject to the rules of Aristotle. The *romans* of 1640 to 1660 were themselves reacting against the adventure romances which preceded them, such as Gomberville's. Mlle de Scudéry demanded more verisimilitude, by which she meant that upon a true historical framework a plausible reconstruction of private lives should be built. Georges de Scudéry formulated the concepts in the preface to *Ibrahim* (1641):

> Mais entre toutes les regles qu'il faut observer en la composition de ces Ouvrages, celle de la vraysemblance est sans doute la plus necessaire. Elle est comme la pierre fondamentale de ce bastiment, et ce n'est que sur elle qu'il subsiste. Sans elle rien ne peut toucher; sans elle rien ne sçauroit plaire; et si cette charmante trompeuse ne deçoit l'esprit dans les Romans, cette espece de lecture le dégouste, au lieu de le divertir. J'ay donc essayé de ne m'en éloigner jamais: j'ay observé pour cela les mœurs, les coûtumes, les loix, les religions, et les inclinations des peuples: et pour donner plus de vray-semblance aux choses, j'ay voulu que les fondemens de mon Ouvrage fussent historiques, mes principaux personnages marquez dans l'Histoire veritable

[39] Arnaldo Pizzorusso, "La Concezione dell'arte narrativa nella seconda metà del seicento francese," *Studi Mediolatini e Volgari*, 3 (1955), 114-25.

[40] See Arthur L. Cooke, "Henry Fielding and the Writers of Heroic Romance," *PMLA*, 62 (1947), 984-94.

comme personnes illustres, et les guerres effectives. C'est
sans doute par cette voye que l'on peut arriver à sa fin: Car
lors que le mensonge et la verité sont confondus par une
main adroite, l'esprit a peine à les démesler et ne se porte
pas aisément à détruire ce qui luy plaist.[41]

The theory was, alas, far superior to the realizations. Late
in the century, numerous critics could be quoted assailing the
romans; Du Plaisir summarizes their faults concisely: "leur
longueur prodigieuse, ce mélange de tant d'histoires diverses,
leur trop grand nombre d'Acteurs, la trop grande antiquité
de leurs sujets, l'embarras de leur construction, leur peu de
vray-semblance, l'excés dans leur caractère. . . ."[42] Some of Du
Plaisir's objections could be ascribed to changes in taste—the
length, the construction modeled on the epic, and even the
complexity. The lack of verisimilitude, however, denotes a
failure of the author's own intentions. Segrais had implicitly
made the same complaint; when his spokesman the Princesse
Aurélie proposes French characters as heroes of fiction, it is
to enhance the author's chances of attaining the desired verisimilitude. This prescription not only contradicts one of the
constant assumptions of the Scudérys, but also runs counter
to the common practice of classical authors in the nobler
genres. In other words, the change in taste was neither toward nor away from classicism, but rather a recognition of
greater affinities between *romans* and comedy than between
romans and the epic.

Pizzorusso observes that the pages of *Clélie* attest to the internal crisis of the *roman héroïque*.[43] In volume ten of *Clélie*,
published in 1661, Mlle de Scudéry attempted to redefine and
defend her conception of the *roman*. The central principle of
an adroit mixture of truth and invention remains at the heart
of her doctrine, but she tries to add nuances to the meaning
of *vraisemblable*. Her effort was doomed to failure, partly

[41] Coulet, *Anthologie*, pp. 45-46.
[42] Coulet, *Anthologie*, p. 88.
[43] Pizzorusso, "La Concezione," p. 118: "Ma le pagine di *Clélie* con-
fermano l'interna crisi del romanzo eroico, e la necessità della sua
trasformazione."

because she had a naive and abstract sense of what was credible, and partly because she restricted the domain of what was true to the most superficial elements—battles and names, for instance. The presence of an apology within *Clélie* speaks eloquently of the pressure Mlle de Scudéry felt to justify her art, but it is perhaps even more significant that some years before she had in effect abandoned her own principles, and begun using *Artamène* and, later, *Clélie* as vehicles for portraying herself and her friends under pseudonyms. In 1661 she herself wrote a short work entitled *Célinte, nouvelle première*, and published several more afterwards. Thus the long romance authors themselves had started to move in the direction of a new type of fiction, more familiar in subject, and therefore more readily credible. Moreover, Mlle de Scudéry's long *romans* already had entered a field that the French *nouvelle* was soon to adopt as its main subject, the minute analysis of the human heart. Both the matter and the form of the *nouvelle* were largely present in Mlle de Scudéry's *romans*, and in her later works they made the transition into the new form virtually intact. Even though it may not be obvious to twentieth-century readers, the theory of the *roman* pointed fiction in the direction of greater realism in our modern sense, and both authors and readers of the seventeenth century appreciated the superiority of the realistic elements for achieving the kind of verisimilitude they sought from fiction.

For the classical writer, aspiring to have his art taken seriously, the newness of the novel was nonetheless a drawback. It lacked ancestors, and therefore had escaped the legislative attention of Horace and Aristotle. A genre without rules was always in danger of excess, and the absence of fixed standards seemed to paralyze critics, when it did not provoke scorn, as from Boileau: "Dans un Roman frivole, aisément tout s'excuse."[44] The prefaces of the Scudérys responded to this general attitude, by attempting to place the *roman* within the epic tradition. Critics and theorists of fictional genres failed to comprehend the changes that the authors were making.

[44] Nicolas Boileau-Despréaux, *L'Art Poétique*, Chant 3, line 119.

Huet, for example, although he wrote as a friend of Segrais and Mme de Lafayette, drew his own conception of the *roman* from the Scudérys; and his *Lettre sur l'origine des romans* (1670) was regarded as authoritative well into the eighteenth century. Naturally, Huet reaffirms the epic origins of the genre.[45] The authors of *nouvelles*, then, appear to have considered the *roman* tradition at least a partial blessing, insofar as it allowed them claim to some status as artists.

Du Plaisir is unique in giving serious consideration to the actual practice of the *nouvelle*, and in attempting to base some rules thereupon. Even he, however, looks for a tradition and associates *nouvelles*, which he sometimes calls *romans nouveaux*, with historical writing. So completely does he assimilate the *nouvelle* into history that he would require complete objectivity on the part of the author, refusing to permit a novelist to call his hero "ce grand Prince," even in speaking of the king.[46] Moreover, he asks that the author portray his characters by their words and deeds, insofar as possible. Finally, he recommends a usage of history comparable to Georges de Scudéry's, that is, as a framework on which to build a story of private emotions. Unlike later historians, however, Du Plaisir shares many of the classical prejudices. He does not approve of physical details in descriptions:

> Outre que ce détail de nez, de bouche, de cheveux, de jambes, ne soufre point de termes assez nobles, pour faire une expression heureuse, il rend l'Historien suspect de peu de verité. Les Lecteurs sçavent que tous ces traits ne consistent que dans son imagination. . . . Enfin ces sortes de peintures ne plaisent point universellement; s'il est des Personnes qui aiment dans les Hommes une taille fine, il en est qui aimeront davantage une taille pleine; et ainsi l'Auteur peche contre le dessein qu'il a de faire aimer de tout le monde, ceux dont il parle.[47]

For the same reasons, he wants heroes in good health, except when they die, but heroines of only modest strength.

[45] Coulet, *Anthologie*, pp. 66-69.
[46] ibid., p. 91.   [47] ibid.

Romans, Romances, *Nouvelles,* and Novels

Thus the theorists, whether of the *roman* or the *nouvelle,* bound the novel to the severe limitations of classical aesthetics, which are in precise opposition to the particularizing realism associated with the novel. Fortunately, the authors listened to their own inspiration more than to critical counsels. Yet they did not protest against the critics, for these misguided and unperceptive pedants did provide the "lettres de noblesse" for the *roman.* To the classical way of thinking, mere copying of reality fell short of being art of any sort; what was valued in the *roman* was what was imagined. The old *romans* had stressed the true historical content as a means of creating verisimilitude. The early authors of *nouvelles* actually moved away from the depiction of reality in this sense; Mme de Villedieu regularly prefaced her *nouvelles* (which she usually called *romans*) with a confession of their fictitious nature. With that exception, however, she too remains in the tradition of the old *romans.* As Bruce Morrissette says, she "attempts to retain most of the outward forms of the heroic novel, and yet to describe only what is reasonable and *vraisemblable.*"[48] Mlle de Scudéry, of course, had had no other object; Mme de Villedieu's effort represents less a break with tradition than an extension of it, as did virtually all the authors who turned to the *nouvelle.* The temper of the times did not favor a radical break with tradition, especially in the direction of realism in a modern sense; rather, the writers who recognized the need for renewal were more disposed to make minor technical adjustments and shifts of emphasis.[49]

[48] Bruce Morrissette, *The Life and Works of Marie-Catherine Desjardins (Mme de Villedieu), 1632-1683,* Washington Univ. Studies in Language and Literature, no. 17 (St. Louis: Washington Univ. Press, 1947), p. 124.

[49] René Godenne, in his *Histoire de la nouvelle* reaches substantially the same conclusion, albeit with somewhat different emphases. The term by which he designates the type of *nouvelle* in vogue during the last part of the seventeenth century is "nouvelle romanesque," and his general opinion is summarized (p. 108) in the following sentence: "Quand on examine à présent les nouvelles qui parurent au cours des années 1671-1699, on constate que les auteurs ne suivent guère les préceptes d'un Du Plaisir, mais reprennent, au contraire, des procédés en honneur auprès des romanciers de la première moitié du siècle."

Evolution of the French Novel

Huet's erudite genealogy and the Scudérys' neo-epic theory seemed less a stifling limitation than a necessary protection, at least to most of the first wave of *nouvelle* writers.

If the *roman* contained within itself some predisposition to evolve in the direction of the *nouvelle*, and also offered the *nouvelle* writers a worthwhile precedent and theory, other factors were working to obscure the most revolutionary elements in the *nouvelle*. By all odds, Cervantes exercised the greatest influence of any writer on French fiction of the seventeenth century; from the first translation of part one of *Don Quixote* (1614) he was acknowledged as a genius. Spanish influence in France was strong anyway, witness *Le Cid* and *Don Juan*, to cite only two of the best known examples. Of the many Spanish *novelas* translated into French during the seventeenth century, Cervantes' *Novelas Exemplares* were the most important. Georges Hainsworth has devoted an entire book to a study of their impact on France, and I will do no more than summarize his conclusions here.[50]

Cervantes' originality consisted largely in bringing the techniques of the romance to what had previously been a largely comic genre. The Italian tradition, illustrated by Boccaccio, and in France by Marguerite de Navarre, emphasized the surprise twist in the plot. Cervantes concentrated on the art of the narration, on the analysis of passions. But to accomplish this, he borrowed from the romance:

> En effet, l'on trouve employés dans le roman, avant Cervantes, tous ces procédés qui servent à rehausser l'intérêt des choses racontées. De même les digressions, les longues conversations rapportées textuellement, et la convention d'après laquelle l'auteur est omniscient en tout ce qui concerne son histoire, ces particularités de la nouvelle cervantesque avaient été jusque-là le fait du roman seul.[51]

[50] George Hainsworth, *Les "Novelas Exemplares" de Cervantes en France au XVIIe siècle*, Bibliothèque de la *Revue de Littérature Comparée*, no. 95 (Paris: Champion, 1933).

[51] ibid., p 26.

Sorel, whom Hainsworth regards as the first French author of *nouvelles,* also translated Cervantes. To him *nouvelles* were hardly distinguishable from little *romans*:

> En un mot, nous voulons des nouvelles: le mot l'emporte: Ce sont des nouveautez. Ce nom est attribué aux contes de Boccace et de la Reyne de Navarre de mesme qu'aux Histoires amoureuses de Cervantes, et d'autres, ce qui monstre que pour se donner un tel divertissement l'on peut aussi bien raconter des avantures agreables et merveilleuses en maniere de Roman, comme des nouvelles facetieuses.[52]

Thus Sorel tends to emphasize the *romanesque* elements of Cervantes' *nouvelles* both in his translations and his imitations. Other translators followed suit; again quoting Hainsworth: "Les nouvelles de Lancelot [translations from the most famous Spanish authors (1628)] sont surtout importantes en ce qu'elles renforcent l'influence de la partie romanesque des *Novelas Exemplares,* et cette influence, nous allons le voir, ne tarde pas à être affermie par d'autres traductions."[53] The next important translations came from the pen of Scarron, and while he shunned the most extravagant, he displays no interest in the most "realistic" ones either.

Cervantes, Sorel, and Scarron all share a curious sort of blindness to the impact of their own work; or at least so it seems to the modern reader. All three wrote burlesques, which now seem like direct ancestors of the realistic novels of the nineteenth century, but which they themselves apparently regarded chiefly as satires. The old forms, the medieval romances for Cervantes, the pastoral romances for Sorel, the heroic romances for Scarron, needed to be replaced; but *Don Quixote, Le Berger extravagant,* and *Le Roman comique* are demolitions, not reconstructions. Both within these works and in separate collections, the three authors offer the public a new, and presumably more satisfactory genre: the *nouvelle.* Yet in their settings, these *nouvelles* maintain a considerable

[52] Charles Sorel, *La Maison des jeux* (1642), quoted by Hainsworth, p. 127.
[53] Hainsworth, p. 162.

distance from what we now regard as realism, and this distance guided the evolution of the *nouvelle* in France, if not the novel in England.

The promise of renewal through imitation of the *novela* thus failed, because the *novela* could not resist assimilation by the *roman*. The *roman* tradition was powerful; the *novela* from the outset shared many elements with the *roman*. Godenne says, in fact, that the authors of *nouvelles* "se mettent franchement à l'école des romanciers" in the last third of the seventeenth century.[54] The French persistently admired and imitated the most *romanesque* elements of the *nouvelle* or *novela*, because these elements fit in better with the classical theories of art. These elements were, in particular, a seriousness of tone and manner, and a self-conscious artistry in style and technique. Neither is inconsistent with the novel as we think of it today, but for the moment, realism in our sense had taken refuge in works which provoked laughter, and which mocked the art of the *roman*. Most important, the authors of *nouvelles*, except for Mme de Lafayette, lacked genius. Coulet says of them: "Sans être vraiment classiques, ils ont connu les circonstances qui ont aussi produit le classicisme, mais n'en ont ressenti que les effets négatifs."[55]

The great irony is that the French, obsessed with the notion of clear distinctions between genres, failed completely to identify and establish genres within the realm of fiction. The most prestigious form of *nouvelle*, that practiced by Mme de Lafayette, bore close kinship to the *romans*. Mlle de Scudéry had pointed the way for these minute analyses of the human heart, where the realism is all psychological. Circumstantial detail was deemed unnecessary, even undesirable, for it lessened the likelihood of the reader's identifying herself—the reader was always assumed to be a woman—with the heroine. In some ways, progress was accomplished. The settings came to be nearer home, but without getting much more detailed in their description. The characters

[54] Godenne, *Histoire de la nouvelle,* p. 120.
[55] Coulet, *Le Roman jusqu'à la Révolution,* tome I, p. 272.

tended more and more to be French men and women, with plausible French names, although with little progress in particularization of character. The events related included less and less exaggeration and generally excluded the impossible; but coincidences still abounded. The *nouvelle*'s claim to relate more familiar and commonplace events was at least partly true; but the differences were so superficial and vague that no one succeeded in defining them effectively.

The demand for more verisimilitude remained strong, and the failure of the *nouvelle* to provide it did not escape notice. The satires on the *roman* were reedited, and new ones kept appearing; *La Fausse Clélie* (1670), *Le Roman bourgeois* (1677), *Pharsamon* (1712), *Fan-Férédin* (1735), and others attest to the continuing refusal of the more acute readers to be satisfied. Unfortunately the presence of realistic techniques in satirical and burlesque works only tended to keep those techniques identified exclusively with lower genres, and out of serious novels. Instead, the fiction writers looked elsewhere for a way to win belief from the readers.

In this temporary stalemate there arose a genre which concentrated its efforts on the narrator rather than on the events. It took several different forms, which can be described collectively as forged documents. The most famous types are, of course, the memoir and the epistolary novel. Travel accounts, journals, chronicles, and the like are minor variations. In the hands of a clever practitioner, like Courtilz de Sandras, such works could in fact so completely hide the line between truth and fiction that to this day some doubt persists. Nonetheless, the credibility of a narrator ultimately depended on the credibility of his tale. The publisher of the *Memoires de la comtesse de Tournemir* (1708) may affirm: "Je donne au public ces petits Memoires que l'on a trouvez fort singuliers, et que je sai être très-veritables . . . ," and the comtesse may begin: "Aprés avoir éprouvé tout ce que la fortune a de plus bizarre, de plus cruel et de plus honteux, je veux donner au public, mais je le veux faire de bonne foi, l'histoire de ma miserable vie qui paroitra peut-être tenir de la fable et du Roman, et qui sera cependant aussi veritable que j'ai été malheureuse,"[56] no one is likely to believe that, having escaped beheading for the murder of her brutal husband, who was in reality killed in a duel he had unjustly provoked, the heroine should meet the man she had wanted to marry all along—but, as fate would have it, he is by then a monk. It was still, all too obviously, a *roman*, and no one was fooled.

Indeed, the *romans* were on the whole superior works, compared to these obscure *nouvelles*. In retrospect it is quite just that their prestige should have imposed their name on the genre. Mlle de Scudéry displays some talent as an observer of humanity, at least within the limited scope of social intercourse among gentlefolk, and when she invents, her imagination discloses some breadth. She probably knew much better what she was doing, moreover, and had fewer illusions about winning total belief in her fictions than most of the now forgotten novelists who repudiated her. With exceedingly rare and minor exceptions, the proliferation of subgenres in the late seventeenth century in France does not denote much actual experimentation. Only the names are changed. The *romans*, the *nouvelles*, the *histoires*, the *mémoires,* whether *historiques, galants,* or *véritables*, were virtually indistinguishable from each other.

This conclusion will not surprise scholars of the period. At a colloquium held by the Association Internationale des Etudes Françaises, published in 1966, much the same conclusions were reached.[57] A. Kibédi Varga sought a definition of the *nouvelle* and failed to find one. R. Godenne in a discussion of the relationship between *nouvelle* and *roman* remarked that "Tout se passe comme si les nouvellistes voulaient composer un récit, qui serait comme une sorte de roman en réduction, un 'petit roman' selon l'expression de certains"; his more recent book on the *Histoire de la Nouvelle*

[56] Anon., *Memoires de la comtesse de Tournemir,* 1708, "Avertissement du Libraire," and pp. 1-2.

[57] *Cahiers de l'Association Internationale des Etudes Françaises,* 18 (1966). The quotation from Godenne is on page 74, the one from Fabre on page 257.

en France aux XVIIe et XVIIIe siècles amply documents the same point. J. Rustin had no more success defining *histoire véritable*, and Jean Fabre observed in the discussion afterwards "Ecrire des 'histoires véritables', ce n'est pas tellement réagir contre le romanesque que donner au romanesque une garantie (ou pseudo-garantie) de vérité." I have tried to search out some of the causes for this confusion of genres, all the more surprising because of the desire the period had to separate them, and the fact that in the beginning they were separated to some extent. The English, who knew the Spanish *novela* largely through the intermediary of the French, seem to have accepted the beneficial ideas of artistry and seriousness in prose fiction, while remaining much more open to redefinitions of the concept of familiar subject matter and verisimilitude. In its superficial concern for realism, the English novel diverged from the French, at least temporarily; but in their deeper ambitions, the two traditions remained close together.

— II —

Purposes of the Novel

Efforts to define a genre require looking toward the past. The French novelists of the early eighteenth century, like all their contemporaries, took the question of genres very seriously. Their failure to recognize the novel as a new genre stems from the fact that it was only partly new; its constituent elements could be found in many diverse works of fiction, history, even poetry and satire. Moreover, they were hoping to find a continuity extending back to Antiquity, and this wishful bias further obscured the originality of the emerging "realistic" novel. Even various attempts to describe new fashions in fiction by contrast to past works led finally to the persistence of the old genre, at least in name; and the name carried with it enough tradition to influence and perhaps delay the evolution of the genre in the direction of realism.

To speak of delay, of course, introduces a historical fallacy. The novelist of 1700 had no way of knowing that he was supposed to be groping toward realism. Nor, on the other hand, does this imply that the novelists had no ideas about what the novel should become. Quite the contrary, for hardly a novel came out without a preface in which the author stated his or her purpose, and these statements could be taken all together as a program for the development of the genre. Some of the more important prefaces have been studied in detail by modern scholars; Deloffre has made much of the ideas expressed by Challe and Marivaux in the opening pages of *Les Illustres Françoises, La Voiture embourbée, Les Effets surprenans de la sympathie,* and *Pharsamon.* In the 1920's Daniel Mornet quoted extensively from lesser known works in the introduction to his edition of *La Nouvelle Héloïse,* and more recently Georges May has used these minor works as evidence for what he calls "the dilemma of the novel."[1] In all these cases,

[1] See Frédéric Deloffre's introductions to his editions of Challe, *Œuvres,* 1967; Pierre Carlet de Chamblain de Marivaux, *La Vie de*

Purposes of the Novel

however, the prefaces have been searched for signs of a particular outlook for the future, which we know to be the eventual course of the novel. I will attempt to study them without any such perspective, simply as one indication of the state of the genre when they were written. Furthermore, while scholars have heretofore selected prefaces according to the author's skill (and obviously, the opinions of Challe or Marivaux deserve more attention than those of Pallu de Doublainville), it is also instructive to be able to view the totality of a given period; and to that end, I have examined not only the text but also the prefatory materials in at least three-fourths of all the works listed by S. Paul Jones for the first twenty years of the eighteenth century.

My view is still not complete, to be sure, and Jones's list poses a number of problems in itself. The two-page pamphlet, *Le Marchand devalisé par une femme* (1704), is plainly not a novel. Neither are a number of short collections, such as the *Nouvelles galantes des eaux de Bourbons* (1703), and a series of satirical works directed against the *partisans*, such as *Pluton maltotier* (1708). In rejecting these works, I have injected some of my own historically determined prejudices into the discussion; but I can say with great confidence that any works I have overlooked or eliminated could only further strengthen my conclusion; for the situation of the novel at the beginning of the eighteenth century is highly confused, if not totally chaotic.

The Dilemma of the Novel

Georges May has characterized as the dilemma of the novel a conflict that was particularly acute and therefore formative in the eighteenth century, but that he believes to be inherent

---

Marianne, Classiques Garnier (Paris: Garnier frères, 1963); and Marivaux, *Le Paysan parvenu*, Classiques Garnier (Paris: Garnier frères, 1959); and his article, "Premières Idées de Marivaux sur l'art du roman," *Esprit Créateur*, 1 (1961), 178-83; Daniel Mornet, introduction to Jean-Jacques Rousseau, *La Nouvelle Héloïse*, Grands Ecrivains de la France (Paris: Hachette, 1925), Vol. 1; Georges May, *Le Dilemme du roman*, 1963, ch. 4.

in the very nature of the novel. This conflict opposes, on the one side, a moral obligation upon the author to respect or even reinforce the society's standards of propriety and good conduct, and on the other side an artistic obligation to depict the world as he sees it. May argues that the pressure from the moralists in the 1730's forced the novelists to improve their techniques and to clarify their ideas. Similar pressures in the years from 1650 to 1670 had produced an earlier period of progress. Between 1700 and 1720, there was no particular pressure on the novelists, and that may partially explain why it is a relatively poor period in terms of fiction.

May shows that the progress accomplished by working novelists of the 1730's was accompanied by the elaboration of four critical theories of the novel, each one a reconciliation between morality and realism. The first theory May terms "l'argument du tableau de la vie humaine"; it reframes arguments that had been advanced to justify comedy in the seventeenth century, and holds that a true picture of society will have moral utility. The second argument, "la supériorité de l'exemple concret," is a corollary to the first; it contrasts the effectiveness of abstract moral predication to that of dramatized moral problems. The argument "de la justice immanente," or poetic justice, supplies a formula by which the novel can apparently insure its moral propriety: the good shall be rewarded and the wicked punished. Finally, the argument "du piège dénoncé" claims that even the depiction of vice may be morally useful, because it forewarns the innocent. All four of these theories were current in the first two decades of the eighteenth century.[2]

The "tableau de la vie humaine" is the most sophisticated argument. Crébillon *fils* applied it to the novel with striking forcefulness in the preface to *Les Egarements du cœur et de l'esprit* (1734-36); but May recognizes that the argument itself had been stated before the end of the seventeenth century, and he quotes a passage from the *Mercure galant* of 1694, which claims that there had already been a noticeable

[2] May, *Le Dilemme du roman*, ch. 4.

evolution of the novel in that sense.[3] May points out the influence of La Bruyère, especially on Lesage's *Diable boiteux* (1707); one might equally well quote the "Déclaration de l'auteur" in *Gil Blas* (1715):

> Comme il y a des personnes qui ne sauraient lire sans faire des applications des caractères vicieux ou ridicules qu'elles trouvent dans les ouvrages, je déclare à ces lecteurs malins qu'ils auraient tort d'appliquer les portraits qui sont dans le présent livre. J'en fais un aveu public: je ne me suis proposé que de représenter la vie des hommes telle qu'elle est....[4]

Lesage is visibly more concerned with denying (or hinting at) satirical intentions than in defending the moral usefulness of his work. Challe uses the argument for moral purposes in the preface to *Les Illustres Françoises* (1713):

> Presque tous les romans ne tendent qu'à faire voir par des fictions que la Vertu est toujours persécutée, mais qu'enfin elle triomphe de ses ennemis ... Mon roman ou mes histoires, comme on voudra les appeler, tendent à une morale plus naturelle, et plus chrétienne, puisque par des faits certains, on y voit établi une partie du commerce de la vie.[5]

Among less famous novelists, the chevalier Louis Rustaing de Saint-Jory in the preface to *Les Galanteries angloises* (1700) and the anonymous author of *La Foire de Beaucaire* (1708) both express similar ideas.

May believes that the argument "de l'exemple concret" appears later than the "tableau"; but Rustaing de Saint-Jory had already drawn that conclusion in the work just mentioned, for he calls it " ... une vingtaine de petites histoires ... desquelles les innocentes beautez de nôtre siécle pourront aisément tirer d'utiles instructions, pour peu qu'elles soient disposées à profiter de l'exemple d'autrui."[6] In the same year,

---

[3] ibid., p. 114.
[4] *Romanciers du XVIIIe siècle*, Vol. 1, p. 493.
[5] Challe, *Œuvres*, p. lix.
[6] Rustaing de Saint-Jory, *Les Galanteries angloises*, 1700, p. vii.

1700, appeared the anonymous *Mylord *** ou le paysan de qualité*, with an "Epistre dédicatoire à la jeunesse de France" recommending that the readers consider "ce Volume comme un modèle sur lequel vous devez régler votre conduite envers ceux qui vous ont donné le jour, et ceux qui vous ont touché le cœur."[7] And Challe, too, seems to have drawn the corollary when he concludes his list of moral lessons with the comment: "Voila je croi une bonne partie des rencontres qui se trouvent ordinairement dans le monde, et la morale qu'on en peut tirer est d'autant plus sensible qu'elle est fondée sur des faits certains."[8] May himself points to *Télémaque* (1699) as one of the first novels written on this principle; but the other instances suggest that in reality it was already rather widespread at that time.

May, relying on Moses Ratner, places the first appearance of the argument "de la justice immanente" around 1730,[9] but the passage from Challe quoted earlier—"presque tous les romans ne tendent au'à faire voir par des fictions que la Vertu est toujours persecutée mais qu'enfin elle triomphe de ses ennemis"—would seem to suggest that the formula of poetic justice had been not only used but abused well before 1713. Paul François Nodot's *Histoire de Geofroy surnommé à la grand'dent* (1700), a historical novel, would appear to bear this out; Nodot says of the adventures he relates, "La vertu y paroist toûjours triomphante; le vice condamné, les sciences occultes tournées en un ridicule serieux, suivant leurs principes."[10] Guillaume Castri's *L'Amant libéral dans l'Isle d'Amour* (1709) concludes naively that his tale " . . . marque comme dieu ne laisse point les bonnes actions sans récompense, ayant avant son arrivée enlevé du monde son Rival, et mis Leonor par là en liberté de se choisir un Amant à son gré. . . . Cette Histoire montre aussi qu'il n'y a point de crimes

---

[7] Anon., *Mylord *** ou le paysan de qualité*, 1700, p. ii-iii.
[8] Challe, *Œuvres*, p. lxi.
[9] May, *Le Dilemme du roman*, p. 119.
[10] Nodot, *Histoire de Geofroy surnommé à la grand'dent*, 1700, "Préface."

impunis."[11] Challe, however, was probably thinking primarily of the *nouvelles* of the late seventeenth century, which were the inspiration for his own work, much more than the edifying stories of Nodot or Castri. And whether or not these *nouvelles* stated explicitly that they preserved moral proprieties by means of an arbitrary poetic justice, Challe leaves no doubt that the public knew it.

The final argument, that of "le piège dénoncé," is the least common, both in the 1730's and in the early years of the century. This can probably be attributed to the fact that, as May remarks, the argument can so easily be made "*a posteriori* et de mauvaise foi," and furthermore it can be used to justify almost anything. Catherine Bédacier seems to have had such a rationale in mind when she wrote the preface to *Les Belles Grecques* (1712), which did indeed invite that sort of defense, since the heroines are five courtesans. Challe might well have used the defense for the last two stories in *Les Illustres Françoises* (1713), but at best he only alludes to it. The reviewer of the *Journal Littéraire de la Haye*, however, gave it as clear a formulation as one would ask:

> La septième Histoire, fort inférieure à toutes les autres, est le récit de tous les tours d'un Libertin. On ne trouve pas ce récit trop bien à la suite du précédent, à moins qu'on ne le considère comme une farce à la suite d'une tragédie. Cette Histoire, toutes fois, peut avoir beaucoup d'utilité. Le Caractère du Conteur qu'on y fait parler est si scélérat à l'égard des femmes, que celles qui s'en instruiront pourroient en tirer de justes sujets de méfiance, pour se garder de la fourberie de leurs amants, si lorsque le cœur est pris, la réflexion pouvoit conserver le reste.[12]

The argument is all the more impressive because it is plainly from a disinterested source; moreover, it confirms May's observation that the critics preceded the novelists in using it.

The four types of argumentation just reviewed are all

[11] Castri, *L'Amant libéral dans l'Isle d'Amour*, 1709, p. 40.
[12] Challe, *Œuvres*, p. 576.

peculiarly apt as a realist's response to the charge of immoralism, for they all turn the weapon around—the realistic fiction becomes the necessary tool of the moralist. The popularity, or occasional appearance, of these arguments before 1720 does not alter May's thesis significantly, and indeed may actually support it. What May discovered in the 1730's was a political campaign against the novelists, which spurred them to innovate so long as it remained a mere threat, but discouraged them once it reached the status of theory itself. Nothing of the sort was operating against the novelists of the first decades of the century, so that they were experimenting at their own and their readers' whim. In this relative freedom they did not formulate any of the arguments as clearly and forcefully as the later novelists, which is to say that they had probably not thought about the problem as deeply or as systematically. Moreover, their works remain at a considerable remove from their prefatory claims in most cases, which suggests that the critical pressure on them was weak. And finally, they did not hesitate to advance justifications which would have seemed ridiculously inadequate in 1737, when the state imposed a ban on the whole genre.

For many novelists, the only purpose of a fiction was to amuse the reader. Such is the justification offered by the anonymous author of *La Flandre galante* (1709). A prefatory dialog in the anonymous *Histoires galantes de diverses personnes qui se sont rendues illustres par leur savoir ou par leur bravoure* (1709) has Philinte say: "Le Public croira ce qu'il voudra; pourvû que je fasse passer agreablement quelques heures de temps à mes Lecteurs, ils ne me pardonneront pas seulement, mais ils loüeront mon ouvrage."[13] Too heavy a reliance on this principle could, and no doubt did, all too often lead novelists into the error that Boileau had denounced: "Dans un roman frivole, aisément tout s'excuse." The more serious novelists tried at least to avoid the trap, even while doubting their own worth. Marie Jeanne l'Héritier de Villandon writes, rather pathetically, in the preface to *La Tour ténébreuse* (1705): "Je sçay bien qu'on me peut dire que la

---

[13] Anon., *Histoires galantes de diverses personnes*, 1709, p. 5.

Purposes of the Novel

Tour Tenebreuse n'étant qu'un Ouvrage de divertissement,
on se met peu en peine que j'aye suivi si exactement la
verité."[14]
All the countless novels that promise extraordinary adventures are based implicitly on the idea that the novel's primary
function is to amuse; but to find the argument by itself is rare.
Thus the publisher of the *Memoires de la comtesse de Tournemir* (1708) says: "Je donne au public ces petits Memoires que
l'on a trouvez fort singuliers, et que je sai être très-veritables."[15] The claim of veracity promised a special kind
of amusement, and of course leads back to the question of
realism. Occasionally authors tried to define other sorts of entertainment. Marivaux presents *La Voiture embourbée*
(1714) with the comment that its strange mixture of styles
gives it "un air extraordinaire, qui doit faire espérer qu'il
divertira plus qu'il n'ennuiera,"[16] and the work which follows
is a comic novel with several different styles of narration. In
another work, *Les Avantures de *** ou les Effets surprenans
de la sympathie* (1713), Marivaux stresses the emotional
effect of the fiction: "... et puisque le Roman n'est fait que
pour le cœur, quand il le touche, doit-on s'en plaindre?"[17]
Later in this very sophisticated preface, Marivaux makes
some fine distinctions: "Je trouve à mon gré qu'on a retranché
des Romans tout ce qui pouvoit les rendre utiles et souvent
même interessans. Ceux qu'on compose à present ne sont que
de simples avantures racontées avec une hâte qui amuse le
lecteur à la verité, mais qui ne l'attendrit, ni ne le touche...."
As Marivaux's language implies, for an author concerned
with the quality of the amusement he provides, amusement
is not far distant from utility. With very slight modifications,
Marivaux's statement can be transformed into an argument
for the "tableau de la vie," or for the "exemple concret."

[14] L'Héritier de Villandon, *La Tour ténébreuse*, 1705, "Préface."
[15] Anon., *Memoires de la comtesse de Tournemir*, 1708, "Avertissement du Libraire."
[16] In Marivaux, *Romans*, ed. Marcel Arland, Bibliothèque de la
Pléiade (Paris: Librairie Gallimard, 1949), p. 3.
[17] Marivaux, *Les Avantures de ****, 1713, Vol. 1, "Avis au lecteur."
Listed as anonymous by Jones.

45

The last widely used argument bears some relation to that of the "piège dénoncé": it treats the novel as a school of manners in the most practical sense. It is quite possibly the most obsolete of all the arguments and seems to have been in particular esteem in the seventeenth century. The literal-minded application of fiction to life lies at the heart of the quixotic theme, which was often imitated in France. In *Francion* (1623-33) the hero relates:

> Il me souvient qu'estant a Paris j'avois un laquais qui estoit fort amoureux d'une servante du quartier. Ayant trouvé dans mon cabinet les amours de Nerveze et de Desescuteaux [both were active novelists between 1600 and 1610, and published several works entitled *Amours*], que je gardois pour me faire rire, il en dechira les fueillets où il y avoit des complimens. Il les apprenoit par cœur pour les dire a sa Maistresse, et les portoit tousjours dans sa poche pour y estudier, de peur de les mettre en oubly.[18]

In *Le Roman bourgeois* (1666) Furetière created the comic hero Nicodème, who "auroit bien voulu faire l'amour dans les formes; il n'auroit pas voulu oublier une des manieres qu'il avoit trouvées dans ses livres, car il avoit fait son cours exprés dans Cyrus et dans Clelie."[19]

It was not only a joke for the satirists, however. When Choisy undertook to abridge the gigantic *Astrée* in 1712, he explained that he had done so at the request of a lady, because "Elle avoit ouï dire, qu'une jeune personne, qui veut avoir de l'esprit, doit lire et relire le Roman d'Astrée."[20] Furthermore, in the *Histoires galantes* . . . (1709) already quoted, while Philinte considers entertainment a sufficient justification, he responds to Timante's criticism by adding:

[18] In *Romanciers du XVIIe siècle*, ed. Antoine Adam, Bibliothèque de la Pléiade (Paris: Librairie Gallimard, 1958), p. 432. Hereafter cited as *Romanciers du XVIIe siècle*.

[19] *Romanciers du XVIIe siècle*, p. 911.

[20] Choisy, *La Nouvelle Astrée* (Amsterdam: Pierre Humbert, 1713; first edition 1712), "Avertissement."

" . . . ils apprennent du moins par cette lecture l'usage du monde et à s'énoncer aisément."[21]

The expression of these various theories about the educational purposes of fiction did not serve to orient the novel in any particular direction. The prefaces do demonstrate that from the beginnings, even the minor writers were aware of different possibilities and gave some thought to their art, if only after the fact. Posterity would soon show that the "tableau de la vie humaine" opened the most promising avenues, but not until after the others had been shown to fail, notably the formula of poetic justice. It would be satisfying to discover that the best novelists sensed that from the start, but such is not the case. The young Marivaux was drawn toward the sentimental *romans* of the old school, Challe believed that precise morals could be drawn from his stories, and only the satirist Lesage set out to portray society. Had all three done so, the evolution toward realism would no doubt have been much faster, for the next generation—Prévost, Crébillon *fils*, Duclos, et al.—would have had different models.

The moral aspect, moreover, is only half the dilemma. There was as much debate and confusion about the nature of realism as about the purpose of the novel. Of the three elder authors just mentioned, Challe, not Lesage, comes closest to a modern conception of realism, despite his edifying intentions. Thus there is another group of standards to analyze, before it is possible to say what was the range of choices confronting a novelist in 1700.

Realism

The concepts associated with the term realism, when applied to fiction, are so elusive even today that it would be astonishing to find any widely accepted theory of realism in 1700. For general usage, realism signifies a fundamental plausibility, usually created or reinforced by the multiplication of physical details and the choice of ordinary subjects. I have been

---

[21] Anon., *Histoires galantes de diverses personnes*, 1709, p. 7.

using the term in this sense. The literary notion of realism contains at least two separate ideas, however: one of subject matter and one of technique, each of which may be diversely interpreted. A novel which seems realistic in 1970 must ordinarily seem true at many different levels: true to our sense perceptions, true to our reasonable expectation of how things happen, true to our emotional sensibilities, true to our philosophical understanding of the world; but in all cases it is the content or subject which seems true. There are in fact many techniques capable of producing this effect, only one of which is usually called realism, the one that emphasizes the physical detail and the everyday subject, and was predominant during the nineteenth century. This technical definition can henceforth be designated by giving Realism a capital R; but the general terms "reality" and "realistic" remain as elusive as ever, even in relation to a Realistic novel.

Novelists throughout the seventeenth century were interested in the question of how to make their works realistic, and they tended to limit their requirements to only one level of truth. It is therefore relatively easy to classify the approaches to the question, on a theoretical basis, although such a classification often leaves a modern reader perplexed when he considers the novel that presumably realizes the prescription. The disparity is due to the fact that most of the discussion centered on the nature of reality, or at least on the type of reality that was suited to the novel, with very few implications for the technique. The techniques can be studied only in the works, for there are virtually no treatises or even isolated comments on the craft of fiction until quite late in the eighteenth century. Much of what appears to be technical advice or criticism is in fact part of a debate on the nature of reality. I have, of necessity, devoted a long and independent chapter to the development of the techniques of Realism; but from the prefaces I will try only to give evidence for the different concepts of reality, and the novelists' attitudes toward it.

Hardly anyone argued that the novel had no need of "le vrai." Later in the eighteenth century, when the gap between the triumphant moralists and the clandestine realists was at its widest, Baculard d'Arnaud could write, in the preface to his *Nouvelles historiques* (1774): "Ayons donc, s'il le faut, recours aux artifices de la fiction; c'est dans cette circonstance qu'il faut bien se garder d'exposer le vrai dans une nudité dangereuse à voir; laissons croire aux hommes que cette vertu les mènera aux plaisirs, aux richesses, aux dignités; c'est un roman: eh bien! ardents sectateurs de la vérité, ne nous ôtez point notre roman."[22] Such an attitude was unnecessary in the early years of the century, for the dilemma had not been pushed to the point of opposing morality to truth, even a fictional truth, much less the real truth, as Baculard d'Arnaud seems to imply. By the same token, however, the most diverse authors acknowledged the need for "le vrai," and sought to persuade their readers that they had provided it.

At one extreme stand the classically oriented authors, who distinguish sharply between "le vrai" and "le vraisemblable." Historical reality may well be implausible, and indeed many of the circumstances and accidents of life mock credibility. To an author of this school, the historical fact is less interesting than the universal truths that can be abstracted by reason from the mass of facts. Such an attitude of course presides over much of the seventeenth century, and was shared by the great dramatists and moralists of the Age of Louis XIV. It is perhaps the greatest enemy of Realism, because it has an equal artistic validity but a completely opposite approach. Its lingering prestige was certainly one factor in delaying the entry of English Realism into France, thereby somewhat delaying the evolution of the novel.

At its most extreme, this vision of truth leads to allegory, and the individual becomes a pure type. It is, then, the spirit behind a tale like *Florine ou la belle Italienne* (1713) which has a key to the names at the conclusion: Agatonphise represents "le bon sens," Achakie "l'innocence," Agnoïse "l'ignorance," etc. Similarly, the use of impossible or highly improbable stories may be justified in the name of an abstract

[22] Baculard d'Arnaud, *Nouvelles historiques* (Paris: Delalain, 1774), Vol. I, p. xxii.

moral truth. Bruslé de Montpleinchamp, for example, in *Le Diable bossu* (1708), constructs an elaborate frame using various demons and gods, all of which he excuses by saying that "on a pris l'air de Roman, mais on s'en est distingué en racontant de pures veritez sous quelques voiles dessennuians."[23] And in fact, the tales all involve little moral lessons.

Nodot, in *Histoire de Geofroy* (1700), first refers to the historical bases for his work, but he adds: "Ces évenemens ont servi de sujet à cet Ouvrage: ils sont mêlez de plusieurs avantures fort extraordinaires; mais qui contiennent une morale, dont les reflexions peuvent estre utiles."[24]

The most successful novelist in this style is Lesage. *Le Diable boiteux*, which inspired *Le Diable bossu*, is certainly an example, even though Lesage did not include any statement to that effect in the first edition (1707); in the 1726 edition he described it as "un tableau des mœurs du siècle," and it has been described as La Bruyère put into novel form. In *Gil Blas* there is a similar statement: "Je ne me suis proposé que de représenter la vie des hommes telle qu'elle est; à Dieu ne plaise que j'aie eu dessein de désigner quelqu'un en particulier."[25] That Lesage should hold at the same time the most advanced moral position, and the most backward view of reality, is at first glance paradoxical, and reflects a typical consequence of "the dilemma." In practice, classicists like La Bruyère, Molière, and Lesage tended to group individuals, and to minimize the differences; "les grands, les femmes, les esprits forts" might conveniently classify large numbers of people with many common characteristics, and "le misanthrope, l'avare, le bourgeois gentilhomme" might name a universal type. The authors who presented them, however, knew that each representative had his own individual characteristics, and the art of Molière or La Bruyère or Lesage

---

[23] Bruslé de Montpleinchamp, *Le Diable bossu*, 1708, "Préface," p. xiv.

[24] Nodot, *Histoire de Geofroy surnommé à la grand'dent*, 1700, "Préface."

[25] *Romanciers du XVIIIe siècle*, Vol. i, p. 493.

consists in preserving just enough of the individuality to make the character live, while bringing out fully his type. A very slight increase in the attention one pays to the individuality can transform this classical aesthetic into a Realist aesthetic. The eighteenth century did more or less just that. The number of types seems to proliferate; this tendency is obvious already in La Bruyère and has gone quite far in *Le Diable boiteux*. At the same time, the whole class seems to be better illustrated by its most eccentric member, the "original," of which Rameau's nephew is the best known example. And finally, it must be borne in mind that Lesage is not telling the whole truth. Some of his best pages describe real individuals who were only too recognizable, and Lesage was using the classical disclaimer as a ruse.

The classicists, then, although they prefer general to particular truths, admit both aspects of an artistically necessary reality. The group which came closest to denying any need for fidelity to reality looked on fiction as an imaginative art. Its function was to exalt the reader's sensibilities, either through stylistic brilliance or through surprise. At one pole, this theory merges with the classical point of view just discussed; for example, a *conteur* like Voltaire succeeds by delighting rather than convincing his readers, but of course his tales are meant to convey a serious truth. At the other pole, the theory must lead toward Realism, because the fiction's capacity for moving the reader's emotions or imagination depends ultimately on its persuasiveness. In other words, this position really begs the question. Nonetheless, it was occasionally advanced by novelists to justify works of fantasy, like the very popular fairy tales, or new versions of an old story, like Choisy's *La Nouvelle Astrée* (1712) or Mme ***'s *La Nouvelle Psyché* (1711). The already cited *Histoires galantes* (1709) explicitly denies the importance of being believed: "Timante: . . . croyez vous que sur vôtre parole le Public croira que *Solon* et *Socrate* etoient des gens à bonne fortune? Philinte: Le Public croira ce qu'il voudra; pourvû que je fasse passer agreablement quelques heures de temps à mes Lecteurs, ils ne me pardonneront pas seulement, mais il loüeront mon ouvrage."[26] The tone of the stories is, in fact, so close to parody that the author may have intended to make fun of the historical novelists of more lofty pretensions.

The most serious proponent of this justification was the young Marivaux. As has been pointed out, he was several years behind the times in his literary tastes when he first began to write. *Pharsamon*, for example, written around 1713, satirizes La Calprenède's *Pharamond* which came out in twelve volumes between 1661 and 1670, and was the last of the long *romans*. Similarly, the enchantments and chivalric adventures of *La Voiture embourbée* (1714) belong to an earlier age; it can be appreciated today because of a few realistic scenes in the frame, which Marivaux no doubt regarded as "comiques" at the time. His preface describes the work as follows: "la tournure m'en paraît plaisante, le comique divertissant, le merveilleux assez nouveau, les transitions assez naturelles; et le mélange bizarre de tous ces différents goûts lui donne totalement un air extraordinaire, qui doit faire espérer qu'il divertira plus qu'il n'ennuiéra." Later, having failed to write a satisfactory preface, he states: "Sans l'embarrassant dessein de faire cette préface, j'aurais parlé de mon livre en termes plus naturels, plus justes, ni humbles, ni vains: j'aurais dit qu'il y avait de l'imagination; que je n'osais décider si elle était bonne; qu'au reste, je m'étais véritablement diverti à le composer, et que je souhaitais qu'il divertît aussi les autres. . . ."[27] The key terms are therefore imagination and entertainment; but these elements, at least in fiction, were already relegated to separate and inferior genres like fairy tales by most readers and authors, unless the author took the trouble to justify his fantasies by grounding them in some kind of truth.

Another of Marivaux's early works, *Les Avantures de *** ou les Effets surprenans de la sympathie* (1713), emphasizes emotional involvement rather than amusement: "Quand un Roman attendrit les Dames, en vain on crie qu'il ne vaut rien,

[26] Anon., *Histoires galantes de diverses personnes*, 1709, p. 5.
[27] Marivaux, *Romans*, Bibliothèque de la Pléiade, pp. 3-4.

le cœur est gagné, il est persuadé, peut-il se tromper? et puisque le Roman n'est fait que pour le cœur, quand il le touche, doit-on s'en plaindre?" But Marivaux realized very quickly that for the heart to be persuaded took more than mere imagination, and a few lines later he concedes that "quand les Dames lisent un Roman, en vain l'amour en est la matiere, si cet amour n'est dépeint dans le vrai."[28] In formulating the novel's purpose as winning the heart, and in defending the evocation of love as a means, Marivaux actually comes somewhat ahead of his time, perhaps through naiveté, for he was exposing his works to the most persistent of the moralists' attacks. Despite his admiration for the seventeenth century's independence from reality and reliance on a pure creative imagination, Marivaux's own perception of the novel's effect led him toward the realism of the 1730's, emphasizing fidelity to reality instead of imagination, and utility instead of entertainment.

Both of the preceding arguments were relatively uncommon and near disappearance; their chief interest lies in the fact that authors as promising as Marivaux and Lesage still found value in them. The dominant approach to reality in fiction, however, relied on the novel's assumed kinship with history. A satisfactory theoretical statement of historical verisimilitude had been achieved by Georges de Scudéry in his preface to *Ibrahim* in 1641. It held that the novelist was bound to respect known historical events: battles, treaties, deaths, marriages, and the like; but that the circumstances, such as conversations, and the private lives, especially the secret love affairs, could be imagined by the novelist within the historical framework. The genre is, of course, still thriving. It admits of great variety in execution, from the highly fanciful romances of the Scudérys to the very plausible *nouvelles historiques* of Mme de Villedieu, which Bayle condemned because they were often mistaken for history. To judge by their prefaces, however, writers of this school did not by and large intend to deceive their readers; they quite

---

[28] Marivaux, *Les Avantures de *** ou les Effets surprenans de la sympathie*, 1713, Vol. i, "Avis au lecteur."

openly admitted that they were embroidering upon the truth, while insisting that they had not invented anything in direct contradiction to it.

Mme de Villedieu provides as clear a statement of principles as anyone; here is part of the preface of her *Annales galantes* (1697):

> J'avoüe que j'ay ajoûté quelques ornemens à la simplicité de l'Histoire. La Majesté des matieres Historiques ne permet pas à l'Historien judicieux de s'étendre sur les Incidens purement Galants. Il ne les rapporte qu'en passant, et il faut une Bataille fameuse ou le renversement d'une Monarchie pour luy arracher une digression. J'ay dispensé mes Annales de cette austérité. Quand l'Histoire d'Espagne m'apprend qu'une Comtesse Souveraine de Castille suivit en France un Pelerin de saint Jaques, je presuppose que cette grande resolution ne se prend pas dans un moment, il faut se parler, il faut se voir pour s'aimer jusques à cet excez. J'augemente [*sic*] donc à l'Histoire quelques entrevuës secretes et quelques discours amoureux. Si ce ne sont ceux qu'ils ont prononcez, ce sont ceux qu'ils auroient dû prononcer."[29]

The work is accompanied by an index giving sources, with such entries as this:

> Othon III, petit fils d'Othon le grand, et Marie sa femme Frisin. liv 6, Sigon. liv. 7, et pour plus grande commodité abrégé de l'Hist. Universelle de Turcelin, anné 384 [*sic*]. Il y a plus d'invention dans cette Histoire que dans aucune autre, mais si le Lecteur veut prendre la peine de l'examiner, peut-être trouvera-t-il le deguisement de la verité assez juste, pour ne pas blâmer l'Auteur de l'avoir fait.

One could scarcely be more straightforward, but this candor did not prevent critics like Bayle from complaining that Mme de Villedieu had made it impossible to tell truth from fiction.

---

[29] Marie-Catherine Desjardins, called Mme de Villedieu, *Annales galantes* (Lyon: chez Hilaire Baritel, 1697; first edition 1670), "Avant-propos."

The confusion would not have been so easily made had the historians themselves showed more respect for historical fact; but as Paul Hazard has shown, the late seventeenth century lost faith in history because it realized that historians wrote on principles not much different from Mme de Villedieu's.[30] Bayle was trying to establish the bases for a new science of history; he was not speaking for the traditional practice of historians.

Quotations similar to Mme de Villedieu's abound. The chevalier de Mailly wrote in *Anecdote ou Histoire secrete des Vestales* (1700): "Au reste il n'y a dans cette histoire que quelques traits de galanterie qui soient de mon invention, et peut-être mon imagination a-t-elle dicté la vérité."[31] Née de la Rochelle wrote in the preface to *Le Czar Demetrius* (1715): "J'avoue qu'en quelques endroits, j'ay substitué des Episodes à la vérité qui ne me paroissoient pas vraisemblables: mais je l'ai suivie avec trop d'exactitude en mille autres, pour ne donner à mon récit que le simple titre de Nouvelle Historique."[32] One could add Catherine Bédacier's *Anecdotes galans* (1702), Mlle de la Roche-Guilhem's *Histoire des Favorites* (1703), or her *Jacqueline de Bavière* (1707), Marie Jeanne l'Héritier de Villandon's *La Tour ténébreuse* (1705), Cusson's *Les Pieux Délassements de l'esprit* (1711), Jean de la Chapelle's *Les Amours de Tibulle* (1712-13), and the sieur La Paix de Lizancour's *Le Prétendant Perkin* (1716), and many others which are less explicit but plainly within the same genre.

This very popular genre had a double line of descendants. As René Bray put it, "La règle du vraisemblable conduit au romanesque par le canal de l'infidélité à l'histoire."[33] Née de

---

[30] Paul Hazard, *La Crise de la conscience européenne* (Paris: Boivin, 1935), especially Part 1, ch. 2. Georges May has discussed the relationship of the historical crises to the novel in "L'Histoire a-t-elle engendré le roman?" *RHL*, 55 (1955), 155-76.

[31] Mailly, *Anecdote ou Histoire secrete des Vestales*, 1700, "Préface historique," p. 46.

[32] Née de la Rochelle, *Le Czar Demetrius*, 1715, "Préface," p. iii.

[33] René Bray, *La Formation de la doctrine classique en France* (1927; rpt. Paris: Nizet, 1951), p. 209.

la Rochelle is quite openly taking that risk, and in the hands of an imaginative author, like Prévost, the historical framework can serve as pretext for the most outlandish adventures. Nothing in the original theory of historical verisimilitude inescapably predisposes the work toward modern Realism. The true elements are not necessarily important to the plot, and in any case are very limited in nature and function. In a very real sense, the historical framework hindered the development of realistic fictions, by forcing the author to exercise his reconstructive imagination on small, discrete fragments of the story. The multi-leveled sense of truth is harder to construct out of isolated parts than from a single conception, however far removed from historical reality.

At the same time, to writers who were so oriented for other reasons, the theory of historical realism did offer some kind of theoretical foundation and posed no obstacle to the use of realistic detail. The process of developing a realistic novel meant reducing the historical element to the status of background, while emphasizing more and more the imaginary circumstances. *La Princesse de Clèves* had illustrated the successful adaptation of this technique as early as 1678; a rapid further step would be to lower the rank of the major figures. One striking characteristic of this sort of fiction, however, is that it confesses to being fiction. The reader enjoys the author's art, and apparently enjoys it most when it is most realistic; but he enjoys it as art, not because he thinks he is reading history. This is essentially the form of the nineteenth- and twentieth-century novel. In the eighteenth century it was overshadowed by works in the then undifferentiated subgenre that has also continued to thrive as the historical novel, and had in those days the stronger pretensions.

The Scudérys had advocated the use of history solely as a source of real incidents, but in 1641 there was no conflict between the historical and the epic view of reality. Both historians and poets reconstructed, making liberal use of their imaginations. In the 1650's the epic structure had been tested and found unsuitable for the novel. The critics did not immediately discard their epic genealogies, but the novelists began more and more to ally their genre with history rather than with the epic, in practice if not always in theory. Consequently, the novelists' attitude toward reality evolved in close parallel to the historians' during the late seventeenth century, and at the very moment when the novelists were turning to history for respectability, history itself was being discredited. Armed with Cartesian skepticism and critical reason, historical scholars like Bayle challenged all that civilized man thought he knew about his past, and demanded that henceforth an affirmation be accompanied by proof. That meant, of course, returning to the sources of history, the documents and the eye-witness accounts that had survived.

Numerous authors of *nouvelles historiques* continued to write in the traditional historical manner. What Mme de Villedieu had termed "the majesty of historical matters" nonetheless put severe limitations on the range of this technique. Du Plaisir, who has already been quoted, called his poetics for the *nouvelle "Sentimens sur les Lettres et sur l'Histoire,"* and he enjoined the novelists to observe the absolute impartiality of a historian.

In addition, discretion made it awkward to write formal histories of recent events; authors had to resort to transposed settings and pseudonyms. For example, Grandchamp's *Le Telemaque moderne* (1701) advises the reader: "Le Heros qui va paroistre ici masqué sur la Scene, sous le nom de Telemaque moderne, a fait tant de bruit dans le monde par ses Intrigues, que le Public n'aura pas de peine à le reconnoistre."[34] Catherine Bédacier makes almost the same comment in *Les Petits Soupers de l'été 1699* (1702) as an introduction to the "Histoire du duc de Dardelle et de la comtesse d'Orselac." The *Histoire de la Dragone* (1703), another third-person narration, purports to be by the wife of the publisher, who wanted to refute inaccurate versions of the same story which were circulating. It claims the unique advantage of several letters from the heroine—now fighting in Italy—to the author, which are published at the end. To be sure, similar pretexts were required of first-person narrators. The "Aver-

[34] Grandchamp, *Le Telemaque moderne*, 1701, "Avertissement."

tissement" to Olivier's *L'Infortuné Napolitain* (1704), a memoir-novel, explains that the author-hero had to write in order to forestall someone else's doing it. Similar examples are the *Memoires de la comtesse de Tournemir* (1708) and Grandchamp's *La Guerre d'Italie* (1702, 1710); and Philip Stewart gives many more in *Imitation and Illusion in the French Memoir-Novel*, with an impressive variety of reasons.[35] Obviously, it was far easier for the hero to justify telling his own story than for anyone else to do so, especially if secrets were to be revealed.

Readier pretexts for writing were not the only factor that made it expedient for novelists to take the same course as the new historians and forge documents instead of inventing histories. It had been felt even by the heroic romance writers that believability increased as the subject drew closer to home in time and space. Fictitious memoirs opened up a much more extensive area for the novelists to work in than if they had felt obliged to compose formal histories of recent times. Furthermore, the first-person document permitted free range to the emotions. Unlike the historian, the memorialist was expected to have a bias; and as the favorite form gravitated away from the chronicle and toward the private diary, authors could make more direct appeals to pity, compassion, fear, delight, and all the other sentiments that build sympathetic identification. Finally, when the author did his work well, the novel came close to realizing an ancient ambition: total illusion. The experience formerly reserved to madmen like Don Quixote could be imposed on everyone, with an incalculable gain in influence for the novelist.

Frédéric Deloffre has argued, largely on the basis of prefaces by Marivaux and Challe, that by 1700 the attempt to create a total illusion was no longer a primary goal of novelists.[36] It is certainly true that none of the three most impor-

[35] Stewart, *Imitation and Illusion in the French Memoir-Novel*, pp. 84-101.

[36] Deloffre, "Le Problème de l'illusion romanesque et le renouvellement des techniques narratives entre 1700 et 1715," in *La Littérature narrative d'imagination*, ed. Albert Henry, Colloque de Strasbourg

tant novelists writing between 1700 and 1715—Challe, Lesage, and Marivaux—had this intention; and indeed, none of the three used the historical techniques which were numerically dominant. Their unusual theories can not, however, be regarded as a genuine evolutionary phase. Marivaux was unquestionably looking backwards, not forwards, in his earliest works; so, to some degree, was Lesage. Challe's ideas are the most original and the most fruitful for the future, but they are relatively isolated. The vogue of the historical novel, both the admitted fictions and the attempted illusions, was still very much alive. Courtilz de Sandras was actively publishing, with some dozen titles in Jones's list between 1700 and 1716, most of them memoirs. Hamilton's very popular *Mémoires de la vie du comte de Gramont* came out in 1713 and was frequently reedited. Within a few years, Prévost and others instilled new life into these old techniques of the historical novel. If there was a general feeling of dissatisfaction with the historical novel around 1700, it was probably less with its aims than with its results. The theory really gave no counsel at all about how to produce an effective illusion of truth, but once some of these techniques were discovered, novelists like Rousseau and Prévost hastened to use them to dupe the reader. It is possible that Challe, Lesage, and Marivaux, finding the historical novel of 1700 inadequate, were casting about for a better way in a more or less systematic manner. If so, it was Challe who found a genuinely productive direction for the novel to take.

Challe's *Les Illustres Françoises* is undoubtedly the most realistic work of French fiction published during the first two decades of the eighteenth century, but neither Challe's theory nor his accomplishment is entirely without precedent. Challe's posture before reality approximates that of a nineteenth-century Realist: he has a profound respect for detail and circumstance, for the integrity of the event, and for the reality of the commonplace world. In the opening lines of his preface, he claims to have written down stories he has heard,

23-25 avril 1959 (Paris: Presses Universitaires Français, 1961), pp. 115-29.

59

without knowing precisely who was involved; other remarks seem to contradict this claim, however, at least for certain stories. In general, he says: "Je n'ai rien voulu dire qui ne fût vrai,"[37] and he defends specific incidents, like Dupuis's attempted suicide, on the grounds that they were true. On the other hand, he claims to have transposed names, dates, and settings, so as to hide the identities of the people involved. This very act reveals the importance he attached to these details, which many of the novelists of the era would have dispensed with entirely. Challe places the burden of persuasion on the teller, that is, on the style and construction of the story, not on the external guarantees of veracity. These, of course, are matters of technique, and while Challe's technique is supported by his conception of reality, it is neither entirely dependent upon it nor always dictated by it.

A number of other authors, with less talent than Challe, had expressed similar ideas. The chevalier Rustaing de Saint-Jory began his *Galanteries angloises* (1700) by explaining that he had originally intended to be a chronicler of great men and memorable events, but found that it required too much work. Hence he has taken love among ordinary people as his field. The work consists of some twenty-one little stories, some mere anecdotes, some in the tradition of the Italian *novella*, but most susceptible of becoming real novels. The author says of them, " . . . je ne veux rien écrire que je ne sçache trés certainement, et dont je n'aye été pour ainsi dire le témoin Oculaire. . . ."[38] Alas, his laziness or lack of talent prevent him from doing much more than telling the plot. On the other hand, the two little stories in *Les Intrigues parisiennes et provinciales* (1700) are not without merit. The author claims to have heard them from a friend in the Tuileries and the Palais Royal, and he repeats them with the apology, "La curiosité fut toujours permise aux personnes qui ne cherchent qu'à s'instruire."[39] The first tells of Hyacinte, a

[37] Challe, *Œuvres*, p. lxi.

[38] Rustaing de Saint-Jory, *Les Galanteries angloises*, 1700, p. 214.

[39] Anon., *Les Intrigues parisiennes et provinciales*, 1700, "A Madame D ∗ ∗ ∗."

merchant's daughter, who loves a poor nobleman but lets ambition guide her choice of a more distinguished marquis; but
then she gets smallpox, is abandoned by the marquis, and
marries her true love after all. The account of Hyacinte's
fears of catching the disease, and her efforts to escape it, is
unusual but convincing—just the sort of detail that converts
the providential disease into a realistic incident.

La Foire de Beaucaire (1708) is an even more interesting
work. The preface is long, but deserves to be quoted:

> En me servant du Titre de la Foire de Beaucaire, je n'ai
> point prétendu faire le détail des Marchandises qui s'y
> vendent, des spectacles qu'on y voit, ni de ce qui s'y passe
> publiquement, mon unique dessein étant de raporter les
> Evenements veritables qui y sont arrivez, et que je sai de
> bonne part. Si je n'en marque point le tems positivement,
> et si je ne me sers pas des propres noms, cela ne fait rien
> à la certitude des choses. Ceux qui trouveront quelque
> ressemblance entre cette Histoire et leur fortune me
> voudront peut-être du mal; mais s'ils savoient mon inten-
> tion, elle leur paroîtroit innocente. On écrit aujourd'hui sur
> toutes sortes de matieres: rien n'est plus commun que de
> faire des Livres, et pour en fournir les Libraires, on n'est
> pas toûjours obligé d'en puiser les sujets dans l'Histoire. Le
> cours de la vie présente en fournit qui ne sont pas moins
> propres pour divertir que ceux des siécles passez. J'en
> laisse faire le jugement aux personnes de bon sens, sans
> m'arrêter à combattre les entestez. Les avantures des
> hommes ordinaires peuvent aussi-bien remplir des volumes
> que celles des Princes et des Heros. J'en prends les Espa-
> gnols à témoin qui dans leurs Nouvelles galantes n'ont
> affecté ni le merveilleux, ni le magnifique. Ce sont d'assez
> bons modelles, et on ne seroit pas méprisable en les imitant
> avec un genie qui pût approcher du leur.[40]

The stories are far from perfect; the first, that of the marquis
de Chalantes and Mlle de Saint-Alais, later Mme de
Montalan, begins well. Their love is opposed, and she, under

---

[40] Anon., *La Foire de Beaucaire*, 1708, "Préface."

threat of a convent, marries Montalan. In a well conceived scene, Chalantes disguises himself as a painter in an effort to see her, but she sends him away. The story ends, however, with several unbelievably providential deaths and reunions. In the second, Riberac loves Mlle d'Elbiac, and the family favors him, but she just does not want to marry. Riberac fights a bloodless duel with a rival, who is no more favored than he, and the account of it sparks Mlle d'Elbiac's interest, so that she finally agrees to marry Riberac. In a third tale Mme de Verdezi was a Protestant orphan, whose Catholic relatives had her put in a convent to get her inheritance. She is then rescued by a Protestant friend of another nun. There are moments when the characters are quite unusual and interesting, and the characterizations, even of minor figures, like Mme de Montalan's mother, well done. The general themes and tone bear some resemblance to *Les Illustres Françoises*—the intrepidity of the heroines, the antipathy to convents, the sympathy for Protestants. In any case, the author has applied the principles of the preface to a remarkable degree.

Other works which could be cited in this category include *Mylord *** ou le paysan de qualité* (1700), Cavard's *Mémoires du comte de Vordac* (1702), which is full of childhood memories and some Rousseauistic accents, and De Sacy's *Histoire du marquis de Clemes et du chevalier de Pervanes* (1716), which the author claims is true, and in which he says he has deliberately used "des hommes privez" as heroes. It is a remarkably graphic story of adultery, which ends with the guilty wife receiving "vingt-trois coups d'épée."

Deloffre has shown that the "histoire véritable," as this sort of tale was most often called, exerted a major influence on both Marivaux and Prévost, perhaps on Richardson as well. In quantity of works written, it was still a minor genre in 1713, but it already incorporated the basic principles of Realism, combining the Spanish attention to the lower elements of society with the French seriousness of purpose. It located reality where we would locate it today, all about us, and thus focused the problem on the techniques of the writer. As I have observed before, the technical problems could be, and were, dealt with separately. There were elements of a new realism in Lesage, in Marivaux, in all the historical fictions, but also in the comic novels and satires; the next chapter will deal with their evolution amid such dispersion. It is probably not an accident, however, that some of the most dramatic signs of progress occur among this last group of writers; for their theory put the greatest burden on technique.

Good theory does not produce good literature; no one has even demonstrated that it helps. The best theories and analyses seem to appear after the best works have been written. By the same token, bad theories do not prevent progress; many an author has written well in spite of himself.

In the first twenty years of the eighteenth century, virtually all the major doctrines regarding the genre of the novel, its moral purpose, and its relationship to reality had not only been stated, but had achieved wide currency. Brilliant intuitions for the later development of fiction can be found in a close reading of Marivaux's prefaces, but they can also be found in the prefaces to obscure works by anonymous or forgotten authors. Statements of principle can be found which Balzac or Dickens need not have disclaimed, but as often as not, the work that they accompany did not find favor even with its contemporary readers. The importance of the theoretical and critical statements may, therefore, legitimately be doubted. Two factors prevent their being completely discounted. The first, as Georges May has proven, is that the hostile critics had political and social power which they brought to bear on the novelists, going so far as to ban the entire genre. Under such conditions, the writer obviously had to make some allowance for what the critic said. The second, a more evident point, is that the prefaces denote concern and interest in the problem, however confused their ideas and however irrelevant their advice may be.

It is nevertheless hopeless to try to trace an evolution of the novel through the critical writings. A change in the predominant tone of the critics is more likely to follow and reflect a change in the novels themselves than to bring such a change about. Even more than with the novels, a modern scholar is likely to be misled, by the apparent modernity of a preface by Scudéry or an essay by Du Plaisir, into tracing a line of steady progress through them. Yet the works written under the guidance of Scudéry's ideas are really responsible for the derogatory implications of the term "romanesque," and Du Plaisir's essay went practically unnoticed in its own time. One is tempted to ask why, if good theories had been formulated, they failed to assist the evolution of the genre. And an answer can be provided, although the question is badly put; one should ask how the theories could have helped.

It might have worked if all the good elements could have been combined in one major doctrine. If a scholar with Huet's prestige, Segrais's conception of the distinction between *roman* and *nouvelle*, Lesage's ideas on the utility of fiction, and Challe's attitude toward the reproduction of reality had written a defense of the novel, perhaps more progress would have occurred sooner. I rather doubt it, however; such a work would have reduced the confusion and, one can say with hindsight, would have encouraged novelists to work in the right vein. The real difficulty, nevertheless, lay elsewhere.

The rarest thing in these early years of the novel is to find a work which lives up to the claims of its preface. Today we notice especially that authors claiming to tell the truth, or to show life as it is, fail miserably; but we overlook the fact that those who profess the more modest desire only to amuse do not succeed any better. And still more significantly, those who promise extraordinary adventures and great wonders usually fill their volumes with predictable clichés, which would be more credible if they were more, not less, extraordinary. One successful application of a theory had more impact than several clear formulations of it; that is the secret of the continued prestige of the long romances. For all their faults, some of these works displayed real imagination. Most of the time, as one would expect, even praiseworthy attempts were flawed, which is to say that the principles were applied intermittently. Even the greatest novels of the eighteenth century have these lapses—critics worry over the "Old Man of the Hill" in *Tom Jones*, the moral digressions of *La Nouvelle Héloïse*, and the arbitrary ending of *Les Liaisons dangereuses*. In earlier works by far less gifted writers, such anomalies abound.

The anomaly, moreover, was not always readily perceptible as such. Indeed, the more successful the work was as a whole, the more difficult it was to demarcate its weaknesses. To take one well-known example, the worst elements in *Clarissa* are probably its long-winded preachiness and its epistolary form. Yet the French imitated both extensively, and did not recognize the value of Richardson's meticulous concern for everyday circumstances until much later. Even Diderot, who did recognize the importance of Richardson's realism, and was able to formulate the most advanced ideas of the century on fiction in France, nevertheless overestimated the worth of the predication by a wide margin. And in lesser works, if the faults were more glaring, the qualities were harder to detect.

The situation of the novel, in terms of theory, can then be summed up as chaotic. Most of the theories were derived by deductive logic from purely external sources, the rules of history or of the epic, or again, the dictates of morality. Inevitably, some of the theoretical discussions were not bad, but the novelists had little way of knowing which ones. In any case, the novelists almost without exception proceeded by imitating other novels, not by following precepts. This was no doubt a happy consequence of the fact that no theorist of the novel had the dogmatic authority of a Boileau. With a proliferation of advice to choose from, they could and did experiment, within the limitations of their own talents. Clearly, there existed a general pressure from the public for more and better fiction, and a general desire on the part of novelists to elevate their genre above the status of mere entertainment for idle women and fops.

Progress was constantly taking place in the novels. Among the several hundred minor novels published in French, in this period, there are literally scores in which a modern reader will find some detail, some incident, some character to surprise and delight him. Most of these passed unnoticed into oblivion. A few, and nobody will ever know which few, undoubtedly struck the attention of the growing new generation of novelists, and emerged later in some other form. It is certainly through this evolutionary mechanism that Realism finally emerged as the dominant trait of the novel. Each successive step in that direction was perceived, amid the confusion, as possessing exceptional power. Hence it survived, in the memory of other writers.

—III—

Techniques of Realism in Early Fiction

Introduction: Critical Methods

The techniques of any art are by and large conventional. That is to say, a work of art represents something to its audience by means of mutually agreed upon signs. Since every element in that statement is susceptible, not only of diverse interpretations at a given time, but also of interpretations that change in time, the study of techniques requires a very careful definition of its terms.

Surely no form of art is more conventional than literature, for its very medium is conventional. There is no apparent logical relationship between the sound of a word and the concept or object it designates; and further, there is no apparent logical relationship between the written symbols of a language and the sounds or the concepts and objects. The entire system of language from which literature is fashioned is itself a conventional system, a very complex one, with semantic, auditory, and visual components, arbitrarily linked by the general consent of all who use the language. Some other art forms occasionally attempt to renounce their conventionality, by taking the "found object" as a piece of sculpture, or by calling natural sounds music. Of course, some convention remains, if only in the isolation of the "work" from its natural environment; but such efforts at evasion can scarcely be imagined in literature, and needless to say, the seventeenth century never even contemplated the possibility, at least in those terms.

On the other hand, writers of the period tried very hard to define what the work of art ought to represent, and then to codify the signs by which the representation would be made. In the preceding pages, I have tried to show that the novelists were in great confusion about what their works ought to be representing; to some extent, other literary genres, like the theatre, suffered from a similar confusion. But as I argued in the opening section, the novelists were equally confused about their genre; unlike the dramatists, they did not know which set of conventional signs, if any, was appropriate for their use.

One of the things that art might represent is reality, meaning the physical world, events in logical sequence, and human actions with plausible motivation. Other subjects for art might be fantasy, or moral truth, or the supernatural, or some more restricted version of reality. Whenever a writer sets himself the goal of depicting reality in the definition just given, he ought logically to be called a realist; and it is clear that there were realists writing what are now called romances at least as early as George de Scudéry's preface to *Ibrahim* in 1641. The reason Scudéry is not generally considered a realist is chiefly that the techniques he devised, based on a combination of historical and epic conventions, do not much resemble the techniques of the nineteenth-century Realists.

Alongside Scudéry's realism there existed many other theories about the purposes of the novel and the nature of its subject. If it were possible to determine precisely for each work what theory its author was applying in it, one could isolate the realistic fictions and study just the evolution of realism. The problem, alas, is not nearly so simple. It is not just that the author's intention often can not be determined, nor that the theories were ambiguous; even within a single work, the author's direction often appears to change abruptly. At first glance, it seems that the only way to make sense of the confusion is to inject a later perspective into it, to take the knowledge that more realism was coming as a proof that any instance of realistic writing belonged in an evolutionary chain. This approach, as I have argued, badly distorts the true situation in which a novelist of 1700 found himself.

Ian Watt has attempted an alternate approach on the English novel, and achieved some very brilliant results. The originality of his method consists in disregarding the literary antecedents and concentrating on the audience. Since the conventions are consented to by the readers, their motives can be analyzed to explain how the conventions evolved.

Techniques of Realism in Early Fiction

While admitting the great worth of Watt's work, I can not put full faith in it. For one thing, as Georges May and others have long since pointed out, Watt has to find a pretext for ignoring French fiction during the period he studies, and the pretext he finds is not very convincing.[1] Indeed, this approach depends initially on being able to consider the novel as an entirely new phenomenon, and I explained in the first section why this is simply not true of French fiction. A second point which weakens Watt's argument is the cosmopolitanism of fiction in the eighteenth century. If exclusively English factors produced the novel, how did it happen that the French liked English novels so much right away? And conversely, why did the English continue to demand translations of French fiction? Is it plausible that novelists of the two nations could have been following such different paths, when there are so many cases in both directions of mutual influence—and occasional occurrences of similar themes almost simultaneously?[2]

On a different level, Watt's arguments depend too heavily on speculative relationships between the reader and the novel. It is by no means certain that readers generally, or eighteenth-century British bourgeois women readers particularly, prefer to read about themselves; and even granting that as a very plausible assumption, it remains to determine what sort of things people like to read about themselves. To illustrate, Watt writes of *Pamela*: "The marriage of the protagonists usually leads to a rise in the social and economic status

[1] Watt, *The Rise of the Novel*, p. 30; cf. May, *Le Dilemme du roman*, pp. 7-8.

[2] To cite only some well-known examples: Lesage was extremely popular in England and was translated by Smollett; Fielding read widely in French Fiction; Prévost's *Manon Lescaut* (1731) and Defoe's *Moll Flanders* (1722) are similar enough to have inspired a controversy over whether Prévost copied Defoe; the same is true of Marivaux's *La Vie de Marianne* (1731-45) and Richardson's *Pamela* (1740); Rousseau's *La Nouvelle Héloïse* (1761) was widely admired in England, although less than in France; Defoe's *Robinson Crusoe* (1719) became an immediate classic in France; Richardson was translated by Prévost and widely imitated in France; Fielding was also popular, although less than in England; and finally, Sterne was particularly appreciated and imitated by Diderot.

of the bride, not the bridegroom. Hypergamy, though not a convention of modern society, is a fairly constant convention of the novel; and its ultimate cause is surely the preponderance of women in the novel-reading public, a preponderance which this crucial detail of its matrimonial mystique directly reflects."[3] One might just as plausibly argue that since there is a preponderance of male authors, this matrimonial mystique represents a masculine fantasy; with the creator of Lovelace and Clarissa, an imaginative obsession must surely be granted considerable importance. That the subject matter of the novel roughly parallels social changes is not mere coincidence; but the precise nature of the relationship has yet to be determined. Watt has vastly increased the documentation of the parallels, and has given superlative readings of the novels from the perspective of eighteenth-century society; but he has not been able to demonstrate *how* society produced change in the novel, or even *that* it did.

Watt's approach is out of the question for French fiction, in any case, because of the scanty sociological information now available. There is virtually no general study, for instance, of the social and economic background of seventeenth and eighteenth-century novelists. Only the major men of letters have inspired such investigation, and most of them only recently.[4] With regard to the reading public, the prospect seems hopeless. It is barely possible to establish a complete bibliography of separate editions of the better known novels. They were often printed on cheap paper, and simply disintegrated. By and large, libraries contained only more serious works. Then to determine how many copies were printed and sold is pure speculation. Many editions were contraband to begin with, and few records survive of the ones that were not. Finally, even the make-up of the general reading public remains unknown. The cliché of the time, which is often quoted still today, held that most readers were women or fops: "Que peut-on penser dans les pays étrangers lorsqu'on voit la plu-

---

[3] Watt, *The Rise of the Novel*, p. 154.

[4] Jacques Proust's *Diderot et l'Encyclopédie* (Paris: Armand Colin, 1962) stands as a model for such studies.

Techniques of Realism in Early Fiction

part des ouvrages qui paraissent aujourd'hui? Ce ne sont que des *Histoires galantes*, dont les meilleures ne sont tout au plus utiles que pour amuser quelques petits maîtres et quelques femmelettes."[5]

It is nevertheless obvious that every major writer had read widely among the contemporary fiction, whether he approved of it, like Huet, Fontenelle, and Diderot, or claimed to disapprove, like Boileau, Voltaire, and Rousseau. The novelists, as tabulated by S. Paul Jones for the years 1700 to 1750, are predominantly male, three hundred and one to forty-three.[6] Daniel Mornet's study of library catalogs of the eighteenth century disclosed that, in some five hundred collections, one of every forty books was a novel, fourth best of the ten classifications.[7] The single work most often found was Bayle's *Dictionnaire*, with two hundred and eighty-eight copies; *La Nouvelle Héloïse* with one hundred and sixty-five led all the novels, and placed ahead of such works as Voltaire's *Le Siècle de Louis XIV*, Locke's *Essay on Human Understanding*, and the *Dictionnaire* of the Académie. Taken all together, the old *romans* of the mid-seventeenth century, supposedly out of fashion since 1660, produced the respectable total of one hundred and four, ahead of *L'Encyclopédie*; and *L'Astrée* appeared eighty times, putting it ahead of Voltaire's *Eléments de la philosophie de Newton* and Rousseau's *Discours sur l'inégalité*. In short, there is enough evidence for a broader and more respectable reading public to warrant at least some hesitation before attributing to the "frivolous" public of women and their young admirers the preponderant influence among the readership.

In the absence of reliable information about the readers, the works must serve by themselves. If they offer little insight into what the audience wanted, they do at least show what the writers provided and, occasionally, what the writer

---

[5] D'Argens, *Lettres juives*, 1738, Vol. VI, p. 63, quoted by May in *Le Dilemme du roman*, pp. 216-17.

[6] Jones, p. xv.

[7] Daniel Mornet, "Les Enseignements des bibliothèques privées," *RHL*, 17 (1910), 449-96.

wanted to provide. The difficulty lies in trying to look at what seemed significant then, rather than what seems significant now. The ultimate triumph of realism implies strongly that it consistently succeeded best. The aim of the chapters that follow will be to analyze the evolutionary mechanism by which, at a time when realism was ill defined, lacking any great illustration, and quantitatively one of the minor sub-genres, the devices of realistic writing nonetheless survived and even improved. Thus I will concentrate on certain specific areas of reality, which may or may not be treated realistically, but which must be present, if only implicitly, in any work of fiction.

The devices of realism constitute too extensive a subject to cover completely, even for a short period; but a still greater problem is the subjective or arbitrary nature of many so-called realistic elements. David Hirsch has recently taken Ian Watt to task for having failed to keep this in mind.[8] I believe that Watt is on the right track when he says that "logically the individual, particular case is defined by reference to two co-ordinates, space and time," and then draws an analogy between realistic techniques in fiction and evidence in a court of law. But Hirsch scores a telling point when he quotes Watt using the term "real" consistently without recourse to his own definition. What does Watt mean when he says that "Pamela's residences in Lincolnshire and Bedfordshire are real enough prisons"? or that, in *Moll Flanders*, "The gold watch is a real object"? Hirsch concludes that "when Watt comes to speak about realism in the novel he can speak of it only as a feeling or a belief or an intuition."

The greatest danger in relying on such feelings is not, in my opinion, that different critics will be of different minds. On the whole, readers agree about what is and is not believable. The danger is that feelings may be swayed by the wrong criteria. Works may very well win the reader's belief, or the

[8] David H. Hirsch, "The Reality of Ian Watt," *Critical Quarterly*, 11 (1969), 164-79. The parts of *The Rise of the Novel* alluded to specifically in my text are pages 26 to 34 and 96 to 97.

willing suspension of his disbelief, without being what we normally mean by realistic. Such, for example, are the great plays of Racine. They take place within the two co-ordinates of space and time, but with a particular literary definition: the place is often a hypothetical room, communicating with all others, and serving both as a public hall and as a private chamber; and the time is dramatically compressed. Once a reader or spectator acknowledges these co-ordinates, the play will convince him of the reality of the characters, their feelings, and their actions. This example is extreme; it is useful because classical theory shows so clearly that the space and time co-ordinates are there. Yet everyone understands that Racine's tragedies are not realistic; they aspire to the universal, not to the particular. Consequently, they are conspicuously lacking in detail.

The amount or type of detail, however, can not serve as a standard either. Within the most undeniably realistic works there are vast differences in the amount and type of detail given about different objects. Neither Balzac nor Flaubert nor Zola tried to describe everything; neither Joyce nor Butor succeeded. Yet in trying to trace the early evolution of realistic techniques, we will have to compare the works of different authors. It is a fact that Challe describes in much more detail than Mme de Lafayette; yet one can not contrast the undescribed settings of *La Princesse de Clèves* to more fully described settings in *Les Illustres Françoises*, without first proving a rough equality of thematic need for such description—and on no precise object can one justify such a precise comparison.

What is clearly needed is an object of description that runs throughout fiction and exists in the readers' world as well. Then we could adopt the quasi-judicial approach Watt discusses, and measure the degree to which each novelist accurately renders the object. Even this kind of verification could apply only to certain kinds of objects. Characterization, for example, will not serve, because one's understanding of character in reality depends on the optic of the age; our view

73

is inevitably colored by the theories of Freud, as the eighteenth century's was by the ideas of Descartes or Locke. Watt's two co-ordinates, space and time, do in fact permit objective measurements, at least to a very considerable degree. Moreover, they are such universal elements of human existence that any story—even a fantasy—must treat them somehow. I propose then to adopt as a skeleton definition of realism the effort to reproduce within the novel the same time-space co-ordinates that exist outside the novel. Therein lies the crucial difference from Racine, who consciously employs other co-ordinates. If we limit consideration to the rigorously defined and invariable systems by which people measure time and space, then we can effectively compare the degrees of realism in different works, at least on these matters.

It is a plausible assumption that an author concerned with rendering time and space faithfully would also be aiming at realism in other areas too. It would be better, of course, to have some proof, and as it happens, Watt suggests a third element, less rigorously defined than time and space, but nonetheless belonging to a rather stable social system and always present in fiction: names. Yet another, not always present but very common, and very well defined, is money. Both systems can be applied equally to fiction and to history, so that a double verification is possible: the novel can be checked for internal consistency and for compatibility with its historical context.

A fifth element may seem out of keeping with the others: the narrator. The narrative structures of eighteenth-century fiction have been discussed more than almost any other aspect, but usually from one of two perspectives: either the superficial narrative structure is taken as a genre definition—epistolary novel, memoir-novel, *Ich-Roman*—or the point of view is studied as a factor in developing the theme. The former does little more than provide a means of classification, while the latter frequently leads to flagrant anachronism,[9]

[9] See, for example, Ian Watt's article "The Recent Critical Fortunes of *Moll Flanders*," *ECS*, 1 (1967), 109-26.

and at best explicates only isolated works without showing why so many unsuccessful novels were written with the same devices. I will demonstrate that the narrative devices and complications of early fiction in fact resemble very closely the other elements of reality that novelists tried to incorporate. Like the other elements, the narrative structure can be scrutinized not only for its internal consistency, but also for its compatibility with historical reality; that is to say, by and large the novelists attempted to prove that the characters lived, the events occurred, *and the story was recorded* in a real context. What makes this device stand out most strikingly is the fact that from the late eighteenth century onward, the conventions of realism excepted the writer, so that today the ingenuity of early novelists to explain the documentary sources of their story seems absurdly misplaced.

In the romance tradition, money was never mentioned at all. Names tended to be exotic or allegorical. Geography was treated much the way names were: real places might be mentioned, but the spaces separating them and the interior features were largely ignored. All of this can be explained as necessary to the freedom of the romance hero. He was conceived to illustrate a moral or sentimental problem in its purest state. Anything that placed limitations on him rendered the illustration less universal, and therefore less useful. Chronology was harder to ignore; the characters might be exempt from aging or forgetting, but the events had to come in some kind of sequence. The seventeenth-century French romances generally resorted to epic chronology: the action begins *in medias res*, there are one or more narrations of the preceding events by the characters themselves, and the present time is limited to one year. The narrator was taken from the same tradition: the primary story was told by an author who might reveal his presence through first-person interventions or through stylistic flourishes, while the other narratives were quoted from characters in the story, most often a squire who told his master's story. These romance techniques do not actually prevent plausible fictions from being written, but when, as happened more and more often, a novelist attempted to portray contemporary reality through such devices, certain predictable problems arose.

Chronology, as I use the term here, is not the intuitive or conscious philosophical conception of time, which Georges Poulet has studied so instructively. From earliest antiquity to the present, no human being has been able to escape having some sense of time, whatever it might be; and in a writer, this sense informs his works implicitly if not explicitly. Chronology belongs to a much more superficial order of knowledge. Western man measures time in a linear fashion, using divisions like years, days, and hours, when the measurement is sophisticated, or seasons, days, and recurrent cycles like hunger and sleepiness, when it is unsophisticated.[10] It is entirely possible to write fiction in which clock or calendar time is ignored, or is mentioned only to show its inapplicability. Much of the fairy tale fiction of the late seventeenth century belongs to this tradition; an example, intended as parody, might be Marivaux's "Histoire du magicien" from *La Voiture embourbée* (1714): "Sachez donc, Seigneur, lui répondit cette dame, que c'est ici la retraite d'un fameux magicien et de sa sœur; il y a près de deux cents ans qu'ils sont tous deux retirés dans ces lieux affreux, que leur art a rendus comme inaccessibles: tous ceux qui sont ici vivants, y sont du même temps que lui, et malgré la jeunesse que vous voyez peinte sur les visages de ces dames infortunées qui languissent dans cette salle, et sur le mien même, nous y sommes toutes entrées au même moment que nos deux magiciens."[11]

The first systematic attempt by novelists to incorporate calendar time seems to have derived from the theory of the

[10] To my knowledge, there is no general study of fictional chronology in this sense. However, chronologies have been established for numerous individual novels, and these commentaries will be cited where they are relevant. See also Stewart, *Imitation and Illusion in the French Memoir-Novel*, pp. 240-62.

[11] Marivaux, *Romans*, Bibliothèque de la Pléiade, p. 47.

historical novel, as in Scudéry's preface to *Ibrahim*. The first difficulty to arise from this principle involves the synchronization of the two time schemes, the historical and the fictional. That is to say, the events from history occurred on known dates, and these dates willy-nilly break the novel into time segments, during which the characters are active and must be accounted for. They must not do anything which would require more time than the dates allow, and if they are major characters, they must have some occupation which fills the time. As the handling of chronology grew more sophisticated, of course, the difficulty arose not only from history, but also from the parallel lives of different characters.

The second step in recording chronology in fiction was to take account of the daily, or even hourly, passage of time for the central characters. Obviously the novelist must face a problem of equilibrium: if his plot takes him through long periods of time, he can not afford to detail each day's trivial actions. Conversely, if he is detailing a day, he can not afford to omit certain regular occurrences. As novelists became more and more adept at dealing with this sort of chronology, which was not excessively difficult to work into a memoir novel, they found themselves encountering the problem of synchronization, already mentioned above, more and more frequently.

The third step, which actually represents a temporary by-way of the novel, led novelists to try to synchronize in some way the characters' time with the narrator's time. This step obviously depends on a special conception of the narrator, which will be explained later. When the narrator was supposed to be writing a memoir or a letter, it was relatively easy for him to account for his own time. When he was merely a persona of the author, however, it was more difficult to account for his activities. By the nineteenth century, novelists really had ceased worrying about this problem, which seems rather eccentric today; but its very oddity makes it especially instructive regarding the way in which the techniques evolved.

Geography bears some relationship to chronology: part of

the historical element was a date, and part was a place.[12] An obvious difficulty would be that the hero did not have time to get from one place to another. That sort of incoherence arose chiefly out of ignorance, for many novelists apparently had no knowledge of geography at all, even though they delighted in speeding their heroes about the globe. The problem becomes interesting, however, only when more localized geography becomes a concern. Once a character has been put in a recognizable setting, the rest of his movements can be traced from that spot. In a reasonably complicated story, the first mention of setting almost inevitably leads to the establishment of an entire geography. The difficulty is far less acute than with chronology, but the evolution is very similar, and the lapses, when they occur, are all the more instructive.

Money, according to Marshall McLuhan, is stored energy.[13] Just as the romance hero possessed unlimited physical energy, and could defeat whole armies singlehanded, so too his other energies were unlimited. Time is one limit on a man: he can be active only for so many hours before he must sleep or eat. Place is another: he can be in only one place at a time. In any realistic world, money is a third: a finite amount will sustain a man for a finite period of time, after which he must somehow acquire more. Eighteenth-century novelists quickly recognized this principle, but had great trouble applying it. To my knowledge, there is no novel in French before 1800 which focuses more than incidentally on a man earning his living. One could perhaps cite *Gil Blas*, or *Moll Flanders* in English, but even here the emphasis falls on their unusual adventures. This was therefore a technical problem that the novelists developed ways of evading rather than solving.

Even in romances the characters had names, but they were

---

[12] For some general discussion of geography in early French fiction, see Stewart, *Imitation and Illusion in the French Memoir-Novel*, pp. 205-12.

[13] My article, "Money Matters and Early Novels," *YFS* 40 (1968), 118-33, contains a preliminary version of the remarks I have included here.

exotic and obviously fictional.[14] As the novelist sought to win belief on the one hand, or sought to give a faithful picture of his observations on the other, he had to name his characters in accordance with his own society's practice. At the same time, the names had to match the other conditions, notably the narrator. Thus, when the narrator was an authorial voice, the hero could receive a plausible contemporary name; but when the narrator pretended to be a real living person, he had to pretend that his characters were too, and this required a different technique. Many solutions were tried during the eighteenth century, including the famous and already archaic pseudonyms, initials, dashes, and asterisks. This is a problem which even now sometimes embarrasses authors, for a character named too appropriately loses credibility as surely as one named inappropriately. Men have almost mystical relationships to their names, and to name is in part to create. This leads into a subjective area, where the kind of technical study I am pursuing becomes impossible. Novelists did begin to exploit this aspect of naming very early, but the aspect that I will deal with must be limited to their efforts to reproduce society's names in the novel.

The narrator belongs to this list of techniques, because the novelists of this period regarded the narrator as another factual link between the fiction and the reader's sense of reality. Like chronology or geography, the narrator had to give the impression of being objectively verifiable. The rules of evidence forbid the use of hearsay, and the eighteenth-century novelists came very close to adopting that rule. There have been many discussions of the narrator in eighteenth-century fiction, some of them very illuminating, especially with regard to individual authors like Marivaux or Laclos, who derive significant artistic effects from the point of view adopted. In general studies, however, like Vivienne Mylne's *The Eighteenth-century French Novel* or Philip Stewart's more recent

---

[14] Two worthwhile studies of names in early French fiction can be cited: Laurent Versini, "De quelques noms de personnages dans le roman du XVIIIe siècle," *RHL*, 61 (1961), 177-87; and Stewart, *Imitation and Illusion in the French Memoir-Novel*, pp. 263-80.

Imitation and Illusion in the French Memoir Novel, it is simply assumed that the readers wanted to be deceived and that these techniques actually did deceive them. Evidence for the latter, in particular, is very slim indeed. True, many readers believed in Clarissa Harlowe and in Julie d'Etange; but these cases stand out because they were so exceptional. Moreover, while the argument might be defensible regarding *La Vie de Marianne,* an oral narration like *Manon Lescaut* or a third-person frame narrative like *Les Illustres Françoises* is no more literally believable than a third-person omniscient story. The narrator belongs to a set of conventions, and the different postures of the narrator can be explained by reasons similar to those that governed the use of money or chronology. The entire first-person current must be regarded as a temporary aberration of the novel, albeit a rich and productive one. The nineteenth century discarded the highly rationalized narrator, and returned, with no loss in the power to create illusion, to a third-person omniscient author. The first-person tradition, which still thrives, has had for almost one hundred fifty years a completely opposite function to the one assigned it by the eighteenth century. Then, it opened up realms of experience which convention closed off otherwise; now it closes off irrelevant realms.

To summarize briefly the types of narration, the third-person omniscient author is the most obviously conventional. Such a narrator is susceptible of considerable variation, although the early novelists were not much given to exploring these possibilities. The narrator may be more or less intrusive and garrulous, making himself more or less of a character in his own right. Fielding, in *Tom Jones,* is very intrusive; Scarron, in *Le Roman comique,* is relatively discreet; but both have basically the same position relative to their story and to their readers. This narrator may fall silent altogether, and he may explicitly or implicitly put limits on his knowledge, without altering his basic position.

At the opposite pole, the supposed author of a document, such as a letter or memoirs, is the least obviously conventional. The found packet of letters comes close to the found object as a convention-free art form; but when one of these forged documents has value as a novel, it is almost always because it has violated the conventions of its own form. Both the memoirs and the letters succeed as novels by eliminating all the irrelevant sub-plots, and very often by suppressing hindsight or violating some other principle of the genre as well. Nonetheless it is at least marginally possible that such a narrator should have really existed, and that he should have produced such a document for real reasons (not as a novel), and that it should have somehow been published and thus communicated to the reader.

Between the poles there are no doubt many possible variations, but two occur with some frequency in the eighteenth century. The historian writes in the third person, and the historical novelist imitates him, but makes no claims to omniscience. Whatever the historian says must be attributed to a source, although in the great majority of cases, the source is implied without being specifically identified; that is, most of what the historian relates is more or less common knowledge, since it takes place in the public view. Any information about motives or emotions, however, must be derived from a source. The historical novelists (and sometimes the historians themselves) took liberties with this principle, supplying exact quotations where there was no record of them, on the grounds that it was a plausible reconstruction. Some went farther, and invented secret intrigues and love affairs to explain actions that history had to regard as mysterious. Nevertheless, even in imagining these conversations and plots, they maintained the same narrative stance as someone who had obtained the information from a documentary source. When the story involved contemporary events and more ordinary characters, the sources tended to be personal informants or gossip or public opinion, rather than historical documents.

Finally, stories related orally might be recorded, or more accurately, reconstructed by some intermediate narrator. This is the case with *Manon*, and with the stories in *Les Illustres Françoises*. Many are found within other stories, and are not regarded as works in themselves. The convention which permits this type of narration is called the convention of perfect or faithful memory. Otherwise, it is indistinguishable from the forged document.

Comic Fiction

The history of French fiction has long been confused by the mistaken designation of certain seventeenth-century works as "romans réalistes," notably Charles Sorel's *Histoire comique de Francion* (1623), Scarron's *Le Roman comique* (1655), and Furetière's *Le Roman bourgeois* (1666). By a merely descriptive definition of realism, they do indeed appear to be examples of realism: their heroes often come from the lowest classes, and they are full of physical details. Ian Watt is correct in terming these "inverted romances," however, for the author's intention, at least in the beginning, lies directly opposite that of a true realist.[15] These so-called realists were actually attempting to demonstrate the radical incompatibility of reality and a certain kind of literature, namely, the romance. Their own term for their genre was *roman comique*, as can be seen in two of the titles, and in the subtitle of *Le Roman bourgeois*: "ouvrage comique." I will henceforth refer to this kind of fiction as the "comic novel."

The fundamental device of the comic novel consists in maintaining intact all the rules or conventions of the romance (or some other kind of fiction), while utilizing the most incongruous subject matter that the author can find. The comic novel is then a subgenre of the burlesque or parody, and it is not surprising that comic novelists occasionally practiced the method in other areas as well, as in Scarron's *Virgile travesti*. The comic novel, however, possessed several qualities which tended to set it apart from the ordinary burlesque. One could not say that they were rules of the genre, but beginning with Cervantes, who really created the genre in *Don Quixote* (first French translation 1614), the same phenomena recur, and will serve to define the genre for the purposes of this study of techniques.

[15] Watt, *The Rise of the Novel*, p. 11.

Techniques of Realism in Early Fiction

Don Quixote satirizes an earlier genre of fiction by opposing to its unreality the recognizable reality of contemporary everyday life. The main character, Alonso Quixano the Good, makes the opposition possible by reading the chivalric romances, by believing them to be true, and by taking them as guides for his own conduct. Don Quixote does this partly as a matter of conscious choice, where some later quixotic heroes will be unwitting victims of their reading. Either way, the comic novelist often starts from the premise that the novel acts powerfully on the reader, however grotesque its influence. In some cases, the author may regard this as no more than an amusing hypothesis, but the other two characteristics of the comic novel give it more claim to reality.

Cervantes quite apparently comes to see more in Don Quixote and Sancho than two puppets who serve as targets for his satire on the chivalric romance. The characters come to life at a point which can not easily be defined, although I believe it occurs symbolically between chapters eight and nine of Book One, where the original narrator stops and Cide Hamete Benengeli begins. Prose fiction may be peculiarly apt to produce this effect for reasons such as those which Ian Watt gives in the first pages of *The Rise of the Novel*, that is, because it can successfully imitate the mode of discourse which is persuasive in real life, as in a court of law. Another reason might be that the romance's power over the reader was not merely hypothesis, but to some extent an observed fact. No one is likely to have gone mad like Don Quixote, to be sure, but there is no reason to suppose that readers of romances were not swept away by their imaginations as they read, just as modern readers are swept away by Balzac, Proust, or Malraux. In any case, the comic novelist's satirical purpose grows more and more ambiguous in a number of instances. It is as if the novelist had been caught in his own trap. In order to oppose reality to the romance, he had to find some literary representation of it; and it then turns out that his representation has great powers of persuasion. Hence the satire recedes and more straightforward narration takes its place. After Cervantes, who was of course never equalled, the better the novelist, the more likely it is this change in conception will take place.

To regard the comic novelist as the unwitting accomplice of a genre he meant to attack clarifies part of the situation but it falsifies the rest completely. Cervantes meant to attack the chivalric romance, but he also offered a new and better kind of fiction, the *novela*. Cervantes' imitators commonly have the same intention, and like Cervantes, they illustrate the superiority of the new genre by including one or more examples within the comic novel. In *Don Quixote,* such were the "Novela del Curioso Impertinente" and the captive's tale. The second half of *Don Quixote* does not contain any more of these, so that one may conclude that Cervantes at least eventually recognized the comic novel itself as a superior genre. French readers, however, saw only the satirical aspects throughout the seventeenth century, and novelists were more impressed by the *novela*. Consequently, as has already been seen in the discussion of the terms *roman* and *nouvelle,* the French tended to borrow what had been most *romanesque* in Cervantes—the complicated plot, the dramatic coincidence —rather than the realistic elements, which seemed too crude for good literature. Thus the comic novel did not gain recognition as a realistic novel, but continued to serve as a purely negative force, neutralizing the bad effects of an earlier genre so as to permit the new one to emerge.

The comic novel is then a friendly criticism of the novel. Often the novelist overtly states his belief that serious fiction can be written; even if he does not, he may well allow the strength of his own imagination to seduce him; and finally, at the very least, the quixotic theme in comic fiction implies that the novel possesses great potential. Consequently, within any given comic novel, there are likely to be some satirical elements, and some which are more serious and direct. In discussing the comic novel here, I will try to limit myself to the satirical side. Later, in discussing the devices of serious fiction, I will likewise neglect their appearances in comic fiction, even where they seem realistic rather than comic, because of the ambiguity of the genre. On some points, for example, one simply can not be sure whether Scarron is seriously concerned or whether he wishes to make a joke. By the end of the seventeenth century, however, there is clear evidence that a merger was taking place between the comic and the serious styles. The lessons which Cervantes could have taught were finally heeded and adapted to French tastes, which is to say that a number of novelists began writing in the comic tradition and moved into the serious novel, taking with them techniques which they had originally developed as satire.

Sorel's *Francion* (1623) is more rewarding as a funny story than as a satire. The only significant rule for fiction in Sorel's time was the epic narrative form; and so *Francion* begins *in medias res*, proceeds to a long narration of the hero's earlier adventures, and then moves forward. The nature of Francion's adventures is calculated to make this structure seem funny, and the opening scene is a fine parody of the epic beginning. Afterwards, however, Sorel makes very few specific allusions to the parodied form.

Scarron's *Le Roman comique* (1651-57) fits almost all the particulars of the comic tradition as founded by Cervantes. By Scarron's time, the heroic romance was in its heyday, and the Scudérys had elaborated some rules for the genre. Thus Scarron shows much more concern for specific questions, such as the narrator, than did Sorel. Scarron, moreover, played one of the largest roles in introducing Cervantes' *Novelas* to the French public, and *Le Roman comique* contains several independent tales in the Spanish style, besides several first-person narrations.

Furetière, on the other hand, remained a pure satirist in *Le Roman bourgeois* (1666). The conventionality of the *roman* had been solidly established, so that he had an easy time exposing the genre's weaknesses. Even more than in Scarron, the specific concerns of the novelists are made visible by Furetière's parody. His own realism never affects him, though, and instead of moving toward the novel, he allows the work to disintegrate. The last part is a collection of portraits, with the plot more or less abandoned. Needless to say,

Furetière has no new genre to suggest as an improvement, although he does revive the device of using a novel-reader as central character.

At about this time, the comic novel began to merge with the serious novel, represented then by the relatively new *nouvelle*. One of the first examples was the anonymous sequel to *Le Roman comique*, called "la suite d'Offray," published in 1663. Roughly a third of this sequel is given over to the "Histoire du prieur de Saint-Louis," a contemporary story of unhappy love, which clearly foreshadows the subsequent trend. Antoine Adam says of this story that "elle représente, dans le développement de l'art romanesque, un fait si neuf, si particulier, si riche d'avenir, qu'à lui seul il excuserait la publication de cette suite anonyme du roman de Scarron."[16]

An even more striking mixture of comic and serious fiction came with the publication of Subligny's *La Fausse Clélie* in 1671. As the title suggests, the initial impulse was to parody Mlle de Scudéry; but the work is actually a collection of *nouvelles*, loosely connected by means of a frame in which one character does imagine herself to be Clélie. This work is a clear anticipation of the *nouvelle* as it was practiced around 1700, in *Les Illustres Françoises*, for example; Challe's first biographer, Prosper Marchand, noted the resemblance in 1748, and a recent article has demonstrated a number of likely borrowings.[17] Thus some of the earliest *nouvelles* have a close connection to the comic tradition.

About the same time, *Don Quixote* was retranslated, and the new version ushered in a period of much greater popularity for Cervantes' masterpiece.[18] The number of editions, imitations, and sequels between the first translation in 1614

[16] Antoine Adam, "Le Roman français au XVIIe siècle," in *Romanciers du XVIIe siècle*, p. 42. This essay is a good general introduction to Sorel, Scarron, and Furetière.

[17] Alain Garsault, "Une Source des *Illustres Françoises* de Robert Chasles: *La Fausse Clélie* de Subligny," *Dix-septième Siècle*, no. 79 (1968), 57-66.

[18] See Maurice Bardon, *Don Quichotte en France au XVIIe et au XVIIIe siècles*, Bibliothèque de la *Revue de Littérature Comparée* (Paris: Champion, 1931).

and the second in 1678 is less than half the number in the same amount of time after 1678. To a twentieth-century reader, the 1678 version, attributed to Filleau de Saint-Martin, is inferior to the first one, by Oudin and Rousset. Filleau adapted the work to French classical taste, sacrificing much of its vigor; but by eliminating the cruder aspects, perhaps he helped to focus attention on its more serious side. In any case, around 1700, three of the eighteenth century's most significant novelists were learning their art by imitating *Don Quixote*: Lesage, Marivaux, and Challe.

Lesage's work, entitled *Nouvelles Aventures de l'Admirable Don Quichotte de la Manche*, is the least interesting, because it is not an entirely original work. Lesage presented it as the translation of Avellaneda's sequel, which first appeared in 1614, even before Cervantes had completed the original work; but Lesage's translation is so free that adaptation seems a better term. He obtained the censor's permission to publish it and a copyright in October 1702, and the work appeared in 1704. It seems to have had a modest success, since it was reprinted several times.

This success is hard to understand today. Lesage, already at the disadvantage of having an inferior imitator to translate, comes nowhere near the spirit of Cervantes. He does not seem to have any message of his own, either; he is to a disastrous degree exercising his function which, at the moment, was that of a hack; it was not until 1707 that he would publish any original works. Unlike the other comic novelists, moreover, Lesage had no desire to attack any predecessors; rather, the influence of his Spanish translations would remain with him always, and he would transpose his own works into a Spanish setting. In his version of *Don Quixote,* the dominant elements are picaresque and Byzantine. The heroes' movements are almost random, and ultimately play a very secondary role to the other actions. The subplots involve either the lowest classes, like the prostitute Barbe la Balafrée, or exceedingly complicated stories of recognitions and misunderstandings. Don Quixote's madness is tolerated, even encouraged, by his companions, but his role is that of a bore.

Lesage's main literary criticism is directed against Cervantes, whom he accuses of not having sustained the character of Don Quixote as well as Avellaneda. One can infer from this remark that Lesage remained strongly attached to the seventeenth-century conception of character, which kept him from realizing one of the novel's greatest qualities, the development of a character in time. This weakness marred all of Lesage's fiction, even his best, *Le Diable boiteux* and *Gil Blas,* which tend to be portrait galleries. On the other hand, their continued popularity and their strong influence on the novel well into the nineteenth century attest to some strengths as well as weaknesses, and at least one comes from *Don Quixote*: a concern for the discrepancy between reality and the individual's perceptions of it.

Marivaux's *Pharsamon* was not published until 1737, but it had been passed by the censors and even announced for publication in 1713.[19] It is just one of several experimental works by the twenty-five-year-old unknown, freshly arrived in Paris from the Provinces. He chose as the object of his satire La Calprenède's *Pharamond*, the last of the long heroic romances, published from 1661 to 1670. Marivaux's technique comes straight from *Don Quixote*: the hero has been educated on *romans,* and has refused all the girls proposed to him as wives; one day, in a wood, he meets a beauty, and from then on he and his servant, under the names Pharsamon and Cliton, live as if they were in a *roman,* although experience often enough gives them the lie. *Pharsamon*'s most notable feature is its garrulous narrator, although the roguish Cliton and a girl who appears late in the story foreshadow some of Marivaux's later creations. Thus *Pharsamon* is a very unsatisfying work in itself, and was actually disavowed by its author; but it shows how the transition was being made from the comic to the realistic. For once, the most realistic scenes are not those where Pharsamon's illusions are destroyed, but the inserted stories, like Cliton's story of his boyhood. And throughout, the insipid story is given some life by the per-

[19] See Mario Matucci, *L'Opera Narrativa di Marivaux* (Napoli: Pironti e figli, 1962).

sonality of the narrator, a discovery which Marivaux would put at the heart of his masterpieces, *Marianne* and *Le Paysan parvenu*.

Challe, like Lesage, wrote a continuation to *Don Quixote*; but unlike Lesage, Challe invented his, and drew farther and farther away from his predecessor as he went along.[20] The publishing history of *La Continuation de l'Histoire de l'admirable Don Quichotte de la Manche* is obscure; Challe's authorship has been challenged, but seems probable. The sequel came out in two volumes, the first in 1695, the second in 1713. The 1678 translator had evidently projected a sequel, for he eliminated the hero's death from the conclusion. Challe's initial project, quite possibly undertaken just to earn money, seems to have been no more than an extension of the adventures, of which he had a typically superficial understanding. Challe's Don Quixote is first and foremost an "honnête homme"; his insanity embarrasses the author, who cannot quite bring himself to let Don Quixote be the victim of any of the jokes. Sancho, on the other hand, being a peasant, hardly deserves contempt; he pays the price for all their misadventures. It is not hard to imagine that progress is slow in the beginning, for the author has nowhere to go. Eventually he brings in a group of French travelers, who tell their story, and suddenly the whole direction of the work changes. The travelers' story is a first version of one of the major stories of *Les Illustres Françoises*, and there are two more similar *nouvelles* in the last part. It appears that Challe has grasped the profound lesson of *Don Quixote*, that his madness is symbolic of all individual perspectives on the world, especially those which are highly colored by passion. Love, jealousy, and honor all seem to be forms of quixotic behavior. It is at this point that the comic novel fully merges with the serious novel for the first time.

Diderot's *Jacques le fataliste*, composed around 1774 but not published until 1796, illustrates the fusion of the serious

[20] See English Showalter, Jr., "Did Robert Challe Write a Sequel to Don Quixote?" *RR*, 62 (1971), 270-82.

and the comic strains.[21] Many scholars have written of this novel as if it were intended to win the reader's belief in the same way that *La Religieuse* is; but Diderot adopts poses and uses tricks that are even more evidently satirical than Furetière's. The narrator's commentary on his art and his fellow novelists makes up a significant part of the book, yet his attitude varies widely and rapidly, and no systematic doctrine or theory emerges. Nonetheless, in the context of Diderot's other works of fiction and of his other writings about fiction, *Jacques le fataliste*'s parody must be regarded as a sympathetic if unusual study of the novelist's craft. Diderot resembles Scarron, in that the latter also used one of his illustrative *nouvelles* to comment on his new techniques. Unlike Scarron, however, Diderot emphasizes the basic similarity of the principal burlesque plot of *Jacques* and the illustrative *nouvelles* like the stories of Mme de la Pommeraye or the *père* Hudson. *Jacques le fataliste* is probably the best of all the French comic novels. I have paid less attention to it than to the others, because it follows the period under study at too great a distance. Diderot's prime targets are the novelists of the 1730's, especially Prévost. The same technical devices continued to pose problems, however, and it is sometimes helpful to glance at the later manifestations.

Throughout the seventeenth century the comic novel is moving toward the serious novel, approaching reality from an opposite attitude. The technical problems of the serious novelist are not solved by the comic novelist; they are exposed. To some extent one can trace the evolution of serious fiction by looking at what the comic writer satirized. This is the primary interest of the analysis which follows, in which I will trace the five "real" systems through some of the comic novels. The brazen insistence of the comic novelist on displaying his difficulties contrasts sharply to the evasiveness and discretion of the serious authors.

Although *Don Quixote* relies heavily on the impression of

[21] Among many recent works on *Jacques le fataliste*, the most informative on its comic aspects is Robert Mauzi, "La parodie romanesque dans *Jacques le fataliste*," *Diderot Studies*, 6 (1964), 89-132.

anachronism which the hero creates, Spanish history does not contribute more than a few passing allusions. In the first part, the Captive tells the story of his adventures, which like Cervantes' own included participation in the Battle of Lepanto.[22] In the first pages of Book Two, Don Quixote hears of a new threat which the Turks are posing. The first narrator, when he comes to the end of his first manuscript, deduces that the story is modern because of the books which were found in the knight's library. These few details suffice to fix the date somewhere in the late sixteenth or early seventeenth century. Careful reading and scholarship would surely turn up other historical details, such as the fact, noted by D. B. Wyndham Lewis, that windmills were first brought into La Mancha in 1575.[23]

Cervantes evidently intends to contrast his hero's ideals with the general customs of the time, not with any specific events. Not only the date, but most of the other specifics are left vague at the start. The situation resembles the romance setting, wherein the hero is exempted from all the normal limitations of the real world. And this is natural, for *Don Quixote* is an inverted romance. The Captive represents an intrusion of reality, inspired by Cervantes' personal bitterness. Using his tale as a basis, one can deduce that since he left home in 1570 or 1571, the latter being the year of Lepanto, and has been away twenty-two years, the date of Don Quixote's adventures is 1592 or 1593. Perhaps some leeway should be given for rounding, but there is no way to make this calculation fit the dates on the letters written during Sancho's government: July 20 and August 16, 1614.[24] It would be false to imply that Cervantes made a great deal of this incoherence; it is not even clear that he noticed it. The unexpected precision of the dates does suggest that he meant them to stand out, but this is in the general context of the novel's movement toward reality, symbolized by Barcelona, where Don Quixote

---

[22] Miguel de Cervantes Saavedra, *Don Quixote*, I, ch. 39.

[23] D. B. Wyndham Lewis, *The Shadow of Cervantes* (New York: Sheed and Ward, 1962).

[24] Cervantes, *Don Quixote*, II, chs. 36 and 47.

will finally be defeated. In Book One, the turning point of the expedition occurred in the isolation of the Sierra Morena, a realm of fantasy.

If Cervantes pays little attention to the historical inconsistency of his dates, it is probably because the chivalric romance paid the question no heed at all. On the other hand, Cervantes took great interest in the daily passage of time. During the Inquisition of the Books *Tirante the White* is spared because of its excellence in this respect: "here the knights eat and sleep and die in their beds, and make their wills before they die, and other things as well that are left out of all other books of the kind."[25] To be sure, chronology is not the only aspect of realism which is involved, but it is the easiest to isolate and trace. Don Quixote also eats and sleeps, dies in his bed and makes his will before his death, but not without explaining to Sancho how the other knights had managed:

> I would have you know, Sancho, that it is a point of honour with knights errant not to eat once in a month; and when they do eat to take what they find nearest to hand. You would have realized this if you had read as many histories as I have. For in all the many I have read I have never found more than a passing mention of what knight errants ate, except at those sumptuous banquets they used to be given.[26]

[25] "Aquí comen los caballeros y duermen y mueren en sus camas, y hacen testamento antes de su muerte, con otras cosas de que todos los demás libros de este género carecen." All English translations are taken from Cervantes, *Don Quixote*, tr. J. M. Cohen, Penguin Classics (Baltimore: Penguin Books, 1950); this one is from I, ch. 6, p. 60. The Spanish texts, given in the notes, are taken from Miguel de Cervantes Saavedra, *Obras Completas*, ed. Angel Valbuena Prat (Madrid: Aguilar, 1956); this one is on p. 1053.

[26] ibid., I, ch. 10, p. 83. ". . . hágote saber, Sancho, que es honra de los caballeros andantes no comer en un mes, y, ya que coman, sea de aquello que hallaren más a mano; y esto se te hiciera cierto si hubieras leído tantas historias como yo; que aunque han sido muchas, en todas ellas no he hallado hecha relación de que los caballeros andantes comiesen, si no era acaso y en algunos suntosos banquetes que les hacían . . ." p. 1065.

Techniques of Realism in Early Fiction

The point Don Quixote is leading up to is that it will be permissible for him to eat some of Sancho's food. Hunger is one of those base facts which romance preferred to ignore; it links man with animals and things. It also marks his submission to the clock, for the appetite returns as regularly as the sunrise. Having made the point, Cervantes characteristically does not pursue it in comic fashion, but illustrates the opposite; most, if not all, the days are accounted for, and the characters are shown eating and sleeping on a fair number of them. One would think that the difficulty was thereby solved, and would disappear; but this solution worked only for this kind of narrator, who posed as historian, but without historical dates. When, for entirely independent causes, authors resorted to other types of narrator, new solutions had to be found.

Just as the matter of dates gave Cervantes little pause, the idea that the narrator lived in time like the characters did not seem to bother him much. This attitude can be partly attributed to the historian's traditional manner, for nobody expected the historian to match his writing time to the lifetimes or centuries he was relating. Nonetheless, at the end of chapter eight of Book One, where the first narrator claims to have reached the end of the manuscript he was translating, Cervantes does insert a several-page account of how the new manuscript was found. He does not say how long he spent looking for it, but once he had found it, it took six weeks to translate. As I observed before, I regard this shift in narrators as symbolic of Cervantes' change in attitude toward his creation; but whatever the significance, the device which brings it to the reader's attention is a brutal contrast between the patient search for the manuscript, and the split second which elapses between where one leaves off and the other begins. The swords which were poised aloft in chapter eight come crashing down in chapter nine several pages later. By choosing this obvious moment of suspended animation, Cervantes directs attention onto the narrator much more forcefully than he could have by making the change, say, at the beginning of chapter seven, just before the second expedition. The freedom he felt about his narrator did not survive in France, and what was a literary effect in Cervantes became a problem for Marivaux.

Scarron's *Le Roman comique* has even fewer allusions to historical events than *Don Quixote*, although it was written while the Scudérys' historical romances were enjoying their greatest vogue, and indeed was written as an attack on them. Scarron, however, chooses a different approach: he treats the ridiculous fistfights and love affairs in his troupe of provincial actors as seriously as if they were affairs of state. There are some literary allusions which can be dated, but they were certainly not meant to serve as chronological cues, and it would falsify the perspective to take them as such.

Scarron does adopt the epic chronology, which was also part of the long romance. The action begins with the mock heroic arrival of the troupe in Le Mans, and their present tense adventures dominate the work, with Destin's story of his life serving as the delayed exposition. Other secondary narrations are inserted, too, and several independent tales are read or told; the effect is very like *Don Quixote*. Scarron has compressed the action intensely, however, so that the whole story takes only three days; the *Suite d'Offray* takes it two days farther. Not surprisingly, all the expected activities, like eating and sleeping, are accounted for; there are even some details about La Rancune's urination.[27] Scarron's purpose is not realism, however, as the style and tone of the last mentioned incident would prove at a glance. The triviality of these details ought to seem comic in itself, especially in a form usually reserved for the elevated deeds and thoughts of Mlle de Scudéry's heroes.

Scarron, unlike Cervantes, never appears to recognize his main plot as anything more than a burlesque. He had other ideas about serious fiction, to which I have already alluded: they came from the Spanish *novela*. As a result, the inserted tales bear all the responsibility for showing the way to serious fiction. The first one, "Histoire de l'amante invisible," serves

---

[27] *Romanciers du XVIIe siècle*, p. 544.

as a sort of demonstration model for the author.[28] Unlike the others, which are by and large quite ordinary as far as their form is concerned, this one is full of satire and criticism directed at the heroic romances. Scarron, who takes over the narration from Ragotin ("Ce n'est donc pas Ragotin qui parle, c'est moy."), makes fun of historian-narrators, use of the confidant, detailed descriptions of furniture, lengthy conversations quoted in their entirety, and the use of soliloquys. Of particular interest here, he says: "Je ne vous diray point exactement s'il avoit soupé, et s'il se coucha sans manger, comme font quelques faiseurs de Romans qui reiglent toutes les heures du jour de leurs Heros . . . " and again a few pages later: "Ne disons point, si vous voulez, ce qu'il fit jusqu'au disner, qui valut bien le souper, et allons jusqu'à la rupture du silence que l'on avoit gardé jusques à l'heure." These quotations make it plain that Scarron regarded trivial detail as unsuitable in a story of elevated sentiments and noble actions. This first tale is sacrificed to the needs of the critic and innovator, so that he can make it clear where he has done something new. The rest of the tales illustrate how they ought to be written. It is worth noticing, though, that both Scarron's theory and practice are a step backward from the heroic romances. Mlle de Scudéry's handling of the daily use of time was no doubt awkward, and therefore unrealistic. Scarron succeeded where she had failed, in the main plot of *Le Roman comique*, but he did not take that seriously, nor did his readers. Consequently his influence tended to move interest away from circumstantial detail, and onto the plot and the characters.

Marivaux, in his maturity, wrote some of the most genuinely realistic novels of the French eighteenth century. In both *Marianne* and *Le Paysan parvenu*, the narrative point of view becomes an important element of the structure, while the chronological ordering seems to pose insurmountable

---

[28] ibid., pp. 552-67. Since all the quotations and allusions that follow in this paragraph come from these few pages, I have not identified them more precisely.

problems. In the early comic novel *Pharsamon*, the narrator's development as a character is already evident, and so are his difficulties with chronology. Marivaux had as much trouble as Mlle de Scudéry in scheduling daily activities, and perhaps more, because he shows increasing interest in the trivial. At the time he wrote *Pharsamon*, this detail was not one of the novelist's major concerns, however; the narrator had preempted everyone's attention. As a result, the problems of chronology in *Pharsamon* are considered from the perspective of a narrator whose reality is assumed. Marivaux mocks the narrator, too, but he nonetheless makes him responsible for the chronology.

Thus, the narrator hesitates at one point to repeat a long dinner conversation, but finally consents to give it. After two pages, he can no longer stand it, and bursts it: "Oh, c'en est fait, je m'ennuye de ces fades compliments, dont presque tous les Romans sont remplis; Pharsamon et le Solitaire ne s'en feront plus, il y a déjà près d'une heure qu'ils sont à table, ou du moins mon intention a été qu'ils y demeurassent tout ce tems-là. . . ."[29] Scarron also had mocked the long conversations, and their insipidness was target enough for derision. Marivaux plainly alludes to a further problem, though, in modifying his statement that the characters had been at the table for an hour. As is typical of a comic novelist, he underlines the difficulty of the situation, first by beginning to handle it in one style, and then shifting abruptly to another; and secondly by explicitly calling it to the reader's attention, but without providing any solution. Is it desirable to give all the information? Is it enough to say they were there for an hour? The same problem can work in reverse; much later, the narrator observes: " . . . au reste ces réflexions que je lui fais faire, étoient bien plus promptes dans sa tête qu'elles ne le paroissent, lorsqu'il les faut mettre sur le papier: car, en un instant, Pharsamon réfléchit, raisonna, et jugea tout ce que je n'ai pû dire moi, qu'en beaucoup de mots" (p. 314). One serious solution, which Marivaux will adopt, is to make the nar-

[29] Marivaux, *Pharsamon* (Paris: Prault, 1737; 10 parts in 2 Vols., pages numbered consecutively), p. 165.

rator's time the only significant one; the richness or poverty of his memories, the complexity or simplicity of his comments and analyses, will entirely govern the pacing of the story—so much so that the timing of the narrated events goes askew, as I will demonstrate later.

In *Pharsamon*, the problems of time's passing are just one aspect of the whole problem of the narrator's time compared to the story's time. Habitually, the narrator of *Pharsamon* attacks the problem by moving from the time scale of his story into his own, and then back out again at the appropriate moment. Examples are numerous, but one deserves to be quoted for its precision. "Voilà tous mes gens couchés, il n'est encore que trois heures du matin pour eux, mais il n'est que neuf heures du soir pour moi, et ainsi je vais les faire agir tout comme s'ils avoient ronflé vingt-quatre heures."[30] Such a pose, which Diderot also strikes a number of times in *Jacques le fataliste*, hardly makes intelligible satire unless the narrator has been strongly emphasized in serious fiction. Chronology, at this stage, seems relatively less significant to novelists than other problems, and as a result, many of the serious novels make extraordinary chronological mistakes. It is really a sign of this neglect that among the comic novels there have been so few instances of historical dates' being confused. This reflects the fact that serious novelists were not using such precisions with any regularity. Late in the century, Diderot finally makes it the object of some obviously intentional lapses in *Jacques le fataliste*. For example, the spurious conclusion which the narrator appends makes Jacques fall in with Mandrin, who was executed in 1755, when Jacques has already talked about events which took place in 1756, like the Battle of Port Mahon. On the other hand, Jacques supposedly left the army after being wounded in the knee at Fontenoy, in 1745, yet he shows up both at Port Mahon and at Berg-op-Zoom in 1747. Jacques's story is so filled with contradictory dates that one has to conclude finally that he made it all up. *Jacques* is one of the last comic novels, but at any earlier date,

[30] ibid., p. 518; other examples pp. 280, 334, 348.

there would have been no basis for a satire of dates in the novel.

The evidence of the comic novels suggests that from the beginning all the basic problems of chronology had been noticed. Cervantes seems to have taken day-dy-day reality quite seriously, and it was still important enough in Scarron's time to be worth mocking. History, on the other hand, never really breaks into the novel as an important factor in chronology. Both of these problems tend to be subsumed under the problem of the narrator, which had precedence in critical importance.

Geography, although less acutely felt as a problem in the novel, bears some relation to the problem of chronology and has similar dimensions. The name of the particular location of the setting corresponds to the historical dating of the action, and the degree to which motion through space is accounted for corresponds to the day-by-day activity. The easiest form of satire consisted simply of naming a place which was amusing by its humbleness or banality, but this supposes already that the novelist gives his places names. To some extent, however, the novelists were reluctant to give names, or unable to account for their characters' movements accurately, and these errors were also satirized.

Cervantes began *Don Quixote* with a remark of this sort: "In a certain village of La Mancha, which I do not wish to name. . . ."[31] Beyond this village, however, all the places are real and are designated—El Toboso, La Mancha, the Sierra Morena, and Barcelona. Moreover, the movements of Don Quixote and Sancho through this landscape are given in exact detail, just as the days are counted. The joke is hardly worth laboring. On the other hand, the imaginary geographies of certain fantastic narrations are the target of a later brief incident. Dorothea, pretending to be the Princess Micomicona, claims to have landed at Osuna; but Don Quixote objects that

---

[31] Cervantes, *Don Quixote*, I, ch. 1, p. 31. "En un lugar de la Mancha, de cuyo nombre no quiero acordarme . . ." p. 1037. It is perhaps worth noting that the French translator eliminated this remark in the 1678 version, although it had been kept in Oudin's translation.

Osuna has no port, and the priest has to explain that she really landed at Malaga, but first heard of Don Quixote at Osuna (I, 30). The space between Malaga and the kingdom of Micomicona is roughly the border between the novel and romance.

The same hesitancy before geographical names appear in *Francion*. The hero journeys to Italy, and Sorel narrates the journey:

> Je ne veux point vous dire s'il passa des rivieres ou des montagnes, s'il traversa des villes ou des bourgades. Je ne suis pas en humeur de m'amuser a toutes ces particularitez. Vous voyez que je ne vous ay pas seulement dit en quel lieu Nays estoit aux eaux, si c'estoit a Pougues ou autre part: Je ne vous ay point apris le nom de la forteresse où Francion fust prisonnier, ny celuy du village où il fust Berger, et celuy de la ville où demeuroit Joconde. C'est signe que je n'ay pas envie que vous le sçachiez, puis que je ne le dy pas, et que l'on ne s'aille pas imaginer que ce soit une faute de jugement si je ne mets pas tout cecy.[32]

Obviously the reader might expect to be told by another novelist. Indeed, in other parts of *Francion* Sorel is less discreet; Francion says that he first saw Laurette in the streets of Paris, and he followed her until "Enfin elle s'arresta dessus le pont au Change" (p. 94), and the mention of Pougues shows how easy it would be for Sorel to overcome any difficulty. Yet the habit was strong that prevented particularizing details too close to one's real experience. An interesting variant shows that Sorel wrote in 1623 "me donna en pension a un Maistre de College" but changed it in 1626 to "du Collège de Lysieux" (pp. 170, 1278). The remarks in *Francion* suggest that the problem lay really in varying the scale, so to speak—that Sorel felt embarrassed about naming some places and not others. It would seem quite acceptable today that he should refrain from saying anything about Francion's trip to Italy except, "He went to Italy," and Sorel apparently sensed this. At the same time, the story of his college days is so full

---

[32] *Romanciers du XVIIe siècle*, pp. 395-96.

of trivial details that the names of places are called for. So long as the literary theorists tended to think in terms of rigid, universal principles, however, it was logical that an author should feel some compulsion to regulate all his methods according to one fixed standard.

By the time Scarron wrote *Le Roman comique*, the novel had a theoretical formula, based on the epic and history. Scarron thus has very specific objects for his satirical thrusts. Most of the action takes place in and around the town of Le Mans, and the descriptions are accurate and detailed enough so that Antoine Adam can identify most of the places mentioned. This apparent realism, however, must be put in the context of the very first lines: "Le soleil avoit achevé plus de la moitié de sa course et son char, ayant attrappé le penchant du monde, roulloit plus viste qu'il ne vouloit." Scarron develops this mock-heroic image to a degree which is comic in itself, and then triggers the reader's laughter with an anti-climax: "Pour parler plus humainement et plus intelligiblement, il estoit entre cinq et six quand une charette entra dans les Halles du Mans" (p. 532). In short, all the allusions to Le Mans must be regarded as partly inspired by a desire to deflate the pompous epic pretensions of the *roman*.

The historical claims receive the same treatment. In the second part of the novel, Scarron locates Ragotin's house in the following style:

> Quoy qu'un fidelle et exact Historien soit obligé à particulariser les accidens importans de son Histoire et les lieux où ils se sont passez, je ne vous diray pas fort juste en quel endroit de nostre Hemisphere estoit la maisonnette où Ragotin mena ses confreres futurs. . . . Je vous diray donc seulement que la maison estoit au deçà du Gange, et n'estoit pas loing de Sillé-le-Guillaume (p. 758).

The anti-climax here punctures the novelist's fraudulent claim to historical exactness.

Furetière's *Le Roman bourgeois* begins on a similar burlesque of the epic: "Je chante les amours et les advantures de plusieurs bourgeois de Paris" (pp. 903-904); and he goes on to state that he wants to have a mobile setting, sometimes one section, sometimes another, beginning with the most bourgeois, the Place Maubert. To further exploit the comic effect, Furetière includes an elaborate architectural description of the Place Maubert, in the style of the Scudérys' descriptions of Roman monuments and palaces. Again, the seeming realism is quite clearly meant primarily to make the conventions of the novel look ridiculous.

Challe, in his sequel to *Don Quixote*, returned to the device Cervantes had used in Princess Micomicona's story, but Challe's version evidently owes as much to more recent fictional voyages as to the mythical geography of the chivalric romances. The surgeon tells Don Quixote a tale like Dorothea's, which contains lines like: " . . . je le suivis, nous allâmes au Pérou, et en allant notre Vaisseau se brisa contre le Mont Caucase, et nous pensâmes boire plus que de raison. Nous en prîmes un autre, et nous arrivâmes en huit jours sur la côte de Malabar, à trois lieues du Pérou, et nous fîmes le reste à pied."[33] In the next chapter, Don Quixote objects, and everything is explained by enchantment. Challe, who had been to India, and the New World, knew his geography; when his ship touched in at the Canary Islands, he recalled that Gomberville had set *Polexandre* there, with liberal use of his imagination. True to the comic tradition, he demonstrated in an inserted tale how geography could be used. The Parisian setting, and the journey from Paris into Spain, from the "Histoire de Sainville et Sylvie," point the way unmistakably to *Les Illustres Françoises*.

The increasing skill with which Challe, Marivaux, and Prévost used local geography did not, however, entirely solve the problem. Diderot opens *Jacques le fataliste* with an obvious reminiscence of *Don Quixote*: "D'où venaient-ils? Du lieu

---

[33] Cervantes, *Histoire de l'Admirable Don Quichotte de la Manche* (Paris: Compagnie des Libraires, 1771; first edition in six volumes, 1713), Vol. V, Livre Iᵉʳ, ch. 15, p. 136. Hereafter cited as Challe, sequel to *Don Quixote*.

le plus prochain. Où allaient-ils? Est-ce que l'on sait où l'on va?"[34] And a few pages later he shows that the basic problem has persisted, having changed only its form. The novelist still feels awkward before the literal-minded reader, who asks "Where?" "Où? lecteur, vous êtes d'une curiosité bien incommode! Et que diable cela vous fait-il? Quand je vous aurai dit que c'est à Pontoise ou à Saint-Germain, à Notre-Dame de Lorette ou à Saint-Jacques de Compostelle, en serez-vous plus avancé?" (p. 513). In this case, the reader's insistence drives the author into an allegory, which he consents to abandon, offering in its place a wide selection of realistic places his characters could have spent the night. Ultimately it will turn out that they spent the night in the town of Conches, at the home of the lieutenant-general. The delay in revealing the truth serves to protect the suspense of the incident; but the author's coy evasions serve to underline the conventionality of this kind of realism.

The naming of characters has much in common with giving geographical names. On the one hand, literary elegance seems to require a certain kind of name, which is inconsistent with everyday reality. On the other hand, too precise a name, like too precise a location, may provoke disbelief on the part of readers who either know the person, or know that no such person existed. The comic novelist thus can apply the same sort of satire, either giving grotesquely inappropriate names, or else making the naming process visible.

Cervantes does both. In the first pages, he feigns ignorance about Don Quixote's real name: "They say that his surname was Quixada or Quesada. . . ."[35] The hero's name, like his home, remains unknown to the reader at the start. Besides calling attention to the novelistic convention of naming, this device helps emphasize the universality of the hero. The main point of the satire really falls on Don Quixote's naming himself Don Quixote de la Mancha (with the later variations),

---

[34] Denis Diderot, *Œuvres romanesques*, Classiques Garnier (Paris: Garnier frères, 1962), p. 493.

[35] Cervantes, *Don Quixote*, I, ch. 1, p. 31. "Quieren decir que tenía el sobrenombre de Quijada, o Quesada . . . " p. 1037.

naming his horse Rocinante, and his mistress Dulcinea. These are all parodies of the fanciful names which knights bore.

Most of the names which Scarron gives to the townspeople of Le Mans have a Rabelaisian ring: La Rappinière, La Garouffière, Roquebrune, Ragotin, Bouvillon, La Baguenodière. Moreover, they all serve largely as butts of slapstick pratfalls. The appearance of such names in the novel is comparable to Cervantes' use of Rocinante. Scarron plays with another set of names, however—those of the actors, which are all pseudonyms: Mlle de l'Estoille, Le Destin, La Rancune, and La Caverne. While the practice of actors using stage names was real enough, these were not at all typical, and "La Caverne" is unmistakably ridiculous because of its obscene implications. When it is first pronounced in Le Mans, "Ce nom bizarre fit rire quelques-uns de la compagnie; sur quoy le jeune Comedien ajousta que le nom de Caverne ne devoit pas sembler plus estrange à des hommes d'esprit que ceux de la Montagne, la Valée, la Roze ou l'Epine."[36] Scarron seems to have been laughing at his own expense to some degree. In the tales he adapted from the Spanish, the names were common contemporary given names, like Dom Carlos, Victoria, Dom Fernand, Elvire, Dorotée, Féliciane, Dom Diègue, Dom Sanche. Such an effect was more difficult to achieve in French, where first names were not in general usage. A young girl could be so named, as Mlle de l'Estoille is—her name was Léonore before she went on the stage. Otherwise, the French novelist had to find one of those vague, euphonious combinations of name fragments, like Verville, Saint-Far, and Saldagne, the names Scarron gives to the characters in Le Destin's past. Marivaux's M. de la Vallée and Challe's Mlle de l'Epine really belong to the same tradition that Scarron is parodying with La Caverne.

The new style of names was slow to win acceptance in France; Challe and Subligny still had to defend the practice in their prefaces. Furetière remains at approximately the same stage as Scarron in naming his "realistic" characters Vollichon, Villeflattin, and Bedout. He attacks the historical

---

[36] *Romanciers du XVIIe siècle*, p. 533.

novelists more directly than Scarron on this point, for his bourgeois heroes and heroines have classical names like Nicodème, Pancrace, and Lucrèce. Of the last, Furetière writes: "Cette Lucrèce, que j'ai appellée la Bourgeoise, pour la distinguer de la Romaine, qui se poignarda, et qui estoit d'une humeur fort differente de celle-cy . . . " (p. 917), which is to say that she got pregnant out of wedlock. Furetière also has a heroine with the colloquial and even vulgar name Javotte. As she is presented, after a parody of the idealized portraits in the romances, the final revelation of her name is a comic anticlimax, like the naming of the Place Maubert. She is thus only a distant ancestor of Challe's and Prévost's Manons.

The same is true of the Babet who appears in Marivaux's *Pharsamon*. The title itself is a punning joke on *Pharamond*. The rest of the names, presumably all pseudonyms, belong to the French précieux tradition: Cliton, Cidalise, Clorine, Fatime, Félonde, Tarmiane, Oriante, Célie. Marivaux rather disconcertingly neglects the realistic side of his imitation of *Don Quixote*. What the reader knows of reality, as opposed to the hero's monomaniac view of it, he must guess by inference. One of his few clues occurs in Book Five. Pharsamon and Cliton find Cidalise and Fatime, for whom they have been looking, and they play out a scene which concludes with everyone swooning. The honest rustic who is supposed to help them at this point turns out, however, to be a real honest rustic, and he bursts out laughing, leaves them lying on the floor in great perplexity about what to do next, and greatly offends Cidalise by addressing her as Babet.[37] This is surely less an instance of realism than a comic way of exposing Cidalise.

The methods of naming became more codified during the eighteenth century, and some new variations were invented. One of the most famous was the blank, meant to give the impression that a real person was being protected. Fielding demolished that convention in his comic novel *Joseph Andrews* (1742), when he took Richardson's Mr. B----, and

[37] Marivaux, *Pharsamon*, p. 338.

gave his full name as Booby. Diderot harks back to Cervantes once again, as he asks in the opening lines of *Jacques le fataliste*: "Comment s'appelaient-ils? Que vous importe?"[38] As a matter of fact, the name of the master is never supplied. Diderot uses all the different devices for naming in *Jacques*, using some first names like Jacques and Denise, some *nouvelle* style names, like Des Arcis and Mme de la Pommeraye, some real names like Mlle Pigeon and Prémontval, and some blanks like "le maître" and "la veuve." And finally, in a passage reminiscent of Scarron's comment on La Caverne, and perhaps also of Fielding's Booby, Diderot discusses the appropriateness of the name Bigre (pp. 701-702).

Here again, the problem seems easy to solve—indeed, at times it seems that it has been solved—and yet it crops up again and persists throughout the century. The variations in comic treatments roughly parallel the new conventions of the serious novel, and the continuation of the search for new conventions suggests once more the depth of the novelists' insecurity.

Money would appear to have less profound connections to man's fundamental notions of existence than time, space, or names. It has always been regarded as a mere circumstantial detail. At times when financial problems have constituted a major source of plot material, as in Balzac, this has been taken as a reflection of social change. Money does have in common with the other themes both its systematic quality and the universality of its presence. By virtue of its very superficiality, it can serve here as a kind of control; the fact that the money problem parallels all the others guarantees that the problem lies in the nature of the genre, not just in the inexperience of the writers.

Cervantes, as always, dealt with it first. On his first excursion, Don Quixote meets an innkeeper, who asks if he has any money:

Don Quixote replied that he had not a penny, since he had never read in histories concerning knights errant of any

---

[38] Diderot, *Œuvres romanesques*, p. 493.

knight that had. At this the innkeeper said that he was wrong: for, granted that it was not mentioned in the histories, because their authors could see no need of mentioning anything so obvious and necessary to take with one as money and clean shirts, that was no reason for supposing that knights did not carry them.[39]

Don Quixote's attitude was to remain more or less the hero's attitude, however; the author simply assumed that he had enough. Cervantes puts Sancho beside the hero, however, to remind him occasionally about such things as wages. This contrast recurs continuously in France: characters from the lower classes are obsessed with being paid, while those from the upper classes disdain the subject. In *Francion* money is mentioned quite often, but in the adventures of the schoolboys and their mercenary master Hortensius, or in the adventures of the whores Agathe and Laurette, or when the main characters bribe a peasant couple to copulate in public. The mention of money seems to have the same burlesque effect as the grotesque names.

Furetière carries this type of satire quite far in *Le Roman bourgeois*. In the opening scene Nicodème wins Javotte's affection by scooping all the *deniers* out of her alms basket, and replacing them with a *pistole*. Furetière terms this a "nouvelle sorte de galanterie."[40] A few pages later he drops any pretense of writing a fictional satire, and turns to pure social satire: "Sçachez donc que, la corruption du siecle ayant introduit de marier un sac d'argent avec un autre sac d'argent, en mariant une fille avec un garçon, comme il s'estoit fait un tariffe lors du decry des monnoyes pour

---

[39] Cervantes, *Don Quixote*, I, ch. 3, p. 42. " . . . respondióle Don Quijote que no traía blanca, porque él nunca había leído en las historias de los caballeros andantes que ninguno lo hubiese traído. A esto dijo el ventero que se engañaba: que, puesto caso que en las historias no se escribía, por haberles parecido a los autores de ellas que no era menester escribir una cosa tan clara y tan necesaria de traerse como eran dineros y camisas limpia, no por eso se había de creer que no los trajeron." p. 1043.

[40] *Romanciers du XVIIe siècle*, p. 909.

l'évaluation des espèces, aussi, lors du decry du merite et de la vertu, il fut fait un tariffe pour l'évaluation des hommes et pour l'assortiment des partis" (p. 919). The table follows, and matches the size of the dowry to the importance of the man's position.

Both Lesage and Challe make avarice one of Sancho's dominant traits in their sequels, and the attitude which Challe expresses in his letters to the *Journal Littéraire* shows how little regard for the working classes even a rather poor bourgeois like Challe had:

> Je vous avoüe, Messieurs, que votre remarque m'a fait rire au sujet des horions que j'ai fait recevoir à Sancho chez le Comte de la Ribeyra et le duc de Medocq. Regardez les richesses que je lui donne, la maniere dont elles lui viennent, la génerosité des François et des Espagnols, son caractere à lui, et l'amitié que lui portoient [*sic*] la niece de la gouvernante, outre que ce n'est qu'un païsan, et vous avoüerez qu'il étoit à propos de lui faire payer devant Pluton dans les Enfers, et dans le monde devant toute la compagnie, le moyen d'aller chez lui passer en paix le reste de ses jours, et qu'il étoit juste que sa Thereze . . . eut part au moyen de gagner cet argent puisqu'elle en devoit profiter.[41]

Challe did not entirely disdain the subject of money; *Les Illustres Françoises* goes into some detail about the financial circumstances of the characters. Sancho's burlesque windfall, however, aptly satirizes the only device which the novelist had to enable his character to earn a living or to rise above his station.

Late in the century, Diderot still found it appropriate to set up the same situation. Jacques leaves home to join the army with five *louis*. His spending them is quite well accounted for, but once he is penniless, help arrives as if sent by fate—a

---

[41] Frédéric Deloffre, "Une Correspondance littéraire du début du XVIIIème siècle: Robert Challes et le *Journal Littéraire* de la Haye (1713-1718)," *Annales Universitatensis Saraviensis, Philosophie-Lettres*, 3 (1954), 175.

good deed has been witnessed by a rich nobleman, who takes Jacques in. Diderot comes very near to treating Jacques's fortunes realistically; not only his previous expenses, but also the savings he has by the time of the novel's present, seem plausible. This rapid turn of fortune, however, while uncharacteristic of *Jacques*, occurs over and over in the serious novels of the eighteenth century. Since Diderot goes out of his way to interrupt this narration at the crucial moment, interjecting for no apparent reason: "Lecteur, si je faisais ici une pause . . . ,"[42] he seems to be making fun of it. The naive master has already allowed himself to be so involved in the story that he imagines himself to be living at that past time, and Diderot begins the digression by denying that he is stuck for a way to get Jacques out of his distress. This is, in short, one instance where Diderot does write as if he were Prévost. In some ways, the narrator's interruption makes the implausibility of the incident all the more striking; in others, by separating the two parts of Jacques's autobiography, it preserves the plausibility of the work as a whole, because individually the parts are acceptable. Typically, Diderot experiments rather than merely satirizing.

Money is the least important of the themes being traced, but it follows the same evolution. Its appearances in the comic novel are more noticeable than in the serious novel, because the comic novelist deliberately exposed to ridicule what the serious novelist hoped to conceal or evade. It may even appear that the comic novelist foreshadows the developing realism of the serious novel, but that is an illusion. New perceptions were equally present in both, and in most cases, the comic novelist is only responding critically to the serious novelist's efforts to write better. All four of the themes discussed so far seem very easy to solve, and their continuing presence as problems has repeatedly suggested some underlying difficulty. That difficulty came to focus in the problem of the narrator.

Cervantes' narrative techniques are subtle and not particularly intrusive. The first author, who poses as historian, as-

---

[42] Diderot, *Œuvres romanesques*, p. 575.

sumes the primary responsibility for the first eight chapters. In the beginning he writes as if he were compiling his story from various sources; thus he reports that there is debate about Don Quixote's real name or about his first adventure:

> There are authors who say that the first adventure he met was that of the pass of Lapice. Others say it was the windmills. But what I have been able to discover of the matter and what I have found written in the annals of La Mancha. . . .[43]

"The annals of La Mancha" is the term that can designate the supposed real life sources of this part of the story.

At the end of chapter eight, however, the last document of these annals leaves Don Quixote in the thick of a battle. The author-historian then goes in search of the rest of the document, for he can not believe that so important a work should have been lost. Much later, in Toledo, he chances on some old papers in Arabic, which turn out to be the missing continuation. It bears the title: "History of Don Quixote de la Mancha, written by Cide Hamete Benengeli, Arabic historian,"[44] and takes up the story precisely where the annals left off. Cide Hamete relates the rest of the story, through the offices of an anonymous translator hired by the author and with an occasional remark by this author.

At the end, Cide Hamete's relationship to the story grows very ambiguous. The characters have already read the first part, and so they refer to him; for instance, the priest has a notarized statement of the hero's death made to prevent any other historian from reviving him. Cide Hamete himself concludes with the remarkable apostrophe to his pen, in which he says: "For me alone Don Quixote was born and I for him.

---

[43] Cervantes, *Don Quixote*, I, ch. 2, p. 37. "Autores hay que dicen que la primera aventura que le avino fué la del Puerto Lápice; otros dicen que la de los molinos de viento; pero lo que yo he podido averiguar en este caso, y lo que he hallado escrito en los anales de la Mancha . . . " p. 1041.

[44] ibid., I, ch. 9, p. 77. "Historia de Don Quijote de la Mancha, escrita por Cide Hamete Benengeli, historiador arábigo." p. 1962.

His was the power of action, mine of writing. Only we two are at one. . . ."[45] Cervantes thereby confesses to the trick he had used when Cide Hamete was first mentioned, and invites the reader to meditate on the mysterious relationship between the author and his work.

Cervantes' parody of these historical elements is always gentle, and only rarely interferes at all with the story. Don Quixote was mad to consider the chivalric romances as historical accounts, but Cervantes emphasizes the implausibility of the stories, not the impossibility of the historian's existence. In his *novelas* Cervantes uses a third-person omniscient narrator, and one may assume that Cervantes considered the imaginative reconstruction a sufficient justification of itself, when it was done with enough art to seem real. Cide Hamete is a direct and not too distant ancestor of the garrulous narrators of the nineteenth century; the majority of narrators in the seventeenth and eighteenth centuries are collateral kin.

Don Quixote himself approaches the question from a somewhat different angle. He begins with the assumption that the chivalric histories are true, and it follows that every logical consequence of them must also be true. Much of the comedy results from his stubborn faith in this truth, when it flies in the face of the facts. Among other things, Don Quixote wonders about the mechanism by which the stories came to be known and written down. His first thought as he rides out is to imagine the opening lines of his own history, which will certainly be written by a "Sage." Then he speaks directly to the imaginary sage: "And you, sage enchanter, whoever you may be, to whose lot it falls to be the chronicler of this strange history. . . ."[46] The first author, with evident irony, shares Don Quixote's opinion about how the knights' his-

---

[45] ibid., II, ch. 74, p. 940. "Para mí sola nació Don Quijote, y yo para él; él supo obrar y yo escribir; solos los dos somos para en uno . . . " p. 1523. Since the French translation of 1678 omitted Don Quixote's death, in anticipation of a sequel, this apostrophe was also omitted. It had been included in the earlier translation, however.

[46] ibid., I, ch. 2, p. 36. "¡Oh tú, sabio encantador, quienquiera que seas, a quien ha de tocar el ser coronista de esta peregrina historia!" p. 1040.

tories came to light. When he comes to the break in the manuscript, he comments: "It appeared to my mind impossible, and contrary to all sound custom, that so good a knight should have lacked a sage to undertake the writing of his unparalleled achievements, since there never was one of those knights errant who—as the people say—go out on their adventures, that ever lacked one. For every one of them had one or two sages ready at hand, not only to record their deeds, but to describe their minutest thoughts and most trivial actions, however much concealed."[47] Don Quixote not only believes that the Sage knows all his deeds and thoughts, but even credits him with some magical ability to influence the story. After Sancho calls Don Quixote "The Knight of the Sad Countenance," Don Quixote explains that "the sage I mentioned has put it into your thoughts and into your mouth to call me now *The Knight of the Sad Countenance*...."[48]

This sage clearly arises out of Don Quixote's insanity. No one else would expect such literal truth from a story. Yet the evolution of the genre in the seventeenth and eighteenth centuries is increasingly dominated by this quixotic approach to the narrator. In its strictly rational analysis, it resembles the already noted insistence that time go by with the objective regularity of the clock. Obviously the spirit behind it also moved the theorists of the dramatic unities. Don Quixote looked on the ideal narrator as an enchanter; it is not by accident that by the end of the century, fairy tales were in vogue, and soon even "realists" were using such unrealistic devices as *Le Diable boiteux* or *Le Sopha*.

[47] ibid., I, ch. 9, p. 75. "Parecióme cosa imposible y fuera de toda buena costumbre que a tan buen caballero le hubiese faltado algún sabio que tomara a cargo el escribir sus nunca vistas hazañas, cosa que no faltó a ninguno de los caballeros andantes, de los dicen las gentes que van a sus aventuras, porque cada uno de ellos tenía uno o dos sabios, como de molde, que no solamente escribían sus hechos, sino que pintaban sus más mínimos pensamientos y niñerias, por más esconidas que fuesen . . . " p. 1061.

[48] ibid., I, ch. 19, p. 147. "Y así, digo que el sabio ya dicho te habrá puesto en la lengua y en el pensamiento ahora que me llamases *el Caballero de la Triste Figura* . . . " p. 1099.

Scarron does not go far beyond Cervantes, but the narrator's role was apparently troubling the novelists of his day. One of Scarron's common poses is that of a contemporary historian, working from authentic accounts. Usually the indications are no more than a phrase: " . . . et pour Destin, je n'ay pas bien sceu l'effet que cela fit sur son esprit"; "Pour revenir à cette grosse petite femme, qu'il me semble que je voy toutes les fois que j'y songe . . . "; "Il se nommoit la Garouffiere, ce qui me fait croire qu'il estoit plustost Angevin que Breton. . . ."[49] Finally he relates a complicated version of how he wrote about Ragotin's disgrace, how a priest saw the text in proof, and gave him some more particulars, and how this proved to the printer that the story was true, to his astonishment, "car il avoit creu, comme beaucoup d'autres, que mon Romant estoit un Livre fait à plaisir" (p. 762). In view of the inconsistency of this pose, for the narrator usually is omniscient, and of the farcical nature of most of the incidents, there can be little doubt that Scarron meant the historical narrative pose to seem comic.

Another of Scarron's poses is that of the artist, which is to say that his intervention deals not with what was true and how he knew it, but with the way in which he is composing his book. To suppose such a narrator does not necessarily preclude his telling true stories, but it reveals a different concept more closely akin to the epic theory than to the historical theory of the novel. In the most important comment of this type, the narrator says: "peut-estre . . . qu'un Chapitre attire l'autre et que je fais dans mon Livre comme ceux qui mettent la bride sur le col de leurs chevaux et les laissent aller sur leur bonne foy. Peut-estre aussy que j'ay un dessein arresté. . . ." (p. 575). Whichever it may be, this commentary can only make the reader more aware of the writer's problems and of his presence; it is the very opposite of realism.

As I have already mentioned, Scarron imitated Cervantes by adapting various Spanish tales, several of which are inserted in *Le Roman comique*. Although Scarron makes a pre-

[49] *Romanciers du XVIIe siècle*, pp. 539, 693, 705.

text for each one, by having some character tell or read it, the main author says that he will retell it in his own words. Most of them, like Cervantes', are third-person omniscient narratives, with no narrative peculiarities. The first one, however, has a very intrusive narrator, who moralizes about lovers meeting in churches, explicitly evades quoting a conversation, claims to know someone who knew the characters, refuses to follow clock time, makes fun of the conventional confidant, refuses to describe the furniture, and explicitly omits other irrelevant circumstances (pp. 552-61). This tale has been sacrificed for the purposes of satire; most of the attacks are directed against the heroic romances of the Scudérys' style. The net effect of the interruptions is to prove that these awkward elements can be eliminated. In the next such tale, they are eliminated, but before the tale begins, the characters discuss fiction and praise Cervantes' *nouvelles* while ridiculing the heroic romances (p. 645). The narrator is somewhat intrusive, especially in the first tale, but Scarron is still looking primarily at other problems, notably of plot and character.

The narrator and his logical plausibility as a person had become such a problem for Furetière that *Le Roman bourgeois* is constantly being interrupted for comments on the telling of it. Antoine Adam comments in his introduction:

Furetière ne peut décrire l'émotion de Nicodème parce que personne ne lui tâta le pouls. Il ne comprend pas non plus qu'un romancier rapporte une conversation entre deux amants s'il n'existait de témoin pour la rapporter. L'histoire exacte de ce qui se passa entre Lucrèce et le marquis, nous devons renoncer à la connaître. "On ne sait rien de tout cela, parce que la chose se passa en secret." Furetière semble exiger que le roman soit le récit d'une histoire, telle que le narrateur l'a apprise, et veut que le romancier laisse dans l'ombre toute la part de réalité que ce narrateur imaginaire ne pouvait atteindre. En fait, Scarron s'était amusé, dans *le Roman comique*, à feindre une exigence du même ordre.

Mais ce n'était qu'un jeu de sa verve. On devine, chez Furetière, quelque chose de plus systématique, et, pour tout dire, de plus pédant (p. 47).

There can be little doubt that Furetière is vastly inferior to Scarron as a storyteller and as a humorist. Nevertheless, it seems to me that Adam fails to take adequately into account that Furetière is writing to satirize the serious novel. It is not so much the author Furetière who is limited to his knowledge, as it is "the Novelist," a creature imagined by Furetière to be an object of ridicule. As we will see, the exigency of a consistent and plausible narrative source had become a critical standard; Mme de Lafayette among others was taken to task for violating it. Furetière himself violates it without scruples much of the time; he even uses the famous *style indirect libre*, as in this line from the opening description of Javotte: "Quant à son meneur, c'estoit le maistre clerc du logis, qu'elle avoit pris par necessité autant que par ostentation; car le moyen sans cela de traverser l'Eglise sur des chaises, sur lesquelles on entendoit le sermon, à moins que d'avoir une asseurance de danceur de corde?" (p. 907). These pages could provide many ordinary examples of authorial omniscience, such as "Cette nouvelle sorte de galanterie fut remarquée par Javotte, qui en son ame en eust de la joye, et qui crût en effet luy en avoir de l'obligation" (p. 909). The very passages alluded to by Adam seem to me deliberately coy poses; while claiming not to know, the author does in fact tell what happened: "Cet homme donc n'eut pas si-tost jetté les yeux sur Javotte . . . qu'il en devint fort passionné. . . . Je ne vous sçaurois dire précisément quelle fut l'émotion que son cœur sentit à l'approche de cette belle (car personne pour lors ne luy tasta le poux), mais je sçay bien que ce fut ce jour-là précisément qu'il fit un vœu solemnel de luy rendre service" (p. 908).

On a number of occasions, the respect for narrative limitations is just a pretext for mocking the banality of the usual *roman*. Such is the moment when Furetière writes:

Je croy que ce fut en cette visite qu'il luy découvrit sa passion; on n'en sçait pourtant rien au vray. . . . Par mal-heur
pour cette histoire, Lucrece n'avoit point de confidente,
ni le marquis d'escuyer, à qui ils repetassent en propres
termes leurs plus secrettes conversations. C'est une chose
qui n'a jamais manqué aux heros et aux heroïnes. . . . Nos
amants n'estoient point de condition à avoir de tels officiers,
de sorte que je n'en ay rien pu apprendre que ce qui en
a paru en public; encore ne l'ay-je pas tout sçeu d'une
mesme personne, parce qu'elle n'auroit pas eu assez bonne
memoire pour me repeter mot à mot tous leurs entretiens;
mais j'en ay appris un peu de l'un et un peu de l'autre, et,
à n'en point mentir, j'y ay mis aussi un peu du mien
(p. 936).

He continues by saying that in other novels the lovers' conversations are taken from *Amadis*, *Astrée*, or *Cyrus* anyway.
After a similar refusal later on, he writes: " . . . vous n'estes
gueres versez dans la lecture des romans, ou vous devez
sçavoir 20 ou 30 de ces entretiens par cœur. . . ." (p. 1017).

In short, the rigorous plausibility of the narrator was a rule
which Furetière took from the novels he satirized, and he
took it because he found it absurd. When he protests ignorance, he intends to make us realize how strained are the devices by which novelists get around the problem of secret
meetings and private conversations, not to mention a character's innermost thoughts. The narrator's commentary often
leads into a further attack on the novel, moreover, for its
banality, repetitiveness, implausibility, or triviality. Furetière
does carry this sort of satire much farther than the earlier
comic novelists, partly in response to an ever greater attention to the genre and its rules, but also partly because of his
own weaknesses as a writer. Both Cervantes and Scarron balance their satire with illustrations of a better style of fiction—
or at least they considered it better, and in the short run the
public vindicated their taste, since both are pioneers of the
popular *nouvelle*. But Furetière is not won over; on the contrary, his novel disintegrates. Book Two opens with an address to the reader:

Si vous vous attendez, lecteur, que ce livre soit la suite du premier, et qu'il y ait une connexité necessaire entr'eux, vous estes pris pour duppe. Détrompez-vous de bonne heure, et sçachez que cet enchaînement d'intrigues les uns avec les autres est bien seant à ces poëmes héroïques et fabuleux où l'on peut tailler et rogner à sa fantaisie. Il est aisé de les farcir d'épisodes, et de les coudre ensemble avec du fil de roman, suivant le caprice ou le genie de celuy qui les invente. Mais il n'en est pas de mesme de ce tres-veritable et tres-sincere recit, auquel je ne donne que la forme, sans alterer aucunement la matiere. Ce sont de petites histoires et advantures arrivées en divers quartiers de la ville, qui n'ont rien de commun ensemble, et que je tasche de rapprocher les unes des autres autant qu'il m'est possible. Pour le soin de la liaison, je le laisse à celuy qui reliera le livre. Prenez donc cela pour des historiettes separées, si bon vous semble, et ne demandez point que j'observe ny l'unité des temps ny des lieux, ny que je fasse voir un heros dominant dans toute la piece. . . . Ne l'appelez plus roman, et il ne vous choquera point, en qualité de recit d'aventures particulieres (pp. 1025-26).

It is tempting to see in this a manifesto of genuine realism, as opposed to the satire we have seen elsewhere. Whereas the others had thought the future lay in the conventional and not very realistic *nouvelles*, Furetière alone would have tried to reproduce reality. But reading the novel, we are quickly undeceived. Furetière merely wished to train his satire on specific individuals, primarily Charles Sorel, rather than on the literary genre. He is certainly right to counsel that we drop the name *roman*, insofar as that implies a plot, a linking of episodes and a continuity of characters, however loosely defined. Furetière is thus a marginal figure. His comments are highly provocative, and there is good reason to suppose that the voluble comic narrators of the eighteenth century owed him a great deal. Yet it was in a sense in spite of himself; Furetière could see only the negative side, and his refusal to structure his work places him even farther from the main current of development than those who were looking for help in the rules for history and the epic.

No less an authority than Wayne Booth has called the narrator of *Pharsamon* the most important use of the dramatized narrator between *Don Quixote* and *Tom Jones*.[50] This praise is, I think, exaggerated, partly because Marivaux's work remained so obscure, and partly because it does not do full justice to Scarron and Furetière. Nevertheless it gives us an idea how intrusive and interesting the narrator is. Marivaux differs from the other comic novelists in one significant respect: from the beginning, his ultimate purpose is to defend the genre, not to attack it. His first work, *Les Effets surprenants de la sympathie*, included in its *avis au lecteur* an important defense of the genre. Marivaux most notably decries the role of reason, which makes rules, and argues that taste and feeling should preside; and he maintains that an admitted fiction can move as much as truth, so that verisimilitude is only a limited virtue in the novel.[51]

In light of these principles, it is not surprising then that Marivaux's self-conscious narrator spends little time pretending to follow rules. Only once or twice does he pretend the kind of ignorance which Furetière displayed; for example: " . . . je ne sçai point ce que Pharsamon répondit à cette nouvelle attaque qu'on faisoit contre son cœur; mais je me doute aisément qu'il y répondit en galant Chevalier."[52] But this isolated example is probably just a variant on his constant evasion of relating conversations completely, not because he does not know what was said, but because he finds them boring. Another example, obviously meant only to amuse, is this parenthetical comment: " . . . il n'est pas jusqu'aux chats de la maison, qui, dans la bagarre, craignant pour leur vie à laquelle ils s'imaginent qu'on en veut (je dis

---

[50] Wayne Booth, "The Self-Conscious Narrator in Comic Fiction before *Tristram Shandy*," *PMLA*, 67 (1952), 170-75.

[51] See Frédéric Deloffre, "Premières Idées de Marivaux sur l'art du roman," *Esprit Créateur*, 1 (1961), 178-83. This preface was discussed in the preceding chapter.

[52] Marivaux, *Pharsamon*, p. 261.

s'imaginent; car je n'ai point à présent d'autre terme pour exprimer le raisonnement d'un chat) . . ." (pp. 403-404).

Much more common and much more extensive are the passages where the narrator talks of his difficulties as an author. A narrator telling a true story will, of course, encounter certain artistic problems. The chronological problem of dealing with simultaneous events, or of synchronizing the author's time and the characters' time, or the acceptability of digressions and moral commentary—all these can plague the historian as well as the novelist. What is unique to the creative writer, however, is the invention of the plot, and Marivaux's narrator discusses his difficulties with that.

In Book Three, the two heroes begin an adventure with two mysterious people whom they find living alone in a wood. The dramatized reader objects that "voici une avanture qui sent le grand . . . c'est du comique qu'il nous faut, et ceci n'en promet point." The narrator confesses that he has perhaps made a mistake, considers erasing what he has just written, but eventually demands that the reader be patient: "Suivez-moi, mon cher Lecteur, à vous dire le vrai. Je ne sçai pas bien où je vais; mais c'est le plaisir du voyage. Nous voici dans une Solitude; restons-y puisque nous y sommes, nous en sortirons comme nous pourrons avec nos Personnages" (p. 155). The same idea is developed in Book Four, where the author affirms not only that he does not know where he is going, but that his merit is based on his ingenuity in getting out of these situations: " . . . je me suis . . . quelquefois trouvé dans l'embarras: qu'importe, si je m'en suis bien tiré, je n'en aurai que plus de mérite, quand on ne sçait où l'on va, s'il arrive qu'on se conduise passablement, on est plus adroit que ceux qui marchent la carte en main; je serai . . . assez content de moi, si je puis tirer Pharsamon d'ici avec autant de succès; allons, allons toujours le hazard y pourvoira" (pp. 261-62).

Knowing the role which coincidence plays even in Marivaux's mature novels, we may well take that as an accurate statement of his methods of composition. They do not on the whole satisfy twentieth-century readers, even those with a taste for freewheeling adventure or for the intricate implausibility of the mystery; the conventions of the genre have changed too radically to admit *Pharsamon* as even a faintly amusing ancestor. The pride with which he sets up and then unravels a farfetched set of circumstances is rather naive, in the instances already cited, and again in Book Six. The conclusion is, almost literally, produced by a wave of a magic wand. Marivaux's real interest was not structure, but style, as the narrator says: "La manière de raconter est toujours l'unique cause du plaisir ou de l'ennui qu'un récit inspire. . . ." (p. 514). Marivaux had the originality to see that this justified realism, and indeed, the quotation comes from a defense of Cliton's life story, which resembles no other in the novel: instead of adventures and catastrophes, he tells of stealing apples and shooting sparrows as a boy.

Whether his concern be structure or style, however, the teller of the story must be conceived somehow by the author. Marivaux here toys with a movement away from the rule-bound narrator, toward a third-person omniscient narrator. Conditions were not yet right, though, for such a narrator to be accepted universally; in fact, the most remarkable third-person narrators of the eighteenth century are all comic. The novelists' artifices were still too crude to be concealed. The best hope then was to make an honest confession of them, and aspire only to keep the reader entertained, as Marivaux has his narrator say: " . . . si vous me prenez pour un auteur, vous vous trompez, je me divertis, à la bonne heure, si je vous divertis quelque fois aussi. . . ." (p. 517).

The effects of the rules can be observed with particular clarity in Challe's continuation of *Don Quixote*. Needless to say, the closing words of Cide Hamete Benengeli had been cut out, in the first edition of Filleau de Saint-Martin's translation in 1678. The new part alludes to that conclusion, however, to say that another Arab had gone to La Mancha to see for himself if Don Quixote was dead as Cide Hamete claimed. And of course he was not. This new historian was born Zulema, but changed his name to Henriquez de la Torre when he became a Christian. The most remarkable detail about him is the care with which Challe explains how he obtained the new story: " . . . il le suivit pied à pied, et gagea des gens pour l'observer."[53] Henriquez de la Torre eventually leaves for the Indies, and entrusts the manuscript to a friend; the sequel is made up of their contributions combined. Challe does not dwell on Zulema's spying, but he takes much more trouble than Cervantes to justify his knowledge. In chapter eight, Sancho and Don Quixote have a conversation, in the course of which Sancho remarks: "A propos de l'Historien, Monsieur, je rirois bien s'il alloit continuer notre Histoire, et qu'il y mît tout ce que nous venons de dire; mais je l'en défie, où diantre le prendroit-il, quand il n'y a ici que vous et moi?" But the author has reminded us in the first pages of that very chapter that Zulema had "observé de Sancho jusqu'aux moindres mouvemens" (Vol. V, Livre 1, ch. 8, pp. 63-64, 73), and while the movements alluded to are emotional rather than physical, the reminder of his constant presence is nonetheless significant. In later pages the truth comes back to us through various intermediary narrators or through written accounts (Vol. V, Livre 1, chs. 20, 21, pp. 205, 216; Livre 2, ch. 28, p. 317). The last volume of the sequel begins by naming Zulema's friend, Cid Ruy Gomez, and describing the way by which the manuscript came to France, having passed through the hands of several lackeys and of two Frenchmen, the last of whom translated it. In some ways this is no more than an uninspired imitation of Cervantes' story of discovering Cide Hamete's manuscript, but with a crucial difference. Cervantes makes no effort to explain how Cide Hamete acquired his information, nor for that matter how the manuscript came from his hands into the shop in Toledo. Challe provides the complete chain from Don Quixote's deeds, to the observer, to the author-historian, to the translator, and thus finally to the reader.

Like Cervantes and Scarron, Challe sensed the potential value of fiction, and illustrated a new and better style by the tales he scattered throughout his sequel to *Don Quixote*. Several of them foreshadow *Les Illustres Françoises*, and one in particular, *L'Histoire de Sainville et de Sylvie*, dominates

[53] Challe, sequel to *Don Quixote*, Vol. V, Livre 1, ch. 1, p. 2.

the whole sequel. In it, Challe treats with complete seriousness the problems of narrative credibility he parodies in
Zulema and Cid Ruy Gomez. These narrative complexities,
just as in Marivaux's case, will constitute one of the most important qualities of Challe's later work.

More than half a century later, when Diderot wrote
Jacques le fataliste, all of the old narrative problems were
still hanging over the novelist. An age of exceptional novelists
had come and gone. Their great discovery, the first-person
narrative, had yielded some excellent results, but it sacrificed
one of the novel's greatest assets—suspense, or the feeling of
reliving without foreknowledge; Diderot had discovered that
for himself in writing *La Religieuse*. The epistolary novel,
despite the prestige of Richardson and Rousseau, was obviously a technical dead end—its masterpieces themselves were
evidence of it. Looking for a new departure, Diderot went all
the way back to Cervantes. The narrator of *Jacques* is pro-
tean; at one point or another he embodies all of the poses
which had been assumed up until then. In the early pages, he
resembles Marivaux's author-narrator: "Vous voyez, lecteur,
que je suis en beau chemin, et qu'il ne tiendrait qu'à moi de
vous faire attendre un an, deux ans, trois ans, le récit des
amours de Jacques, en le séparant de son maître et en leur
faisant courir à chacun tous les hasards qu'il me plairait. . . .
Qu'il est facile de faire des contes!"[54] Marivaux might not
have shared that last reflection—indeed, Diderot's narrator
boasts of what Marivaux's confessed, but it is the same power
and freedom to move the story, or not, as they see fit.

This freedom begins to erode very quickly in *Jacques*, for
within a few pages the narrator begins to talk as if he were
in a position like Don Quixote's sage, that is, a reporter and
recorder, limited by the facts of what happened, but whose
actual physical presence would be difficult to explain. In this
pose he says, for example: " . . . il ne tiendrait qu'à moi que
tout cela n'arrivât; mais adieu la vérité de l'histoire, adieu le
récit des amours de Jacques" (p. 505). He dwells much more
than Cervantes on the problem of the stylist—what to tell,

---

[54] Diderot, *Œuvres romanesques*, p. 495.

what to eliminate—and intervenes so often that he makes rather a nuisance of himself. It is worth noting, however, that he profits from the ambiguous reality of this "sage" to be present at whatever level of the narrative he chooses; for example, when Jacques tells of his stay with a peasant woman after Fontenoy, the narrator comments in a digression, "Lorsque j'entendis l'hôte s'écrier de sa femme: 'Que diable faisait-elle à sa porte!' je me rappelai l'Harpagon de Molière. . . ." (p. 507). Sometimes the dramatized reader objects to this narrative ubiquity: "Là, j'entends un vacarme. . . .—Vous entendez! Vous n'y étiez pas; il ne s'agit pas de vous" (pp. 577, 586, 592, 622). This supposed reader has taken a dogmatic position, like the critics in Furetière's time, but he is no more consistent than the narrator he attacks.

After the night in the inn, the narrator begins to change again, reducing his role still farther to that of the gatherer of hearsay we have seen in *Le Roman comique*. He notes that there are two versions of the night Jacques was drunk, and he claims to have gotten some of his story directly from Jacques himself. Finally he assumes the position of the first narrator of *Don Quixote* working in the archives—there are gaps in the manuscript and the narrator finally stops abruptly with the comment: "Et moi, je m'arrête, parce que je vous ai dit de ces deux personnages tout ce que j'en sais" (pp. 653, 670, 718, 777). As in *Don Quixote*, the narrator goes in search of new documents, finds them, and continues—although in *Jacques* the narrator considers them to be spurious, and indeed they do not really fit the rest of the story very well.

The effect of these changes is to destroy the credibility of the narrator, whatever we consider his proper role to be, and this may well have been Diderot's purpose. Within *Jacques*, as in *Don Quixote* and *Le Roman comique*, the satire of bad narration is accompanied by illustrations of good narration. Jacques is a good story-teller, but he is working within the first-person autobiographical tradition, and it is worth noting that like Marivaux and Crébillon *fils*, Diderot fails to bring the story continuously into the present. Jacques jumps over the ten years of his life between his love for Denise, and the journey where we see him. A more original story is the hostess' famous tale of Mme de la Pommeraye. We know how she heard the story, but she is not an eyewitness or participant; yet she does not call any attention to her distance from it by admitting ignorance. On the contrary, she relates word for word private conversations and thoughts, and possesses exactly the omniscience necessary to maintain the suspense. This is the *conte historique,* as Diderot termed it at the end of *Les Deux Amis de Bourbonne,* a descendant of the *nouvelles* of Cervantes, Scarron, and Marmontel. As Diderot puts it, the author "veut être cru; il veut intéresser, toucher, entraîner, émouvoir, faire frissonner la peau et couler les larmes. . . ." (p. 791). To do this, the narrator had to get out of the way by fading into a conventionally accepted background role. *Jacques le fataliste* destroys all his other pretenses, and the story of Mme de la Pommeraye illustrates his superfluity.

At the conclusion of the hostess' tale, the master admits that he has enjoyed the tale, but he is perplexed. The hostess narrates well, but, the master tells her, "Vous avez péché contre les règles d'Aristote, d'Horace, de Vida, et de Le Bossu" (p. 649). The rules in question concern character portrayal rather than narration; but all the rules were alike in posing awkward problems for the novelist. For Diderot, the real interest of the novel lay even beyond the interesting, touching, tearjerking *conte* as the hostess told it. After the master and Jacques have discussed the tale, the primary narrator intervenes and undertakes to defend Mme de la Pommeraye: "On ne vous a pas dit qu'elle avait jeté au nez du marquis le beau diamant dont il lui avait fait présent; mais elle le fit: je le sais par les voies les plus sûres" (p. 651). Only when the novelist is free to exploit these mysterious but sure ways of knowing will the genre be adequate to its real mission, to reveal the most hidden recesses of the human soul.

Although I have thought it worthwhile to refute convincingly the claim that French comic novelists were realists, that has been only a secondary function of this survey of comic fiction. The more important purpose has been to highlight the technical problems raised by the five real systems that will subsequently be traced through serious novels. The comic novelist affords the advantage of summarizing; burlesque treatments of money in Furetière or of narrators in Marivaux guarantee to some extent that these same subjects were being dealt with in serious novels generally, so that we can have confidence that the examples cited will not be mere oddities. The comic novels also flaunt their actual or feigned ineptitude; this pinpoints the sources of difficulty for serious novelists, who for obvious reasons did their best to dissemble them. Taken together, the comic novels give an abridged history of the technical problems of early novelists. It should be clear, however, that the comic novelists tell very little about the progress of serious fiction, except by inference. Contrasting *Jacques le fataliste* to *Don Quixote*, one might deduce that Diderot's immediate predecessors used domestic and contemporary settings and avoided plot turns based on sorcery, which was an advance over the chivalric romances mocked by Cervantes. Such inferences are difficult and often doubtful, however, for the truth is that the comic novelists—at least in the comic parts of their stories—did not even attempt to make progress, and frequently resorted to deliberately archaic devices. The problems are now more or less in the open. To see how they were resolved, we must undertake the more difficult analysis of the techniques of serious fiction.

Serious Fiction

Serious fiction is a great deal more nebulous a concept than the comic novel, which can be limited to a dozen or so major works. A serious novel is one in which an effort is made to reproduce reality, however it be defined. As I have pointed out, most comic novels contain examples of serious novels; furthermore, the comic novelist almost unwittingly has to reproduce reality as part of his burlesque of some serious form. I will omit these serious elements of comic fiction from the rest of the discussion, however, so as to avoid ambiguous cases, even though a mistake would only introduce some confusion, not undermine the argument. Most other fiction I take to be serious in intent. As I have already showed, novelists of this era had many different ideas about the nature of reality and the novel's proper relation to it. In principle, I am imposing no *a priori* standards of realism on the novels, as part of the definition of seriousness. *Le Diable boiteux* is a serious novel, despite its fantastic frame, and so are many less known allegories, romances, and tales. I have looked for the five elements of reality—chronology, geography, names, money, and narrator—in all the two hundred and some works I located from the years 1700 to 1720. It was quickly apparent that this standard does in fact separate realistic from non-realistic fictions; the latter deliberately violate or ignore at least one, and usually several of the systems. What remains is not by any means all Realistic fiction; but the historical romance, for example, does make an effort to keep the systems of the real world intact, and thereby sets the direction for its evolution toward Realism.

From the point of view of technique, serious novels stand in direct opposition to comic novels on the central question of realism. The comic novelist deliberately keeps his fictional forms intact, while forcing into them realities which are incongruous and therefore grotesque. The serious novelist moves in the opposite direction. He perceives reality through the filter of literary forms, or attempts to describe it in literary terms; but his intention is neither to ridicule the literary viewpoint, nor to seek out incongruity. On the contrary, he writes because he thinks there is a deeper knowledge of reality to be gained from the literary analysis of it. Thus, while the comic novel tends to move from romance to its diametric opposite, from the gallant hero to the crude peasant, or from exotic settings to the nearest gutter, the serious novel tends to move by smaller steps, from the aristocratic hero to a wealthy bourgeois hero, from the palace into the townhouse. This is less an invasion of literature by ever more plebeian characters and commonplace events than an invasion by literature of ever wider areas of reality.

As I suggested before, the serious novelist resembles Don Quixote—his education and literary formation determine the way he sees his world. Don Quixote represents an extreme case, where the education excludes any lessons of experience; but Cervantes wanted to use his hero as a comic figure. The novelist need not imitate Don Quixote's intransigeance to share his outlook, although it is probably true that the more unconscious the novelist's own perspective, the more convincing the portrayal. Where the bias is too obvious, the novel seems to have a thesis, although of course the author's artistic skill may compensate for his intellectual prejudices.

In the first chapters, I have given some elements of a history of serious fiction. The whole history is much too complex to undertake. In the limited area which I want to examine, the comic novels have afforded a useful summary by indirection. Every comic novel tends to touch on all the problems of the recent past. The author satirizes everything he has found ridiculous, and goes out of his way to have a pretext to mention it. The serious novelist, on the other hand, avoids any problem not essential to his theme, and often tries to conceal those he can not escape. Each comic novel gives a static picture of the condition of the novel at that time, or slightly earlier, whereas any given serious novel probably contains no more than fragmentary indications of the general situation.

The evolution implied by the comic novels starts with all the significant problems already present to some degree. The development of the genre leads to heavier and heavier emphasis on rules, derived by and large from some other literary genre. Moreover, the work itself is extended by logical deductions into the real world. Again, this is a quixotic process; the literal truth of the novel is assumed, and the consequences deduced. As these consequences came to light, the concern of the comic novelist shifted away from style, which was Scarron's chief interest, toward the narrator, which was the dominant interest of Challe, Furetière, and Marivaux. Diderot finally attacks the narrator's domination, and restores the other elements of Realism to a position of importance.

A consideration of the serious novel will reveal that progress occurs only in a very limited sense during the eighteenth century. The novel had encountered the fundamental difficulties of realism by the early years of the century, no later; yet the solutions are never satisfactory, and seldom applicable to other works, in all the five areas I have singled out. The most durable contribution in many fields was to have exhausted most of the blind alleys, notably in the conception of the narrator.

It is generally recognized that the first flowering of French rationalism occurred in the decade of the 1630's, marked by such events as the publication of Descartes's *Discourse on Method*, the founding of the French Academy, and the quarrel over *Le Cid*. Well before the triumphant years of French classicism, scholars and critics were formulating, and popular taste was imposing, the doctrine of rules. For all its lowliness as a genre, the novel did not escape the examination of reason, and it is here that the problems begin. In 1641 Georges de Scudéry published a long theoretical preface with his novel *Ibrahim*. Although I have already referred to this preface several times, its date as well as its intrinsic merit make a fuller consideration worthwhile. Scudéry frequented the famous salon of the Hôtel de Rambouillet, where he would have met such literary legislators as Vaugelas, Chapelain, and Ménage; and as Henri Coulet observes: " . . . comme Chapelain, comme d'Aubignac, Scudéry croit à l'infaillibilité des règles."[55]

If one is accustomed to the common idea of the Scudérys' novels as monuments of extravagance, the theory behind them is indeed astonishingly and outstandingly rational, laying heavy emphasis on such concepts as nature and verisimilitude. The writings of the Scudérys and La Calprenède are so sound as theory, that they have been cited by Arthur Cooke as possible sources for Henry Fielding's theories. As Cooke observes, "Mlle de Scudéry and Henry Fielding enunciated principles which were in many respects almost identical; yet there is certainly little resemblance between *The Grand Cyrus* and *Tom Jones*."[56] Cooke explains this by referring to

[55] Coulet, *Anthologie*, p. 44.

[56] Arthur L. Cooke, "Henry Fielding and the Writers of Heroic Romance," *PMLA*, 62 (1947), 994.

changes in the meanings of terms like probability, unity, and morality; and no doubt this semantic vagueness played a role. Another factor, however, is almost certainly the difference in approaches; the Scudérys seem to have the idea that the novel can be derived from the rules, not vice versa, whereas Fielding tries to derive a theory which will justify what he instinctively knows to be a good novel.

The apparent excellence of the Scudérys' theory is misleading; they did not invent the modern novel, any more than did Horace and Aristotle, from whom they took their theory. The main significance of the preface to *Ibrahim* is, I believe, the proof it affords of the new seriousness with which authors were treating the novel. In a short time this theory would contribute to the downfall of the genre it was written to defend—just as Descartes's method was eventually used to overthrow his physics, and just as the emulation of the ancients finally produced the moderns. The reader of the 1660's held ideas of reality and verisimilitude similar to Racine's. It was natural that they should favor a novel which incorporated similar qualities—density, psychological intensity, dramatic crises, abstraction—and prefer the short *nouvelle* to the long *roman*.

The preface to *Ibrahim* touches, sometimes indirectly, on the themes I have been discussing. Scudéry admires the epic chronology, because it enables the author to preserve a unity of time: " . . . et pour s'enfermer dans des bornes raisonnables, ils ont fait (et moy aprés eux) que l'Histoire ne dure qu'une année, et que le reste est par narration. . . ."[57] Although, as Scudéry states, he is merely copying Homer, Virgil, Tasso, and Heliodorus, it is worthwhile to note his justification for the principle of a unity of time: "Ils n'ont pas fait comme ces Peintres qui font voir en une mesme toile un Prince dans le berceau, sur le Trône, et dans le cercueil, et qui par cette confusion peu judicieuse embarassent celuy qui considere leur Ouvrage." The rationale for the unity of time lies outside the work, in the reader's perception. He must be able to embrace the work within a clear rational framework.

[57] Coulet, *Anthologie*, p. 45.

Similar demands of reason, all purely external to the work itself, will be made regarding the narrator and even the details of the story; and it seems probable that this rationalism, more than anything else, led to the collapse of the long *roman*. *Ibrahim* was more than three thousand pages long, *Clélie* over seven thousand, and *Le Grand Cyrus* over thirteen thousand. No factitious structure could overcome the truly embarrassing confusion of such works.

A second element of chronology is the use of historical facts. Scudéry proposes to combine historical facts with poetic beauties to create the novel. History serves primarily to lend verisimilitude, which Scudéry calls "la pierre fondamentale de ce bastiment . . . sans elle rien ne peut toucher; sans elle rien ne sçauroit plaire. . . ." (p. 46). Scudéry's method is described plainly: ". . . pour donner plus de vraysemblance aux choses, j'ay voulu que les fondemens de mon Ouvrage fussent historiques, mes principaux personnages marquez dans l'Histoire veritable comme personnes illustres, et les guerres effectives." This doctrine did not, however, extend to the chronological veracity of the events; Scudéry is explicit about that: "Or de peur qu'on ne m'objecte que j'ay raproché quelques incidens que l'Histoire a fait voir plus éloignez, le grand Virgile sera mon garant, luy qui, dans sa divine Eneïde, a fait paroistre Didon quatre Siecles aprés le sien" (p. 48). The same application can of course be found in the classical theatre. By verisimilitude, the classicists clearly had in mind only the possible existence of a thing, or the possible occurrence of an event, and the possibility was to be judged by reason. Historical realism was a partial guarantee of verisimilitude, but the possibility of a battle, or of a heroic deed, was extra-temporal once it had occurred. In the classical spirit, the rules of art take precedence; it is better to sacrifice the chronology than the unity of time. Clearly, though, a major self-contradiction underlies the doctrine, and the arbitrary unit of time would increasingly yield before the demands of historical veracity.

Money, geography, and names are fairly technical matters, and do not receive much attention from Scudéry. Money, indeed, is not mentioned, except that any but the most general allusion to it would be banned from the novel by the following precept on style: "sans parler comme les extravagans, ny comme le peuple, j'ay essayé de parler comme les honnestes gens" (p. 49). Geography is touched on; but the epic of antiquity had had no discernible unity of place, and so the question did not much concern Scudéry. He rejects the use of mythical kingdoms, asking: "comment seray-je touché des infortunes de la Reine de Guindaye, et du Roy d'Astrobacie, puisque je sçay que leurs Royaumes mesmes ne sont point en la Carte universelle, ou pour mieux dire, en l'estre des choses?" (p. 46). The judge of plausibility once again turns out to be a pedantic form of reason, and the places, like the historical events, have an abstract existence. To name them is to make them exist in the reader's mind, which has accepted them on the authority of the historians. Passing to personal names, Scudéry remarks that "l'imposition des noms est une chose à laquelle chacun doit songer, et à laquelle neantmoins tout le monde n'a pas songé" (p. 48). Scudéry has carefully given Turkish names to Turkish characters, where in the past many authors had used Greek names. We are still in the distant exotic past, and Ibrahim, Artamène, Clélie, or Pharamond may pass for realistic names because real people once bore them. But the principle will constitute a grave problem once the novel begins to treat subjects closer to the present and closer to home. Then the reader will still want to know where and who (and perhaps even how much), and the author will be hard pressed to stay in the no-man's-land between particular realities and general possibilities.

Since Scudéry relates the novel to the epic, he accepts the epic narrator, who is a creator and who can therefore go beyond the limits of a single point of view. In the preface he appears even to advocate a fuller usage of this power by authors in saying: "Aprés avoir descrit une avanture, un dessein hardy, ou quelque évenement surprenant, capable de donner les plus beaux sentimens du monde, certains Autheurs se sont contentez de nous asseurer qu'un tel Heros pensa de fort belles choses, sans nous les dire, et c'est cela seulement que je desirois sçavoir" (p. 47). The main thrust of his argument is toward the matter of the novel, however, not its style of narration; Scudéry opposes the piling up of adventures and favors psychological analysis. This in itself looks to the future and shows the kinship between the long novels and the *nouvelles* which succeeded them. Scudéry comments on the adventure stories: "cette narration seche et sans art est plus d'une vieille Chronique que d'un Roman ... " (p. 46), and therein lay the difficulty. As novelists sought more and more to take shelter under the rules of historical writing, the historical narrator became more and more dominant, and he did not have the right to explore the mind. Even Scudéry is ambiguous, for although he wants to know the thoughts and feelings of the heroes, he talks most about their speeches. For example, he writes: "Ce n'est point par les choses de dehors, ce n'est point par les caprices du destin que je veux juger de luy; c'est par les mouvemens de son ame, et par les choses qu'il dit." Or again he writes: "Or pour les faire connoistre parfaitement, il ne suffit pas de dire combien de fois ils ont fait naufrage, et combien de fois ils ont rencontré des voleurs: mais il faut faire juger par leurs discours quelles sont leurs inclinations ... ," and he cites with approbation the sentence: "Parle afin que je te voye" (p. 47). In short, he at least leaves the way open for such devices as the overheard soliloquy and the confidant, the conventions by which the seventeenth-century novelist tried to accomplish the study of the human soul.

CHRONOLOGY: Scudéry's epic rule for the unity of time enjoyed a short prominence. It was applied in the long romances, and therefore satirized by Scarron, Furetière, and Marivaux. When the *nouvelle* came into vogue, however, this principle ceased to be relevant.[58] It does not, in fact, have any

---

[58] René Godenne, in *Histoire de la nouvelle française*, argues that the *nouvelle* quickly adopted all the conventions of the *roman*, including the epic chronology, and preserved them intact well into the eighteenth century (pp. 108-110). I do not challenge the accuracy of his facts, but question the value of his rigid genre distinctions, for he analyzes only works designated "nouvelle" on the title page or in the preface.

relation to the question of realism, but is a purely formal matter. The decline of the long romance and the rise of the *nouvelle* indicate the growing dominance of the historical element over the epic.

If the rule for the unity of time had little future after 1660, the principles of historical verisimilitude were full of consequences. Scudéry, under the sheltering authority of the Ancients, argued that the historical precedent guaranteed the possibility of the event; he did not really intend to put his novels into a real historical chronology. At sufficient distance in time and space, the method works reasonably well. The average reader is likely to know that the events took place, and that the characters existed; he is not likely to know precisely when.

La Princesse de Clèves (1678) perfectly illustrates the application of this principle, and it is also one of literature's most ambitious, and on the whole most successful, attempts to combine history and fiction. Scholars have long since traced Mme de Lafayette's sources and demonstrated the care with which they were utilized. Nonetheless her first concern was psychological truth, not historical; as Dédéyan puts it: "Elle a fait servir l'humble précision historique à l'art supérieur de la psychologie."[59] Specifically, this means that she took a number of real events and purposely misdated them—the death of the duc de Nevers hastened by three years, Lord Courtenay's life prolonged by four years, to cite two examples; more, with details, are given by Dédéyan. The range of alteration is small, and the events for the most part minor. The reader of 1678 was not likely to know exactly

As I showed in chapter one, the *roman* actually absorbed all the innovations presented by the *nouvelle* around 1660, as well as later innovations associated with subgenres like the *nouvelle historique*, the *histoire véritable*, the *mémoires*, etc. The persistence of an archaic technique like the epic chronology, even in works designated *nouvelle*, does not alter the fact that around 1660 the sudden vogue of the *nouvelle* signaled a shift in interest from the epic approach to the historical.

[59] Charles Dédéyan, *Madame de Lafayette* (1956; 2nd ed., Paris: Société d'édition d'enseignement supérieur, 1965), p. 186.

when they had occurred. The principle is identical to Scudéry's, but as the subject moves closer to the reader, the permissible liberties grow smaller; Mme de Lafayette alters dates by a few years, not a few centuries.

Mme de Lafayette then conceived of herself as an author of fiction, and did not scruple to tamper with facts if she found it useful. It is all the more significant therefore to discover that she was still unable to adjust the historical chronology satisfactorily with the private chronology of her story. Dédéyan once again exposes the following inconsistencies. The earliest events in the story take place between the end of November, 1558, and January, 1559, that is, between the real negotiations of Cercamp and the real marriage of Claude de France. In that space these fictional events happen: Mlle de Chartres and her mother appear in court; Monsieur de Clèves sees the new beauty the next day and falls in love; a day later the chevalier de Guise falls in love with her; both the Clèves and the Guise families oppose the marriage of their sons; Mme de Chartres tries a third marriage which also fails; Monsieur de Clèves's father dies, and after a suitable mourning he declares himself, is accepted, and the marriage takes place. Dédéyan concludes: "L'artiste peut ainsi en imposer au lecteur par sa précision, mais, à l'examen critique, la tentative s'avère infructueuse" (p. 175).

In pointing out these inconsistencies, I do not in the least mean to criticize *La Princesse de Clèves*, but rather the opposite. Mme de Lafayette is obviously an author of superior genius, who perceived with great clarity how historical circumstances could lend credibility to a psychological analysis. If she experienced such difficulties, there must have been lurking in the problem a much greater obstacle than would appear at first glance. Dédéyan mentions in passing a curious factor which contributed to the implausible profusion of events in this beginning: the opposition of Monsieur de Clèves's family is a convention, for "un grand amour doit être traversé et désespéré" (p. 179). Otherwise, the wedding could have been arranged and the ceremony performed within the time allotted and without a serious breach of plausibility. It must be admitted, though, that Monsieur de Clèves's love would have lost some of its prestige. Pursuing this line of thought, one discovers that all of the events which precede the return of Nemours to the court are necessary to establish the character of Mlle de Chartres—her virtue, her extraordinary beauty, her isolation. It is all to Mme de Lafayette's credit that she undertakes to show us these qualities, not simply tells us they are there; but the effort merely entangles her in a still more complicated series of difficulties. There is only one setting for *La Princesse de Clèves*, which is the court; one of the themes of the novel is the public nature of what ought to be a private life, at home, even in the country, and so forth. Thus any proof of Mlle de Chartres's preeminence had to come from the court, and yet had to remain unknown to Nemours. Pretexts are therefore found to keep Nemours away, and then to bring him back after it is too late. Now if Mme de Lafayette were less concerned with the historical plausibility of her novel, such pretexts would be easy to find, and would serve for two years as well as for two months—an unnamed illness or a pointless voyage, for example; one of her predecessors or less talented imitators would have resorted to some such device. But the *best* novelists take a literary tradition—in Mme de Lafayette's case, a form of courtly love—and apply it to real situations, and this combination virtually always creates a problem which is solved by some sort of technical awkwardness.

It is really accidental that the awkwardness should be chronological; had Nemours been kept away through the common device of a wound or illness, no conflict of dates need have arisen. Instead, a modern reader would have sensed an improbable coincidence of timing, which would be just as relevant to the evolution I wish to describe, but virtually impossible to demonstrate. Mme de Lafayette avoids the cliché illness, because for her novel the historical setting has its own thematic significance. It is important that the setting be fully realized through constant detailed reminders. She deals with the implausibility by keeping the dates as vague as possible.

Techniques of Realism in Early Fiction

Lesage was a far less careful craftsman than Mme de Lafayette was, and it is not certain whether he had any plan for the conclusion of *Gil Blas* when he began it. At any rate, one can hardly believe that it was the same plan in 1715 that it was in 1735 when the last three books were finally written. The first six books are mainly linear in construction, closely modeled on the Spanish picaresque tales. Gil Blas sets out on life's road, his course dictated by chance and his adventures related to each other only through his character and memory. In Book Seven, however, a new structure begins to appear: on the one hand, Gil Blas's past repeats itself, either through the reappearance of previous secondary characters, or through Gil Blas's revisiting places he had been before, or through the repetition of certain important actions; and on the other hand, Gil Blas finds himself involved in real historical contexts.

When Lesage conceived this new plan, he was applying a complex literary structure to a new situation. It is perhaps a double application, both the picaresque fiction entering history, and the more complex pattern entering the life of the lower class hero. Lesage really took few pains to make his historical allusions fit his plot, one reason being that behind many of the Spanish names he was describing a French contemporary. Even if it is only to follow fashion, however, he does make a pretense of being historical and real, and soon runs afoul of the facts. Putting together the details of his service under the duc de Lerme and Olivarès, it appears that by the end of Book Twelve, Gil Blas is over eighty years old, yet he marries and fathers two children. While this may lie within the realm of possibility, it clashes with the tone of Lesage's presentation. He has simply neglected to calculate the age of his hero, or else has assumed that his readers will neglect to. Moreover, as Vivienne Mylne points out, the time Gil Blas claims to have spent serving Olivarès—some twenty years—is scarcely accounted for in the novel; we have only a few anecdotes from these two decades, when Gil Blas had his greatest power and influence. Mylne explains the contradictions by the fact that Lesage is a derivative author, often a mere hack; and the hack, more than any other, repeats the clichés of his time.[60] Lesage approaches reality with no profound artistic vision; rather he brings to it a set of well-worn devices. *Gil Blas* exhibits the sort of slipshod compromise this often entailed and which was accepted by the readers of the time with only slight protest. Though similar in type to Mme de Lafayette's, Lesage's errors of chronology seem less forgivable today than hers, because they do not seem to have arisen from anything more than technical incompetence.

The abbé Prévost has much in common with Lesage. Both wrote in order to earn a living, and as a result had to sacrifice art to quantity. Both published in installments, and therefore employed the kind of open-ended plotting which made a successful novel infinitely extensible. And both encountered the same difficulties with chronology, although with Prévost one feels that the artist's vision is operating, just as with Mme de Lafayette. Prévost claimed the right to alter the facts of history in favor of the novel, if he needed to; for example, he writes in *Le Pour et contre* that there are in his novels "quantité de faits qui sont vrais dans leurs principales parties," but "il y en a peu dont je n'aye étendu ou raccourci les circonstances, suivant que je l'ai jugé nécessaire pour le seul dessein que j'ai eu de faire passer quelques maximes de morale, à la faveur d'une narration agréable. Voilà le fait, simplement exposé."[61] Since this was Prévost's conscious method, it is perhaps superfluous to cite examples, but it is worth noting first that he could choose between precise historical events or a general context, and sometimes chose the former; and second that he himself expressed some qualms about his errors in chronology.

The hero of *Cleveland* (1731-39) is supposed to be the bastard son of Cromwell; this sets the story in an extremely

[60] In Vivienne Mylne, *The Eighteenth-Century French Novel* (Manchester: Manchester Univ. Press, 1965), pp. 49-72.

[61] In *Le Pour et contre*, 6 (1736), 342-43, quoted in Jean Sgard, *Prévost romancier* (Paris: Librairie José Corti, 1968), p. 134. Sgard treats the question of chronology in Prévost's novels very fully; I will comment only very briefly on his findings.

definite chronological scale. Yet Cromwell is not a real figure, but rather what Sgard calls "une obsession saturnienne de vieillard libidineux et mangeur d'enfants."[62] He is needed to persecute the hero, and his influence implausibly survives after his death—his henchman Will is still pursuing Axminster and Cleveland two years afterwards. Even in volume one of *Cleveland*, Prévost, in Sgard's terms, had forgotten the reality of Cromwell, and had inserted an episode involving him which took place in 1659, even though he had died in 1658. Prévost attributed this error of several months to a lacuna in the manuscript, which proves that he felt some embarrassment about the inconsistency. Later in the story, a different sort of inconsistency occurs, when the story jumps from 1662 to 1667. Sgard explains this by Prévost's wish to pass the mantle of legitimate authority to a new figure, Henriette d'Angleterre—in other words, by an extension of the obsession with the father-tyrant (pp. 136-46). These errors do perhaps result from the obsessional quality of Prévost's father figures throughout his works, but they are not on that account necessary to the structure of the novel. Cromwell's persecution of Cleveland could have ended at his death without being any less severe, and Cleveland could have joined the court in exile of Henriette without omitting five years of his life.

Prévost in fact had extraordinary difficulties with chronology. Sgard states bluntly of the *Mémoires et Avantures d'un homme de qualité* (1728-31) that "l'utilisation du temps est très malhabile" (p. 99). Here the causes are more complex, but turn around the theme of the cloister: "le cloître bénédictin, qui a soustrait Prévost à la vie réelle, semble avoir détruit en lui la conscience d'un temps homogène." Prévost sees time as magic, the same events repeat themselves from generation to generation, and from friend to friend for those born under the same star. There is no doubt a great deal of truth in this analysis of Prévost's perception of time, which parallels Poulet's; it recalls the entire phenomenon of pre-romantic sensibility, which seemed to have no awareness of its exist-

---

[62] Sgard, *Prévost romancier*, p. 137.

ence except when emotion or sensation were acute. Prévost, or his characters, appear to have no memory of themselves except in terms of dramatic episodes that provoked powerful passions.

At the same time, however, one should not forget the technical side of the phenomenon. Sgard says: "Chacun évoque la durée avec des moyens qui lui sont propres . . . " (p. 100), and he even points out that Marivaux had many of the same difficulties as Prévost. The means available at any given time depend on the work of one's predecessors, and it is this aspect of the works that I would like to illuminate. Part of Prévost's difficulty arose from the fact that no previous novelist had solved the problem of duration with entire success. Sgard cites Mme de Lafayette and Lesage; but I have just shown how both these major novelists failed to achieve a correspondence between objective chronology as measured by historical events, and the interior chronology of the novel. Prévost makes an important contribution to the art of treating chronology—his is at times a truly subjective chronology. The incomprehension of Prévost's narrators before the adored woman, and before their own feelings, extends to their sense of time. They remark that they do not know how long things went on, or that they do not remember when something began. Moreover they explicitly color their time sense with emotional tones, especially with the feeling that they have exhausted themselves and grown old of a sudden. Subjective time-distortion is a fictional commonplace today; Prévost's innovation found immediate echoes in Rousseau and Sterne. Here, the story is made internally coherent, while most of the allusions to history are rather vague and distant. *Manon* (1731) obviously takes place against the background of Law's bank and the fever of speculation and free spending which it created. Historically this fixes *Manon* in the years 1719 and 1720 for its central action. The Classiques Garnier edition includes a chronology, established by Paul Vernière and rectified by Frédéric Deloffre, which puts the first scene of the story (Des Grieux meeting Manon in Amiens) on

July 28, 1717.[63] A month later, Des Grieux is back home, betrayed by Manon after two weeks. About two years pass while Des Grieux attempts to forget Manon, and begins a promising career as an ecclesiastic. The second meeting, after Des Grieux's public sermon, takes place in September, 1719. They remain together for the fall in Chaillot, but return to Paris for the winter, and run afoul of old G . . . M . . . . Three months pass while they are imprisoned. Free again in early summer, 1720, they again get in trouble with the G . . . M . . . family, and by the end of the summer are bound for Louisiana. The first meeting with the marquis de Renoncour takes place at this point, the second, after the death of Manon, almost two years later.

As Deloffre points out, this chronology is upset by Prévost's revisions in 1753. The insertion of the episode of the Italian prince, after the escapes from St-Lazare and La Salpêtrière, stretches the happiness of the summer from a few days to a few weeks; but Prévost forgot that Des Grieux wrote a letter to his father immediately after his freedom was assured, and that his father came to find him in prison again, barely a week later. This mistake is revealing of Prévost's methods, which are typically episodic. The links between parts are sufficiently fragile to allow maximum freedom in plotting. *Manon*, for all its careful planning and compactness, repeatedly begins again from the zero point, just like the longer novels. Deloffre calls it a "chance vraiment étonnante" which restores to Des Grieux his freedom of movement after his escape from St-Lazare, the murder of a guard, the escape of Manon, and the death of Lescaut. The same good luck, or rather episodic plotting, gives Des Grieux his liberty after his first flight to Paris, and when he arrives in the New World. The number of times this cycle could be repeated is infinite, subject only to the will or taste of the author. Angus Martin, discussing an

[63] Abbé Antoine-François Prévost, *Histoire du Chevalier des Grieux et de Manon Lescaut*, ed. Frédéric Deloffre and Raymond Picard, Classiques Garnier (Paris: Garnier Frères, 1965), p. xc. Hereafter cited as Prévost, *Manon Lescaut*.

apocryphal sequel to *Manon*, has shown that Prévost either deliberately or instinctively wrote the death of Manon so as to leave open the possibility of reviving her and continuing the story.[64] It is not surprising that such a conception of structure led to errors whenever it met calendar time. A perfect example is the anachronism of *Manon*'s presence in the *Mémoires* of the marquis de Renoncour, who meets Des Grieux while on his way to Spain; once in Spain he hears of the death of Louis XIV, which occurred on September 1, 1715. More obviously than in most cases, *Manon* is a purely separate work, complete unto itself, and the bonds between it and the *Mémoires* are only a pretext.

In all three of the novels just discussed, it is clear that the author has a literary method which he tries to apply to historical reality. In the case of Mme de Lafayette, it is the evocation of courtly love. In the case of Lesage, it is an originally picaresque plot, overlaid with progressive cycles. In the case of Prévost, it is an episodic plot with an obsessively emotional point of view. When the objective time scheme will not tolerate the literary vision, Mme de Lafayette and Lesage rely on the vagueness of the dating to keep the reader from noticing. Prévost actually has his narrators talk about their difficulties with chronology, thus inviting the reader to overlook the errors in return for candor.[65]

Internal chronologies could be just as troublesome. Gil Blas lets about twenty years go by with hardly any comment, for example, and Prévost forgot that he had limited the time Manon and Des Grieux could be free. When the problem seemed to be one of organization, authors very often just confessed to the difficulty in their prefaces or in direct commen-

[64] Angus Martin, "Une Suite de *Manon Lescaut* et les intentions de l'abbé Prévost," *RSH*, no. 117 (1965), 51-57.

[65] Stewart, in *Imitation and Illusion in the French Memoir-Novel*, gives further examples of chronological errors in chapter eight, pp. 240-62. He regards these lapses as a simple matter of inexperience or incompetence, and concludes: "The emergence of the well-wrought novel came only after a long apprenticeship" (p. 262). It is hard to contradict such a statement, but I believe that it fails to recognize the real source of difficulty.

tary. Catherine Bédacier writes in *Les Mémoires secrets de la cour de Charles VII, Roi de France* (1700): "On a été obligé de transposer toutes ces choses pour suivre les differens Ministres qui parurent successivement, et en si peu de tems: ces Memoires ne s'écrivent pas comme une histoire particuliere."[66] Hamilton announces that he will take the same kinds of liberties, in the first chapter of his *Mémoires de la vie du comte de Gramont* (1713; written around 1703): "Je déclare de plus que l'ordre des temps, ou la disposition des faits, qui coûtent plus à l'écrivain qu'ils ne divertissent le lecteur, ne m'embarrasseront guère dans l'arrangement de ces Mémoires."[67] To be sure, these are purportedly true stories, and probably really were closely based on fact; the authors reject chronological order for greater clarity or effect. Their obligation to justify this procedure shows, however, that the reader expected a systematic and continuous chronology.

Authors of pure fiction utilized the same device, moreover. Subligny's *La Fausse Clélie* (1671) has a preface in which the author admits to being a "mauvais Chroniqueur pour l'ordre des temps."[68] Challe says in the preface to *Les Illustres Françoises* (1713): "J'ai fait exprès des fautes d'anachronisme."[69] Although Challe gives an example, it is not fully clear what either of these authors has in mind; Challe's example is so obscure that no one would have noticed it if he had not pointed it out. Challe does, as will be shown later, provide a fairly precise date and chronology for each of his separate stories, and in fact they do not all jibe very well. Subligny's are much less precisely dated, although the present tense of the frame is about 1664. Apparently he was referring mainly to the profusion of narratives which begin in the past and end in the present. The device itself is not remarkable, but it is striking that the authors have to apologize for it.

[66] Bédacier, *Les Mémoires secrets de la cour de Charles VII, Roi de France*, 1700, p. 364.
[67] *Romanciers du XVIIIe siècle*, Vol. I, p. 29.
[68] A. P. Perdou de Subligny, *La Fausse Clélie* (Amsterdam: Jacques Wagenaar, 1671), "Préface."
[69] Challe, *Œuvres*, p. lxi.

It is Marivaux, however, who best illustrates the central problem of internal chronology. Marivaux completely escapes the historical difficulty by avoiding any specific allusion to a datable event. He is then free to concentrate on the private events in his characters' lives. Marivaux's interests were primarily moral and psychological; unlike Prévost and Lesage, he did not pay much attention to his plots. He cared less about what happened than why, and each incident leads him into a complex web of motivations. Moreover, each event reorders the webbing, and the reordering itself becomes a kind of event, with conceivably infinite ramifications. Every moment therefore tends to expand infinitely.

In Marivaux's novels there is considerable action, most of it taken without alteration from the old romance tradition—unexpected deaths, coincidental meetings, chance encounters. Marivaux explores each incident in such depth, however, that he has difficulty proceeding from one to the next. The best-known case is *Marianne* (1731-42), in which Book One ends with Marianne preparing to go to church in the morning of a day that does not end until the last pages of Book Three. In this one day the heroine has enjoyed her triumph in the church, met Valville, realized that Climal was Valville's uncle, returned secretly to Mme Dutour's, been caught by Valville with Climal at her feet, denounced Climal to the priest, and finally been adopted by a lady who will turn out to be Valville's mother, but who for the moment merely sponsors Marianne's entry into the convent. At this rate Marianne would clearly never finish her life story.

The situation in *Le Paysan parvenu* (1734-35) is very similar. After leaving his first situation because of his master's death and bankruptcy, Jacob meets Mlle Habert on the Pont-Neuf. Near the end of Book One, Marivaux evidently is planning another stay of some duration for Jacob, in the house of the two pious sisters. Thus Jacob is astonished at the first meal, because while no one has any appetite, the food disappears; and Jacob comments, "Je ne savais les premiers jours comment ajuster tout cela. Mais je vis à la fin de quoi j'avais été les premiers jours dupe."[70] But the hypocritical director immediately clashes with Jacob, who leaves with Mlle Habert and they take lodgings elsewhere. In fact he spends only a day there; and this rhythm continues for the remainder of the book. The marriage, the appearance before the magistrate, the trip to Versailles, the imprisonment and vindication, the interrupted rendezvous, the meeting with the young comte d'Orsan after saving him from bullies—all this occurs within a week or so. The stages along the road to success are symbolic, for they have no duration.

For all his intricate psychological analysis, Marivaux builds his plots just as Prévost and Lesage did: each episode is a separate event, linked to the next primarily by the continued presence of the main character. At the end of Book One, Jacob is freed from a moral and physical predicament by several strokes of good luck, just as Des Grieux is on several occasions. Later, a new illness, the intruder at the *petite maison*, the imminent death of Mme de la Vallée, and some fortunate chance encounters, give support to Jacob's moral revolt at Versailles, so that he is once again free of the mistakes of his past. In *Marianne* the successive impediments to the marriage are overcome one at a time—Climal repents, the magistrate decides in her favor. After each one, Marianne is apparently free to enjoy her successes, only to meet some new, unlucky obstacle—Mme Dutour betrays her identity, Valville becomes unfaithful. Since the novel is incomplete, we should perhaps reserve judgment on the last incident. Rather than creating a new obstacle, perhaps Valville's elimination opens the way for the next step upward. In any case, the study of how an ambitious young person succeeds in society is hampered by Marivaux's inability to suggest duration of time. His imagination functions by episodes, just as Prévost's and Lesage's did. Marivaux examines the significance of the episode in more detail, maybe with more profundity than either of his contemporaries did; but he brings to the real

---

[70] Marivaux, *Le Paysan parvenu*, p. 52.

situation the same literary methods they used, and meets exactly the same problem.

The last chronological problem discussed in the comic novel does not really come up in serious fiction: the synchronization of the narrator's time with the narration's time. The third-person omniscient narrator had been ridiculed into obscurity by 1700. With the reliance on first-person narrators, the problem changes form, and can be discussed best as a narrative problem. The question arises repeatedly in the novels whether a character who is telling or writing a story ought to stop and rest, or whether a character who is writing a letter would have had time to write so much, and the like. On the whole, the temporal condition of the narrator is imperfectly rendered. Challe, for example, has to contrive for Des Ronais to go on doubting Manon Dupuis's fidelity long enough (seven months), so that the reconciliation may occur as part of the round of storytelling. The adult Marianne, comtesse de ***, begins almost every chapter with a comment on how long it has taken her to write it; but even though she is one of the best characterized narrators, she gives no hint of what she has been doing between chapters. Similar weaknesses mar Rousseau's *Julie, ou la Nouvelle Héloïse* (1761); the rapid collapse of Julie's peace of mind seems very slow indeed, because the letters about Clarens are so long. This is particularly ironic in view of the great care Rousseau took to date the events; but the variants in the text reveal that he too was sensitive to the clash between the calendar time and the apparent time as the reader experienced it. The *reductio ad absurdum* of this problem is Tristram Shandy, who never succeeds in telling the story he set out to.

The novelists were evidently aware of the difficulties but equally aware that an accurate chronology would have great value in persuading the reader. Their profound desire to win the reader's belief demanded that they return to the problem, and deal with it as well as they could. Readers were not so demanding as they are today. Mme de Graffigny's *Lettres d'une Péruvienne* (1747), one of the century's great bestsellers, is based on an incredible anachronism. The story opens with the Spanish conquest of Peru, thus in the sixteenth century; but after crossing the Atlantic, the heroine lands in eighteenth-century France. Critics like Fréron and Clément noticed and forgave the blunder; so did readers like Prévost, Turgot, Duclos, and Marmontel. When the revised version appeared in 1752, no effort had been made to eliminate the anachronism, although some major changes had been made. Instead, a long historical preface was included, giving all the sources for the Incan details, and thereby plunging the work still deeper into the error. Obviously, most of the public still looked on literary reality as a series of plausible episodes, joined by almost any link. Conscientious authors knew that they had to produce an integrated work. Chronology was, of course, only one aspect, albeit a significant one. The concern over the narrator pre-empted a great deal of attention, however, and in many instances effectively stalled progress. By the end of the century, there were enough partially successful chronologies in fiction to guide the next important wave of authors: in the individual components of *Les Illustres Françoises*, in the first version of *Manon Lescaut*, in *La Nouvelle Héloïse*, and in *Les Liaisons dangereuses*, novelists had managed to achieve near equilibrium between the calendar time of the story, the experienced time of the narrator, and the sensation of time in the reader.

GEOGRAPHY: The imaginary exotic kingdoms which Cervantes and Challe had satirized soon disappeared from serious fiction, but in giving them up, the novelists sacrificed nothing at all. The actual accounts of explorers in America, Africa, and the Orient contained facts as incredible as any the novelists had ever invented. Consequently, these real countries replaced Micomicona and the like, but only the names are changed. An example is Mlle de la Roche-Guilhem's *L'Amitié singulière* (1710), which is set in Mexico. Montezuma I marries Irmizene, but on their wedding day he sees her friend, the captive Zelinde, and they fall in love. After some time, Irmizene finds out, and persuades Montezuma to marry Zelinde too. All three live happily ever after. There is not a shred of evidence that Mlle de la Roche-Guilhem had any real knowledge of Mexico; she certainly makes no effort to convey any sense of the country or its customs. Only the detail of plural marriages attracted her attention, and this anthropological curiosity provided a surprise twist for the classical triangle.

The abbé Prévost is famous for his exotic settings, many of which are purely imaginary. Even the real ones, however, bear slight relationship to reality. Cleveland's wanderings through the American wilderness defy analysis; he moves from Cuba to Virginia, lives among the savages, is sold into slavery, and returns to Cuba, without giving the reader any sensation of the distances covered or the difficulties of travel. At the time, Prévost probably had little concept of them himself. Even in *Manon*, the couple flees the New Orleans colony and plans to seek refuge with the English, whom they expect to find after several days of walking, when several months would be closer to the truth. Since Manon dies on the first day, this is no great implausibility, but Prévost very likely did not know any better; Cleveland appears to follow the same map.

The fictional imitations of real travel narratives led to a new vogue at about this time, the imaginary voyage. By and large, its purposes are satirical or philosophical, rather than novelistic. Pierre de Lesconvel's *Relation du voyage du prince de Montberaud dans l'Ile de Naudely* (1705) is one such; the author describes what he regards as a utopian society. To the degree that the author endeavors to make his imaginary country seem real, his effort does fall within the range of techniques of the novelist. The most striking cases are those where in an otherwise fairly plausible story the characters suddenly go to a mythical land. Prévost was of course the most prolific practitioner of this device, but he was not the first.

In 1703, the otherwise unknown Mlle Daunois published *Histoire véritable de Monsieur du Prat et de Mademoiselle Angélique*.[71] As the names suggest, the work begins with a

[71] See Shirley E. Jones, "Robert Chasles serait-il l'auteur de

fair amount of plausibility. Du Prat is noble and poor, Angélique bourgeois and rich—and she limps a little. The marriage is arranged to everyone's satisfaction, except a rival, who attacks Du Prat, and is killed by him. Fleeing, Du Prat meets Du Genest, who has a similar story to tell, about Mlle des Conces and the now dead marquis de Cerman. In Paris they meet Cerman's brother, save his life, and then have to flee again. Obviously, the coincidences are too numerous, and the plot devices too repetitious; nonetheless, the story has some believable scenes and characters. At this point, however, the two men sail to India, nearly lose their lives in the Inquisition at Goa, but come back rich. Du Prat learns that Angélique has been unfaithful, and plans to marry another; Du Prat gets his revenge by spreading the rumor that he has already slept with her. A bit more exotic than the first part, this part still has a basic credibility. The final part, however, shows the two friends as kings of a lost colony of Greeks, descendants of Alexander's army, who are now being oppressed by the Onuphres. Du Prat and Du Genest save them, marry princesses, and plan to live there the rest of their lives. One is reminded of Sancho's Island.

Prévost's works contain several utopian countries. Cleveland, before he even reaches America, hears the story of Bridges, who had been part of a secret colony on Saint Helena. In Virginia, Cleveland lives among a tribe of genuinely noble savages, the Abaquis. In the *Histoire de la jeunesse du commandeur de* *** (1741), the hero rescues a shipwreck victim who tells how he became king of the Maniotes, a tribe descended from the Spartans. These fantastic places demonstrate the survival of the romance outlook within the novel. The authors still looked upon their works to some extent as pure examples; any circumstances made the moral less widely applicable. Hence certain situations could be dealt with only through the device of an idealized society.

l'*Histoire véritable de Monsieur du Prat et de Mademoiselle Angélique?*" *RSH*, no. 137 (1970), 39-50. The attribution of this work to Challe, while plausible, remains unsupported by any positive evidence, but this article gives a good account of the novel.

Prévost's utopias always disintegrate; he does not intend to hold them up for the reader's emulation. The King of the Maniotes loses his kingdom because the law requires him to marry, and he does not want to; he is thus the counterpart of the hero, a Knight of Malta, who is legally prevented from marrying. The utopian societies of *Cleveland* illustrate steps along the way to the hero's ultimate wisdom, and their unreal perfection is necessary to the clarity of the theme, just as it was necessary for the hero to spend his childhood in a cave, thereby acquiring a "perfect" education. At the same time, Prévost sees the spiritual dilemma in the real world, and he portrays it there too; his flights into fantasy are designed to make certain that the reader understands the point.

Prévost's *Manon Lescaut* has one of the most satisfactory geographies of any eighteenth-century novel. Prévost's acquaintance with the New Orleans settlement and the American wilderness was weak; but in the context, that is, as a dream of escape for Des Grieux, even the American passages ring true. Prévost neglects the possibilities of exotic color, and the scarce details he gives are inaccurate. On the other hand, the vision of a new world, free of the prejudices of Europe, is convincingly followed by a disenchanting encounter with the indifferent harshness of the wilderness. The Parisian settings, moreover, are evoked with considerable precision. The couple's first lodging on the rue Vivienne, their later stays at Chaillot, are the bases of operation for their movements around Paris, and Prévost specifically mentions Saint-Sulpice, the Sorbonne, the Opéra, the Palais Royal, the quai Malaquais, Saint-Lazare, La Salpétrière, the Cours-la-Reine, the rue Saint-André-des-Arts, the Pont Saint-Michel, the Châtelet, the Luxembourg gardens, the porte Saint-Honoré within the city, besides Amiens, Mantes, Pacy, and Le Havre. One can reconstruct a fairly broad guide to Paris from these indications.

Since *Manon* was apparently inspired by Challe's *Les Illustres Françoises*, it is not surprising that the same sort of specific geography can be found in the earlier work. Challe had actually begun to use the names of Paris streets in the

Histoire de Sainville et de Sylvie, which appeared in the sequel to *Don Quixote*. The story begins with an accident in the rue Saint-Antoine, and much of it takes place around the Croix-Rouge crossroads. Challe was not the only one to have felt the usefulness of place names to give authenticity. In the anonymous *La Comtesse D*** et le courrier galant* (1700), the story "La Restitution d'Histoire" tells of a young nobleman, Saint-Alvar, involved with an intriguing adventuress, Mlle Lingendre; several streets, such as the rue de Montmartre and the rue de la Villette, are mentioned. Still other novels use other regions: *La Foire de Beaucaire* (1708) uses the fair as background, although not extensively; *Mylord *** ou le paysan de qualité* (1700) alludes to several real cities and battles in Holland; *La Belle Hollandoise* (1679) likewise uses a siege in Holland to good effect. All of these works have in common a fundamental orientation toward a recognizable realism; they have not only real places, but plausibly named characters and at least partially believable plots. None of them, however, can fully sustain this style; sooner or later the story veers into the *romanesque*, the exotic, or even the fantastic. The frequent combination of these realistic details from different areas suggests that they tended to lead from one to another, while the combination of realistic elements with traditional romance elements suggests that the author's motive was not just to describe something real, but rather to make visible the *romanesque* in the real.

Various other novels illustrate better the difficulties and awkward solutions. Just as the historical novelist took actual events and people, and imagined for them a personal and emotional life, so too they took real public places, and imagined private ones surrounding them. *Les Intrigues parisiennes et provinciales* (1700) affords a perfect example. The frame for the first of the two stories is set in the Tuileries, where two friends meet; they then go into the courtyard of the Palais Royal, where the story is told. The story itself is quite believable, but no further details about setting are given. These real public places will go on appearing in novels throughout the century, from *Les Egarements du cœur et de*

l'esprit to *Le Neveu de Rameau* to *Les Liaisons dangereuses*,
but the homes to which the characters then retreat remain
mysterious. Depending on the nature of the plot, the location
might be ignored completely, beyond such vague allusions as
"chez mes parents," or "une maison à la campagne," or "un
couvent." The lengths to which a novelist might go in avoiding a precise name can be demonstrated by a quotation from
Marivaux's *La Vie de Marianne*. The young girl, dressed in
her first finery, and on her first outing, has had the good luck
to twist her ankle in the presence of a handsome young man,
Valville. He has taken her to his house: " . . . sa maison n'était
qu'à deux pas plus loin. . . . Enfin on me porta chez Valville . . . ,"[72] had her pretty ankle cared for by a doctor, and
obviously been touched by her charms. Marianne, however,
must now return to her dwelling, which is Mme Dutour's
linen shop, and naturally she does not want Valville to know
how humble her circumstances are. She demands to go home
alone: "J'avais compris qu'on m'enverrait chercher une
voiture; je comptais m'y mettre toute seule, en être quitte
pour dire: Menez-moi *dans telle rue*; et, à l'abri de toute
confusion regagner ainsi cette fâcheuse boutique . . ." (p. 77).
As I will show in discussing the treatment of money, this is
not the only case where Marivaux resorts to such a transparent
evasion.

As a device it is surely no more transparent than the use of
initials instead of the name. This was of course primarily a
device for implying that characters were real, but Prévost
makes inspired use of it in *Manon*. Des Grieux and Manon
take a room in the rue V . . . when they first light in Paris. No
one can doubt that this was the rue Vivienne, financial center
of Paris. Similarly, much later, Prévost refers to the proprietor of the Hotel de Transylvanie as M. le prince de R . . . ,
and everyone would have known that the real proprietor was
Prince Rakoczy. By pretending to conceal two obviously real
names, Prévost hoped to win more credence for the fictitious
characters Monsieur de B . . . , de G . . . M . . . , de T . . . , etc.

Both Subligny and Challe use another tactic, similar to

[72] Marivaux, *La Vie de Marianne*, pp. 65, 67.

their open admission of inaccurate chronologies. Subligny says in the same sentence, that he is "mauvais chroniqueur" and "mauvais Geografe des environs de Paris."[73] He goes on to state that he had to make some changes after he had set the stories down, and that this explains the inconsistencies, which he does not regard as very important anyway. Challe says, "Quoi que je pose la scéne de toutes les histoires à Paris, elles ne s'y sont pas toutes passées, les provinces m'en ont fourni la plûpart."[74] Neither author really needs to make any apology for his geography, Challe because his seems to be quite accurate, and Subligny because his is so incidental that it hardly matters. Their very confessions of errors and changes, however, claim that the story itself, in its essential parts, is true. And further, they imply that the geographical details are one way by which a reader can judge of the story's truth.

The geography of a story is, on the whole, relatively easy to deal with, whether one wishes to be precise or to avoid precisions. It was therefore much less noticeable as a problem than the narrator or the chronology, when it went awry. Yet the novelists appear to have associated the geographical problem with the others, and their efforts to make fiction of real life around them led them to describe the settings. Until Balzac, no author in France had the concern for physical settings which Richardson had. If one were to study the question of space in the eighteenth-century novel in great depth, it would no doubt appear that the problems I have pointed to in their most obvious manifestations would underlie many other commonplace features of fiction at that time. For example, the tendency toward episodic plots has a geographical aspect; the character has to move on, and having done so, coincidence will be needed to reintroduce a previous character. That is to say that space became a structural factor by separating elements of the story which the novelist had to bring back together as best he could. That is one reason why Prévost's characters are constantly meeting in odd corners of the

---

[73] Subligny, *La Fausse Clélie*, 1671, "Préface."
[74] Challe, *Œuvres*, p. lix.

world. On the other hand, he might want to keep them apart; this problem has been mentioned in connection with *La Princesse de Clèves*. Mme de Lafayette resolves her spatial difficulty by warping her time dimension, so to speak. The shipwrecks and storms needed to prolong a quest are part of the same general problem. So also are the constant goings and comings of Saint-Preux and Claire in *La Nouvelle Héloïse,* not to mention the famous letter written in the closet. Rousseau had to shuffle his spatial aspects to preserve his narrative unity. The elements of Realism are so interrelated that they can not be discovered one by one, or even bit by bit; the whole problem really had to be conquered at once.

MONEY: Money can be more easily omitted from a novel than any of the other themes I have isolated. Especially in the seventeenth and eighteenth centuries, there are novels where the subject is never mentioned. *La Princesse de Clèves* is one example; everyone must assume that all the characters are rich enough to do whatever they wish to. Even here there is enough concern for reality, however, to provide very close equivalents to financial problems. At this aristocratic level of society, marriages are arranged for social or political reasons, but the procedure hardly differs from the financial matches among the bourgeoisie. Money also signifies independence; the prince de Clèves needs the moral freedom which results from his father's death, rather than the inheritance, but again the situation is similar to that of a magistrate's son inheriting a position, like Challe's Des Prez. In *Les Egarements du cœur et de l'esprit*, the narrator-hero Meilcour begins by explaining that at age seventeen, he entered society with an important name, left him by his father, and the expectation of "biens considérables" from his mother. All the other characters seem to be in more or less the same situation.

It can readily be seen that if the plots of *La Princesse de Clèves* and *Les Egarements du cœur et de l'esprit* are to be applied to more ordinary people, some attention must be paid to their financial condition. Challe handles the theme very naturally in *Les Illustres Françoises*. It is by no means the main subject of the stories, but when relevant it is introduced. In the first story, Des Ronais relates that his prospective father-in-law proved his genuine affection by offering a badly needed loan of twelve thousand *écus*. Money has no real function in the plot of Des Ronais's story; the hero is richer than the heroine, and is master of his own affairs. The question of money occurs only to shed light on the characters—old Dupuis, the father-in-law, is possessive toward his daughter in part because he has had financial troubles in the past. Some of the other stories use financial problems as plot elements. Contamine and Angélique ought not to have been allowed to marry, under the normal customs of their society, because she had no money at all. In the case of Jussy and Mlle Fenoüil, she is rich and he is poor. Challe quite often cites a precise figure, and shows no hesitation about bringing money into the story for illustrative purposes or simply as a realistic detail. Nonetheless, the milieu remains largely free of day-to-day concerns with money; in every couple, at least one person has the available wealth to do as he or she pleases. The social or moral obstacles count more heavily—Manon Dupuis will not leave her father, Contamine will not displease his mother, Babet Fenoüil and Des Prez are not yet adults and are thus subject to their parents' or tutors' wishes. The solution to the financial problem is thus accomplished by some radical change of circumstance, a parent's death in Des Prez's and Manon Dupuis's cases, or the attainment of majority in Babet Fenoüil's. Challe has maintained a very high degree of plausibility in all his stories, including the financial circumstances, but he has done so by finding plausible substitutes in the bourgeois world for the clichés of the older romance.

Throughout the eighteenth century the same sort of treatment prevails. Few novelists attain the credibility of Challe, and few mention money as often as he does. *Les Liaisons dangereuses*, because of its general excellence, is perhaps a useful example. Money is almost as absent in the world of Valmont and Mme de Merteuil as in that of the princesse de Clèves. The editor, in an obviously sarcastic preface, says that he knows the work is fiction, because "nous ne voyons point aujourd'hui de demoiselle, avec soixante mille livres de rente, se faire religieuse."[75] With such an income, Cécile was very wealthy indeed, and in the tradition of her class, nothing is ever said about the mechanics of getting and spending the money. Valmont perfectly illustrates the aristocratic attitude in the famous scene of almsgiving, where he pretends to do a work of charity so as to dupe Mme de Tourvel. In Valmont's own words, " . . . cédant à ma généreuse compassion, je paie noblement cinquante-six livres, pour lesquelles on réduisait cinq personnes à la paille et au désespoir. . . ." The entire passage would be worth quoting, for the tone of disdain which Valmont keeps throughout. Admitting that he felt some pleasure in the spectacle of gratitude he had created, he concludes ironically that maybe the virtuous are not so virtuous as they claim, since it is such an agreeable experience to do good. Valmont goes on, " . . . j'ai trouvé juste de leur payer pour mon compte le plaisir qu'ils venaient de me faire. J'avais pris dix louis sur moi; je les leur ai donnés." Ten *louis* were worth two hundred forty *livres*, and one or two *livres* was the daily wage of a worker. Laclos has brought his characters into one brief contact with the real conditions of life around them; they react with an indifferent levity that is repugnant—Valmont ends the story by saying that Mme de Tourvel "vaut bien dix louis" (pp. 44-45). The marquise de Merteuil would supply another example, if one were needed. At the end of the novel, she flees in disgrace, taking with her a fortune in jewelry that belonged to her husband's estate, and leaving behind 50,000 *livres* in debts; this appears to have caused as much scandal as her debaucheries. The money in this case becomes a symbol of the general irresponsibility of the aristocratic class; they have their freedom at the expense of everyone else.

The most complete and convincing account of a character getting and spending money is in Prévost's *Manon Lescaut*, which is to a certain extent a novel about money. There is

[75] Pierre-Ambroise-François Choderlos de Laclos, *Les Liaisons dangereuses*, ed. Yves Le Hir, Classiques Garnier (Paris: Garnier Frères, 1961), p. 1.

never any question of whether Des Grieux will win the love
of Manon or not; there is only the question of whether he can
afford to keep her. The novel is set in 1719, at the height of
the speculations in Mississippi, when the Old Régime knew
for a brief moment the sort of financial delirium that is everywhere in Balzac. The result, as Deloffre says in a note, is that
"la vie matérielle fait irruption dans le roman galant."[76]

When the couple flees to Paris the first time, they take with
them one hundred fifty *écus*, probably the three-*franc* variety. After three weeks in Paris, they have spent over two-
thirds of their resources, and Manon sacrifices Des Grieux to
the financier Monsieur de B . . . . Two years later, Manon has
put aside over sixty thousand *francs*. Des Grieux estimates an
annual budget of two thousand *écus*, on the basis of which he
counts his happiness secure for ten years. Deloffre has deduced that two-thirds of the figure would have been spent on
luxuries, like a coach and the theatre. Des Grieux's plan is upset by Manon's appetite for amusement, which leads them to
take a second apartment in Paris; the arrival of Manon's
brother, with his debts; and finally the robbery and fire of
which Manon and Des Grieux are victims. Des Grieux is back
down to twenty *pistoles* (two hundred *francs*). Manon's
brother thinks he could sell Manon's favors for a thousand
écus, but Des Grieux prefers to borrow one hundred *pistoles*
from Tiberge (about a third of his annual benefice, according
to Deloffre). Des Grieux invests one hundred *francs* joining
Lescaut's gang, and rebuilds his fortune at the gaming table,
with no loss of plausibility, since luck presumably has nothing
to do with his success. Manon meanwhile has been listening
to the offers of G . . . M . . . , to wit: two hundred *pistoles*
(two thousand *francs*) as an opener; a pension of five thousand *francs* a year, half to be paid at once; jewelry, worth at
least one thousand *écus* (three thousand *francs*). Later,
young G . . . M . . . , who has forty thousand *livres* a year in
his own right, offers Manon a carriage, a townhouse, a maid,
three lackeys, a cook, and a permanent bank balance of ten
thousand *livres*. Between these dazzling sums, Des Grieux has

---

[76] Prévost, *Manon Lescaut*, p. 109.

to haggle with coachmen, ask Tiberge for another loan, pay ten *pistoles* (one hundred *francs*) to have G . . . M . . . kidnaped. He borrows fifteen hundred *francs* to rescue Manon from deportation, and spends all but one hundred fifty of it. The guards charge him one *écu* (three *francs*) an hour to talk to Manon. At Le Havre, after getting four *louis* (one hundred and forty-four *francs*) from the Man of Quality, Des Grieux has seventeen *pistoles* left, and spends seven on necessities for Manon.

This outline demonstrates both the care and precision with which Prévost documented Des Grieux's struggle to survive. A modern scholar can verify the accuracy of Prévost's picture of society by looking up the quoted prices; Deloffre has done this, and concluded that everything appears to be plausible. The figures cited are always compatible with the circumstances. *Manon* illustrates how money could be used, but Prévost had few imitators with equal interest in that subject. *Manon* itself contains many remnants of the romance style. Des Grieux and Manon tend to pass from extremes of wealth to extremes of poverty; it is certainly not a novel of the working man. As I have already remarked, Prévost tended to begin each part of his novel from scratch. After escaping from jail, and committing murder, Des Grieux nevertheless regains complete liberty of movement in Paris. Similarly, the loss of their first fortune does not lead to a slow rebuilding, but rather to a new windfall, after which they begin over as before. Only in the New World does Des Grieux attempt to hold a regular job, while Manon moderates her spending, and then a rival destroys their happiness. The success of the novel is due in part to the fact that the characters are brilliantly, and unexpectedly, suited to this romance plot. It is even more surprising how well history supplies the means for Des Grieux and Manon to obtain a *romanesque* state of freedom and irresponsibility: it is a criticism of French society in the days of Law's Bank.

Manon is then a very exceptional success. Prévost's other works belong to a much more visibly outdated tradition. By and large, the novelist sought to escape the necessity of an elaborate financial documentation, by endowing the character with enough money to be free and then making sure that he stayed free. A rough classification of the devices would include the inheritance or successful lawsuit, or wealthy marriage, or death of a wealthy spouse—most obviously devices when they occur at just the right time to eliminate some obstacle; the windfall, such as a gift, a discovery, or a large sum won at gambling—by and large not very plausible in any situation, especially not if the hero needs the money badly; the little treasure rescued from the disaster—significant chiefly because the author felt an obligation to mention it; and finally charity—the conventional sign of total despair.

It can easily be seen that even in *Manon* these devices appear. In *Cleveland*, Prévost carelessly furnishes whatever money is needed, and the fortunes survive shipwrecks, exile, and other disasters. *Gil Blas* is a kind of prototype for the handling of money. Early in the story, Gil Blas loses his small savings to a swindler; not long afterwards, he rescues Doña Mencia from thieves and receives a thousand ducats as a reward. Then more swindlers get that. These early incidents are not meant to be plausible, but even later, Gil Blas reaches the peak of power and fortune thanks to his protectors, and he loses everything when he is disgraced. The more credible his career becomes, in the sense that he appears actually to be working and earning his recognition, the less precise Lesage is about his rewards. The point always seems to be the moral lesson, and the circumstance distracts from it.

The mentions of money in minor novels are sometimes quite amusing. The chevalier de Mouhy had little talent, but some gift for observation. *La Mouche* (1736) begins in promising fashion, describing how a character named d'Osilly stole petty sums and then five hundred *francs* from his father. Mouhy quickly loses patience, however, and lets d'Osilly win large sums gambling and stumble on a hidden fortune of forty thousand *francs*. The hero of the book, Bigand, earns his living as a spy, as Mouhy apparently did himself; but this again bores the author after a while, and he brings in an alchemist who gives Bigand an immense fortune—it includes a mansion and at least several hundred thousand *francs* in gold and jewels. The dominant force in the book seems to be undeniably the *romanesque* vision, not the intermittent realistic scenes. Baculard d'Arnaud was another hack writer, whose novel *Les Epoux malheureux* (1746) was based on a true story. The plot has promise: a young man, Monsieur de la Bédoyère, marries an actress, Agathe, against his family's wishes, and he is disinherited. The young couple does not, however, go out and look for work; instead, they (and presumably the reader) weep as they sell off their large store of jewels and fine linen. Even on the verge of destitution, their noble natures will not allow them to work, but Agathe's brother sends some money just in time. Mme de Graffigny's Zilia, in *Les Lettres péruviennes* (1747) must depend on the generosity of her rescuer Deterville for many months; but ultimately he restores to her all the gold which the Spaniards had stolen from the Inca temple where she was captured. Zilia is especially happy to be able to return some of Deterville's generosity, because a noble heart is wounded at having to accept gifts it cannot repay. These lofty sentiments seem foolish only because they are misplaced. In trying to fictionalize real events, the authors create conflicts between the pressure of circumstances and the purity of romance ideals. The aristocratic disdain for money is hard to make credible when the author himself is wondering where the money came from and has to explain it. Even when he avoids aristocratic pretensions, he still has to provide his characters with freedom to fulfill the prescribed movements of the plot; and that, too, often seems ridiculous, when the author feels obliged to explain where the money came from. It was not until the source of the money itself became a subject of passionate concern that a fully Realist novel could be written.

One of the most instructive authors in his use of money is Marivaux. Both *Marianne* and *Le Paysan parvenu* invite the subject, since both relate the climb of a young person without family or fortune into the upper levels of French society. At the beginning of *Marianne*, Marivaux describes the heroine's financial situation in specific terms: she has four hundred *livres* in cash, about half of which is stolen from her. She too has noble sentiments, and consequently refuses to go into domestic service; but she does not disdain to work in Mme Dutour's linen shop. Although she does not stay there long, her going there at all demonstrates Marivaux's concern for plausibility, especially by contrast to a writer like Baculard d'Arnaud. Marianne is also humiliated by Climal's gift of several *louis*, since it makes her the object of charity. But the most famous scene in the novel is the debate between Mme Dutour and the coachman. Marianne again manifests her nobility by her indifference to the saving which seems so important to Mme Dutour—namely, twelve or twenty *sous*. In the context of Marianne's poverty, this was not a negligible sum, and the scene is not intended to ridicule the pettiness of Mme Dutour, who is after all doing it for Marianne's sake, not her own. If the figure had been much greater, Marianne's reaction would have been the same. But the precision of the amount, and the pettiness of it, come as a shock in the memoirs of a countess. This scene was deliberately written in a vulgar style, which included not only the money, but also the oaths and brutal gestures. It all serves to heighten the contrast between Marianne's innate nobility and her lowly surroundings; between Valville's house, where she had just been, and the house where she lived; between the countess who narrates and the orphan who lived the story. Not long after this scene, Marianne is adopted by Mme de Miran, and from then on her problem is one of birth, not money.

Since Jacob is a man, *Le Paysan parvenu* offered the possibility of more extensive exploration into the economic situation of the working classes, but Marivaux chose to follow an outline very similar to *Marianne*'s. In the first part, where Jacob is a servant and on the point of marrying Geneviève, a maid, there are some precise figures; but once again, they are present to emphasize the sordidness of the situation. The master has been paying Geneviève for her favors, and she in turn tries to win Jacob as a husband by offering him six *louis*. At this moment, Jacob is still peasant enough to take the money, albeit with some sense of shame. Shortly afterwards, however, when he has realized the implications of the bargain, he refuses to take more money from Geneviève, and handsome offers from their master besides. Jacob, like Marianne, is really above such sordid interests, and again like Marianne, he will find a protector to put him beyond the reaches of need. Mlle Habert, in Jacob's estimation, had more than four thousand *livres* of income, not enough to make her rich, but enough for a comfortable existence. From their meeting onwards, although Jacob continues to seek and receive favors, financial and otherwise, Marivaux refuses, in a very striking manner, to go into details. When Mlle Habert, now Mme de la Vallée, sets out to buy Jacob a wardrobe, the first article is a *robe de chambre*, which they buy from the landlady, Mme d'Alain. The purchase is negotiated as follows:

> La veux-tu? me dit Mme de la Vallée. Oui-da, repris-je; à combien est-elle? je ne sais pas marchander.
> Et là-dessus: je vous la laisse *à tant*, c'est marché donné. Non, c'est trop. Ce n'est pas assez. Bref, elles convinrent, et la robe de chambre me demeura; je la payai de l'argent qui me restait de ma prison.[77]

A few lines later, Mme d'Alain bargains on Jacob's behalf with a tailor, in equally vague terms. In these scenes, by contrast to the coachman scene in *Marianne,* to mention prices would be cheapening. Jacob is soon to give proof of his generous nature by refusing a lucrative position in favor of a needier and worthier man, but for the moment, his motives are suspect and too much concern with figures would be unseemly. He can not ignore money altogether, but he can change his style.

In any given work money seems to be treated similarly to other themes, so that there is a better accounting for expenses in novels like *Manon Lescaut* or *Les Illustres Françoises* that also have accurate calendars and geographies. The pressure for some accounting can be seen even in works still close to

[77] Marivaux, *Le Paysan parvenu*, p. 166.

the classical abstract style, however, and actually grows out of the romance tradition. Once again I have taken money as the easiest in a group of factors to study, but it is just one of many limitations of the hero's or the heroine's personal liberty of action. The romance simply presupposed this freedom; the novel had to explain how it came about.

NAMES: If money is rather easy to avoid in a novel, the names of the characters are no doubt the least avoidable element. Consequently, although in some sense money, geography, and chronology "appear" in the novel at a certain time, names have always been present in fiction. In the mid-seventeenth century, the dominant fashion demanded historical names—Cyrus, Polexandre, Ibrahim, Clélie. At this stage, the fiction amounts theoretically to no more than an elaboration on reality. The historical novel has survived many changes of fashion, and still lives today; in the seventeenth century it evolved with the rest of the genre. When the long romance went out of style, shorter historical fictions adopted the same devices. A very high proportion of the works listed by S. Paul Jones for the early years of the eighteenth century still take a historical figure as their hero. In the year 1700 alone one finds novels about Germaine de Foix, reine d'Espagne; Grégoire VII; le cardinal de Richelieu; la princesse de Condé; la marquise d'Urfé; Charles VII, roi de France; Mr. d'Artagnan; la princesse de Conti; Jeanne premiere et Jeanne seconde, reines de Naples; Geoffroy, surnommé à la grand' Dent; and a "Histoire secrète des Vestales." To say that the names designate real characters implies nothing about the veracity of the stories, although many of the novelists did in fact have great respect for the historical backgrounds. Others, however, like Courtilz de Sandras, mixed imaginary and real elements so freely that to this day many of their works can not be classified with any confidence. Courtilz thus comes near bridging the gap between history and the novel; one of his secrets was to select a character whose real biography was too little known to constitute any obstacle, but whose name was well enough known to furnish some immediate credibility. It is a very small step from there to inventing the name altogether.

Mme de Lafayette must be considered a true novelist on this account, since her central character is invented. Nemours, on the other hand, has been fictionalized more or less as Courtilz was in the habit of doing—the name is real, and to some extent his reputation corresponds to what is said of him. Too little is known, however, to arouse any objections to the purely invented episodes. Even the invented characters, nonetheless, belong to real families; Mme de Lafayette has merely added a few fictional branches to a real genealogical tree.

As the subject came closer to contemporary times, the novelists looked for ways to name their characters without so precisely situating them. One immediate result is that the characters must come from a slightly lower rank in society; otherwise, the purported relatives may be annoyed. Hamilton's *Mémoires de Gramont* is exceptional, and the author, a friend of the hero, explains in his first chapter that he wants to rectify the calumnies and false impressions that Bussy and Saint-Evremond had written. Bussy serves to illustrate the dangers in fictionalizing the affairs of the living; as a result of his indiscretions, he was imprisoned in the Bastille and exiled from Paris. His use of classical pseudonyms was, of course, never meant to fool anyone; if it had, the satire would have lost its savor. The device was required by propriety, even when the author's intention was quite different. Grandchamp wrote in the "Avertissement" of his *Telemaque moderne* (1701): "Le Heros qui va paroistre ici masqué sur la Scene, sous le nom de Telemaque Moderne, a fait tant de bruit dans le monde par ses Intrigues, que le Public n'aura pas de peine à le reconnoistre: Il ne faut pas mesme de Clef pour l'intelligence de cet Ouvrage." Nevertheless, "le respect qu'on doit aux Augustes Personnes, qui sont les principaux Acteurs de cette Scene, ne permettoit pas de les nommer."[78]

This polite reticence, a social rather than a literary conven-

[78] Grandchamp, *Le Telemaque moderne*, 1701, "Avertissement."

tion, no doubt explains why so many works appeared anonymously. Mme de Lafayette had no reason to be ashamed of any of her works, but it was more decorous for a professional man of letters like Segrais to assume the responsibility for publishing them. Segrais's *Nouvelles Françoises* (1656) contain a defense of Spanish realism, but the frame, being based on real people, is told with classical pseudonyms: Frontenie, Aurélie, Silerite, Gelonide, Aplanice, Uralie. These ladies in fact discuss the question of names, and their concern appears to be mainly stylistic: Frontenie claims that "naturellement les François aimoient mieux un nom d'Artabaze, d'Iphidamante ou d'Orosmane qu'un nom de Rohan, de Loraine, ou de Montmorency . . . il n'y auroit gueres plus d'incongruité de donner des mœurs Françoises à un Grec, que d'appeller un François Monsieur Pisandre ou Monsieur Ormedon, comme ces gens dont on n'a jamais ouï parler à Poitiers dans la Comedie du Menteur." Her point is that to write novels about French rather than exotic heroes would be very pleasing, but "les noms donneroient bien de la peine à qui voudroit l'entreprendre." Gelonide retorts that the Spanish novels succeed quite well, and were not any more "dés-agréables pour avoir des Heros qui ont nom Richard ou Laurens," and further "nous avons des noms de terminaison Françoise aussi agréables que les Grecs ou les Romains."[79] They go on to draw the logical deduction that, if one is to set stories in contemporary France, they must necessarily be less heroic than the romances of that time.

Although many authors began immediately to follow Gelonide's advice, the use of classical names also survived for many years. From the early years of the eighteenth century one could cite Pallu de Doublainville's *La Reine Bergère* (1700), Dubois de Chastenay's *Uranie ou les secours inopinés de la Providence* (1716), the anonymous *Cléandre et Caliste* (1720), *Florine ou la belle Italienne* (1713), and finally Brunet de Brou's *Le Tendre Ollivarius* (1717), which deserves some special mention, because the preface claims that the story is true and happened to the author. Notwithstand-

[79] Coulet, *Anthologie*, p. 75.

ing the names, Fulvie, Clarice, Darius, Ariste, besides Ollivarius, the story is both believable and touching. Laurent
Versini notes that Thomas Laffichard published *Histoire de
Florise et de Cléante* in 1746 and Crébillon *fils* named the
hero and heroine of *La Nuit et le moment* (1755) Clitandre
and Cidalise. As Versini observes, however, this sort of name
tended more and more to be used in the *conte*, where fantasy
predominated.[80]

The Spanish style of naming characters had to be adapted
to French manners, because upper-class Frenchmen did not
call one another by their given names, nor did they refer to
each other by them. The widespread social custom of using
pseudonyms was one way of escaping the rigid formality
which etiquette demanded. There are occasional exact imitations of the Spanish technique in France; Sorel uses the
names Francion and Raymond, for example. Women were
more freely treated than men; when the name was slightly
mysterious, like Léonore, its use did not imply any disrespect.
By and large, however, the French characters had to possess
a name with a *particule*. Versini's article cited above discusses the use of these names in the later eighteenth century,
when the profusion of names based on the syllables "val,"
"cour," "sac," "ange," and a few others, had virtually destroyed their original realism. The practice had begun at least
as early as 1655; in *Le Roman comique*'s intercalated tales
one can find the comte des Glaris, the baron d'Arques, Monsieur de Verville, Monsieur de Saint-Far, Monsieur de Saint-
Sauveur, Mlle de la Boissière, Mlle de Saldagne, Mlle de
Lery, as well as several more in the *Suite d'Offray*. Subligny's
La Fausse Clélie has even more, but it was still enough of a
novelty for Subligny to apologize for it in his preface:

> Peu de gens avant moy s'estoient avisez de donner des
> noms François à leurs Heros. Et il est à craindre que
> quelques esprits Romanesques voyant un nom de Marquis
> de Riberville, de Mirestain, de Franlieu, et autres, au lieu

---

[80] Laurent Versini, "De quelques noms de personnages dans le
roman du XVIIIe siècle," *RHL*, 61 (1961), 178.

de celuy d'un Tiridate ou d'un Cleante, ne fassent d'abord le procez à mon Livre. Mais je demande pardon à ces esprits delicats, si pour leur plaire je ne fais pas des Grecs ou des Arabes de ceux que je veux faire passer pour des François un peu galans.[81]

By the 1700's the technique was well established, if not already dominant. Challe had, of course, experimented with it in his continuation of *Don Quixote*, where he used the names Sainville and Deshayes. Other examples are *Mylord *** ou le paysan de qualité* (1700)—baron de la Sarte, M. de Sancergues, Mlle de Pinelle; *Les Intrigues parisiennes et provinciales* (1700)—Angélique de Mongueil, Mlle de Ternan; *La Comtesse D*** et le courrier galant* (1700)—comte de Lanceville, Mlle de Lingendre, M. de Saint-Alvar; *Les Amours libres de deux frères* (1701)—M. de Beaubourg, M. de Clerissais; *Les Petits Soupers de l'été 1699* (1702)—duc d'Ardelle, comtesse d'Orselac; *L'Inconstance punie* (1702)— marquis d'Hermanville, comtesse de Ceriancour; *Histoire véritable de Monsieur du Prat et de Mademoiselle Angélique* (1703)—M. du Genest, Mlle des Conces, marquis de Cerman; *Le Petrone almand* (1706)—M. de Flavigny, M. de Sainte-Colombe; *Memoires de la comtesse de Tournemir* (1708)— M. de Saint-Brice, M. d'Arnonville; *La Foire de Beaucaire* (1708)—marquis de Chalantes, M. de Riberac, Mlle de Saint-Alais, marquis de Montalan, Mlle d'Elbiac, baron de Flesac, Mme de Bobigny, Mme de Blinières. When Challe wrote in the preface to *Les Illustres Françoises*: "A l'égard des noms que je leur ai donnés, j'ai cru les leur devoir donner françois, parce qu'en effet ce sont des François que je produis, et non pas des étrangers,"[82] he was merely placing himself in a tradition, not innovating.

On the other hand, toward the end of the same preface, Challe comments on his use of diminutive first names for girls, like Manon and Babet. His remarks constitute an attack on the morals of the age, for according to Challe, every mer-

---

[81] Subligny, *La Fausse Clélie*, 1671, "Préface."
[82] Challe, *Œuvres*, p. lix.

chant's wife now refers to her own daughter as "Mademoiselle une Telle." Challe is virtually alone in using such names, except to designate women of the lower classes. *Les Amours libres de deux frères* (1701), a more or less pornographic novel, has a character named Manon, who attempts in vain to seduce the younger brother. Even the more romantic names, like Angélique and Marianne, are given only to girls of lower rank; this is the case with the heroine in *Histoire véritable de Monsieur du Prat et de Mademoiselle Angélique*, and she is treated with typical aristocratic scorn when she marries the hero's rival—he claims to have slept with her. In *Les Intrigues parisiennes et provinciales* (1700) Angélique de Mongueil turns down a very presentable *homme de robe* because she wants an *homme d'épée*, has her eye put out by her rival, retires to a convent in shame, and there dies of chagrin. In the same collection, Hyacinte, a merchant's daughter, almost makes the same mistake, but comes to her senses in time. In *La Comtesse D*** et le courrier galant*, Marianne is a nine-year-old girl, who likes fairy tales.

The use of nicknames was therefore restricted by social custom to girls of the lower classes; Manon Lescaut is the best example. Beginning in the 1730's, a small group of libertines and wits wrote stories about the lowest classes of society. The comte de Caylus's *Histoire de Guillaume, cocher* (1737) is typical; the hero tells stories about what he has seen while driving people around Paris. Toward the end, he marries a girl named Javotte, who then runs away with someone else. The main stream of fiction continued to work variations on the Verville model. Versini has sufficiently documented the results, so that I can rephrase his conclusion. The names came to represent stereotyped characters; names ending "-ange" usually belonged to innocent girls, those ending in "-sac" belonged to seducers. Certain female first names were also in vogue: Julie and Sophie for virtuous girls, Adélaïde for women in moral struggles. With rare exceptions, the banality of these names reflected the banality of their characterization.

As the historical novel gave way to the fictional document,

a new naming device became popular, the famous *** or an initial. Such devices had been appearing in novels for some time, but usually legitimately—the real author, for example, might modestly sign with only his initials, or the dedication might be made "A Madame D***," as in *Les Intrigues parisiennes et provinciales*. Courtilz de Sandras's *Mémoires de Mr. L. C. D. R.* (1687) are very famous, but everyone knew that the initials stood for Le Comte de Rochefort. It was an easy and logical step to move these devices into the work itself. Within the *Intrigues parisiennes* there are two characters called Monsieur D***; the "d" presumably stands for the *particule*. One can only speculate whether the dedication is fictitious, or perhaps the stories are true. In any case, although one can find occasional examples of the device before 1710: *Mylord *** ou le paysan de qualité*; *La Comtesse D****; *Le Voyage de Guibray ou les Aventures des Princes de B*** et de C**** (1704), it does not appear to have been widely used until the 1730's. Prévost can not be said to have invented it, but the success of *Manon Lescaut*, first published in 1731, may very well have been responsible for its great popularity thereafter.

Prévost, as I remarked before, had the ingenious idea of giving the initials of a street, the rue Vivienne, and a man, the prince Rakoczy, which everyone would recognize. In this way he increased the credibility of the probably fictitious Monsieur de B . . . , Monsieur de G . . . M . . . , and Monsieur de T . . . . Within a few years Prévost had been imitated by Marivaux, in *La Vie de Marianne ou les Avantures de Madame la Comtesse de **** and in *Le Paysan parvenu ou les Mémoires de M***; by Crébillon *fils* in *Lettres de la marquise de M*** au comte de R****; by Mouhy in several works; by Duclos, in *Les Confessions du comte de ***; and by many lesser and anonymous writers. As with any formula for naming, however, use quickly becomes abuse. So long as the novel was pretending to be a document, someone's memoirs or letters, the blanked name had a certain plausibility. On the other hand, once it had been tried three or four times, it was not likely to win any extra credence.[83] It was then at best a way around a somewhat difficult question: If these are real documents, where are the people? Any pseudonym, however, would serve as well, and what counted was obviously not the three asterisks but the quality of the author's work. Thus, when Laclos poses as editor to preface *Les Liaisons dangereuses*, he remarks: "Je dois prévenir aussi que j'ai supprimé ou changé tous les noms des personnes dont il est question dans ces lettres. . . ."[84] They are then deliberately stereotypical, or perhaps ironic. Laclos is on the point of doing what the nineteenth-century novelists will do: invent a name which somehow symbolizes or expresses the character.

Rousseau, indeed, takes the step, although the symbolic value of the names remains rather private. In *La Nouvelle Héloïse*, the hero's name is never known. At considerable expense of ingenuity, Rousseau never had to give it in the first half of the novel, and in the second, Claire decides that he shall be known as Saint-Preux. For Rousseau names had an almost magical power, and this chivalric pseudonym clearly harks back to some myth of self-discovery and self-fulfillment.[85] Rousseau's manner of accomplishing this reveals how much of the romance still remained in the novel. Rather than give the hero a symbolic name from the start, Rousseau contrives to have the name arise out of the action. Plainly, Rousseau means to confront the reader with a new romance myth.

Naming the character, as Rousseau sensed, lies close to the heart of the creative mystery. The technical impediments of the eighteenth century, notably the desire to make the novel seem to be something else, deprived the authors of that act. Instead of imagining a powerful character, and creating him, these novelists had to feign that he was real. Instead of giving his name, they had to hide it. Therefore the progress to-

---

[83] Stewart, in *Imitation and Illusion in the French Memoir-Novel*, pp. 277-80, cites a few cases where the precaution is demonstrably unnecessary for concealment, and thus seems to be purely imitative.

[84] Laclos, *Les Liaisons dangereuses*, p. 3.

[85] Jean Starobinski has a thoughtful commentary on this question in *Jean-Jacques Rousseau: la transparence et l'obstacle* (Paris: Plon, 1957), Part 3, ch. 5.

ward the Realistic device of using a plausible but symbolic name, like Bovary, was stymied. As we have seen repeatedly before, the efforts to make the novel plausible encountered an insurmountable obstacle in the requirement that they make it literally real at the same time. The key element in this obstacle was the narrator.

NARRATORS: Chronology, geography, money, and names are subjects which, for various reasons, have not been much discussed by scholars and critics. The narrator, on the other hand, has elicited a great deal of comment. In general, the eighteenth century is regarded as the age of the first-person narration. As Le Breton said: "La forme autobiographique du récit . . . est celle qui jusqu'à Richardson et Rousseau s'est imposée aux romanciers."[86] S. Paul Jones concurs, noting that "almost two hundred works in our list are written in the first person singular."[87] Another fifty are epistolary novels. With a grand total of nine hundred and forty-six titles in Jones's list, the numerical dominance of the first-person narration is not nearly as impressive as its qualitative superiority. It is a fact that there is hardly a single novel of any importance that is not either a first-person-singular or an epistolary narrative, either in French or in English, until very late in the century; the possible exceptions, like *Candide*, are tales (*contes*) rather than novels.

The standard explanation of this phenomenon is that the first person added something to the work's credibility. Jones, for example, writes: "Authors, attempting to add an air of verisimilitude to their fictions, begin with the pronoun *je,* whether writing a novel of intrigue, an historical novel, a love story, fictitious memoirs, or an imaginary voyage."[88] Moses Ratner says almost the same thing: "In addition, the better to create the illusion of truth, the expedient of casting the narrative in the form of memoirs, and in the first person, became increasingly popular; witness the works of Lesage, Marivaux,

[86] Le Breton, *Le Roman au dix-huitième siècle*, p. 33.
[87] Jones, *A List of French Prose Fiction*, p. xvi.
[88] ibid., p. xvi.

Prévost, the English novelists, not to mention a host of minor lights."[89] This is of course true as far as it goes, but it says nothing of the specific reasons for preferring this technique to some other.

In the past twenty years, many critics have tried to distinguish between the types of verisimilitude. Philip Stewart, in his very recent study of the memoir-novel, makes a useful distinction between imitation and illusion. Imitation, the normal modern meaning of verisimilitude, is the action of any realist writer who creates a fictional world resembling the real one. Illusion is a special effect, in which the author tries to make the reader believe that he is reading history, not a story. One very obvious way to accomplish this, and one which was widely used in the eighteenth century, is to forge documents; Stewart terms this formal imitation.[90] Vivienne Mylne makes essentially the same distinction in different terms in her chapter on "Fiction, History, and Truth."[91] Both Stewart and Mylne believe that, some of the time at least, the novelists wanted to achieve literal illusion.

Henri Coulet also makes the same distinction, but denies that literal illusion was the goal. His term, equivalent to imitation, is "illusion romanesque," and he comments: "Ils auraient été bien naïfs s'ils avaient cru qu'il suffisait de faire parler un personnage à la première personne et de forger une petite fable sur l'origine du manuscrit pour que le lecteur fût dupe; ils veulent obtenir sa connivence, et non lui en imposer; ils le font entrer dans une convention, ils choisissent celle de la première personne parce qu'elle est la plus capable de créer l'illusion romanesque. . . ."[92] Deloffre likewise uses the term "illusion romanesque," but he regards it as a new sophistication, first articulated between 1700 and 1715, following

[89] Moses Ratner, *Theory and Criticism of the Novel in France from L'Astrée to 1750* (New York: de Palma, 1938), p. 70.

[90] Stewart, *Imitation and Illusion in the French Memoir-Novel*, p. 5.

[91] Mylne, *The Eighteenth-Century French Novel*, pp. 20-31.

[92] Coulet, *Le Roman jusqu'à la Révolution*, pp. 320-21.

hard on a period when literal illusion had been the goal.[93]

Both François Jost and Jean Rousset focus attention on the fact that the third-person narrative had been in vogue before. Jost stresses the negative side: "Ce qui disparaît, c'est l'omniscience de l'auteur; jusque-là tout romancier s'était senti libre de sonder les reins et de scruter le cœur des personnages. . . ."[94] Rousset accentuates the positive side: " . . . la première personne, comme la conscience de soi, serait une conquête. . . ."[95]

With so many similar but conflicting analyses, I think clarity would best be served if I began by defining my own position. Wayne Booth states in the early pages of *The Rhetoric of Fiction*: "Our entire experience in reading fiction is based, as Jean-Louis Curtis says in his brilliant reply to Sartre, on a tacit contract with the novelist, a contract granting him the right to know what he is writing about. It is this contract which makes fiction possible."[96] This contract, however, may have widely varying stipulations, depending on the temper of the times. In our own times, particularly in France, the novelist's right to know has come under attack. The public, or some of its more eloquent spokesmen like Sartre, have demanded unmediated reality from the novel; and while the demand, as Curtis demonstrates, can not be met, it can force the author to write as if he were meeting it. The new novelists have by and large retreated from the third-person, into a highly restricted first-person, narrative. The voice is, to be sure, no longer that of the lucid and rational narrator of the eighteenth century, but instead a confused, self-deluded, often

---

[93] Frédéric Deloffre, "Le Problème de l'illusion romanesque et le renouvellement des techniques narratives entre 1700 et 1715," in *La Littérature narrative d'imagination*, 1961, pp. 115-29.

[94] François Jost, "Le Roman épistolaire et la technique narrative au XVIIIe siècle," *Comparative Literature Studies*, 3 (1966), 399.

[95] Jean Rousset, "L'Emploi de la première personne chez Chasles et Marivaux," *Cahiers de l'Association Internationale des Etudes Françaises*, 19 (1967), 102.

[96] Wayne C. Booth, *The Rhetoric of Fiction* (1961; rpt. Chicago: Univ. of Chicago Press, 1966), p. 52.

inarticulate and even subconscious, but nevertheless eloquent interior monolog. Its conventional nature is incontestable.

Much the same thing, I believe, underlies the eighteenth century's narrative conventions. Perhaps the concepts of authenticity and artistry are two poles between which the novel evolves in cyclic movements. In any case it seems clear that in the late seventeenth century the readers and critics and even novelists began to demand more authenticity, at the expense of such artistic qualities as organization, style, and imaginative re-creation. This is to say that while the novelists did not really expect to create a literal illusion, they had to write as if they did.

To a large degree, then, I concur in the conclusions of Coulet, Jost, and Rousset, although I do not believe that this invalidates the criticisms and analyses of Mylne and Stewart. Their approach is highly formal; the form is designed as if to create literal illusion. Naturally enough, all the critics have concentrated on the advantages of first-person narration. Coulet describes its advantage thus: " . . . répondre à ce que le public veut, par le roman, apprendre sur lui-même, en mettant en lumière le point de vue individuel, la sensibilité, l'adresse, l'énergie, la chance ou la malchance d'un individu; en un mot, l'emploi de la première personne permet aux romanciers une transposition du réel moins forte et plus plausible que celle qu'ils trouvaient dans les romans à la troisième personne des époques précédentes."[97] Rousset, in his much shorter work, concentrates on one point, which he regards as the most important: " . . . l'identité du personnage et de son histoire. . . ."[98] Jost enumerates the various advantages of the epistolary form.

None of these comments, in my opinion, undertakes to answer the question of why those particular qualities seemed more desirable than others, at that given time. The method generally followed, of studying only successful novels, leads to a false perspective. The successful novelist, Marivaux for

[97] Coulet, *Le Roman jusqu'à la Révolution*, p. 321.
[98] Rousset, "L'Emploi de la première personne . . . ," p. 104.

Techniques of Realism in Early Fiction

example, stands out among some two hundred memoir-novelists, because he sensed an advantage and exploited it, while lesser novelists did not. The individual point of view, *sensibilité*, the identity of the character and the story—all these can be legitimately claimed for *La Vie de Marianne*. Not, however, for Mouhy's *La Mouche*, written at almost the same time. Something binds the inferior novelist to the form, even though he fails almost completely to profit from its advantages. This force might be simply fashion, but it would appear that the fashion predates its earliest successes; something must still be explained.

Furthermore, none of the studies makes the necessary connection between the form and the supposed general objective. Rousset's point assumes that the eighteenth century wanted to hear narrators speak mainly about what they knew best, which was themselves; or else, that readers wanted to hear about the individual, and the individual knew himself best and was therefore best qualified to narrate. Given that assumption, the first person has its own logic. It is true, as Coulet suggests, that the eighteenth century saw a rise in interest in the individual, leading ultimately to Romanticism. But here one may be prompted to ask why, if individualism so logically produces a first-person narration, did Balzac return to the third person?

The link, I believe, is neo-classical rationalism, long recognized as the tyrant that enslaved and degraded the nobler genres, poetry and the theatre; and some comparison may be instructive. The pretense of literal illusion in the novel is very closely paralleled by Diderot's efforts to reform the theatre. In his earliest writings, the *Entretiens sur le fils naturel* (1757) and *De la poésie dramatique* (1758), Diderot calls for a simple transposition of life onto the stage. He would like the spectator to feel an urge to walk onstage and join in the conversation. At this moment in his life, Diderot made no distinction between *illusion romanesque* (or *théâtrale*) and illusion pure and simple. In his early art criticism he calls for similar fidelity to life; his first standard of judgment is how real the scene looks. Diderot's dramatic theories were meant to be revolutionary and his art criticism had virtually no tradition behind it. Both, however, in their original formulations, reflect the same rational approach which led seventeenth-century theorists to formulate their rules for the theatre. Jacques Scherer has demonstrated the logical connections between the different unities; René Bray has shown how the application of reason to the rule of verisimilitude produced the *romanesque*. It was thought that all the complex rules of versification answered some logical purpose—that the hiatus offended the French ear, for example. Such a philosophy of art clearly does not preclude good works of art, but the barren eighteenth century stands as proof that these rules were applied as if they would guarantee good works of art, and *that* they do not. In the novel, exceptionally, there were successes and there was progress. This has led to the false assumption that the novel had escaped the stifling effects of classicism's senile years. I think that, on the contrary, the same rationalistic spirit led the novel down a blind alley, but being a latecomer to the world of literature, the novel was able to elaborate its structures in the eighteenth century and therefore to accommodate more of the spirit of the times. At the very least, it had the necessary amorphousness to imitate historical forms very closely, and this by itself enabled the novel to respond to the pressures for more contemporary, more personal, and more believable stories, where the nobler genres were constricted by tradition and convention.

Both Rousset and Coulet, I believe, exaggerate the freedom of the eighteenth-century novelist. Rousset exposes his principle with admirable clarity:

> Quand un principe formel, qui est en même temps un mode de vision et de saisie de l'être, prédomine dans une période donnée, on n'en conclura pas qu'il s'impose tyranniquement, qu'il prédétermine tous les artistes de ce temps. Ceux-ci semblent liés par lui, puisque tous ou presque tous s'y conforment; en réalité, il est le principe de liberté qui s'offre à eux à ce moment-là; il leur permet de se libérer de

formes temporairement usées, et il leur offre un instrument
neuf pour qu'ils puissent s'explorer et se constituer en in-
ventant leur forme individuelle.[99]

With reservations, I can accept this principle, and my reservations are summed up by Rousset himself in what he says of
Hamilton on the preceding page: ". . . il était lecteur, *et
prisonnier*, des grands romans du XVIIe siècle."[100] A novelist
is always prisoner of the great novels which precede him.
The first-person narrative offered a freedom only because the
third-person narrative was at that time subject to even tighter
constraints. There had been at least one brilliant effort to con-
quer that freedom in the third-person form, and it was attacked. The grounds of that attack constituted, throughout
the eighteenth century, a powerful limitation on the freedom
of the novelist.

The third-person narrator had two ancestors, the epic poet
and the historian. As early as 1641, the demands of verisimilitude began to discredit the poetic aspect. The novelist
could not admit to having invented his story, as the poet could;
consequently he began to pose as a historian. The historical
pose dominated the last half of the seventeenth century,
slowly giving way to the first-person forms. Georges May has
pointed out that at the same time, history itself was in a state
of crisis. The historian was an artist rather than a scholar, and
drew on the techniques of rhetoric, oratory, and poetry. He
sought to instruct, by revealing the motives of human actions,
and he explained the moral lessons to be learned from history.[101] Under the scrutiny of critical reason, the traditional
historical methods fell apart. Their facts proved false, and
their teachings therefore unreliable, in far too many cases.
The most important historians of the time did works of demolition, like Pierre Bayle, preparing the way for a new genera-

[99] ibid., p. 104.
[100] ibid., p. 103; my italics.
[101] See Georges May, "L'Histoire a-t-elle engendré le roman?" *RHL*
55 (1955), 155-76; and Claudette Delhez-Sarlet, "La Princesse de
Clèves; roman ou nouvelle?" *Romanische Forschungen*, 80 (1968),
70-83.

tion of historians, like Voltaire and Gibbon. Some of this dis. trust naturally affected the novelist who posed as historian, and led him to retreat to the primary sources of history, the first-person eye-witness account.

These movements in intellectual history are undeniable, and surely relevant to the novel. They do not suffice to explain everything, however. As Voltaire and Gibbon illustrate, history rose again from its grave without bringing the third-person narrator back into immediate favor in the novel. The historian's weakness was not his narrative technique so much as his documentation and his bias. Once these were overcome, the third-person historian regained his credibility. Novelists imitated this technique to some degree; Mme de Villedieu, for example, appended a "Table des Matières historiques" to her *Annales galantes* (1670), in which she gives her sources and comments on their value. The fictional part of the historical novel was lost beyond recovery, however; the more documentation provided for the historical events, the more obvious the falsity of the conversations, monologs, and private thoughts which had been the specific contribution of the author.

In other words, the novel remained subject to the constraints on the historian, which meant that the only area which interested the novelist was forbidden to the third-person narrator. He could not tell what he could not know. The rationalists' exigency for truth, based as it was on premises that had little to do with the internal principles of art or literature, limited the freedom of novelists just as it did other authors. The contract between readers and novelists allowed for no art; the novelist had to account for all his information. The analysis of art by critical reason is a peculiar stance, which characterizes the late seventeenth century. It leads to the doctrine that a work of art must be as close to literal truth as possible. Unless we understand this underlying doctrine, the curious narrative devices of the eighteenth century make no sense. All of them answer the same question: how could this incident have come to light? Under classical doctrine, the answer did not have to be plausible, only possible, and the public was eager to accept any explanation. That is the definition of a literary convention.

The sieur du Plaisir's *Sentimens sur les Lettres et sur l'Histoire* contains one of the most favorable descriptions of the historical novel. It is particularly instructive to observe what constraints he places on the novelist. First of all, the historian must remain objective and unbiased; Du Plaisir is categorical and precise on this matter. The quotation is rather long, but deserves to be given in its entirety:

L'Historien peut bien dans le commencement de l'Ouvrage employer tout son esprit, pour faire estimer, ou pour caractériser ses Héros; mais il ne le pourroit pas ailleurs, et je croy que voicy une raison de cette diférence. Les particularitez sur les tempéramens ou sur le mérite écrites avant les actions, sont simplement regardées comme des traits ressemblans, et comme un portrait nécessaire; mais dans le détail de ces actions, elles font voir que l'Autheur applaudit, blâme, et s'intéresse. La peinture qu'il a faite une fois, doit seule estre le principe de tous les mouvemens qu'il décrira. S'il la retouche dans la suite, il témoignera qu'il a manqué de la finir d'abord, ou fera une répétition inutile, et je serois fâché d'y trouver, *Elle estoit reconnoissante, elle estoit naturellement tendre, elle estoit généreuse, et c'en estoit trop pour résister davantage.*

Ce des-intéressement si necessaire dans l'Histoire, défend aux Historiens de joindre mesme à un nom quelque terme flateur, quoy que facile à justifier. Autrement ils sortiroient de leur indifférence, et parlassent-ils mesme du Roy, ils ne pourroient pas dire *ce grand Prince.* Ce n'est point à eux d'estre Juges du mérite d'un Héros, ils doivent uniquement représenter ses sentimens ou sa conduite, et les Lecteurs seuls peuvent luy donner les loüanges dont il est digne.[102]

[102] This, and the quotations which follow, are taken from Klaus Friedrich, "Eine Theorie des 'Roman nouveau' (1683)," *Romanistisches Jahrbuch,* 14 (1963), 105-32, which includes the complete text of Du Plaisir's essay. The quotations may be found on pages 119 to 129. Some, but not all, of the passages are also in Coulet, *Anthologie,* pp. 87-93.

The apparent solution to the problem is to put such phrases into the mouths of the characters. Du Plaisir writes: "D'un autre costé aussi le Héros a des privileges que n'a pas l'Historien, et ces occasions sont principalement dans les discours d'amour et de civilité. Il peut dire, *Madame, vous estes adorable aujourd'huy*; mais un Autheur ne pourroit sans extravagance, écrire, *ce jour-là elle estoit adorable*." Or again,

Ainsi un Autheur qui par une grande connoissance des sentimens du cœur, auroit fait voir tout ce que soufrent deux Personnes éloignées l'une de l'autre, ne pourroit pas, lors qu'elles se rejoignent, faire un second portrait des mouvemens de l'ame. Leur douleur qu'il auroit dépeinte, feroit assez juger de toute leur joye. On n'est plus curieux alors de sçavoir ce qu'elles peuvent penser, on souhaite seulement connoistre la maniere avec laquelle elles vont se recevoir, et c'est icy que l'Autheur doit estre spirituel sans le paroistre; c'est à dire, employer tout son esprit à former une conversation naïve, où il semble que c'est bien moins luy qui parle, que l'Acteur luy-mesme.

It should be observed that, while Du Plaisir seems to exclude omniscience only because in this situation it would be repetitious or boring, in fact the sort of "mouvemens de l'ame" which he refers to tend to derive from general laws of psychology—as in the last sentence of the first paragraph quoted, which Du Plaisir would allow at the beginning but not in the middle. It appeals to the general laws of human behavior, not to the specific feelings and motives of the woman in question. The change in conceptions of human nature and the growth of interest in the individual could not influence this type of novel, however, because the convention forbade any psychological commentary, or moral commentary, on the author's part.

The historical rules had been formulated long before, and were to some degree in force even in the long romances. There, the hero's inner thoughts had been transmitted by two devices: a squire who was privy to all of them, and who recited his master's life to the other characters, or a soliloquy

Techniques of Realism in Early Fiction

delivered by the hero himself. The first had simply passed out of fashion, according to Du Plaisir: "On ne recite plus dans le Roman. Il n'est plus de Confident qui fasse l'Histoire de son Maître; l'Historien se charge de tout, et en quelque endroit où on lise, on n'est plus embarrassé de sçavoir lequel parle, ou l'Historien, ou le Confident." This confidant was part of the epic tradition; his primary function was to tell the hero's previous adventures when the story began *in medias res*. Greater emphasis on history meant a different principle of organization, which eliminated the confidant's particular function.

Du Plaisir's condemnation of the soliloquy, finally, leads to the real heart of the problem: the historian can not tell what he can not know. The first objections are based on propriety and common sense:

Un Héros ne parle plus seul. Il sçait aujourd'huy que la parole luy a esté donnée pour communiquer aux autres ce qu'il pense, et non pas pour se le communiquer à soy-mesme. Il sçait que dans cet état le plus honneste Homme fait peur, ou fait rire; et il sçait enfin que quand on est capable de parler de cette sorte, on n'est pas plus propre à garder un secret que quand on parle pendant que l'on dort.

The author has completely different reasons for avoiding the device:

L'Historien d'ailleurs craindroit de se rendre suspect de mensonge dans de semblables discours; et en effet, si on luy demandoit d'où il les auroit appris, que pourroit-il répondre? Allegueroit-il que quelques Auditeurs se trouverent par hazard aupres du Héros? Ce seroit faire de leur indiscrétion une avanture trop basse, ou trop commune. Diroit-il que le Héros luy-mesme l'auroit revelé? Ce seroit pecher contre la vraysemblance. . . .

In light of these strictures, Rousset's comment that "La première personne . . . serait une conquête" tells only half of the truth. It was unseemly for the hero to tell his story to other people, by a convention deriving more from social custom than literary tradition. The novelists of the seventeenth century had ways around that obstacle, which history closed off to them. In his monologs, the hero had always spoken in the first person; but some new convention had to be found to allow this kind of speech. The confidant, a sort of surrogate for the novelist, made the first-person narration unnecessary. To be sure, the "extrême proximité du personnage et de son récit" constituted a net gain for the novelist, but not until he had first recovered what he had lost under the rules of literal historical verisimilitude.

The attitude which Du Plaisir outlines theoretically is best illustrated concretely by Valincour's *Lettres sur La Princesse de Clèves* (1678). Mme de Lafayette's novel makes use of the full privilege of the omniscient author, within the limits of seventeenth-century taste. Valincour attacked *La Princesse de Clèves* on many grounds, its structure, the lack of verisimilitude of its incidents, the moral implications, and the style. Although it is a very hostile work, Valincour's *Lettres* does admire certain aspects, like the author's psychological insight. His attitude does not appear willfully obtuse, like Faydit's in *La Télémacomanie*; but rather he seems to have been sensitive to some of the novel's qualities, and to represent a cultivated point of view. Once again, the relevant passage is rather long, but worth quoting in full:

> . . . pour revenir à la Princesse de Cleves, il seroit difficile à ceux qui voudroient la prendre comme une histoire, de deviner sur quels mémoires l'Historien a travaillé. En effet, les principaux faits n'ont esté sceûs que de ceux qui y ont eû part, et il ne paroist point qu'ils les ayent jamais racontez à personne, ni qu'ils ayent pû jamais parvenir à la connoissance de l'Auteur, que par le moyen d'une révelation particuliere. J'avois remarqué cela aussi-bien que vous, luy dis-je, sur le sujet de la premier aventure du pavillon; je ne puis concevoir comment l'Auteur auroit pû la sçavoir. Ce n'est pas là ce qui m'embarasse le plus, me répondit-il en riant: car pour cette aventure, il peut l'avoir apprise en

quelque livre où il me semble l'avoir déja leûë. Mais la jalousie de Madame de Cleves, à l'occasion de la lettre; mais ses conversations particulieres avec Monsieur de Nemours et avec son mari; mais la maniere dont Monsieur de Nemours dérobe le portrait, et mille autres choses de cette nature, comment les a-t-il pû sçavoir? Puis que l'Auteur vouloit imiter les grands Romans, dans les aventures extraordinaires, il devoit aussi les imiter dans le reste, et donner à chacun de ses Heros un confident de qui l'on eust pû apprendre leurs adventures secretes.[103]

Valincour's literalist attitude toward the narrator would induce him to sacrifice the most original and interesting parts of the work.

The same arguments are applied generally to all novels by Bougeant, in his *Voyage merveilleux du Prince Fan-Férédin dans la Romancie* (1735). This work almost becomes a *roman comique*, because Bougeant uses the fiction of an imaginary voyage to link his uniformly hostile attacks. Bougeant never really creates an opposing reality, however; his criticisms remain intellectual and abstract. In one chapter, the prince and his guide go to eavesdrop on lovers, and the prince notices that there are many couples of lovers, each with an author lurking behind a shrub nearby. He protests at this violation of privacy, but his guide replies, "Eh! comment les auteurs qui composent les annales romanciennes pourraient-ils autrement savoir si en détail tous les entretiens les plus particuliers de deux amants jusqu'à la dernière syllabe?" Bougeant pushes the reasoning one step farther, and asks a question which will bother the first-person novelists as well: "Mais avec tout cela je ne comprends pas encore comment des écrivains, par exemple, celui de Cyrus ou de Cléopâtre, peuvent écrire de si longues suites de discours sans en perdre un seul mot."[104]

[103] Jean-Baptiste-Henri du Trousset de Valincour, *Lettres à Madame la marquise de *** sur le sujet de la Princesse de Cleves* (Paris: Sébastien Mabre-Cramoisy, 1678), pp. 117-18.

[104] Guillaume-Hyacinthe Bougeant, *Voyage merveilleux du Prince Fan-Férédin dans la Romancie,* in *Voyages imaginaires, songes, visions*

The critics' and theorists' concerns are constantly echoed within the novels. Subligny's *La Fausse Clélie* offers numerous examples. Many of the stories in it are narrated by characters who took part; their knowledge of the events needs no further explanation most of the time. Subligny, however, has very little sense of the artistic advantages of different perspectives. The story of Mlle de Velzers, the chevalier de Graucourt, and the comte de Valdame relates a comic fraud, the basis of which is that Valdame fancies himself loved by Mlle de Velzers, as a result of Graucourt's trickery. Graucourt composes fake letters, even supplies a substitute girl one dark night, and of course bilks Valdame on the pretext of buying gifts for Mlle de Velzers. The story is told by Mlle de Velzers herself, who actually did not learn of it until the end. Consequently, her narrative has to be sprinkled with comments like: " . . . comment avez-vous pû découvrir tout ce mystere? Vraiment, reprit la Hollandoise, nous n'y sommes pas encore, et il s'est bien passé d'autres aventures, avant que j'y aye pu rien connoistre."[105] The substitution of the other girl, in particular, has to be taken on faith, because, Mlle de Velzers says: "Je ne sçay pas assez les ceremonies qui s'observent en ces rencontres là, pour satisfaire vostre curiosité" (p. 87). The story, which has considerable plausibility and potential interest, does not succeed, because Mlle de Velzers's point of view is the least informed of the three main actors, and her character is the most ordinary.

Similar but less extensive narrative limitations occur in several other stories: that of the marquis de Riberville and a lady from Toulouse, which is told in the third person by Mme de Mulionne; in the story of M. de Greaumont and Mme de Mulionne, told by the heroine, who distinguishes between letters she remembers by heart from having repeated them at the time, and others she remembers only the substance of; and the story of the marquis de Commorgien, told by his close friend Montal, who also quotes letters by heart, because

et romans cabalistiques (Amsterdam et Paris: Charles G. T. Garnier, 1788), Tome 26, pp. 130-31.
[105] Subligny, *La Fausse Clélie*, 1671, p. 84.

he had composed them himself. The most specific challenge to the narrator's authority is directed at the very brief story of the comte de Bermilly. Bermilly loved a married woman, and paid court to her niece as a screen and pretext. One evening, while Bermilly was with his mistress, a rival for the niece's hand was killed. Bermilly let himself be executed rather than use the truth to establish his innocence. Montal immediately objects; and the following discussion takes place:

> Comment vous-mesme le croyez-vous, si ce chef-d'œuvre de discretion n'en a rien dit? Tout ce que vous nous contez s'implique en ce que si la chose a demeuré secrette, on n'a pû mesme le sçavoir. Ha! Monsieur, reprit-elle, on ne l'a découvert aussi que long-temps apres, et ce fut par une femme de chambre qui estoit de l'intrigue, et à qui la Presidente rendit de méchans offices depuis. Mais, repliqua-t-il, ne pouvoit-ce pas estre une vengeance de cette femme de chambre? On sçait ce que ces gens-là sont capables de dire et de faire lors qu'on les mécontente? Hé mon Dieu, dit-elle, il n'y a rien de plus vray que ce qu'on vous dit, et mesme l'assassin fut arresté depuis, et declara tout haut à sa mort que le deffunct n'estoit point coupable du meurtre de son Rival; mais bien luy. . . . (pp. 202-203).

One should note that before beginning the story, the marquis says that it took place a year ago, and the narrator Mlle Barbesieux denies knowing where it took place. Moreover, she opens by admitting, "Je pourrois faire une longue Histoire des amours de ce pauvre Gentil-homme. . . ." All of these remarks seem to indicate that Subligny's chief purpose was to demonstrate the plausibility, or at least possibility, of such a story's coming to light. Mlle Barbesieux reduces the little tragedy to less than two pages, however, and with the limitations on knowledge that are implicit in Montal's criticism, no narrator could give more than the factual outline—unless he adopted some device such as a diary, a letter to a trusted friend, or the like.

Only one of the stories in Challe's *Les Illustres Françoises* is a third-person narration, the story of Angélique and M. de la Contamine. Two others are related as if in the first person, but not really; that is to say, the member of the group who heard the story repeats it word for word. In form, this is theoretically not distinguishable from a first-person story, although the device will warrant special comment very shortly. Challe's use of the third person in only one story of seven suggests that he might have had artistic motives for choosing one mode of narration or the other; and in fact, in the case of Angélique, the credibility of her virtue depends rather heavily on the authorial commentary of the narrator.[106] Des Ronais tells the story, and he is careful to give his sources. The most important one is his own fiancée, Manon Dupuis, to whom Angélique first confessed it. He then became a partial confidant. A few details came from others: "Angélique . . . n'entendit point ce qui se disoit, et ce n'est que de Mademoiselle de Vougy que nous sçavons le commencement de cette scène."[107] Des Ronais's comments are the important element, however; one will suffice as an example: " . . . cette obstination me fait croire qu'elle avoit véritablement vécu sage avec lui" (p. 105). On analysis, it is obvious that Des Ronais has composed the story of Angélique, dramatizing scenes he could not have witnessed. Buried among six first-person stories, this old-fashioned one escapes notice, and even here, the author has to take care that all the sources can be accounted for.

Obviously, the requirement of narrative plausibility placed large areas of human experience out of reach. There would presumably be no human action that no one knew about; but many of the most interesting would be known only to one or a few. Probably the curiosity drive is one of the most powerful sources of the novel's appeal. Regarding the inner life of the emotions, only one narrator was possible as a source: the person who had lived through the experience. In theory, the story could have been retold; but principles of discretion and

---

[106] I will show this in more detail in the chapter on *Les Illustres Françoises*.

[107] Challe, *Œuvres*, p. 120.

rules of historical style prevented such a narrative from imitating fully the original. This is the thought which lies behind statements like Prévost's that "les auteurs des meilleurs romans n'ont pas imaginé de plus puissantes méthodes pour plaire et pour attacher, que de mettre leur narration dans la bouche même du héros."[108] Both Mylne and Stewart discuss this fact, and offer quotations making the same point. From another quarter, the abbé Batteux, writing on the style of history, states: " . . . on a observé que plus les acteurs parlent eux-mêmes, plus le récit est vif et animé. . . ."[109]

Philip Stewart has collected and classified many examples of the various devices used to extend the limited resource that the first-person narration offered. For one thing, the hero or heroine had to have a reason for telling or writing the story, and the more private the adventure, the more necessary became a motive. Likely ones were consolation, edification, or gratitude.[110] The first is especially well suited to the Prévostian type of hero, who affects to have withdrawn from the world, having suffered at the hands of fate. This pretext permits him to ignore the reader to a very large degree. Edification, on the other hand, supposes a reader who will have occasion to profit from the events related. Hence the extraordinariness of the story detracts from its applicability, and the narrator's self-indulgence becomes a fault. Gratitude allows the most glaring violations of modesty and shame. The first encounter between Renoncour and Des Grieux, when the former gives the latter money to help him escape to America with Manon, prepares the whole narration; for when chance brings them together again, Des Grieux says: "Monsieur, vous en usez si noblement avec moi, que je me reprocherais, comme une basse ingratitude, d'avoir quelque chose de réservé pour vous. Je veux vous apprendre, non seulement mes malheurs et mes peines, mais encore mes plus honteuses

---

[108] Quoted by Mylne, *The Eighteenth-Century French Novel*, p. 48.

[109] Abbé Charles Batteux, *Principes de la littérature* (Lyon: Leroy, 1800; first edition, 1765), Vol. 4, p. 239.

[110] See Stewart, *Imitation and Illusion in the French Memoir-Novel*, pp. 84-96.

faiblesses."[111] Presumably no other reason could have forced the repentant young man to recount his shameful past. In the case of *Marianne*, the request to which she responds in telling her story makes her pride less unseemly.

Outside the main narrator, the range of the novel could be expanded through the secondary characters.[112] In the case of a social satire, like *Gil Blas*, the stories told by Scipion, Raphaël, Laure, and others have as much importance as Gil Blas's own; moreover, the loosely linked plot is designed with the clear purpose of moving the hero through as many levels of society as possible. As everyone knows, *Manon* is itself one of these secondary narrations. The device had as many drawbacks as advantages, for it violated all the verisimilitude surrounding the main narration (assuming that such verisimilitude existed), despite the tricks used to legitimize the convention of perfect memory. Besides that, the main plot had to stand still while the secondary narration went on, and this was a serious structural weakness. The epistolary novel appeared to solve this problem, as well as others, by allowing all the characters to express themselves directly.

Yet another means of bringing the secondary characters into the story was through eavesdropping.[113] Stewart cites Challe as one of the experts in this device, because of Dupuis's use of the information he overhears when the widow advises her sister. Marivaux also employed the technique often, as did Crébillon *fils*. A whole novel could be built on the theme—Mouhy's *La Mouche* at least begins in that direction. This device does allow a direct personal expression from a minor character to the reader, but it is severely limited in its usefulness, because the main character also must hear it, and there must be a plausible reason for the speaker to say it in the first place. The lost and intercepted letter is a small variation of the same device. In the theatre, and even in fiction today, the device survives as a means of dramatic revelation;

---

[111] Prévost, *Manon Lescaut*, p. 16.

[112] See Stewart, *Imitation and Illusion in the French Memoir-Novel*, pp. 40-52, 102-20.

[113] ibid., pp. 131-36.

in the eighteenth century, it served as a means of social satire as well. The long scene which Jacob overhears near the end of *Le Paysan parvenu* seems designed primarily to expose Mme de Ferval and her particular style of hypocrisy.

The epistolary novel finally achieved great popularity and tempted many of the best novelists, because it offered the greatest number of escapes from the rigorous prison of the plausible narrator. It allowed a diversity of characters, all speaking in the first person. It allowed a suspenseful plot, in that the character's awareness develops at the same time the reader's does. It allowed somewhat more complicated plots, since the narratives of the secondary characters could be worked in bit by bit, instead of in one long "histoire." Its disadvantages are well known, and in fact the narrative implausibility of most epistolary novels is so great that the convention itself loses all meaning. The readers and authors of the time did not immediately perceive this, however.

The foregoing, all of which are discussed by Stewart, extend the capabilities of the first-person narrator. Stewart does not discuss equivalent techniques applied to third-person narrations. They were fewer in number, and the genre as a whole found the first person more congenial to its main concerns. Nevertheless, the satirists, and the students of social custom rather than psychology, found the first-person forms very unsatisfactory, and weathered the fashion in their own way.

The most obvious expedient was to adopt some fantastic frame and then write realistic stories within it. Lesage's *Le Diable boiteux* was an early example which was widely imitated. The premise is that the hero befriends a devil, who then takes him up above the rooftops of Madrid, from which vantage point he can see through the roofs and into the minds of all the citizens. In Crébillon's *Le Sopha*, the sofa performs the same function as the devil; it has access to scenes which no author or narrator would. Of course, it has no ability to read in the hearts of the people who sit or lie upon it; but then it really needs none. Mangogul's magic ring in *Les Bijoux indiscrets* is the ideal novelist's gadget; not only does it make the wearer invisible, giving him entry to all forbidden places, but it can also force a woman's sex to speak the truth. Alongside the vulgar humor which this leads to, Diderot makes a serious survey of the female half of French society. His parody of Duclos's *Confessions du comte de* *** is on the mark; the limitations of the count's egotism prevent him from delving very far into the lives of the women he seduces.

Voltaire follows a similar procedure in many of his tales, using as hero either some incredible figure like Micromégas, or an indestructible human puppet, like Candide. All the exotic trappings win the author the right to know what he knows, which is very plainly relevant to real French society. It is no accident that philosophically oriented writers should have been drawn so strongly to the fantastic, rather than the realistic, current in the novel. Only the fantasy pretexts gave them the rights they needed.

On a less ambitious level, the novelists of society, whom Peter Brooks has perceptively discussed in his work on the novel of manners, sought other solutions. The best, *Marianne* or *Les Liaisons dangereuses*, work through the first person, utilizing in uncustomary fashion its potential for irony. Some people—the countess, Mme de Merteuil, Valmont, and the reader—know what the others do not; we judge the comic or tragic blunders of Marianne, Cécile, and Mme de Tourvel from that point of view. Very few of the first-person works recognize the distance which is possible; rather, as Rousset argues, the quality sought was "l'identité du personnage et de son histoire." Crébillon's perpetual experimentation with new techniques suggests that he found none of them very suitable. All of his works rely heavily on dialog or on letters, the conventional signs of social interaction. The interest of his best work, *Les Egarements*, derives from the older narrator's commentary on the scenes, much like *Marianne*'s. One can only speculate that Crébillon and Marivaux would both have profited from the freedom to comment as omniscient authors on the conversations they reproduce; it seems very probable.

Most of the characteristic devices of the eighteenth-century memoir and letter novels constitute the machinery by which the conventional plausibility of a first-person narration could be sustained, in the face of great improbability or impropriety. They are most noticeable where they are least credible, although to a modern reader all of them stand out somewhat awkwardly. At the highest level of sophistication, the implausibility serves to show that this conventional narrative technique was used even when it was not especially appropriate. Such is the case in both *Gil Blas* and *Les Egarements*. The tone of the story in each case is out of keeping with the supposed narrator. Gil Blas obviously has no involvement in what he writes; his meeting, marrying, and losing Antonia have no emotional impact at all. Meilcour remembers with too much fascination the style of life he claims to be condemning. More often, the author's general purposes corresponded fairly well to the possibilities offered by the genre he chose, but some element of awkwardness entered in. For example, Mme de Graffigny explains learnedly that the Incas wrote by knotting colored threads, called *quipos*; thus she is technically able to pour out her heart in letters to Aza, but the letters scarcely reflect the circumstances under which they are written—namely, that there is no chance of their being delivered. The epistolary novel is badly suited to the story of people who are completely cut off from each other. At the opposite pole, Saint-Preux's frequent departures furnish obvious pretexts for letter-writing, and the famous letter written in the closet reveals the epistolary novel's greatest weakness: it can not deal at all with people who see each other very much. These examples show that, even when the author found a style of narration generally suited to his aims, he clearly had the aims first, and found a technique second; but he did not have enough choice to find one perfectly suitable.

Occasionally the narrative structure was so strained that it produced a comic mistake. A very well known example is the letter which Suzanne's mother writes in *La Religieuse*. Suzanne's sisters, she relates, had come to visit her on her deathbed, and they suspected that something was hidden in the mattress. Finally they succeeded in getting their mother out of bed, "mais heureusement mon dépositaire était venu la veille, et je lui avais remis ce petit paquet avec cette lettre qu'il a écrite sous ma dictée."[114] Diderot evidently was more impressed with the dramatic value of the incident than the consistency of the narrative convention. As an omniscient third-person narrator, he could simply have related the scene. The charitable reader may excuse the lapse as being Suzanne's; she presumably burnt the letter itself, and was therefore trying to reconstruct it from memory to persuade the marquis to help her. Perhaps the priest told her about the scene, and she remembered it as part of the letter.

Challe is guilty of a comparable lapse, in the *Histoire de Monsieur de Jussy et de Mlle Fenoüil*. The hero told the story to Des Frans when they journeyed from Madrid to Paris together. As was permitted by the conventions, Des Frans repeats it in the first person, speaking as if he were Jussy. Challe takes more pains than most authors to preserve the plausibility of this device. Des Frans does interrupt himself from time to time, for example, when he mentions Mme de Mongey, who is present at the retelling: "Ce furent, Madame, continua Des Frans en parlant à Madame de Mongey, les propres termes dont Jussy se servit."[115] Yet he quotes verbatim the part of Jussy's story which goes: "Je ne vous dirai rien de ma personne ni de mon esprit, l'une est présente à vos yeux, et le long tems qu'il y a que nous sommes ensemble peut vous faire juger de l'autre" (pp. 173-74). Now since Jussy is not present, and since most of the company do not have any acquaintance with him, it might very well be appropriate for Des Frans to offer a portrait. It is in any case rather grotesque to repeat such a circumstantial remark. Challe has evidently written Jussy's story, imagining himself on the spot, not retelling it later. The interruptions testify to his awareness that there was a difference, but the mistake shows that the story was whole before the narrative structure was fit onto it.

[114] Diderot, *Œuvres romanesques*, p. 266.
[115] Challe, *Œuvres*, p. 177.

Techniques of Realism in Early Fiction

In the conclusion to his study of fictional techniques, Stewart compares the eighteenth century to the nineteenth, and concludes that the latter is distinguished chiefly by "the freedom to retain all the advantages of that body of technique (developed in the eighteenth century), while dispensing with the historical pretensions which had given rise to it."[116] My arguments would support that conclusion. I have also attempted to show, however, that the various elements of technique are not separable, and that the first-person narrative technique especially derives from the historical pretensions which dominated all the theory and practice of the major eighteenth-century novelists.

The narrator was, in fact, one of the great obstacles to any further progress toward Realism. The hidden areas of human experience could not be brought to light through any plausible use of the first person. Consequently, novelists trying to explore these areas stretched the conventions beyond plausibility, beyond even logical possibility in some cases. At best, this is a temporary and partial solution.

The several acknowledged masterpieces of fiction from the eighteenth century do not disprove my contention. The first-person narrator has survived right down to the present, and is perhaps more vigorous than ever today. Modern novelists use their narrative stance differently, however, from eighteenth-century writers; beginning in the mid-nineteenth century, such theorists as Flaubert, Maupassant, Henry James, and James Joyce made point of view the controlling artistic principle of fiction. The novelist, free to select from points of view as far apart as total omniscience or imbecilic stream of consciousness, chose the one which best illuminated his theme. The eighteenth-century novelist had no such choice. To have his work accepted at all, he had to pretend that it was a document which might really have been written. If, by happy coincidence or by artistic design, the novelist had a theme for which such a point of view was well suited,

---

[116] Stewart, *Imitation and Illusion in the French Memoir-Novel*, p. 303.

the result might be a masterpiece. This is surely the case with *Manon Lescaut*, where the narrator's self-delusion and incomprehension before the mysterious Manon are the theme of the novel—at least for us. Even in *Manon*, Prévost's moral intentions were not so well served, and in a work like *Mémoires pour servir à l'histoire des chevaliers de Malte*, the narrator's self-righteous assurance that he has acted for the good becomes downright offensive. In just the same way, it appears that *Clarissa* and *Moll Flanders* succeed somewhat in spite of themselves; perhaps this is true also of *Les Liaisons dangereuses*—it is not always easy to define the author's purpose. Marivaux uses the narrator-subject contrast as his theme, thus by brilliant intuition approximating modern techniques; but he was not well understood in his own time.

Rousset argued that the first-person narrative offered to the novelist the greatest amount of freedom. That can not be denied, but it was a very limited amount of freedom. It seems quite obvious that the most original novelists wanted and needed more, but were prisoners of the conventions in an age when such restraints had more force than today. By and large, the eighteenth century did not prize originality in literature *per se*. The novel was in a blind alley in the eighteenth century, as far as technique was concerned. Until the writer was freed from the bondage of the first person, the genre was unable to move forward.

Conclusion

The discussion of techniques has been long and needs recapitulation. The starting-point of the novel was the romance, which is usually thought of as contrasting with the novel on the specific matter of realism: the romance is idealistic and abstract, the novel is realistic and concrete. Yet the romances of the seventeenth century had a theory which aimed at verisimilitude, and which is comparable on many points to the theoretical statements of acknowledged realists. The explanation of this anomaly depends on a clear understanding of the nature of literary conventions and the details of their evolution in this instance. In order to focus on the moral problems which were the usual theme of romance, the conventions provided the novelist with a maximum of freedom from the particulars of reality. The hero of romance had to be free of material cares; consequently, such homely details as money were omitted. This principle had far-reaching effects. Exoticism was necessary, because any local precision—place or family names—risked ensnaring the character in a web of circumstances which would compromise his freedom. Even calendar time could be burdensome. The romance author still considered himself a descendant of the epic poets. His only problems with the narrator were those of propriety.

For various reasons, the mid-seventeenth-century authors of fiction felt compelled to look for historical parallels to the novel. They proceeded to elaborate a theory of fiction based on history. The immediate effect of this theory can scarcely be perceived by a modern reader, and the works of the Scudéry school seem just as far removed from reality as the medieval romances or *L'Astrée*. The new principle led almost inevitably toward Realism, however. At first, the romance had to put its plots and themes into a vaguely historical setting—chiefly a few names and a few famous events, like battles. This alone was sufficient to produce an internal crisis in the romance.

At the same time, pressure was growing for the romance to treat of subjects closer to home. The Spanish *novela* set the example, although here again the modern reader will be perplexed by the apparent lack of difference between the early *novelas* or *nouvelles* and the *romans* which precede them. When the novelists undertook to write contemporary history, however, which is roughly the meaning of the change around 1660, it is fair to say that progress toward Realism was inevitable. Still, the pressure must be observed as trying to bring literary perceptions into "real" life, rather than the reverse. It is entirely false and misleading to suppose that the rising bourgeoisie had any desire to see itself realistically described. When authors like Lesage did this for some of the more notorious bourgeois, the subjects were understandably outraged at being exposed. It does appear likely that the rising new class enjoyed the flattering portrayal of itself as capable of feeling and acting like romance heroes and heroines. It was not just a question of renaming the heroine Blanche Bonnin, however, for this created a comic incongruity. Enough realism was needed to make the tone palatable and the story credible. The romance thus began to invade the world of the bourgeoisie and even the lower reaches of the Third Estate, and this necessarily meant dealing somehow with such elementary problems as the name, address, date of birth, and financial condition of the characters. And the historical pretext required that the novelist cite his sources.

Paralleling this whole evolution was a current of comic fiction. Indeed, the first novel, if such a term makes any sense, may well have been the comic novel *Don Quixote*. Cervantes therein pretends that romances are histories, at least in the mind of Don Quixote. This hypothesis reveals at one time both the ridiculous implausibility of the romances, and the potential power of fiction over men's minds. Throughout the seventeenth century, comic novelists parodied the serious romances, by peopling them with lowborn characters and setting them in ordinary contexts. The best of the comic novelists recognized, like Cervantes, that in the act of satirizing they had to create a literary reality which was in fact very realistic. The faults of the genre lay then in the practice, not in the essential nature. Considerations of style and taste prevented these writers and their readers from making the lowborn characters and their crude adventures the subjects of serious fiction. Instead they looked for an intermediate genre, often modeled after Cervantes' *novelas*, combining some elevation of style with a contemporary subject. These efforts on the whole resemble very much the efforts of romance writers to do the same thing. The so-called realism of their burlesque scenes was not perceived by them as being realism. These scenes are instructive primarily because they reflect the progress of the novel by underscoring its failures. The concerns of the serious novelists and of the comic novelists were by and large the same, but where the serious novelist tried to evade his difficulties and conceal his errors, the comic novelist did everything he could to call the reader's attention to them.

The earliest years of this new trend toward a more historical novel were fruitful. Great advances were made in the direction of heightened plausibility, not only through plausible incidents and individualized characters, but also through increasing attention to specific and sometimes physical detail. Roughly speaking, progress continued into the 1730's, after which the epistolary novel allowed a brief spurt of innovation; but most of the progress had been made by 1740 and the rest of the century merely repeated and imitated, usually less well. The basic cause for this decline was that the question of the narrator had become the only significant technical problem. The narrator had to be rationally possible in that a person who told something had to be capable of knowing it; the writing down of his words had to be explained; the transmission of this writing to the public had to be explained. For the novelist interested in, say, the minute reconstruction of conversations, or the intricate interplay of different psychologies, or in building suspense, or in cosmic irony, these requirements posed almost insuperable problems. Therefore the pressures of the technical problems ultimately exercised a strong influence on the themes of the novel. A novelist was free to write on any theme he pleased; but his greatest hope of success lay always in choosing to study the conflict between one individual's perception of reality and his society's perception of it.

—IV—

Robert Challe's *Les Illustres Françoises*

It seems appropriate, after surveying technical problems scattered among many novels, to look at one successful novel in more depth. The five elements I have been tracing provide only a sample of realistic devices, selected moreover on the grounds of their convenience and clarity. A more thorough examination of a single novel will make it clearer how such devices are akin to less easily isolated elements of realism like description, plotting, and characterization. Furthermore, we will be able to study the crucial point that distinguishes the widespread and even hackneyed appearances of "realistic" writing in unbelievable stories, from the much rarer occurrence of genuinely persuasive realistic novels—the relation of technique to theme.

Les Illustres Françoises offers a unique subject for this study. Its technical aspects confirm that by 1713 the principal devices of eighteenth-century realism already existed. More importantly, Challe evidently selected his techniques in light of his thematic purposes. In some cases, he appears to have felt greater freedom of choice than his successors, so that it is particularly significant to observe what connections he made between techniques and themes. In an exceptional number of cases he anticipated or influenced the better known novelists of the century—Prévost, Marivaux, and Richardson, especially. This suggests that the congruences sensed by Challe were the ones that governed the success or failure of most novels written in the eighteenth century.

Coincidentally another reason prompts me to concentrate on this novel. *Les Illustres Françoises* is that rare surprise of literature, a rediscovered treasure. Virtually unread between 1780 and 1959, it has acquired a very high reputation by now among French-speaking readers. Henri Coulet speaks for the general opinion of critics when he says in *Le Roman jusqu'à la Révolution*: "Mais dans l'ensemble aucune œuvre réaliste jusqu'alors n'avait été aussi solidement construite, aucune n'avait fait paraître cette vérité intéressante et étrange des caractères, cette vivacité des dialogues, cette netteté sobre et signifiante des indications d'heure, d'atmosphère, d'attitudes, cette intensité dramatique des scènes, cette utilisation des récits au développement de l'action."[1] As yet, however, the English-speaking world has remained ignorant of this important novel, which falls just short of being a real masterpiece. Two editions and numerous articles on it have appeared in French, none in English. It is therefore more than commonly useful to bring this work to the attention of English-speaking readers.

Les Illustres Françoises originally appeared anonymously in 1713, from the press of the Dutch publisher De Hondt; this edition has completely disappeared, and its existence is demonstrated only by a long and warm review in the *Journal Littéraire de la Haye*, at the time a new periodical, one of many French-language journals taking advantage of the greater freedom in Holland.[2] The number of editions which followed would indicate that the work enjoyed a considerable success during the first half of the eighteenth century; but only two editions came out after 1750, the last in 1780, and it remained the last until 1959, when Frédéric Deloffre reedited the work and published with it a great deal of new informa-

---

[1] Coulet, *Le Roman jusqu'à la Révolution*, p. 315.

[2] The bibliographical information in these first paragraphs is largely summarized from the introduction and annotation in Deloffre's edition of *Les Illustres Françoises* (cited as Challe, *Œuvres*). The current interest in Challe makes it likely that some of my statements will be incorrect by the time they are published. In particular, Deloffre adopts the spelling "Challe" on the authority of a document discovered by Jean Mesnard—see Frédéric Deloffre, *La Nouvelle en France à l'âge classique* (Paris: Didier, 1967), p. 125; this document has not yet been published nor described. In the same work, Deloffre reproduces without comment the title page of a 1713 edition of *Les Illustres Françoises* (p. 82); I assume this means that a copy of the first edition has been found, and will serve as the basis for a promised new edition by R. Picard, but it has not yet appeared. Finally, I myself expect to have published an article in English, and I am certain that there will be others.

tion regarding its author. Besides the fifteen editions, there were two sequels and at least two adaptations for the stage—Charles Collé's *Dupuis et Des Ronais* and Paul Landois's *Silvie*. Moreover, Penelope Aubin published an English translation in 1727, with a reedition in 1739, and a German translation came out in 1728. Compared to other French novels of the period, *Les Illustres Françoises* enjoyed unusual popularity.

Its eclipse is hard to explain. Many other works of less merit had similar fates—Mme de Graffigny's *Lettres péruviennes* or Duclos's *Confessions du comte de ***, for example —but they were still being republished in the early nineteenth century, and have found among their readers a few admiring scholars even in the twentieth. *Les Illustres Françoises* can boast only three: the mid-nineteenth-century realist Champfleury, who stumbled on a copy and wrote an essay on it; the German scholar Waldberg, who devoted a long chapter to it in his *Der empfindsame Roman in Frankreich* in 1906; and Georges Pillement, who published an excerpt in 1927. Possibly this long oblivion can be attributed to the mystery surrounding the author, for until Deloffre published the results of his research, almost everything about the book and its author was doubtful.

Nothing about the author might ever have been known if it had not been for the *Journal Littéraire*. When Challe read the review, he wrote to thank the editors for their praise, and to correct their impression that the author was dead. Thus began an intermittent correspondence which lasted from 1713 to 1718, and which Deloffre discovered in the library of the University of Leyden and has published in its entirety.[3] Among the editors of the *Journal Littéraire* was Prosper Marchand; in 1748, another Dutch publisher, Marc-Michel Rey, asked Marchand to write a notice for a new edition of

---

[3] Frédéric Deloffre, "Une Correspondance littéraire au début du XVIIIe siècle," *Annales Universitatensis Saraviensis, Philosophie-Lettres*, 3 (1954), 144-82. Parts of it are reprinted in Challe, *Œuvres*, pp. 577-87.

Les Illustres Françoises, and so Challe's authorship was revealed. In 1758 Marchand reprinted the notice in his *Dictionnaire historique.*[4] Marchand's information, however, is far from complete, and he himself admits some reservations and doubts. Among other things, Marchand was uncertain whether the author's name was Challe, De Challe, or Des Challes. The first name Robert has been deduced from the fact that he names his saint's day in his *Journal d'un voyage.*

For throughout his five years' correspondence with the *Journal Littéraire,* Challe refused to divulge his name. The editors wrote to him through a mutual contact in Paris, named Bocheron, and it seems likely that Bocheron eventually told Challe's name to Marchand. It is hard to believe that the editors had made no effort to discover his identity for five years, when they had many chances to do so, as the journal's spokesman pointed out in his letter to Challe. It even seems plausible that they knew from the start, and that some Parisian friend had requested the review, perhaps as a service to Challe. The *Journal Littéraire* reviewed few novels, and almost none favorably. The review states that the editors had seen the manuscript, which proves that they had had a hand in publishing the novel. Their gratuitous supposition that the author was dead touched on one of Challe's obsessive superstitions; it is tempting to think that some friend suggested the remark as a joke, for it would be typical of the humor Challe liked best.

Challe, however, had an extremely prickly personality. He apparently considered *Les Illustres Françoises* unworthy of any further effort, once it was written; despite his surprise at seeing it published, he does not express any amazement that a manuscript was available without his knowledge. Indeed there were other copies in circulation—in 1714, the story of Monsieur des Prez and Mlle de l'Epine was published in Paris in a collection of stories, and the variants show that a

---

[4] Prosper Marchand, *Dictionnaire historique, ou Mémoires critiques et littéraires* (La Haye: De Hondt, 1758), Vol. 1, pp. 182-86.

different manuscript was used.[5] What Challe did care about was a work called *Tablettes chronologiques*, which has disappeared, and was never published. It was, to judge by the comments on it, a sort of historical calendar, serving as a pretext for Challe to discourse on his pet themes, such as the fallibility of the pope and the evil influence of the Jesuits. It must have been very embarrassing to the editors, for they plainly did not think it worth publishing, but could not convey this impression to Challe diplomatically. Challe eventually grew very irritated, and declared that he would not reveal his name except as the author of the *Tablettes*. At this stage, the correspondence broke off.

In the interval, Marchand and his colleagues had got to know Challe's hand and his style, and Marchand not only supplied his name, but also a list of his works, all anonymous, some not published until recently, and all rather unexpected. The first was volume six of a sequel to *Don Quixote*, which Challe claimed as his own in a letter to the *Journal Littéraire* in 1714. This claim has been contested. Challe would not reveal his name so that the *Journal Littéraire* could correct the publisher's attribution of the sequel to Filleau de Saint-Martin; consequently, Marchand tended to doubt that Challe had written it. Actually it seems likely that he wrote both volume five and volume six, the first published anonymously in 1695, the second in 1713, although it had been written much earlier.[6]

Les Illustres Françoises was his second publication. The third, in 1721, was the posthumous *Journal d'un voyage fait aux Indes Orientales*. The voyage took place in 1690 and 1691, but Challe wrote his account during the last years of his life using notes and diaries. The date of his death is not known, either, but the preface to this *Journal* says that he had died shortly before. It is a curious work, containing the usual

<hr />

[5] In Anon., *Avantures choisies*, 1714. See English Showalter, Jr., "Un Extrait des *Illustres Françoises* publié en 1714: *L'Amour innocent persécuté*," RHL, 70 (1970), 103-108.

[6] See English Showalter, Jr., "Did Robert Challe Write a Sequel to *Don Quixote*?" RR, 62 (1971), 270-82.

record of weather and sailing conditions, tourist observations, and accounts of the ship's stores, which was Challe's official responsibility on the journey, but in addition, many pages of personal reminiscences and gossipy stories. A fourth work, which Marchand had seen in manuscript and described, was finally published in 1931 as the *Mémoires de Robert Challes*. Again, the title is misleading. There is some autobiography, but there is much more satirical history directed mainly against the corrupt ministers and financiers of the last years of Louis XIV's reign. Marchand judged Challe's letters worthy of being published as literature; this judgment is a bit too flattering, but for historical reasons the letters did seem worthwhile to Deloffre, who published them in 1954. As already noted, the *Tablettes chronologiques* have been lost. Such is Challe's bibliography.[7] From it, from the hints given by Marchand, and from the documents discovered by Deloffre, one can piece together a sketchy outline of a very atypical biography, which supplies some important background for *Les Illustres Françoises*.

Challe gives his birthdate in the *Journal* as August 17, 1659; no records relating to his family have been found. Challe himself had mentioned that his father was in the Queen's Guard in 1638, and he honors the anniversary of his father's death, May 1, 1681. Deloffre has suggested one Hugues Chasles as the father, but certain difficulties arise in that case, for a document exists saying that Hugues Chasles had no children. This might mean only legitimate children, and since illegitimacy is a frequent theme in *Les Illustres Françoises*, it is not implausible to suppose that Robert Challe was illegitimate. However, Challe also refers in his *Journal* to a sister, who was a nun at Compiègne in 1713. She may have been illegitimate as well, but the hypothesis is at best some-

---

[7] But see Shirley E. Jones, "Robert Chasles serait-il l'auteur de l'*Histoire véritable de Monsieur du Prat et de Mademoiselle Angélique?*" *Revue des Sciences Humaines*, no. 137 (1970), 39-50. Although the similarities between this little known novel and Challe's are striking, no other evidence supports the attribution to Challe, and it must be regarded as doubtful.

what doubtful, and for the time being the question must be left unsettled.

Challe attended the Collège de la Marche, where he made the acquaintance of some influential men, notably Seignelay, Colbert's son, who was Challe's sponsor on his Acadian expeditions later. His education included both the Greek and Latin classics, which he read regularly during his travels, and the great French authors of the seventeenth century, Corneille, Racine, Molière, Pascal, whom he quotes at length from memory. His reading also included works like *Francion* and *Le Roman comique*, *Don Quixote* and *Gargantua*, *Polexandre* and *Les Mémoires de Mr. L.C.D.R.* After his schooling, he took part in a military campaign in Flanders, was at the battle of Mont-Cassel in 1677, and later at the siege of Saint-Omer. But the Peace of Nijmegen, concluded in 1678, forced him to look for employment at home, and he became a clerk in the lawyer Monicauld's office. No doubt he disported himself around Paris like one of the young rakes in *Les Illustres Françoises*; Marchand specifically identified the libertine Dupuis as a fictional representation of the author. Challe mentions in his *Journal* that in 1679 he was having an affair with a prosecutor's wife, at whose house he first met Fanchon, the "belle et heureuse garce" who later told him the scandals of Martinique society.

Challe's father died in 1681.[8] Both his direct comments on the event, and remarks from his novel such as, ". . . il n'y a rien de si dangereux pour un jeune homme, que d'être tout à fait abandonné à sa bonne foi avec du bien à l'âge de dix-huit ans, comme je l'ai été après avoir perdu mon pére . . . ,"[9] give the impression that the loss affected him deeply and badly. His character, under the best circumstances, was difficult; he was easy to offend, quick to anger, slow to forget, and ready to act violently. His bereavement apparently

[8] *Journal d'un voyage fait aux Indes Orientales*, Vol. I, pp. 346-47. The copy I used lacked a title page in Vol. I, but the "Avertissement" is dated La Haye, 15 mars 1721. The title pages of Volumes II and III say only La Haye, 1721. Hereafter cited as *Journal*.

[9] Challe, *Œuvres*, p. 411. The speaker is Dupuis.

brought out the worst in him. The details of the incident are not known, but Challe recounts in his *Mémoires* how a quarrel shortly after his father's death made it necessary for him to leave Paris.[10] Thus he became involved in the French efforts to colonize Nova Scotia.

Challe had some personal stake in the enterprise, but he was also charged by Seignelay with watching the administrators of the colony on behalf of the government; his secret reports have been identified by Deloffre among the French colonial archives.[11] The first project Challe undertook was to buy a ship, in Holland, where he met some of the French exiles and was favorably impressed by the freedom of thought and expression which prevailed.[12] In 1682 he sailed for Acadia, as it was then called, and spent about two years in Canada, making an expedition to Quebec on foot in the spring of 1683.[13] In 1684 he returned to Europe by way of Lisbon, where he witnessed an auto-da-fé, and made his way to Paris overland.[14] In 1685 he sailed again for Acadia, but felt that he had not received the authority due to him, and so returned to France by the next ship.[15] His last journey was in 1687, and it ended with his capture by the British and the loss of the whole colony to England. Challe's hope of earning a fortune of course went with it. The British took him to Boston, and then to London; in London he frequented the colony of French exiles, which included Saint-Evremond, who helped him get back to France.[16]

Seignelay came to his aid again, by giving him the post of "écrivain" on a ship belonging to the East India Company. Challe's job consisted of keeping records and watching the provisions; the latter function particularly offered some possibility for profit. The departure for India was delayed by skirmishes with the English and an expedition to Ireland;

[10] *Mémoires de Robert Challes*, ed. A. Augustin-Thierry (Paris: Plon, 1931), p. 264. Hereafter cited as *Mémoires*.

[11] Challe, *Œuvres*, p. xvi.　　　[12] *Journal*, I, 140ff.

[13] *Journal*, I, 93; III, 176; *Mémoires*, p. 264.

[14] *Journal*, I, 211.　　　[15] *Mémoires*, p. 267.

[16] *Journal*, I, 104, 395.

Challe also found time to beat up a rival in La Rochelle.[17] The ship, *L'Ecueil*, finally set sail in 1690—this is the voyage related in the *Journal*. Challe went to Madagascar, India, Ceylon, Siam, and Martinique, and witnessed several sea battles and a hurricane, before returning to France in 1691. The next year he sailed again on a different ship, but in the same capacity, and so witnessed the battle of La Hougue.[18]

From the absence of information rather than from any positive statements, one can deduce that Challe resigned himself to earning a fairly humdrum living in Paris after 1692. His patron Seignelay had died in 1690, so that his prospects in the maritime service dimmed. In his *Mémoires* he displays considerable familiarity with legal and financial circles, and a few allusions suggest that he was living in the Marais district. *Les Illustres Françoises* adds support to these inferences. As one might expect, Challe was a discouraged and frustrated man at this point. He had spent his life in abortive projects. His military career had been cut short by an all-too-temporary peace. His law career, if that had ever appealed to him, was brought to a halt by his exile. His best hope, the development of the Acadian colony, failed through bad luck and the incompetence of his superiors; at least, so it seemed to him. The possibility of a naval career disappeared finally with the death of his protector Seignelay. To add to his bitterness, he could see all around him corrupt administrators, judges, tax collectors, and moneylenders, growing rich by sapping the strength of the nation, being honored for their ill-gotten gains, while he had worked honestly for nothing.

Challe's literary avocation may have been awakened by Claude Barbin, a famous bookseller and publisher, whose shop was located outside the Sainte Chapelle in the courtyard of the Hall of Justice. This shop appears briefly in Des Prez's story as the setting for a rendezvous. Barbin was distinguished among editors of the time for his perceptive selection of fiction. The two most notable works of fiction in the last half of the seventeenth century both came from his presses: Mme de Lafayette's *La Princesse de Clèves* and Guille-

[17] *Journal*, II, 102.   [18] *Mémoires*, chs. 19, 20.

ragues's *Lettres d'une Religieuse Portugaise*. In 1678 Barbin also published the second French translation of *Don Quixote*, generally attributed to Filleau de Saint-Martin. As was frequently the case, Barbin foresaw the opportunity of cashing in on the success of the original by adding a sequel, and from the first edition, Filleau de Saint-Martin's translation eliminated the death of Don Quixote. For unknown reasons, the sequel did not appear for many years; perhaps the work was slower to win over the public than had been expected, or perhaps Filleau de Saint-Martin simply lacked the imagination to carry out the plan. In any event, the original fifteen-year privilege, or copyright, expired, and the translator died, before any sequel appeared. But in 1695, Barbin reprinted the four volumes of the translation, and brought out a new fifth volume, the *Continuation de l'Histoire de l'admirable Don Quichotte de la Manche*. It is very probable that Barbin engaged Challe as a hack to write this fifth volume, and a sixth also, which was passed by the censor in 1702 but not published until 1713, when Challe wrote to the *Journal Littéraire* to claim it.[19]

Both Filleau de Saint-Martin's translation and Challe's sequel are so far beneath Cervantes' original that modern readers tend to scorn them.[20] If only for historical reasons, however, these French *Quixotes* are worth a moment's consideration. Filleau de Saint-Martin hoped, as he says in his preface, to correct a fault in the first translation, which was a crudeness of style. Thus he sacrificed much of the vigor and life, in exchange for more literary polish. As distasteful as this is today, it pleased the readers of the time, and the second French version of *Don Quixote* was twice as popular for about twice as long as the first had been. Filleau de Saint-Martin was nonetheless bound to some degree by the orig-

[19] The attribution of the sequel (and indeed the translation) is based on very insubstantial evidence. I have examined it in detail in my article, "Did Robert Challe Write a Sequel to *Don Quixote?*" and give only my conclusions here.

[20] Bardon's *Don Quichotte en France* provides summaries and a learned commentary on these works.

inal, so that his improvements consist mainly of cuts and reductions.

Challe on the other hand could follow his own imagination, within the rather wide limits of his conception of the characters. His failure to grasp and prolong Cervantes' inspiration is total. The central figures regress to caricatures of themselves: Sancho is a pure buffoon, who never has an elevated thought or action, while Don Quixote turns into a seventeenth-century French "honnête homme"—Challe even uses the term to describe him.[21] As one might expect, Challe does not share Cervantes' admiration for his hero's obsessive faith; his delusions serve only as a pretext to get the action moving. His insanity in fact becomes much less severe, and could almost be reduced to an anachronism of dress. In the entire sequel, Don Quixote attacks only real villains, always with real skill and valor, and his intervention always produces a favorable outcome. He is no tilter at windmills. His delusions persist, quite understandably, for they are not far removed from reality—until a group of his noble friends disenchant him by staging an elaborate hoax, assisted by a former stagehand from the Paris opera. Dulcinea appears as a beautiful young woman, just as capable as Dorothea of acting the role of a fictional heroine. She, and an enchanter, order Don Quixote to return home and seek peace of mind. Poor Sancho meanwhile is beaten mercilessly and humiliated repeatedly, in order to correct the ignoble lusts of his peasant nature, according to the author. Challe, in his letter, said that he had concluded by having Don Quixote die sane, in his bed, repenting his follies, and he considered this the only acceptable way for such a worthy man to end his life. The published version altered the ending, to make Don Quixote die of an accident while still mad.

[21] Challe, sequel to *Don Quixote*, VI, p. 352. Challe quotes the phrase in a letter to the *Journal Littéraire*, written in 1714; see Challe, *Œuvres*, p. 565. Although Challe is presumably referring to the Amaulry edition of 1713, he gives the same page number, which suggests that most of the six-volume editions are identical except for the title page.

Except as a striking demonstration of how the seventeenth-century Frenchman misunderstood Cervantes, the adventures of Don Quixote and Sancho have little to offer. Challe uses his hero as a spokesman for some of his complaints about France, and through him denounces the tax collectors, financiers, government officials, and the like, who reappear in his *Mémoires*. The knight also discourses on women in terms which resemble Dupuis's in *Les Illustres Françoises*. In short, Challe tried very feebly to recapture the spirit of the original. Instead he diverted the novel to his own ends.

The most obvious innovation is the long tale that bridges the two volumes. Here Challe abandoned all pretense of being Spanish, and introduced a band of French travelers, one of whom tells the story of Sainville and Sylvie. This is a fairly typical French *nouvelle*, about a couple who meet, fall in love, but reach a misunderstanding with disastrous consequences. Sainville introduces Sylvie to one of his acquaintances, a rake name Deshayes, who plots to marry Sylvie to get her money. He is assisted by a wicked baroness, who persuades Sylvie that Sainville is unfaithful. Once the marriage is consummated, Deshayes treats Sylvie brutally; and then the baroness is arrested for an unnamed crime, whereupon she confesses everything in a plea for Sylvie's help. Sylvie flees Deshayes, who pursues her; Sainville saves her from his persecution. Still the misunderstanding continues, but the good offices of a marquise bring the two lovers together. The whole party is traveling to Spain to escape Deshayes, and the conclusion merges with Don Quixote's adventures: bandits wound Deshayes, who repents on his deathbed; meanwhile Don Quixote and his friends kill or capture all the bandits.

In its outlines, the plot resembles the story of Des Frans and Silvie in *Les Illustres Françoises*; there are many similarities of detail. Some of the most significant are the narrative technique, for the original narrator quotes long first-person accounts from different moments within the story, so that the truth is revealed progressively through time and shifting perspective; the details of setting, for most of the action is in Paris, where the addresses and landmarks are cited regularly; general attention to circumstantial detail, for Challe always tries to dramatize such complex events as the slow awakening of love by a series of representative incidents, with much dialog. The other tales in the sequel are more in the Spanish tradition, and are not especially good, but they too develop themes which Challe returned to in *Les Illustres Françoises*. In particular, the story of the "Mari Prudent" presents yet another faithless Silvie, whose husband treats her as Des Frans treats Silvie. Finally, Challe moralizes constantly in his sequel, whether through Don Quixote's speeches or through comments on the tales, and in a number of instances the morals are identical to those in the preface to *Les Illustres Françoises*. The *Continuation* is most interesting as the forerunner of *Les Illustres Françoises*, and is an important moment in the evolution of the novel, for Challe was able to adapt Cervantes' irony to a novel which did not have any burlesque elements. This discovery points the way directly to the great fiction of the nineteenth century.

Virtually nothing precise is known about Challe's life from 1692 until his death around 1720. Around 1708 he must have been writing his *Journal*, since he notes in the beginning that the voyage took place seventeen years before.[22] *Les Illustres Françoises* must have been composed some time before 1713, but there is no way to fix the date more exactly. Challe says in the preface that he wrote it during his spare time, without further explanation.[23] In a letter dated January, 1714, he mentioned for the first time the work on which he had lavished the most time and care, the *Tablettes chronologiques*.[24] By his own account, he spent most of two years on this composition, working in the library of Sainte-Geneviève. He also says that he had showed it to various churchmen, one of whom was probably the abbé Bignon, "Directeur de la librairie" and chief censor from 1700 until 1714. Challe chanced upon the review of *Les Illustres Françoises* in Bignon's library, and asked to have Bocheron deliver his letters to Bignon's ad-

[22] *Journal*, 1, 1.
[23] Challe, *Œuvres*, p. lix.
[24] Deloffre, "Une Correspondance littéraire . . . ," p. 159.

dress.[25] Thus Challe seems to have been affiliated with the literary circle around Bignon, and their advice and interest probably spurred his literary activities.

From 1714 until 1716 he was in Lyons, on unknown business. Several of the letters to the *Journal Littéraire* were written from a city a hundred leagues southeast of Paris; an incident related in the *Mémoires* identifies the city as Lyons.[26] It was there Challe discovered that volume six of his sequel to *Don Quixote* had been printed, by the Lyons publisher Thomas Amaulry. In fact, a syndicate of Parisian editors had put out a six-volume *Quixote* at about the same time. In 1716 Challe wrote his *Mémoires*, but he tends more to relate anecdotes and scandals about famous people than to discuss his own life, and in any case the narrative ends abruptly in the year 1701. Prosper Marchand says that Challe spent the last days of his life in Chartres, where he had been exiled from Paris because of some new quarrel. No trace of him exists there now, and the only clue to the date of his death is the preface to the *Journal*, dated March 15, 1721, which says that Challe was already dead by then.

If more were known of it, Challe's life would surely be as interesting as any novel, and few writers of that era led such agitated lives. It is therefore surprising that he should appear, as an author, more a forerunner of the domestic realists than of the exotic romanticists. Challe had fought in real sea battles and survived a real storm; he had spoken with real savages in Canada and witnessed the bizarre rites and customs of Madagascar. Such material was the common stock of many novelists at that time, yet Challe hardly makes more than a discreet allusion to Italy, Spain, and England in the course of his novel. Still, there is something to be learned about the novel from the biography.

Challe certainly used his own experiences to supply the circumstantial details of his stories. In his preface to *Les Illustres Françoises*, he claims to have heard the stories told, and to have done nothing himself but write them down,

[25] ibid., p. 150.
[26] ibid., p. 171; *Mémoires*, p. xix.

changing the names, dates, and places, so as to conceal the identities.[27] This, however, is merely a conventional disclaimer, designed to make the reader believe the opposite; Des Frans's story is obviously a reworking of Sainville's story in the *Continuation*. But there is a grain of truth in the claim nonetheless, for Challe probably did start from stories he had heard, and elaborate his version on that framework. In the *Journal* he tells of a college classmate he met again in Pondicherry, who had met and, within two weeks, married a Norman girl.[28] In less than two weeks after the wedding, she had deceived him three times with three different men; he forgave her, but she relapsed. He then abandoned her, having contrived to leave her in a house stripped of all its furnishings. The situation, and the outcome, foreshadow Des Frans's story. Or again, Challe's old acquaintance Fanchon, whom he encounters in Martinique, tells him how she duped an honest man into marrying her as if she were an honest woman, and how even then she went on whoring in secret.[29] Challe tells people in Martinique that he and Fanchon had been co-sponsors at a baptism, and that he had known her as maid of honor to one of France's greatest ladies. Both details recur in Des Frans's story, but more important, the theme of the unfaithful wife haunts Challe. His concern is specific: what must a man of honor do, if his wife betrays him? Looking at the happily married Fanchon, he wonders what difference it makes. At other times, he advises forgiveness. But if a woman becomes a slave to her senses, her husband has no choice except to banish her and hide his shame.

A companion on the voyage to India, La Chassée, is a convert from Calvinism, as is Terny in the novel; La Chassée tells Challe a story about abducting a girl from a convent, which parallels some of Terny's story.[30] An unorthodox marriage ceremony related in the *Mémoires* also recalls Terny's and Mlle de Bernay's marriage.[31] Other parts of La Chassée's story sound like Jussy and Mlle Fenoüil's tale. The death of

[27] Challe, *Œuvres*, p. lix.
[28] *Journal*, iii, 53ff.
[29] *Journal*, iii, 331ff.
[30] *Journal*, iii, 236ff.
[31] *Mémoires*, p. 104.

a pregnant woman, who had been beaten, may have led to the scene of Mlle de l'Epine's death.[32] And of course, Challe's own life must have furnished countless details; like Des Frans and Jussy, he had made the journey from Madrid to Paris. Like Des Frans, his father was a man of arms and his uncle a financier. Like Dupuis, he was a young rake. The settings, especially around the Marais, are the parts of Paris Challe knew best. In short, the autobiographical works give some idea of the raw sources of Challe's fiction.

Moreover, one can observe the storyteller in all these writings. Recording weather and sailing conditions does not satisfy Challe. Whenever possible, he relates in full detail his frequent quarrels with other members of the crew. Challe constructed his revenges with great care, and no element goes untold. But when all other subjects are wanting, he simply records the good conversations he had with his friends, or recalls some incident from his past. Thus he retells two of Fanchon's tales about Martinique, which purport to be true incidents; true or false, they sound like tales by some imitator of Boccaccio. In exotic lands, Challe makes the traditional effort to observe the customs, but it is plain that in Pondicherry he is more interested in the story of his cuckolded schoolmate than in almost anything else. It is as if Challe perceived his world through a literary filter; what could not be narrated in some kind of plot quickly lost its appeal for him.

At the same time, Challe was not a professional man of letters. He certainly did not lack education or culture, and sprinkled his *Journal* liberally with Latin quotations. Indeed, his *Tablettes chronologiques* sound like the work of a pedant, at least in part. But Challe did not have the training, and probably not the patience, to carry out such a task, despite the two years he devoted to it. He was a man of action, who wanted to put things on paper as he thought they were in reality. Niceties of style and form required a perfectionist's application; Challe appears to lose interest in the work once it is written down, if the fate of his manuscripts is any clue. On the positive side, he conceived of literature as a social act,

[32] *Mémoires*, p. 43.

not as the intellectual realization of some ideal form. A story was to entertain, to inform, to instruct; its telling changed the lives of the teller and the audience. Fortunately, Challe had few literary prejudices, so that unlike the official men of letters, he did not disdain the novel, the one genre where his conception could be realized. Thus, combining a wide range of experience and observation, a taste and gift for storytelling, and a freshness of attitude, Challe produced one of the most original novels of the eighteenth century.

Even to those who know it well, *Les Illustres Françoises* is confusing. There are seven different stories, each with at least two major characters, most of whom also appear in the frame. To assist readers who are less familiar with the work, an outline of the stories would probably be helpful here.

Frame: Des Frans, returning to Paris after seven years, meets his old friend Des Ronais.

1. *Histoire de Monsieur Des Ronais et de Mademoiselle Dupuis*: Des Ronais tells Des Frans how he and Manon Dupuis met, fell in love, but could not marry because her father hesitated and delayed, without ever actually opposing the match. After old Dupuis's death, a misunderstood intercepted letter led Des Ronais to think Manon is faithless; as the novel begins he is still refusing to see her.

2. *Histoire de Monsieur de Contamine et d'Angélique*: Des Ronais tells Des Frans how the poor but virtuous Angélique married Contamine, by remaining steadfast in her virtue.

3. *Histoire de Monsieur de Terny et de Mademoiselle de Bernay*: Terny tells the assembled group how he met Clémence de Bernay in a convent, abducted and married her in spite of her father's opposition.

Frame: Terny explains that the letter which Des Ronais had read was really from him to Mlle de Bernay.

4. *Histoire de Monsieur de Jussy et de Mademoiselle Fenoüil*: Des Frans repeats word for word the account of how Jussy met Babet Fenoüil, a wealthy orphan living with her tutor; broke off his engagement on her orders,

got her pregnant and abducted her at her request, was almost executed but was exiled instead; finally returned after seven years to marry her.

5. *Histoire de Monsieur Des Prez et de Mademoiselle de l'Epine*: Dupuis, still addressing the group, repeats word for word the account of how Des Prez met Marie Madeleine de l'Epine, wooed her against her father's express orders, and married her secretly; and how the father learned the secret the very day she was to give birth to their child, and precipitated an accident in which mother and infant were killed.

6. *Histoire de Monsieur Des Frans et de Silvie*: Des Frans tells the group how he met Silvie by chance, and despite several suspicious aspects of her past and her current behavior, he married her secretly; one night he returned unexpectedly and found her in bed with Galloüin; he took her to the country, imprisoned her, could neither forgive nor forget her crime, finally left her in a convent where she died; he tried to erase her memory by going into the army, but at last he has decided to come home. (Dupuis later relates this conclusion to Des Frans's story.) Galloüin had seduced Silvie by giving her a magic potion; at the time he did not know of the secret marriage, but guessed the truth afterwards and retired to a monastery in shame. He has just recently been killed by bandits.

7. *Histoire de Monsieur Dupuis et de Madame de Londé*: Dupuis tells the group about his youthful escapades, leading up to a long affair with a widow and then an unsuccessful attempt to seduce Madame de Londé, as a result of which he has reformed and intends to marry Madame de Londé.

Frame: Des Frans eventually marries Mme de Mongey, Dupuis Mme de Londé, and Des Ronais Mlle Dupuis.

Narrative Techniques

The device of frame narration had a strong tradition leading up to 1713: *The Decameron, The Canterbury Tales, The*

Heptameron, are well-known frame narratives while, closer to Challe, Segrais's *Nouvelles Françoises* and Subligny's *La Fausse Clélie* had adopted the technique. In most of these works, the tales are completely independent of the frame situation, which serves as a pretext, but little more. The personalities of the narrators may be reflected in the tales they tell, and the frame situation may bear a thematic relationship to the stories, but these links had always been subtle and generally inessential. Subligny, however, anticipated Challe by having some speakers talk about themselves and each other, and by having one of the stories spill over into the frame.

Challe refined the technique and extended it; in *Les Illustres Françoises,* all the speakers also appear as characters, usually in more than one story. The focal figure is Dupuis; he is a close friend of Des Frans, Des Prez, and Des Ronais, as well as Gallouin, who has an important role in Des Frans's story. All these characters had caroused together as young men. Dupuis also says he knows Jussy, without explaining how. Among the women, he knows Mme de Londé, Gallouin's sister and now his fiancée; Silvie; Mlle de l'Epine, though not well; and Angélique, whom he met thanks to his cousin Manon Dupuis. Manon Dupuis thus provides a link to the Contamines; to Mlle de Bernay, like Angélique a friend from convent days, and her husband Terny; and to Mme de Mongey.

Only a reading of the novel can give an idea of how the characters are made to reappear in each other's stories. In most cases, the appearance is fleeting and incidental. Angélique meets her old friend Manon Dupuis by chance one day, and thus Manon is the first to know of her secret engagement to Contamine. When the princesse de Cologny mistakenly thinks Angélique is a kept woman, the girl naturally turns to Manon for help. Obviously, it could have been someone else, without the story's losing any of its point. Similarly, Des Prez's father, thinking that his son wants to become a monk, asks at a convent if his son comes there often and learns that he does. The son explains that it was only to visit his friend, Gallouin. It could have been any friend, but the allusion gibes convincingly with Dupuis's story about Gallouïn, that he repented his debauched youth and became a monk. Other cases, notably Gallouïn's role in Des Frans's story, are far from incidental, since it is Gallouïn who seduces Silvie.

Even the incidental appearances function effectively to bind the stories together. The casual mentions of Gallouïn in Des Prez's story, or of Mlle de l'Epine in Des Ronais's story, give the impression of a unified society. It is not chance, but design or long habit which has brought the group together. Insofar as he was capable, Challe reproduced the witty banter of such a society; these conversations grow a bit tedious, but they do characterize the speakers consistently, and represent a conscientious effort to dramatize an informal social gathering. The gravest obstacle is, of course, to find a pretext for the long narrations, and Challe solves this by the conventional device of having two characters, Des Frans and Jussy, return from long journeys. Thus Des Ronais tells his own and M. de Contamine's stories, to bring Des Frans up to date, and Des Frans reciprocates by telling his story and Jussy's. The other three, Terny's, Des Prez's, and Dupuis's own, are told to correct an impression—each story brings new information to at least one member of the group. This convention succeeds, because Challe avoids excessive use of coincidence. Des Frans and Jussy have returned to their home, where their friends naturally made them welcome.

The primary purpose of Challe's frame is then to integrate the separate parts of the novel into a whole. The characters share more than a love of good storytelling and an interest in particular ideas. They have a great deal of common experience, a fact that is revealed first because they know each other. But this only prepares the way for other signs of the same unity. The landscape of Paris, recent French history, and French social institutions pervade the novel, each detail adding one more thread in the complicated fabric. The frame is initially a narrative convenience; Challe makes it the basis for a much more complicated unity.

In one of his brilliant pages on *Les Illustres Françoises,* Deloffre comments that the collectivity is a better witness of man than any single point of view, because it combines the global consciousness with the changing limited perspective.[33] Novelists of Challe's era relied on first-person narration almost exclusively, when their object was to study the human heart. Challe himself uses first-person narration primarily. Yet if his object is to examine man in his existential condition of becoming, the mature memorialist reflecting on his past is too limited, and the frame offers the possibility of varying the viewpoints within the first-person narration. The characters make this intention explicit toward the end of the novel, for they begin to compare themselves to others. Mme de Jussy is a heroine of constancy, Mme de Contamine is a heroine of virtue. Dupuis considers all the others heroic in their fidelity; he himself is a hero of libertinage. Moreover, the group judges the stories and the characters. Mme de Jussy was pregnant before her marriage, and then the marriage was annulled and her ex-husband exiled; but she is invited to share their company, because they respect her fidelity to her word. Des Frans is blamed for his hardness toward Silvie, and is encouraged to marry instead of harboring a grudge against all women.

In short, the diversity of characters supplies the needed diversity of points of view, and additionally replaces the omniscient narrator's capacity for irony and moralizing. The quixotic Des Frans tells his story movingly, all the more so because he does not understand himself how it happened, in both a literal and a spiritual sense. Then Dupuis steps in to set the facts straight, while members of the group show Des Frans that the roots of his unhappiness are in himself. The superposition of these different levels of understanding makes the point far better than the omniscient commentary of the author, who gives the moral in his preface: a woman should always be on guard, and an outraged love gives rise to great extremes of behavior.

It might further be observed that the different points of view replace the suspense that is lost when a character narrates his own story. True, the first-person narration either re-

[33] Deloffre, *La Nouvelle en France à l'âge classique*, p. 90.

flected or caused a shift in emphasis from *what* happened to *how* it happened, from the novel of adventure to a novel of psychological analysis. Nevertheless, some element of surprise remained desirable, and Challe achieves it by dispersing the knowledge of what happened among several characters. Two plots thus project out of the narrated stories into the frame. Des Ronais learns from Terny that Manon Dupuis was not unfaithful, and the couple is reunited by Terny's story. Des Frans learns from Dupuis that Silvie had been a victim of black magic practiced by Gallouïn, thus raising the hope that he will find happiness and peace of mind with Mme de Mongey.

Six of the seven stories in the *Les Illustres Françoises* are told in the first person; the presence of the seventh suggests that Challe had a sense of the relative merits of each technique. The earlier stories, Des Ronais's, Jussy's, and Terny's, do not offer much complexity. The hero relates what happened to him, and the plots are fundamentally alike, and quite banal: the young man meets a girl, they fall in love, her parents object, they overcome the obstacle. The only function of point of view is to cast some doubt on Manon Dupuis's fidelity to Des Ronais. Yet Challe has well judged the best perspective from which to view these stories. The events are ordinary, as are the emotions aroused. The characters are reasonably individualistic but hardly eccentric or extraordinary. Challe wants to focus attention on the moral questions which arise from these commonplace situations. As the title clearly indicates, the exemplary figures are the women. But it would be difficult for the admirable person to describe herself; in her own mouth the account of her virtuous deeds would sound self-righteous if not hypocritical.

By having the men tell the stories, the moral import is kept intact. The men, whose inner life is exposed, actually suffer from the technique. Des Ronais comes across as a very shallow young man, whose actions are all typical of his age and social class. He loves Manon Dupuis without extravagance; meantime he makes his landlady's daughter pregnant, which causes him some embarrassment but no thought. When he

thinks Manon is unfaithful, he demonstrates his one quality—
pride. Manon Dupuis, on the other hand, gives evidence of
initiative and intelligence. She in fact makes the first declaration of love, and she plans the strategy for thwarting her
father's attempts to discourage her fiancé. The father is the
most unusual type, domineering, afraid of loneliness, inconsistent, mistrustful, but also generous and loyal; his portrayal
through a few incidents from his past and his speeches to the
young lovers is very vivid. A psychological novelist would
certainly concentrate on the old man or perhaps his daughter;
but the moral novelist has to look at them from a relatively
neutral point of view. If the old man tried to justify his
capricious efforts to upset Manon's engagement, he would become unforgivable; but if Des Ronais himself forgives, the
reader can almost go along with Challe's prefatory moral,
that more parents should govern their children as old Dupuis
did his.

The same basic conditions pertain in Jussy's and Terny's
story. Clémence de Bernay had the courage to denounce her
father, to write a very forward letter to Terny, and to plot her
escape from a convent. The father is an outrageous tyrant,
who has bullied his entire family and does not hesitate to
calumniate his own daughter out of spite. He is seen from a
greater distance than old Dupuis, and is correspondingly less
vivid; but once again, the girl and her family offer much more
material to the psychologist than does the two-dimensional
Terny, who has a soldier's capacity for action, but little else.
The ease with which he changes religions is revealing. For
the moralist, here showing that parents ought not to force
their children into marriages or convents, Terny's uncompli-
cated view serves to insure that Clémence's rebellion against
her father appears just, not disobedient or immodest.[34] Jussy
is a paler figure still; he is a pawn in Babet Fenoüil's hands.
She declares her love, orders him to break off his engagement
to Mlle Grandet, promises to let him make her pregnant, in-

[34] One might compare the lengths to which Richardson must go
to make certain that Clarissa's disobedience does not seem inconsistent
with her virtue.

sists that he carry her off, saves his life by her courtroom plea, resists for seven years her family's pressure to marry someone else, and finally arranges a revenge celebration after the marriage to Jussy finally takes place. She is certainly the more interesting character, but since her story is meant to show that only fidelity can compensate for unchastity, she would appear most immodest telling the story herself.

Dupuis, who tells the last story, is really a chronicler. He tells anecdotes about others, in which he has no role or a secondary role—La Récard's exposure, the Londé ménage, the conversation of the two sisters, Gallouïn's seduction of Silvie. His own adventures are very much alike, involving the indulgence of his often malicious whims, followed sometimes by an unconvincing repentance. He changes his behavior by the end, and Challe's moral holds that a virtuous woman can lure a man away from a debauched life; but when Dupuis describes this as a "conversion," his term is accurate. Challe believed in dramatic changes of character, if his works give a true picture of his mind.[35] Dupuis, for all practical purposes, is defeated in battle by Mme de Londé, who refused to make love to him. In some respects, Challe probably intended Dupuis's life to be an education, from neglected childhood through dissipated youth to wise maturity. The slow interior transformation is not conveyed, however; at best, Dupuis pictures himself at critical moments along the way. All things considered, and with due regard for his wit and energy, Dupuis's study of himself reveals no better a man than the first three. Like the others, he is a moral example, and the grudging respect he acquires for virtuous women foreshadows more celebrated rakes like Lovelace and Valmont; but unlike these descendants, Dupuis has no more depth than the women he seduces.

Des Prez's story, although told as if in the first person, is

[35] From the insanely jealous Osorio, transformed by Don Quixote into a model husband with one blow of the lance, to Challe's real shipmate lieutenant Bouchetière, reformed from a pompous fool to a worthy companion by a single battle, lives appear to Challe to change course because of dramatic moments.

really told by Dupuis. Des Prez shows more character than the four previously discussed heroes; he initiates all the significant acts of his affair. He first declares his love to Mlle de l'Epine, he forces her to declare her feelings, he presses for and arranges the clandestine marriage, against her premonitions. He disobeys his own father, not the girl's. The disaster is provoked as much by a real stroke of fate as by weakness on his part, and his revenge is clear-sighted, unlike Des Frans's. Mlle de l'Epine equals him in boldness and strength of character; they are an admirable couple. The story contrasts the truth, of what Des Prez did and felt, to the common opinion, that he abandoned Mlle de l'Epine to die. It adds credibility that Dupuis testifies to Des Prez's sorrow as a calm observer; when he first sees Des Prez, he finds him weeping, and he marks, as he retells the story, the moments when Des Prez broke down and wept afresh. The Man of Quality plays a similar role in *Manon Lescaut,* guaranteeing to the reader the beauty of Manon, the gentility of Des Grieux, and the apparent sincerity of Des Grieux's feelings. Speaking directly to the reader, or to the society, Des Prez might seem to be pleading his own cause too much. As it is, he benefits from the reticence and solitude into which he has withdrawn; he no longer cares what the world thinks. Dupuis, as a friend, had a right to be informed, and it is Dupuis who pleads the cause for him.

Des Prez has little more insight into his motives and feelings than anyone else in this novel, but he is more conscious of his ignorance. The events leading up to the disaster seem to him the operation of a malevolent destiny. From the first moments of their love, Mlle de l'Epine speaks of presages of death and unhappiness. Des Prez's father discovers the marriage because of a letter, which fell by accident from the young man's pocket; "admirez la fatalité," cries Des Prez.[36] But Challe himself really thought otherwise. The moral of the story is, in part, that passion leads to unhappiness. Des Prez brings about his own misfortunes through tempting fate. He is warned repeatedly, by Mlle de l'Epine, by her mother, by

[36] Challe, *Œuvres,* p. 263.

his father, by their landlady, by the priest, by fate itself in the scene where a peasant catches them making love in a rye-field. Des Prez learns to be wary, but not prudent. He finds ingenious devices to evade most of the traps that are set for him, but he never realizes that real prudence consisted in resisting the urges of his passion.

The narrator's blindness about himself is exploited fully in Des Frans's story, which foreshadows *Manon Lescaut*. The unsuspecting Des Frans is struck by love just like Des Grieux, and from then on is helpless to resist it. His beloved Silvie remains an enigma, just like Manon. Her betrayal is especially incomprehensible; in the novel, it is blamed on a magic potion. Challe believed in black magic, for he defended its plausibility in a letter to the *Journal Littéraire*;[37] moreover, all the audience in the novel accept that explanation and pardon Silvie's crime. Yet the explanation lacks authority, even in the context. Dupuis reveals it, and he has good cause to believe it will restore some tranquillity to his friend Des Frans. Dupuis heard it from Gallouïn, who by that time had guessed the truth and repented; he, too, had a motive for trying to placate Des Frans. Silvie never learned about the magic, and in her letter of farewell to Gallouïn, she accepts responsibility for her crime, while denying the usual motives. She attributes her weakness to God, who was punishing her for the sin of pride, but this disclaimer is scarcely more convincing than the common claim that fate inspires love. There is a nice balance between Silvie's blaming God and Gallouïn's blaming black magic. Consciously or not, they are admitting to ignorance about the real motives for their acts.

Even if the black magic is accepted as literal truth, Silvie must answer for her effort to marry Des Frans by fraud. Whatever her ancestry, she was born out of wedlock. Her good qualities are numerous, but her openness at her first meeting with Des Frans is somewhat suspect. Throughout her lifetime, she has been the subject of rumors and gossip. In short, there is room for doubt about her character. Just as Manon Lescaut's promiscuous sexual affairs reveal nothing

[37] ibid., pp. 579-80.

about her heart, no information from the outside can remove all the mystery of Silvie's character. What is seen of her is primarily the romantic vision that Des Frans recalls.

Des Frans is confused by Silvie, and by his own feelings. In retelling his story he returns over and over to this theme: "Je la quittai tellement changé et pensif que je ne me connoissois pas moi-même" (p. 293). His indecision about giving her up, after receiving the anonymous letters, leads him from the strong resolution never to see her again, to the self-deceiving desire to confound her with the evidence, to the final capitulation before her apology. When Des Frans finds her in bed with Gallouïn, he wavers between the urge to kill them both on the spot, and reluctance, which he first rationalizes as a way to save his honor, and later admits was the result of his love's persisting despite the betrayal. In his revenge, he fluctuates even more wildly between conflicting emotions: "Je vis bien que son dessein étoit de me rengager: je lui en sçus bon gré dans le moment: un moment après je regardai cette avance comme une nouvelle trahison" (p. 391).

Both Des Frans's audience and Challe succeed in drawing a clear, rational moral lesson from Des Frans's unhappy experience. They are not the same, however; Challe emphasizes prudence, and counsels women not to expose themselves to unnecessary risks, while the group tells Des Frans he was wrong not to pardon Silvie and go on living with her. Even within the group, there are differences; Jussy would not ruin his own life because of his wife's crime, Des Ronais (wiser after his own errors) would forgive completely, and Contamine would enjoy the moral advantage he would always have over his wife. Contamine in fact expresses several opinions. Before admitting that forgiveness would have benefits, he claims that he would have killed not only the couple but the maid as well, to insure secrecy. Before that, he had questioned the sincerity of Silvie's farewell letter to Gallouïn, provoking a passionate defense of Silvie from Mme de Mongey. These various comments and conclusions suggest that the ambiguity of the story was deliberate; Challe was fully aware that the beauty of the story lay precisely in Des Frans's uncertainty. The human dilemma confronted by Des Frans is the necessity of choosing without knowing. Challe was one of the first to realize that the novel possessed unique powers to make readers relive that dilemma.

The remaining story, of Angélique and M. de Contamine, proves by contrast that Challe's point of view is not dictated by chance or convention. Angélique may well have inspired Pamela and Marianne; like those well-known heroines, she wins the man of her heart by steadfastness in virtue, overcoming not only his solicitations but the more serious obstacles of social and economic distance. Contamine seems the weakest of all the men; he might have married secretly like Des Prez and Des Frans, except that he would not displease his mother. Angélique finally escapes from the impasse when, having been mistaken for a kept woman, she resolves to sacrifice Contamine, if need be, in order to preserve her reputation. Contamine gives in to her from beginning to end, and receives few favors in return; if he told his own story, Angélique's virtue might well seem a function of his weakness, and the unblemished goodness of both characters would be reduced to excessive timidity.

In fact, however, coming from Des Ronais the story seems quite plausible, mainly because Des Ronais maintains a certain skepticism about it. Angélique's chastity, for so long, and under such conditions, does not seem credible to him, and he believes in it only because it is confirmed by other extraordinary details. Thus he reasons that Angélique would not have dared defy Contamine on the matter of revealing their secret engagement, if she had ever been seduced by him. Later he concludes that Contamine would not have gone through with the marriage unless Angélique had refused him any favors previously. Des Ronais even speculates that ambition or calculation played a part in her virtue, without condemning her for it, if it be so. Thus Des Ronais's cynical narration keeps the story within the bounds of plausibility, and the characters may exercise their virtue without appearing self-righteous, ostentatious, hypocritical, or otherwise offensive.

For all the skill with which he uses points of view and narrators, Challe does lapse. One problem, faced by all memoir authors, is how to make the story fit the mood of the narrator. Prévost allows Des Grieux to use his hindsight; whenever he retells a happy period, he remarks that it did not last long. Challe does not have that sophistication; the bereaved Des Prez recounts some rather embarrassingly intimate incidents from his life with Mlle de l'Epine, notably the love-making in the rye field. Dupuis's supposed reform does not dampen his enthusiastic account of the scoundrelly tricks he played in his youth. The crudest error has already been discussed in the chapter on techniques; it occurs when Des Frans, narrating *verbatim* in Jussy's stead, repeats Jussy's remark, "Je ne vous dirai rien de ma personne ni de mon esprit, l'une est présente à vos yeux, et le long tems qu'il y a que nous sommes ensemble peut vous faire juger de l'autre" (pp. 173-74), to a group of people who have never met Jussy. This trivial error betrays the fact that Challe wrote the stories separately and then put them together. Despite his concern for who narrates, and even who listens (he finds a way to send Gallouïn's sister and the virgin Manon Dupuis outside during Dupuis's account of Silvie's seduction), Challe could not keep all the factors under control at once. No editor bothered to change it in later editions, either. It would appear that, once the formal demands of convention had been met, the reader responded directly to the story, just as we do today.

Devices of Realism:
Money, Geography, Chronology, Names

Challe portrays very few characters who have to earn money, since most of his heroes belong to the wealthy upper bourgeoisie. When such characters do appear, he deals with them forthrightly. Clémence de Bernay wins the affection of a lay sister in her convent with a bribe of one hundred *louis*, plus two hundred to her artisan brother. Des Prez offers his landlady fifty *louis* to arrange his marriage, and a pension of twenty *écus* a month. He offers fifty more to the priest, who is in fact more moved by a good dinner. A hundred *louis* is the price Silvie pays to have Rouvière pose as her father. In other cases, the cone-vendor in Dupuis's story or the mirror merchant in Angélique's story, payment is mentioned but no precise sum is given.

The wealth of the major characters does not prevent their being concerned about money; on the contrary, differences of fortune are one of the major plot complications. Old Dupuis's reluctance to let Manon marry Des Ronais stems largely from his fear of being left dependent on them, so it is natural that money should come up often in their story. The old man reveals his unsuspected affection for Des Ronais by lending him the cash to purchase an office—twelve thousand *écus*, or somewhat more than a third of the cost. Des Ronais had two-thirds on hand, and twenty thousand in the hands of a banker whose death prevented Des Ronais from using it. Des Ronais had paid thirty *louis* to the girl he seduced. Manon Dupuis gives him a gift which he has appraised at two hundred *louis*. Challe relies mainly on round numbers, as can be observed; moreover, the sums are quite large. Because of fluctuating values, and the difficulty of fixing a date for an estimate, a precise equivalence is impossible, but one *écu* was worth roughly ten dollars, and one *louis* twenty. With the lower standard of living however, one *écu* probably represented a week's wages for a workman.

It is somewhat surprising to find alongside these natural allusions to money texts like, "Le Maître de la Poste vous donnera une somme de . . ." (p. 358) in a letter which Des Frans is supposedly quoting word for word. Yet he told the figure of what Silvie inherited from the duchesse de Cranves—ten thousand *francs* in cash, plus an annuity of twelve hundred *livres*. Some strange residual sense of discretion lingers, to prevent Challe from naming an amount where the context plainly demanded it; I have pointed out a similar passage in Marivaux regarding the price of a robe in *Le Paysan parvenu*. Certainly Marivaux knew the worth of a robe, and Challe could have estimated how much to send to Des Frans. Their reticence does not derive from ignorance, but from a feeling of impropriety. Des Frans, trying to give evidence of Silvie's noble generosity, could destroy the effect by citing the figures. Challe displayed a realist's attitude toward plausibility by quoting precise figures where he was able to.

Likewise, in trying to deal with the "rencontres qui se trouvent ordinairement dans le monde," rather than artificial problems, he had to be precise about how the problems arose—that is, how, when, and where his couples met. (Even Mme de Lafayette had had to face that problem, and her choice of a jeweler's shop was criticized on the plausible grounds that Mme de Chartres would not have let her daughter go there.) He chose to set the action in Paris, and once he had the characters circulating in the city, he had to go on accounting for their whereabouts. The result is a highly successful geography. A careful reading of the novel would give a relatively complete and accurate idea of the lay-out of Paris. Many of the characters live near the Porte Saint-Antoine on the eastern end of Paris—Des Ronais, Manon Dupuis, Des Prez, Mlle de l'Epine, Silvie; many of the others live on the northwestern edge of the city—Dupuis, Des Frans, Gallouïn. Contamine apparently lives on the Left Bank; he frequents the Luxembourg Palace and the Saint-Germain Market, and gives Angélique a house on the rue Dauphine. Most of the young men work as lawyers or administrators, and their offices are located on or near the Île de la Cité. Des Frans, returning to Paris from Spain, enters from the south, crosses the Île de la Cité, and gets entangled in a traffic jam; there he meets Des Ronais, dressed in his legal gown, and thus the novel begins. The life of the city, as these people know it, appears to be located in a strip along the Right Bank of the Seine; there one finds the opera, about in the middle; to the west, the Tuileries, where Rouvière and Mme Morin have their rendezvous, and the Capuchin monastery, where Gallouïn retires and where Des Prez is seen by his father; in the center, La Delorme's house of prostitution on the rue Saint-Nicaise where Dupuis traps La Récard, and the Pont-Neuf, where Dupuis and Gallouïn swim in the Seine; on the Île de la Cité, besides the law offices, there was the Hôtel-Dieu, where Mlle de l'Epine is sent to die, and the Sainte-Chapelle and the bookshop where she and Des Prez had their first rendezvous;

stretching to the east was the rue Saint-Antoine, site of the midwife La Cadret's establishment, and at its end lay the Bastille and the ramparts, which were a popular promenade for Mlle de l'Epine, Silvie, Des Prez, and others.

In all cases, this fictional geography corresponds to the real. The eastern end of Paris, the Marais, was the section where the wealthy bourgeoisie was concentrated. Swimming under the Pont-Neuf was popular among young rakes, and the cause of scandals. There was a Capuchin monastery on the rue Saint-Honoré. When Des Prez's father has him arrested, he goes to Saint-Lazare (like Des Grieux), which was especially reserved for disobedient young men of good families. When Mlle de l'Epine plans a pretext to get out of her house, she uses the Mont Valérien, famous as a pilgrimage and as a meeting place for young people. On the peristyle of the Sainte-Chapelle there really was a bookshop, owned by Claude Barbin who probably published Challe's first work.

Not all the stories are so well situated, however; it is not possible to say where Mlle Fenoüil or Mlle de Bernay lived. The references to geography arise as the plot demands them, and then to some degree momentum keeps them going. Challe always explains how his couples met for the first time. Des Ronais met Manon Dupuis because she was a friend of Mlle Grandet, his neighbor. Contamine met Angélique when she accompanied Mlle de Vougy to ask a favor of Contamine's mother. Terny was a close friend of Mlle de Bernay's brother. Jussy was invited to M. d'Ivonne's house because they both liked music, and Mlle Fenoüil was M. d'Ivonne's ward. Mlle de l'Epine came with her mother to ask help from Des Prez's father. Des Frans met Silvie by chance, at the baptism of a foundling in Notre Dame. Dupuis had known Mme de Londé as Galloüin's sister; he meets her again by chance. When, as in the first four stories, this detail does not require Challe to define the place very precisely, the geography of the rest of the story is relatively vague as well; but when the opening scene takes place at a clearly fixed spot, the rest seems to follow in the same style. The needs of the story, rather than some arbitrary obligation to supply realistic detail, thus dictate the presence or absence of geographical references. Fortunately, the stories require enough references to give a very lively sense of the Parisian landscape and ambiance.

Challe claims in his preface to have made deliberate errors of anachronism. He gives an example which is so obscure that it would almost certainly have passed unnoticed otherwise. It appears from the novel that he has in fact taken some pains to establish a suitable chronology for each separate story, and then to make them all gibe with each other. He even tries to make the long-winded oral narrations plausible, by providing suitable pauses and interruptions.

Many of the stories are linked to historical incidents. In the very first, Des Ronais says that old Dupuis was wounded at the Battle of Charenton, which was on February 8, 1649. Thinking he was about to die, old Dupuis agreed to marry his pregnant mistress, and Manon Dupuis was born about six months later. The story begins with her return home from her convent, at the age of nineteen or twenty. Her father dies a year and a half later, and the narration takes place almost a year after that. Thus the time of the narration can be fixed at 1671 or 1672. Angélique's birthday can be placed approximately in 1650; she was around eight when her father died, in 1658. At fifteen, she was placed with Mlle de Vougy, where she stayed an unspecified length of time, leaving to take care of her mother. She spent two years with her mother, two more after her mother died, as Contamine's secret fiancée; at the time of the narration she has been married over two years. Thus her age matches Manon Dupuis's, and again the narration seems to be in 1671 or 1672. Unfortunately, Challe attempted to link Angélique's story to Manon's by having Angélique serve Mme Dupuis until her death; but Mme Dupuis died only four and a half years before the narration, so that an incongruity results.

Similar discrepancies appear in other stories. Terny's letter to Mlle de Bernay was responsible for Des Ronais's jealousy. The time accounted for in Terny's story is internally consistent, and consistent also with the time lapses given in Des

Ronais's; but Terny marks the start of his tale after a campaign which can be dated as 1675, a few years later than the others. Des Frans's story presents a major difficulty. He was orphaned, while in school, by his father's death at Valenciennes in 1656, while Silvie claims to have lost her father in Candia, in 1669, when she was about eight. Obviously, this makes her not only too young to have her story narrated in 1672, but too young for Des Frans to fall in love with. Moreover, in his despair at her betrayal, Des Frans fights in the battle of Raab, which took place in 1664. The anachronism which Challe cited in the preface also involved Silvie, who was singing an air from *Proserpine*, composed in 1680, and her singing had to precede the narration by about ten years. If she were born in 1661, she would be precisely the right age to sing *Proserpine*, since she is nineteen when Des Frans sees her for the first time. It is as though Challe took two characters, from different generations, and put them together without changing any of the facts of their biographies. Very likely Silvie is Challe's fictionalization of a girl from his own experience. In 1680, he was twenty-one himself. Two years later, he had to leave Paris because of some trouble he was in. Ten years later he returned to settle down in Paris. Two of the stories in his sequel to *Don Quixote* have heroines named Silvie, and both women are, or seem to be, unfaithful to their lovers. One suspects a private obsession, which led Challe to depict Silvie in *Les Illustres Françoises* as much like her real-life model as possible, despite the glaring anachronism. Except for this one character, the interlinking of the stories is fairly close in time, and the termination falls fairly close to some date in the early 1670's. The timing of internal events, insofar as it can be worked out, is plausible in every story.

In some stories, the seasons even play a role in setting the mood. Des Prez and Mlle de l'Epine celebrate all the winter holidays together—Martinmas, Christmas, New Year's, Carnival—during their courtship; their happiest days fall in the following summer, including the exceptionally beautiful day when they walk in the rye-field; her death falls, ironically, on the longest day of the next summer, June 19. Des Frans meets Silvie the day of the Nativity of the Virgin, September 8; again the date is symbolic. Des Frans's worst moments come in the dead of winter; it is a pitch-black night when he receives the anonymous letter accusing Silvie, and one of the coldest nights, but crystal-clear, when he goes to confront her. They marry the following October, and he discovers her with Gallouïn sometime the following spring. Dupuis also uses the hot summer months for some of his exploits—swimming under the Pont-Neuf, for example—and frequently gives the time of the year—Sophie gets married during Lent, Célénie's bastard is born in November, he meets Mme de Londé again in the summer. Here again, the subject seems to have influenced the technique. When the story begins with a fixed date, the events continue occurring on a relatively precise calendar. The major difficulties seem to have arisen in trying to adjust the different stories to fit the narrative form he was using.

Challe evidently uses the *nouvelle* style in selecting names, and the unfortunate repetition of the "*de*-plus-name" pattern is counterbalanced by some small details. His use of pet names, like Manon and Babet, is unusual; but if the preface is accurate, a change in social customs deprived that usage of its realism before long. Deloffre has pointed out that the names actually reflect the regional origins of the characters— Terny, Bernay, and d'Orneix are localities near Geneva, appropriate for a story about a former Calvinist. The occasional use of the "évêque de ***" device in the story of Des Frans seems odd, since all the names are admitted pseudonyms; but in fact, in Des Frans's story, several real people figure at a distance—Beaufort, Créqui, for example—lending added force to the device when applied to more or less public personalities closer to the action.

Challe's efforts at characterization are less successful than his other technical innovations, but are nonetheless interesting. The novelist of the time labored under two handicaps: classical psychology held that characters did not change and should always be true to their first conception; and the need to draw a clearcut moral lesson further hindered efforts at a nuanced portrayal. In romance, all characters tended to be alike in their bland perfection; in the realistic fictions, they were sometimes as mechanically bad as the romance heroes were good, but all tended to be flat and indistinguishable.

The heroes and heroines of *Les Illustres Françoises* offer more depth; Challe tried conscientiously to individualize them. Unfortunately, he was hampered by two factors: he continued to use the technique of the portrait, giving a list of the subject's features with a complimentary epithet; and because of the narrative situation he used, the portraits display more tact than accuracy. Nevertheless, Challe managed to convey some distinctive qualities and features.

Manon Dupuis illustrates Challe's discretion quite well. She is the old maid of this group, still unmarried although the same age as the other women. Des Ronais does not spare the flattering adjectives in describing her, but one may wonder about the line: "Pour sa fille, il ne pouvoit pas la nier. C'étoit son portrait; et ce qui me surprend, c'est que plus elle a grandi, plus elle a embelli, et plus elle lui a ressemblé. Cétoit pourtant un des hommes du monde le plus laid" (p. 16). Still more disturbing is Des Frans's remark, " . . . toujours puis-je vous assurer, que le changement que vous avez remarqué dans la beauté de votre maîtresse, ne provient que du chagrin qu'elle a de vos maniéres" (p. 67). In short, reading between the lines, one guesses that Manon Dupuis is a relatively plain-looking girl, whose charm lies chiefly in her wit and vivacity.

Contamine benefits from the same polite treatment. The portrait is too long to quote in full here, but the following passages deserve to be noticed: "Il est d'une taille au dessus de la moyenne, assez bien prise, *mais embarrassée.* . . . Pour de l'esprit, il n'en manque pas; *mais il l'a timide* . . . enfin on peut dire qu'il est ce qu'on appelle un bel homme" (p. 70)—the last speaks plainly enough through its evasiveness. Contamine is an only son, raised by his mother. He keeps Angélique in suspense for four years, fearing to broach the subject of marriage to his mother; when Angélique insists, he gives in. His most remarkable ability is that he can weep at will. Once again, reading attentively, one guesses that Contamine is a weakling, who has been brought to the altar by a stronger and smarter woman; Des Ronais's cynical suspicions about Angélique's motives have already been mentioned. It is a shame that Challe could not have exploited this element of the story more; the moral example might have suffered, but the human interest would have profited greatly.

Almost every story opens with one or two portraits. As a technique, these quickly lose their effect, because too many extraneous elements are included. Challe, however, has occasional flashes of brilliance in these vignettes. The sensuous looks of Mlle de l'Epine strike a note that the rest of her story echoes, yet sensuality seems incongruous in so fair a girl, and this contrast between her outward appearance and her real nature will likewise be reflected throughout. Silvie's long hair, so long she has to stand on a table to have it combed, distinguishes her from all the other women and contributes to her mystery; such extravagant hair seems out of place on a modest girl of good breeding. Obviously, Challe only half sensed the potential which lay in the use of apparently random elements of description, but even that much was an innovation.

It is particularly impressive to find the same methods used in the settings. Angélique has been living for four years on gifts from her secret fiancé Contamine. She has refused to permit him any liberties, and has gone to great lengths to prevent their relationship from being publicly known. Nevertheless, all appearances are against her. One day, by chance, she is seen by the princesse de Cologny, who assumes that she is a rich man's mistress. Immediately Angélique resolves to put an end to the situation, even though she knows it is innocent, and even though it may cost her the chance to marry Contamine. Most novelists of Challe's day would have embroidered that incident with pathetic conversations between the lovers, with long passages describing Angélique's grief after her discovery, and with abundant tears. Challe does all that, but adds one detail which almost no other novelist would have stopped to think about: the place where Angélique was seen.

The incident takes place in a mirror shop. Challe does not insist on the symbolic implications, but they are unmistakable. Angélique sees herself differently after this humiliation, and indeed no longer really considers the relationship innocent. Her honor does not consist solely of her own opinion of herself; her reputation constitutes an important part of it, and her reputation can not be separated from appearances. The key to the moral implications is not the accident by which she is exposed, but the self-knowledge she gains from the exposure. Presumably, she would have eventually reached the same conclusion even without the incident. The narrative structure does not permit Challe to state this idea explicitly. The discussions which follow the stories maintain a more bantering and practical tone. Hence the careful selection of apparently random circumstances furnishes Challe with a new device for implying what can not be directly said, by playing on the natural associations made by the readers.

Des Prez's story offers several examples of this technique. To Des Prez, the origin of his misfortune appears to be fate. From the beginning, Mlle de l'Epine has premonitions of disaster, and it seems that the series of events which led to the discovery was linked together by some malevolent spirit. If Des Prez had not dropped the letter, or if his father had not picked it up, or if it had been any other day, the disaster would have been averted. The unhappy date, which Des Prez recalls bitterly was June 19, the longest day of the year, suggests a cosmic irony in the implacable ruin of his happiness. This date is, of course, an arbitrary choice by Challe, which underscores the pathos of the disaster better than the usual tears and lamentations. It was also Challe's choice to surround the couple at the beginning with symbols of fatality— the gambling which is their pretext for meeting, and the watch which Des Prez gives Mlle de l'Epine. There is another incident, however, which foreshadows the ending, but with somewhat different implications—the interrupted love scene in the rye-field. Here again, the season seems significant, its beauty reflecting the couple's state of mind. Des Prez is so dazzled by his happiness that he forgets his usual caution by taking his wife out for their only walk together, and then demands that she indulge his whim by making love in the open air. The peasant's intrusion is a warning which goes unheeded. One can not condemn Des Prez too severely for loving and marrying Mlle de l'Epine, but he owed something to his father and something to his wife which he failed to pay. In the preface, where direct statement is possible, Challe does not hedge: this story shows the unhappiness that results from giving in to one's passions. Neither Mlle de l'Epine's beauty nor the beauty of a summer's day fully excuses Des Prez's lack of self-restraint.

Des Frans's first view of Silvie is one of Challe's most striking uses of detail. The place is Notre Dame; Des Frans is in Paris waiting until the next spring's military campaigns. Thus the conclusion is foreshadowed in the beginning, for Silvie will die in a convent, while Des Frans goes off to foreign wars to forget. A nun asks Des Frans to stand as godfather to a foundling about to be baptized; he agrees, and suggests Silvie as co-sponsor, for her beauty has attracted his attention. This fatal day was September 8, Feast of the Nativity of the Virgin. In these two circumstances are summed up the dilemma in which Des Frans finds himself. Silvie herself is an illegitimate child, and although her father was of the nobility, her mother was a servant in her father's household. Her heritage is tainted by the conditions under which she was conceived; her parents' passionate nature has come to her in their blood. Yet on the other hand, her conduct seems justifiable, and the rumors against her can be explained as the effects of prejudice. Des Frans wants to see the angelic side of her, the idealized woman whose symbol is the Virgin. Both possibilities are present in their first meeting, and the fundamental ambiguity of her nature is hinted at by the circumstances.

Later in the story Des Frans's state of mind is mirrored in the two winter nights when he hears Silvie accused and then listens to her justification. The first night is so dark that Des Frans can see nothing, not even the man who gives him the letter, for the wind has extinguished his torch. The letter plunges him into total confusion. The second night is calm and clear, but freezing. Des Frans sets out to mock the perfidious Silvie, but instead lets himself be persuaded of her innocence, and his love once again assumes control. This, as his audience points out at the conclusion, is his truth—even when he had the proof of her treachery, he loved her. On this clear night, he might have understood that, but does not; and both times he performs the same gesture of pulling his sword, and both times the sight of Silvie's breast undoes his resolution.

Thus the setting and circumstances add resonance to the stories, reflecting the unconscious preoccupations of the narrator, or arousing associations in the reader. Challe's use of this device is perhaps tentative; certainly he falls far short of Stendhal or Flaubert in what he derives from it. Yet herein lies the fundamental secret of realism in the novel: the details must not only seem true, they must also signify. Superficially, Challe's uses of chronology, geography, money, names, and narrators typify the practices of his time. More and more authors had found that they had to deal with such factors in some manner or other, and none of Challe's realistic techniques can be regarded as a pure innovation. Challe impresses us today as strikingly original, less because of the accuracy of his details or the quantity of them—indeed, he made mistakes like everyone else, was inconsistent, and did not always cover the essentials—than because he chose some details for two functions. The first, obvious function was to seem plausible. The second was to add meaning to the story.

Themes

What has just been said about the aptness of particular elements of technique applies even more forcefully to the general suitability of the methods to the themes. Since theory dictated technique in large degree, there were arbitrary limits on what themes could be treated in depth. The first-person narrative offered the greatest advantages to those novelists who studied the individual. Challe explored the individual's situation in society with a fullness that few others achieved in the eighteenth century. His subjects are not so much unusual or new as renewed by his treatment of them—

brought to life by his realism, given depth by his use of different points of view, and rediscovered by his application of romance forms to real situations. On one side of every conflict are the individual characters, dominating the stories through the narrative structure; and on the other side are society's institutions, Church, courts, army, and family. Between the two, and at the heart of the plot, lies that ambiguous phenomenon, love.

Challe handles the theme of love with unwonted seriousness. The typical love story turned on the question of whether the couple could overcome the obstacles—usually parental—to be married. The marriage ceremony, if the novel ended happily, promised a future of contentment; in an unhappy ending, the obstruction of the marriage meant a lifetime of unhappiness for the couple, frequently shortened by death. This plot surely bespeaks some deep-seated yearning in the human soul, whether it be a Manichean death-wish as Denis de Rougemont claims, or a conflict of the id and super-ego as Freud might say, or some other basic principle of human nature. Such interpretations, however, push the phenomenon farther toward the abstract, while the novel evolved in the opposite sense, realizing the human myths more and more concretely. Challe's plots can be fit into the formula just cited, but his originality lies in his study of the particular conditions under which love flourished around 1670.

It has been pointed out that every story begins by explaining specifically where and how the couple met: through friends, because of business, or by chance. Since much of the difficulty arises from the social differences between the lovers, their ability to meet so easily suggests some inconsistency in social organization. Des Frans's fated encounter with Silvie approaches the mythological, but all the others come straight out of banal experience. Their continued meetings are significant in the same way. Anticipating the opposition of one or both parents, six of the couples contrive to meet in secret. The young men have at their disposal virtually unlimited time and money, but the liberty this implies is incomplete—they must not do anything their parents disapprove with their freedom.

The girls vary more in their ability to move freely; Angélique after her mother's death, Silvie, Mme de Londé after her husband's death, and Dupuis's anonymous widow can be said to have complete freedom of action. Mlle de l'Epine and Mlle Fenoüil have little surveillance, although they are subject to their parents' or guardians' wishes. Manon Dupuis, Angélique and Mlle de l'Epine win their parents' cooperation in arranging to see their lovers. Only Mlle de Bernay has to combat complete opposition and even imprisonment. All of these arrangements sound plausible, yet love can progress quite far before meeting the obstacle; the obstacle then seems out of harmony with society itself, not just with the passions of the lovers.

The obstacles in three cases arise from differences of rank and fortune—Angélique is far below Contamine in both respects, Jussy is of good family but much poorer than Mlle Fenoüil, and Mlle de l'Epine is much poorer than Des Prez. Only in the last case does the obstacle prove insuperable, and even there an element of unfortunate timing may have caused the disastrous conclusion, rather than an implacable opposition. Contamine's mother accepts Angélique with good grace, and Mlle Fenoüil has only to wait until she is of age, for her parents are dead. In all three cases, the parents or guardians defend tradition by opposing an unequal marriage, at least up to a certain point. In two other cases, the girl's father raises obstacles because of a personal whim. Des Ronais and Terny qualify in every respect as excellent matches for Mlle Dupuis and Mlle de Bernay. Old Dupuis delays, because he is afraid of being alone, and because he is an eccentric. Once he was tricked into marriage, and now he hesitates to commit himself. As on the first occasion, he now consents on his deathbed, but this time too late. M. de Bernay simply enjoys tyrannizing others. He imposes on his eldest daughter a husband whom she does not like—and even M. de Bernay does not really like him, for when his daughter dies, he sues the son-in-law to recover the dowry, and they become bitter enemies. He threatens and cajoles his other two daughters, playing favorites to have his own way with their lives, finally trying to force Clémence to take vows. These two cases suggest that the power which fathers possess is excessive; there is no restraint on its abuse, except the resistance of the children.

Thus the most serious obstacles arise out of personality rather than social regulations, but not only because of eccentric parents. After old Dupuis's death, Des Ronais lets an unjustified suspicion delay the marriage. Contamine's reluctance to mention Angélique to his mother appears, at the conclusion, to have resulted from his weakness more than from a realistic appraisal of the situation. Jussy and Mlle Fenoüil overcome the obstacle to their marriage, which is in fact only a delay, through constancy of character; unlike Des Ronais and Des Frans, they do not let separation or temptation weaken their resolution. The social obstacle to Des Prez's love for Mlle de l'Epine is certainly real, but the moral suggests that Challe wanted to blame the couple for their irresponsibility. Clandestine marriage is an evasion, and an illusory paradise. The father's reaction to Mme de l'Epine's heartlessness leaves open the possibility that he might have been won over, like Mme de Contamine or Des Frans's mother; or he might have been beaten by an unconcealed defiance, as in Terny's or Mlle Fenoüil's cases. It is not surprising that Marie-Madeleine turns to her mother in the crisis, or that Des Prez can not get free from his father. The couple act as children, and they themselves left power over them in the hands of their parents. Des Frans's unhappiness follows the conquest of all the obstacles; he is married to Silvie, and his family has accepted her. Then his honor requires him to renounce her for her infidelity, although his heart still clings to her. Somewhat unexpectedly, his friends criticize his action, arguing that his honor ought not to depend on what someone else does, and that he ought to have followed his own feelings. This love is destroyed by Silvie's susceptibility and Des Frans's ignorance of his own mind. Dupuis, finally, meets only the resistance of the women he pursues. The widow insists on retaining her independence, and grants Dupuis all that love can give except marriage; Mme de Londé insists on retaining her virtue, and grants nothing without marriage. Dupuis and the others regard these obstacles as ultimately beneficial—they have reformed the debauched Dupuis—and indeed, in all the stories where the obstacle is met head-on it is overcome to the advantage of the couple.

The conversations which follow the stories orient the interpretation in the direction of moral and social lessons. The long debated question of whether love is compatible with marriage is taken up again, with remarkably modern overtones. Contamine, for instance, states that

> . . . souvent la tendresse d'une femme est à charge à son époux: suivons toûjours mon exemple. Je rentre assez souvent au logis chargé d'affaires. J'y rêve, ma femme croit que je suis de mauvaise humeur, et vient, par des caresses hors de saison, me faire perdre une idée, que je ne ratrape plus. La même chose quand je suis à travailler dans mon cabinet. Je n'ose pas la faire retirer, crainte de lui donner du chagrin. . . . (p. 278).

Except for the tragic story of Mlle de l'Epine, all the stories end with a conventional happy marriage, or at least the prospect of one. The convention loses its artificiality, however, because of the honest evaluation of married life. Contamine has been married two years, longer than any other man in the book; his admission that marriage has drawbacks, however trivial, sets the happy ending in a different light.

Other hints of this cynical view are given. Des Frans is advised to marry Mme de Mongey, whom he does not really love, because "il est bien plus avantageux pour un honnête homme d'épouser une honnête femme qu'il n'aime pas, mais dont il est aimé, que d'en épouser une qu'il aime sans en être aimé" (p. 274-75). Since the conclusion of the novel anticipates the successful conclusion of this match, it would appear that personal happiness depends more on social integration than on satisfaction of the passions. It should be noted, moreover, that Mme de Mongey has been very unhappily married to M. de Mongey; and while Mme de Londé and the widow did not suffer during their marriages, that was only because they accepted a disenchanted view of marriage as reasonable. Both women tolerated their husband's infidelities, and neither woman enjoyed sexual relations with her husband. And since they thought that their own infidelities would jeopardize their honor and domestic tranquillity, neither one had any sexual pleasure during her marriage. The women's attitude toward marriage is even less conventionally optimistic than the men's.

Finally, among the minor characters, unhappy or imperfect unions abound. Old Dupuis never got along with his wife. He had married her under duress, and published his suspicions about her infidelity; the day she died, he went to a masquerade. M. de Bernay mistreats his wife as brutally as his daughters, and Clémence's elder sister is so unhappy married to M. d'Ornex that she thinks the younger sisters did better to stay in the convent. Des Frans's mother, when widowed, resolves to live as well as her sisters-in-law, who are richer than she is because their husbands were financiers, while Des Frans's father was an officer in the army. One senses, behind Des Frans's filial apology for his mother, that the ménage had been strained by conflicts over this question. Dupuis's parents give the impression of a similar hidden strife, for his father openly prefers him, while his mother favors his elder brother.

Dupuis relates many shorter stories of marital problems, some of which he caused. Out of spite, he spreads the word that he once caught Sophie and d'Espinai in a somewhat improper posture together, and then he gives d'Espinai a potion which makes him impotent for the first three months of his marriage, so that Sophie will be more disposed to infidelity. The marriage survives, but obviously not without difficulties. The case of Célénie shows still more vicious behavior on Dupuis's part. After seducing Célénie with promises of marriage, and making her pregnant, he loses interest. She has the baby secretly, and finally succeeds in marrying Alaix, who knows nothing of her affair with Dupuis. Dupuis has his lackey spy on their wedding night, when Célénie pretends to be a virgin, and then sends a letter to Alaix, telling him everything. Once again, however, prudence and forgiveness have preserved the marriage. Finally, Dupuis overhears the widow talking to her younger sister; the latter is a bride of only a year, but already her husband has deceived her many times. The widow counsels prudence and tolerance, and distinguishes between three independent sorts of relationship: marriage, which is a social and legal arrangement; love, which is an emotion, based in part on esteem; and desire, which is an involuntary dictate of the senses. If all three exist at once, the union is very fortunate; but more often, only one occurs at a time. By its position near the end, and by the length and expository form which Challe gives it, this analysis seems to represent Challe's wisdom regarding marriage.

Challe's treatment of love is therefore conventional only in its most superficial aspects. The plot outline has been kept, but it is applied to real circumstances and situations, and the possible solutions which Challe envisions are compromises, not ideals. Challe's work is not so much a drama of married life as *La Princesse de Clèves*, but it has the same orientation. Moreover, Mme de Lafayette offers little solution except self-denial; there seems to be a radical incompatibility between the romantic passion and the ordinary marriage. Challe's characters are not so perfect, nor are their passions so pure and extraordinary, but for that reason they have greater relevance to the problems of the ordinary man.

The now famous generation gap was wider in the novel of Challe's day than in recent years. The parents appeared as obstacles, with almost no balancing parental affection or concern. A universally known example is *Clarissa*: the elder Harlowes are guilty of such tyrannical stupidity that it undermines the moral lesson intended in Clarissa's obedience. Beyond that, one wonders how the same heredity, environment, and upbringing produced both Clarissa and her hateful brother and sister. Richardson makes very little effort to show a family continuity. This was the rule rather than the exception during most of the eighteenth century. Des Grieux's father has every justification for trying to keep his son out of the clutches of Manon; but Des Grieux's passionate nature is all in contrast to his background—nothing in his father's past nor in his education foreshadows the sudden eruption of passion. This is not a real flaw in *Manon Lescaut*, but may be called an opportunity missed.

Challe as a rule does give his characters a family context, which accounts for some of their behavior. Old Dupuis acts at times like a conventional obstacle figure, but his eccentricities, his occasional outbursts of generosity, and his past redeem him as a character. His fear of losing Manon, and of giving up his power over her, can be traced back to the business misfortunes he has suffered, and to the feeling that he was tricked into marriage and then deceived by his wife. This does not make him lovable, but it does make him understandable. His assistance to Des Ronais actually wins the frustrated suitor's affection. Manon has both the innocence which comes of a convent education and the tolerance which comes from living near her father, who does not mince words with her. Her own strong character may be inherited or learned from her father.

Contamine is the only son of two wealthy parents, who loved each other. After his father's death, his mother devoted her life to his upbringing. As one might expect, he is somewhat spoiled, and a weakling. He can not give up the things he wants, particularly Angélique, but he can not demand the right to have her either. Thus for four years, Angélique lives in seclusion while waiting for him to reach some sort of decision. Angélique herself comes from a poor but noble family. Both her parents were younger siblings, thus deprived of any inheritance. When her father was killed, she and her mother both had to go into service. It is not surprising that Angélique has principles above her station, nor that she should have in the back of her mind the advantages of a marriage to the wealthy Contamine.

Mlle de Bernay's father is the most unreasonable man in the novel. His opposition to Terny's suit is purely capricious, and his general behavior is tyrannical. Clémence may be said to resemble him in her bluntness and refusal to be dominated. Challe at least allows Clémence to respond normally to this mistreatment. When she is forced into the convent, she de-

nounces her parents in very strong terms; as her brother retells it, she called her father a tyrant and

> . . . conclut par lui dire, qu'elle voyoit bien qu'elle étoit
> destinée à être malheureuse dans ce monde, soit en
> épousant un homme qui lui déplaisoit, soit en restant dans
> le couvent malgré elle, et damnée par conséquent dans
> l'autre monde, n'ayant pas pu faire son salut dans celui-ci :
> mais que du moins, elle auroit la satisfaction de n'entrer
> pas toute vive dans les bras du démon. . . . Elle fit encore
> pis, car elle ne voulut jamais dire adieu à mon pére quand
> il s'en alla. . . . (p. 134).

True, she nurses her father when he is ill, submitting even to
his humiliating demands, but she was hoping at that point to
get permission to marry Terny. When she realizes that there
is no hope of her father's becoming reasonable, she readily
agrees to the drastic, almost violent means by which Terny
abducts her and makes her his wife. A further sign of the
Bernay family's strife-ridden relations can be seen in the fact
that Clémence's younger sister Séraphine betrays her and
uses Clémence's disgrace to secure her father's preference.
The Bernay family is similar to the Harlowe family, but unlike Richardson, Challe set a limit to the submission which
virtue required of a daughter and admitted that the mere fact
of parenthood did not guarantee love.

Des Prez's father is another who assumes the role of obstacle, but again with nuances. His personality shows in his anti-
monastic outbursts, in his rigid probity as a judge, and in his
regret at the outcome of his intervention. He abuses his power, perhaps, but one can understand why his son respects
him, even as he chooses to disobey him. Mlle de l'Epine is
descended from an Italian family, and this probably accounted in Challe's mind for her passionate and sensual nature. Her mother's fiery temper may also be ascribed to her
Latin ancestry. Mme de l'Epine is portrayed quite unsym-
pathetically, since greed makes her oppose Des Prez's visits,
then guard the secret for them, and finally send her daughter
off to a charity hospital in the midst of a miscarriage. Marie

Madeleine shows no signs of sharing her mother's meanness, but her willingness to enter into a clandestine marriage, and to abuse her mother's permissiveness, probably reflects a desire to flee her.

Dupuis blames some of his excesses on the fact that his father died when he was eighteen, leaving him money and independence too soon in his life. His worst tendencies were surely encouraged by reaction against his older brother, his mother's favorite, and outwardly at least a more disciplined young man. Moreover, because of his mother's disfavor, he was raised largely outside the household, which is also calculated to provoke some spiteful rebelliousness. Among his friends, Galloüin belongs to a very pious family, with a director of conscience living with them. Mme Galloüin, unlike M. Des Prez, is delighted when she thinks her son has plans to become a monk. This is in fact what he does, after pushing his crime to excess, but perhaps the extremes of his character derive from this authoritarian moral education and the proclivity of his parents to total intellectual commitments.

Des Frans has the most complex personality, in relation to his background. His father, killed in the wars, had of course been a military officer; but his uncles were financiers, and thus much richer. Des Frans's mother is jealous of their wealth, and urges her son to let them find him jobs where he too can make a fortune. Des Frans, however, remembers that his father despised financiers, including his own brothers, and longs to emulate his father by becoming an officer himself. Thus his early youth is a series of unpleasant conflicts with his family, in which Des Frans refuses to expend his energy in jobs he detests and soon leaves them in disgrace.

When at last Des Frans meets Silvie, the gap between him and his family is already wide; she is in a sense one more act of rebellion against them. More important, it is clear by that time that Des Frans believes in a romantic ethical system, like the soldiers of the Fronde, in which his father fought. Personal valor, honor, and generosity were a man's virtues; beauty and chastity were a woman's. But France had changed, and one can see plainly enough in *Les Illustres*

Françoises that money and bureaucratic power ruled. Des Frans denounces the moral decline and injustice, but he speaks for an outmoded ideal. He is in short a quixotic figure, whose mad imaginations come not from books (although the seventeenth-century French romances illustrate these ideals) but from his image of his dead father. Silvie even calls him the "Chevalier de la triste figure"; and she of course is his Dulcinea, a mysterious and beautiful girl onto whom he has projected his vision of the ideal woman. Don Quixote is sustained by faith through many disillusioning experiences; Des Frans is not. Twice he has evidence against Silvie, and believes the worst of her. His honor demands that he leave her, yet he can not find the strength to do that, either. For months he flounders in his indecision, punishing Silvie, then regretting it, but he realizes too late what the truth is: he loves the real Silvie, even if she has deceived him, not the ideal image of her. In the end, Des Frans seems to be reconciled to living life as it is, to marrying Mme de Mongey because she will make a good wife, even though he does not love her. Challe obviously regards that as wisdom, but just as obviously shares Des Frans's nostalgic admiration for the dashing heroes of yesteryear.

Thus almost every major character in *Les Illustres Françoises* comes from a distinctive family context. Some of Challe's moral lessons are directed to families: he applauds old Dupuis for holding on to what was rightfully his, and thereby keeping the respect of his daughter and son-in-law, while he condemns M. de Bernay for doing violence to his daughter's inclinations. He discourages clandestine marriages, and warns that once a couple is married, they should rely on each other alone, and no longer on their parents. Whatever the worth of these precepts, the implications of the characterizations and of the stories are certainly more important. Without calling attention to it, Challe delineates some of the influences which parents have on their children, and thereby adds a dimension to the art of character analysis.

The quixotic Des Frans to some extent stands for a special group in *Les Illustres Françoises*: his old friends Des Ronais and Dupuis, his former friends Gallöuin and Des Prez. All these young men have difficulty adjusting to society. Des Prez, in fact, seems to have been permanently alienated by his misfortune, does not plan ever to marry again, and is devoting his life to getting revenge on those he considers responsible for his wife's death; and Gallöuin withdrew from the world into a monastery. After passing through a phase of revolt, expressed mainly through wild debauchery, the other three seem to have accepted the wisdom of compromise. Des Frans has to come to terms not only with his true feelings about Silvie, but also with his opinion of his homeland. He had declaimed bitterly against it to his mother, but confesses on his return that "on ne perd jamais l'amour de la patrie" (p. 400). As it happens, this line reappears exactly in Challe's *Journal d'un voyage* and evidently represents a realization the author had reached himself.[38] Furthermore, his *Mémoires* furnish useful clues to an understanding of the novel, for he regarded 1668 as the year of France's greatest glory, which had all been dissipated by 1713 or earlier.[39] Yet Challe too had reached a compromise between his ideals, hopes, and expectations, and the reality he found when in 1692 he returned to Paris to earn a living, having given up his dreams of making a fortune in America or winning glory at sea.

To a lesser degree, some of the social institutions of seventeenth-century France function as the older generation does. For the most part the Church, the courts, and the tax offices obstruct the path to happiness, while the army proves an illusory means to glory. Like the parents, these institutions are not inflexible, and do not always work against the heroes. Rather, they create problems mainly by being less than what they claim to be. Just as the parents' teaching and principles are belied by reality, so the institutions' purposes have often been perverted by personal ambitions or greed.

Three of the heroes have had military experience, Terny, Des Frans, and Dupuis. Terny evidently comes from a military family; he had been sent to Paris by his Protestant father to learn the arts of war. Although he has been wounded him-

---

[38] *Journal*, III, 315. [39] *Mémoires*, ch. 2.

self, and lost his best friend, Terny does not appear to have any regrets about his service. Nonetheless, he will not imitate those of the previous generations, like Angélique's father or Des Frans's father, who spent their lives serving their country on the battlefield only to leave their dependents in need, or to live a bitter and unrewarded old age themselves. Instead, he has bought an office in the provinces, where he plans to settle with his new bride. Des Frans regarded the army as the honorable profession for a man of his rank, since his father had been an officer, and this prejudice contributed to his distaste for the tax service. Silvie distracted him for two years from pursuing his career, but after her betrayal, he tries to find death or peace of mind in battle. Like Terny, he has little to say about it. His wish to die gave him unusual daring, which in turn built his reputation very high; but he apparently had ceased to consider the army as a career. Until peace left him with nothing to do, he used the army purely as a means of escape. Dupuis speaks the final word on the army as a profession. In his seventeenth or eighteenth year, he had set out for Flanders, but his batallion stayed in the barracks at Amiens. Dupuis was bored, and since a peace was signed shortly afterwards, he never considered it again.

Challe had served in a campaign similar to Dupuis's. In the sequel to *Don Quixote*, he brings in a young man who had been in Flanders, and who criticizes the military life because it has been taken over by self-serving administrators.[40] Don Quixote of course defends it, and Challe probably held the military virtues in high respect. For a young man of his time, however, it was not a fruitful choice; valor and devotion went unrecognized and unrewarded at home, and often enough their effects on the battlefield were undermined by the meddling of bureaucrats. Such at least is the picture Challe paints in his *Mémoires*. In *Les Illustres Françoises*, the fact that none of these young men, despite their backgrounds and their youthful ambitions, has chosen to make his career in the army is undoubtedly an indirect criticism.

Through Des Frans, Challe berates the tax system as a

[40] Challe, sequel to *Don Quixote*, v, ch. 6.

plunderer and persecutor of the poor, echoing what he says in his own terms in the *Mémoires*. Des Frans's brief experience as an administrator in the *Aides*, which collected taxes on beverages, serves to portray the corruption in the system, for his assistant has been cheating and the supervisor has an illegal traffic in wines. Moreover, the mentality of the petty bureaucrat is attacked in the character of this supervisor, who reprimands Des Frans for his failure to observe his office hours exactly. Des Ronais evidently shares this dislike of the *partisans*, who had grown rich through profiteering in the collection of taxes; when he explains the sources of Contamine's fortune, he is careful to specify that Contamine's father had acquired his money legitimately, not from the *partis*, or tax contracts. The tax service has even less role in the novel than the army; it appears chiefly to be condemned. Historically, the *partisans* were taking advantage of their enormous wealth and power to break into the highest social circles. Contamine's mother had, in fact, inherited her fortune from a *partisan*, but this seems to have been forgiven because of her lack of snobbery and ambition—she even consents to her son's marriage to the penniless Angélique. Des Frans's uncles were also involved in the tax offices, although perhaps at not quite so high a level. In short, this relatively new class of men was threatening the older order, based on more feudal ideals. Challe's heroes have become disenchanted with the ideals they were taught, but have not become sufficiently opportunistic to accept this new ethic, based on money.

The legal profession was more honorable than finance, although less so than the army. Once again, Des Ronais's introduction of Contamine shows the distinctions: ". . . une maison qui s'est toujours distinguée par son attachement à la personne de nos Rois, mais plus connuë dans la robe que dans l'épée, quoi qu'il en soit sorti de très-braves gens, et qui ont servi dans les armées avec éloge" (pp. 69-70). Jussy's and Des Prez's fathers were also men of law. All three sons follow in their fathers' footsteps, and Des Ronais too is a *conseiller*. Challe himself was in this profession, and knew the Hall of Justice from personal experience. The milieu of the novel is most strongly marked by this middle class, between the old warrior aristocracy and the new financial aristocracy. In his *Mémoires* Challe attacks the administration of justice, which was venal and notoriously slow.[41] In the novel the quirks of the legal system do not come in for criticism, no doubt because these are men who know how to protect themselves and to exploit the system.

Des Ronais's story offers an excellent illustration of the judicial system in operation. While he is engaged to Manon Dupuis, Des Ronais satisfies his physical desires with a maid at his boarding house. She gets pregnant, and threatens to sue Des Ronais, to make him marry her. Old Dupuis counters by charging the girl with seduction, and gets a warrant for her arrest, which he uses to frighten her into accepting a cash settlement. Doubtless the girl was scheming and justice was basically done, since Dupuis does not exercise his warrant; but Des Ronais goes to the heart of the judicial system when he explains that "Il avertit cette fille, qui se trouva forte embarrassée, voyant bien qu'on lui feroit de terribles affaires, si malgré des gens infiniment plus riches qu'elle, et bien plus puissans, elle s'obstinoit à vouloir m'épouser malgré moi" (p. 44). Rich and powerful friends tell the whole story.

Jussy nearly loses his life by judicial order, for seducing and abducting Mlle Fenoüil, which was a capital crime. Being a lawyer himself, he explains to her that it would be preferable to make her pregnancy known:

... qu'attendu sa jeunesse de près de dix années moins que moi, et la différence du bien et de la naissance, on ne manqueroit pas de m'accuser de subornation et de rapt. Que si nous étions arrêtez, le moins qu'il pouvoit lui en arriver, étoit d'être renfermée toute sa vie dans un couvent, et moi finir la mienne par la main d'un boureau. Que ce n'étoit point un crime digne de mort que de faire des enfans; mais que le rapt en étoit un qui ne s'étoit jamais pardonné (p. 185).

[41] *Mémoires*, chs. 11, 16.

Under the laws of the Old Régime, Jussy's exposition is completely accurate. Moreover, his prediction is nearly realized, but Mlle Fenoüil herself pleads in court for him, with such passion and sincerity, that the judges are moved toward leniency: Jussy is merely banished for seven years, condemned to pay court costs and child support, while Mlle Fenoüil is sent to a convent, and their mutual written promises of marriage declared null. At a later date this sentence might have served to wring tearful protests from readers about the severity of the laws in pre-Revolutionary France, but for Challe and the heroes of his novel, the judgment is a model of enlightened justice. Jussy himself states that the law was interpreted in his favor, and that the prosecutor had acted with the integrity of a true magistrate in reducing the sentence. The blame falls on the couple for having put themselves in jeopardy, although by courage and constancy they vindicate themselves in the long run. The courts showed exceptional wisdom in allowing Jussy to live. The law itself is beyond challenge.

In the story of Des Prez and Mlle de l'Epine, the courts do not serve justice so well. Des Prez's father possesses all the power, and while he is a judge of great integrity, he uses his office to thwart his son. Mlle de l'Epine first appears when she accompanies her mother to the judge's office, to ask his help in her case. In theory, these visits enabled the judges to form an opinion on the rights and wrongs of the case, but it was not even thought improper for the judges to accept gifts as part of the process. The young Des Prez says that he would have considered Mlle de l'Epine's beauty a strong argument on her behalf, and he does indeed do what he can to help them. Nonetheless, in the context of the times, all of this was regarded as ethical. When the father threatens Mme de l'Epine with an obstruction, if she does not stop her daughter from seeing his son, then he is abusing his office—although Des Prez expresses doubts that he would actually have done anything. Des Prez himself does not disdain to block the settlement of the lawsuit, in order to get revenge on the mother; it is his intention that only the daughters shall have the benefit of the favorable decision. However understandable his motives, it is difficult to condone such intrusions of personal interest into the administration of justice. It is equally unacceptable on principle for his father to have him locked up in Saint-Lazare without recourse, but this was a common practice at the time, and the possibility was open not just to judges but to any father who wanted to discipline his son (or other members of his family).

Although laws and courts play a greater part in the action than do the army and the tax offices, Challe's implied judgment is similar. The administration of justice is imperfect, but tolerable. The intent of most laws is sound, but the application depends on human beings, who may act wisely or foolishly. Both as author and as man of law, Challe had a particular interest in the means of judging one's fellow man, and no doubt a particular appreciation of the difficulty in judging. The novel itself becomes a kind of courtroom, where the inner motives and hidden facts can be brought to the attention of the judges. Challe makes the parallel explicit, first by using the legal system in the novel, by making his heroes lawyers, and by setting scenes in the Halls of Justice, and then secondly by constituting his frame audience as a court. After each story, the hearers render their verdict, and assess the penalty, insofar as they have the power. Des Ronais is guilty of jealousy and mistrust; he must beg forgiveness. Angélique has deserved her good fortune. Mlle de Bernay is justified in disobeying her father; he on the other hand has behaved unjustly to the young couple. Mlle Fenoüil has justified her disobedience and her pre-marital pregnancy by keeping her word; the company consents to receive her as a friend. Des Prez has been maligned by public opinion; he deserves pity, while Mme de l'Epine deserves his ill will. Silvie is exonerated on the basis of Dupuis's testimony. Des Frans is therefore in the wrong, but his reasons mitigate his offense; certainly the appearances favored his conclusion. Still, to earn full acceptance in the company, he will have to indicate his return to stability, probably by marrying Mme de Mongey. Dupuis is pardoned for his many offenses because of his reform. Galloüin is forgiven by most, but Mme de Contamine still protests; even though his repentance was sincere, she finds his crime too heinous to overlook. In most cases, there are nuances of opinion, and the moral drawn in the preface may not agree with the opinions expressed in the discussion. The evidence, however, has been presented to the reader, and the arguments made; now the reader must exercise his judgment. In *Les Illustres Françoises* what might have been just a bit of setting, or an instance of social criticism, develops into a general confrontation of society and the individual, and beyond that into a general questioning of the nature of man.

Challe's inquiry into the nature of man might have led him to use the Church as a major element in the novel, as did Prévost in *Cleveland* and *Manon Lescaut*, where the author tries to answer questions about the ultimate destiny of mankind. Religion in Challe is disappointingly secular, and in fact the characters have little spiritual dimension. Challe's interest really stops when he has explored the social and moral behavior of his era. Thus the Church must be considered as simply another institution, whose influence is somewhat wider than that of other institutions, but which has no greater claim to prestige than the others.

Churchmen appear in virtually every story, sometimes in a favorable light, sometimes not. Old Dupuis's confessor tries to help Manon and Des Ronais persuade the old man to consent to their wedding; but the intervention serves only as a pretext for old Dupuis to deliver a tirade on his reasons for refusing. This priest had also given Manon the occasion to make her love known to Des Ronais, by his remark that co-sponsors at a baptism ought not to marry. He turns into an obstacle when the old man, on his deathbed, wishes to see his daughter married. The dispensation from banns arrives too late, and the priest will not honor it since the cause for which it was issued disappeared with the father's death. Thus the Church makes its demands on the characters' lives; its rules must be followed and its representatives consulted. Yet there is no hint of a religious element in their lives. When Dupuis dies, he leaves behind a poem expressing his feelings about death; its inspiration is Stoic, not Christian. He regards life as suffering, not as service to God. Death promises peace, with no threat of judgment or damnation. Allusions to death are frequent in *Les Illustres Françoises*, mainly when parents die, but also at the deaths of Silvie and Mlle de l'Epine. In no case is any religious feeling evident.

The most common role of a priest is to perform marriages, at least in fiction. The poverty-stricken Norman priest who marries Des Prez and Mlle de l'Epine in secret becomes a sympathetic and convincing character. His reluctance to bless such a union melts during a hearty meal, although he had not been moved by money. His homilies and care to protect the girl, in case Des Prez tries to leave her, testify to his fundamental goodness. Des Prez's father reveals a rather surprising streak of anti-religious sentiment, when he suspects his son of wanting to become a monk; he would in fact prefer to have his son philandering. No other character speaks out so openly against the Church; most simply ignore it.

Terny would have good cause to attack it. He was raised a Protestant, but the superficiality of his faith can be seen in the facility with which he converts—he had postponed doing it, he says, in order to get the inheritance of a Protestant aunt. In his *Journal* Challe tells of a friend who had converted under somewhat similar conditions; after the Revocation of the Edict of Nantes, his military career was jeopardized by his Protestantism, so he eventually abjured it.[42] But Terny's wife, Mlle de Bernay, is almost forced to take vows by a conventionally avaricious group of nuns, abetted by her own father. Mlle de Bernay tricks them and thereby escapes. She and Terny declare themselves man and wife during the ceremony when she was meant to take her vows. Apparently this irregular ceremony was legal; the presence but not the blessing of a priest was required, provided there were witnesses. Terny seems to look upon all this as administrative obstruction, and it has no relationship to his religious faith.

Des Frans is aided by a kind friar, who tries to reunite him with Silvie. This Carmelite preaches forgiveness, and con-

[42] *Journal*, III, 236.

vinces Des Frans that he should pardon both Silvie and Galloüin; but his logic is very worldly, and in fact the other members of the little society reach the same conclusion for purely
secular reasons. Since Silvie had died, Des Frans cannot be
reunited with her. In his despair, he lives for some time with
the friar in a monastery, but the monotony bores him. His
spiritual crisis has to be resolved in action, not in meditation;
he joins the army.

The most pious family in the novel is Galloüin's, and Galloüin does in fact become a monk. He is, however, only a secondary figure, and little is ever said of his inner feelings
about his crimes. Nor does the shock of his guilt spread to his
companions, notably Dupuis, who only moderates some of his
wilder tendencies, while continuing his generally undisci-
plined and morally reprehensible way of life. In fact, Galloüin's reasons for becoming a religious smack strongly of
paganism, since he fears that an astrologer's prediction of his
death on the gallows may be realized unless he reforms.
Moreover, the audience of Dupuis's story appear very little
concerned with Galloüin's chances for salvation, and whether
his penitence would be adequate in God's eyes; rather, they
are concerned with his reputation in the world, and whether
Des Frans will forgive him or not.

The realistic uses of the Church in *Les Illustres Françoises*
may have suggested to Prévost that he could use the novel to
study man's place in creation, but this is only speculation. It
is very plain that Challe goes no farther than the moral nature of man, which in turn is determined by society. The
characters have little sense of guilt, but a very strong sense
of propriety. Like the other institutions, the Church has
partly failed in its mission of supporting a proper morality.
Too often, as in the case of Mlle de Bernay, the same sordid
motives govern the churchman and the tax collector. Stupidity and incompetence are rampant; virtue and goodness are
often uncompensated.

Collectively, the institutions make up a coherent social context within which the characters act and react. Challe sees
neither the institutions nor the characters in black and white.

Where the individual clashes with society, his advice seems to be: adapt. In the end, almost everyone does adapt. Still, though this conclusion is inescapable, all the interest lies in the futile struggle. Des Frans's disgust with working as a tax official, Dupuis's hypocritical pose as a future monk, Des Prez's revenge on the *exempt* are all revolts against the inadequacies of society. So, too, are the debauches and escapades of the young rakes, Dupuis, Galloüin, Des Frans, and occasionally Des Ronais and Des Prez; the romantic fantasies of Des Prez and Des Frans; or the delusion that the army holds promise of adventure and glory. The qualities that these young men have been taught to prize highest have lost their utility, and they all feel the frustration of their own superfluity. Some, like Des Frans, retreat into quixotic romanticism, only to be disillusioned; others, like Dupuis, turn cynical by reaction. For both, ultimately, even a flawed reality offers something worthwhile, so one reforms and the other returns from exile. Here wisdom begins, and the story ends.

Men are not the only characters who have to contend with society. *Les Illustres Françoises* is in fact about women, as the title clearly states. Challe's most original ideas concern women's place in society, and some of the statements in his novel could have been made by the most advanced Enlightenment thinkers, such as Diderot. By tradition and by law, women were subjects, to the will of their fathers until marriage, thereafter to the will of their husbands. Besides being obedient, a woman had to be chaste. In practice, to be sure, things often did not follow the precepts. The very existence of the precepts, and the insistence on them by contemporary moralists, indicate that pressure for change was strong. Few novelists made as clear a statement of the problem as did Challe in *Les Illustres Françoises*.

The women in the novel demonstrate that obedience is not a natural tendency in their sex, and indeed, not even a desirable habit. One after another, they must take the initiative in order to realize their own and their lovers' happiness. Manon Dupuis makes the first declaration of love, and persists until she overcomes Des Ronais's jealousy at the end. Angélique sets the conditions under which she will see Contamine and demands the public revelation which leads to the happy resolution. Clémence de Bernay writes a bold letter to Terny and plots her own abduction from the convent. Babet Fenoüil invites Jussy to make her pregnant and forces him to run away with her. Silvie completely rules Des Frans, especially in persuading him that the accusations of Valeran are lies. Dupuis, by his own admission, has been brought back to the paths of virtue by two women, the widow and, most important, Mme de Londé. By and large, the women have stronger characters than the men.

Their forcefulness shows not only in their relationships with their lovers, but everywhere else as well. Manon Dupuis and Clémence de Bernay stand up to their fathers' authority and, on occasion, trickery or tyranny. Mlle de l'Epine displays the same independence from her mother, and Babet Fenoüil from her uncle. Outside their families, Angélique displays great courage and poise in seeking to justify herself to the princesse de Cologny; Babet Fenoüil appears before the court on Jussy's behalf, and her plea saves his life.

More than a similarity of personality, these women share a conviction that they should determine their own destinies. To be sure, this right can never be absolute, for other people with an equal right are always involved. At a minimum, a woman possesses a veto, and must not be forced into marriage or into a convent against her will. If, however, women must concede that society demands some infringement on their absolute right of self-determination, the very same principle demands that the infringement be socially necessary. M. de Bernay's arbitrary rejection of Terny's suit has no moral authority behind it; Terny meets every social qualification, and society ultimately allows Clémence to marry him against her father's orders. Most of the stories show that where tact and patience are employed along with resolution, society can be forced to accept the individual's choice.

The cases of the widow and Mme de Londé provide further exploration of the question in a more difficult situation—

after a marriage of convenience. Mme de Londé respects her husband, who is in all ways a good man, but she has no love for him. They agree that society's expectations must be met—they will live together, she will be faithful to him—so that a kind of cordial alliance exists between them. But M. de Londé recognizes that to ask for his sexual rights is a violence to his wife; consequently, although she says she will not refuse him, he refrains from asking her. Instead, she tolerates with an amused curiosity his extra-marital affairs. Finally, his death frees her to marry Dupuis, whom she does love; but she is as adamant about maintaining her independence from him as from her former husband. Although she is sexually attracted to Dupuis, she will not grant him any liberties before their marriage. Her firmness finally vanquishes Dupuis.

The widow endured a very similar situation in her marriage. Afterwards, she follows a different course from Mme de Londé, and takes Dupuis as her lover, but under conditions which insure his discretion and fidelity. Their arrangement is somewhat utopian; it assumes that time and money are no obstacle, and that all parties can be trusted on their honor. Furthermore, the liaison does not last, although it ends by mutual consent and with mutual esteem after some five years. Challe doubtless intended it to be significant that Dupuis was reformed by two women who could act independently. Responsible to no one but themselves, they acted with more prudence than the dutiful daughters—except possibly Angélique, but she too is on her own for two years.

Both the widow and Mme de Londé can deal with a fundamental fact of human nature, male or female, which ordinary morality and parents seem to ignore or deny: sexuality. Several of the stories underscore the fact that women are sexually attracted by men; for some, like Mlle de l'Epine, sensual pleasure seems to be a dominant aspect of their character. This does not necessarily imply promiscuity or unchastity, but it ought to lead to some reconsideration of social customs and their moral value. The widow explains her views in a long conversation with her sister, which Dupuis overhears. The sister, a bride of only a year, has already been partly abandoned. The widow blames her grief on injured vanity, rather than loneliness or unrequited love. Perhaps a measure of sexual yearning plays a part as well. Society tolerates the infidelities of husbands, but not those of wives, and there are some valid reasons for the distinction, according to the widow. Consequently, she herself always acted virtuously while her husband lived, and even concealed his misbehavior, because she admitted to herself that she would have done as he did, except for the fear of pregnancy, disease, and scandal.

Dupuis later adds a commentary on male responsibility. Since most of the social consequences follow the woman, laws are designed to discourage women from causing disorder in society. Women are punished severely for infractions, while men may lead them into crime with impunity. Dupuis hypocritically declares that a man who breaks a promise to a woman has no honor himself. Moreover, as the widow had pointed out, virtue consists in resisting a penchant in the name of reason, and women are thus in general far superior to men. The Church's categorical condemnation of sexual relations outside marriage gets little sympathy from these people; their discussion is limited almost exclusively to the social considerations.

In their actions they bear out their doctrine. Angélique is much admired for her chastity, but Babet Fenoüil is almost as much admired for her long constancy, and she is welcomed to the society despite the fact that for some seven years she was the mother of a bastard. Dupuis reserves his greatest respect for his future wife, Mme de Londé, who remained chaste as a widow; but he accords almost as much to the anonymous widow, who was his mistress for five years and bore him several illegitimate children. Dupuis mentions in passing two prostitutes he knew, La Récard and an unnamed woman. The latter returned to a more virtuous way of life, and protected her husband's honor, after the incident with Dupuis; he honors her reform by withholding her name. La Récard, on the other hand, has forfeited her claim to respect by her brazen wantonness. Finally, the company agrees that Des Frans ought to have forgiven Silvie's infidelity and taken her back. The mitigating circumstances of course affect their decision, but the Carmelite and Des Frans himself had already reached the same conclusion in ignorance of the magic potion's role. Furthermore, the act was real, even if the motive could be explained, so that to forgive it is to deny that the act is of crucial importance.

The women deserve to be called illustrious for reasons that vary from story to story, but as a rule they overcome unfavorable circumstances to take their place in society. In some cases, the difficulty arises from poverty, in others from parental opposition, and in others from still more exotic causes, like Silvie's mysterious birth, or Mme de Londé's unhappy marriage. Much more than the men, the women have to work for what they want. Only Jussy is the social inferior of his wife, and she is the most aggressively dominant girl in the novel. Moreover, the women have a more delicate balance to maintain between their true feelings and propriety. The pathetic failures of Silvie and Mlle de l'Epine show how hard the task is. They thought they had taken every precaution, and their conduct may deserve no blame, yet happiness was denied them. The success of the others merits all the more admiration, and as Challe observes with justified pride in his preface, their stories illustrate problems which arise in the world, and the moral has all the more impact because the facts are so realistic.

The great similarities between Challe's plots and those of *Manon Lescaut*, *Marianne*, and *Pamela*, whether they prove influence or merely affinity, show that Challe had sensed the direction the novel was taking. As the century progressed, the individual's resistance to society came to seem more and more heroic; in *Manon* there is an apparent conflict between the stated moral lesson and the clear emotional sympathies of the author for the immoral couple. Later, Rousseau's Julie, Diderot's Suzanne Simonin, Bernardin's Virginie, and even Laclos's Mme de Merteuil will be martyrs to the hypocrisy and narrowness of society. At the beginning, however, for Challe and his contemporaries, society embodied goodness. The novel relates the hero's or heroine's entry into his or her rightful place. The novelist thus must present two fundamental points of view: the hero's perception of himself, his society, and his place in it; and the society's view of the hero.

Because of the large number of characters he uses, Challe presents a relatively complete view of society. Moreover, at the time of the narration, these characters belong within society. Their conversations before and after each tale set the moral standards and social rules by which they live. Conflicts between individuals and society are common, but upon analysis most conflicts seem to have their roots in some other individual's abuse of his power—or indeed, in the main character's own abuse of it. The institutions which presumably govern behavior, the Church, the law courts, and the family, possess considerable flexibility. Only when the person performs his job badly does the institution appear hostile—the ignorant and literal-minded priest who delays Des Ronais's and Manon Dupuis's wedding; Des Prez's father, who uses the law in an arbitrary and selfish way; Clémence de Bernay's tyrannical father. Since there remains little or no conflict between the characters and society as a whole, Challe has few problems in conveying a sense of social approval. In most cases, the institutions eventually grant their official blessing. Where they have not, as in Des Prez's and Des Frans's cases, the group itself expresses the judgment.

The individuals can of course speak for themselves. Most of them feel, with good reason, that the outcome has vindicated them. Thus the memory of their rebellions and perils are pleasant to recall. There is no question, though, that the most moving of these stories are precisely the ones in which the hero remains alienated—Des Prez's and Des Frans's. Our foreknowledge of Jussy's safe return to Paris transforms the pathos of his story into nostalgia. A more fertile vein is Des Prez's sense of irrevocable loss. To close with a happy ending, a story requires some suspense along the way, and first-person narration does not lend itself well to that effect. On the other hand, a story that ends in disaster often comes across admirably as a pathetic confession or complaint. The happy man is likely to see his good fortune as his own creation; the unhappy man will blame fate and see all institutions

—even nature and providence—as hostile. The persuasive power of this attitude depends on emotion, and was therefore especially appealing to readers with pre-romantic sensibilities. The more optimistic attitude requires more intellect and analysis; it too had an audience, especially in the 1730's. Both are illustrated in *Les Illustres Françoises,* which thus stands as the headspring of the major themes as well as techniques of eighteenth-century fiction.

— V —

The Individual Against Society in the
Eighteenth-Century French Novel

Challe's recent rediscovery grew out of researches into the sources of better known novels, notable *Pamela* and *Manon Lescaut*. Henri Roddier and Claire-Eliane Engel pointed out the obvious plot similarities between the stories of Angélique and of Pamela, of Silvie and of Manon. *Marianne* also resembles the story of Angélique de Contamine in several particulars. Whether or not the later writers actually read *Les Illustres Françoises* and imitated it matters very little; Challe's contribution to the genre was not a powerful innovation, but rather a competent exploitation of the available resources.

Well before Challe's time, romance had developed internal pressures that strongly influenced the eventual trend of fiction. Given a fairly limited number of conditions in the literary world, the techniques of fiction almost inevitably had to produce greater documentary realism; and at the same time, authors had to rely more and more heavily on first-person narration. These technical factors then determined the range within which excellence was possible. To some extent, of course, there was mutual influence; the deep concerns of an age are sure to shape its literature. It is very likely, however, that in any period a new intellectual force will become manifest soonest and most strikingly in the genres most susceptible to change. In eighteenth-century France, the prestigious dramatic genres remained fundamentally impervious to evolutionary forces, and so declined precipitously from the excellence they attained under Louis XIV. The great writing of the new era went into lesser literary forms—the essay, the informal letter, to some extent the novel. The novel's accession to prominence was not owing to a total lack of ancestry or technique; it did not offer complete freedom to the En-

The Individual against Society

lightenment thinker. But its particular capacity suited the concerns of the age rather well, and therefore attracted new interest.

Challe had some ambitions for the novel that went unfulfilled until the nineteenth century. One of these was the wish to depict a complete society. Deloffre has called attention to the affinities between Challe's methods and Balzac's.[1] It would also appear, from the handling of the story of Silvie, that Challe desired a complex suspenseful plot. Neither ambition could be adequately realized with the means he had at his disposal. Moreover, these two goals did not receive much further attention in the eighteenth century; or rather, the efforts made to fulfill them were condemned to produce uniformly poor fiction. The exceptions, *Clarissa*'s meticulous social details, or *Les Liaisons dangereuses*'s elegantly structured plot, stand as oddities. They succeed in spite of their methods.

First-person narration works best as a means of confession or apology. The central figure explains his secret motives or reveals his hidden frustrations. If the technical problems are handled with skill, so that the narrator speaks with a credible, consistent voice, the reader is inevitably drawn to this new point of view. Wayne Booth has analyzed this mechanism exhaustively and concludes: "Yet regardless of how much we may reason about it, we have, in the course of our reading of this book, been caught. Caught in the trap of a suffering consciousness, we are led to succumb morally as well as visually."[2] First-person narration is highly subversive, and the eighteenth-century novelists brought the genre to prominence by exploiting this quality more than any other.

Challe himself had developed the theme of the individual in conflict with society. Like other novelists of his age, he probably first sensed the appeal of this situation in *Don Quixote*. Cervantes' novel is, of course, not a first-person narrative in the same sense as the others. The author, or at least his fictional stand-ins, regulate the distance between the read-

[1] Deloffre, *La Nouvelle en France à l'âge classique*, p. 88.
[2] Booth, *The Rhetoric of Fiction*, p. 383.

er and the hero, maintaining an ironic perspective which prevents the reader from accepting the Knight's madness as sanity, without qualification. Nonetheless, the privileged views one gets into Don Quixote's mind are seductive. He begins the novel as a buffoon, and leaves it a tragic hero. In the various adaptations and continuations produced in France by Challe, Lesage, and others, the loss of ironic distance stands out as the greatest single failing. One wonders if the authors had any capacity at all for self-criticism. This tendency grew during the eighteenth century; the author disappeared altogether, leaving the hero behind to tell the story. Its effect on the readers' sympathy is all the greater. The dangers in this type of narration have, again, been amply discussed by Wayne Booth.[3] Modern novelists often purposely conceal their own feelings, expecting that the readers—or at least the "happy few" of the enlightened élite—will judge the story in the light of their own unstated principles. But these principles are subject to change and misapprehension, and for the uninitiated such novels are quite simply corrupting. It seems doubtful that before Sterne any eighteenth-century novelists made deliberate use of this device, although an argument over *Moll Flanders* has persisted.[4] Certainly in France, the novelists had their fictional spokesmen go straight to the point in most cases, so that the author's intention seldom raises much difficulty of interpretation.[5]

The radical relativism that has made the twentieth century deny the reliability of any narrator had not been conceived of in the early eighteenth century. Indeed, the novelists of the first third of the century generally conclude with the hero's acceptance of, and by, the society he opposed in the beginning. That is to say, many of the early novels relate a young character's struggle to find his place within society;

[3] ibid., Part III, especially ch. 13.

[4] See Ian Watt, "The Recent Critical Fortunes of *Moll Flanders,*" *Eighteenth-Century Studies*, 1 (1967), 109-26.

[5] There are some important exceptions. See, for example, the "Introduction" by Frédéric Deloffre and Raymond Picard to Prévost, *Manon Lescaut*, pp. xciv-clvi.

The Individual against Society

Challe's stories all move toward this conclusion. The basic structure allows of only two endings: the hero may triumph over the obstacles or he may be defeated by them. The social and intellectual history of the eighteenth century exercised some influence on the evolution of this structure. Triumphs predominate in the early years, defeats in the later ones. This reflects in part the spread of the Enlightenment, ever bolder ideas confronting an ever more inadequate political and social system. At the same time, the individual began to emerge as a significant philosophical and moral concept; and well before the philosophers made the novel into a vehicle for their ideas, novelists like Marivaux, Crébillon *fils*, and Duclos had observed that society exacted a heavy price from the individual. Thus four stages can be discerned in the transformation of the one basic theme: 1) in the closing years of Louis XIV's reign, the novelist concentrates on society, and chronicles the hero's education and admission into it; Challe and Lesage both illustrate this stage; 2) in the 1730's, the ways of society have become more stereotyped and consequently less interesting; the hero wins entrance as before, but now goes beyond and recognizes that the loss of innocence was a genuine loss; 3) in the 1760's, conflict between the individual and society dominates the best novels; Prévost had treated the theme in the 1730's, and his influence was strong on Diderot, Rousseau, and Voltaire, whose heroes find their own ideals and society's fundamentally incompatible; 4) in the last years of the century, society once again becomes an important subject, but as the target of attacks; Diderot (in his tales) and Laclos make the suffering of an individual the pretext for a hostile analysis of society.

The continuity of this theme makes it possible to focus on a rather small number of crucial techniques. The novelist must be concerned with communicating two points of view, the hero's and the society's. The first is accomplished through the first-person narrator, and has already been much discussed here and elsewhere. Since the whole evolution of the genre depends on the reliability and authenticity of first-person narration, it is not surprising that irony is rare. There is virtually no self-criticism, and no implicit criticism of the individual as moral authority.

The presentation of society's point of view requires more sophisticated methods. The attitude toward society is, in fact, much more variable and more ambiguous than the very constant sympathy for the hero. The most traditional method is to introduce an authority figure, most often a father, or another relative, or in some cases a priest or an official. The advantage is that he may speak unequivocally for himself, but the disadvantage is that his position must still be shown to represent the general view of society, all the more if he strongly opposes the hero. The risk is great that such a character will simply become a villain, and that his personality will overshadow his social significance. Examples can be found in most novels—Prévost, Lesage, Diderot, Voltaire, Rousseau all used minor characters this way. A very similar device is to use a rather secondary character, or even a group, as a kind of chorus. The frame characters serve this function quite effectively in *Les Illustres Françoises*.

Yet another method is to rely on the stereotypes to such an extent that the reader can be assumed to know what the conventional point of view is. Peter Brooks's excellent study on *The Novel of Worldliness* demonstrates this procedure in Marivaux, Duclos, Crébillon *fils*, and Laclos.[6] Some of these same authors, and Diderot even more, refer explicitly to the opinions of society—that is, to the fictional society's opinions about the fictional events. There is nothing very ingenious about having a character say what "people" thought, except that in several cases the public's opinion is elevated almost to the level of a protagonist. This is most notably the case in Diderot's story *Madame de la Carlière*, which Naigeon first printed with the accurate title *Sur l'inconséquence du jugement public de nos actions particulières*.

Finally, the most dramatic method is to bring the hero before some kind of tribunal or court. In such a situation, all the other methods achieve a sort of synthesis. At its best, the

[6] Peter Brooks, *The Novel of Worldliness: Crébillon, Marivaux, Laclos, Stendhal* (Princeton: Princeton Univ. Press, 1969), ch. 1.

courtroom represents society's most conscientious effort to discover the truth about human affairs, to observe and analyze the very sort of evidence that Ian Watt calls realistic in the novel. Scenes of this type occur in the novels of Challe, Marivaux, Prévost, Diderot, Voltaire, and Laclos. The novelist, of course, retains the right to overrule the court, and a great deal can be told about his attitude toward society from the way he makes his judges act.

Challe and Lesage: Adaptation

Challe's *Les Illustres Françoises* and Lesage's *Gil Blas* illustrate how novelists treated the individual's conflict with society early in the eighteenth century. Both works have a strong tie to the spirit of the seventeenth century, having been published at least in part during the last years of the reign of Louis XIV. Challe specifically set his stories in Paris around 1675. Lesage of course pretended to set *Gil Blas* in Spain around 1600, but only to mask his satire of contemporary France. *Gil Blas* is further complicated by the fact that it appeared in installments, in 1715, 1724, and 1735; but while the later sections differ from the earlier ones in sophistication of technique—the work becomes more unified as it goes along —Lesage's basic outlook does not seem to change radically.

The seventeenth-century view of society provides the framework for the exemplary societies described in the novels. Society as a whole is organized so that the most enlightened members rise naturally to the top. It is then a highly aristocratic society, at least in theory, as was French society in Paris and Versailles. The nobleman under Louis XIV had rank, privilege, and sometimes wealth by virtue of his birth; but he had also to perfect his taste and to lead a certain style of life. The example of the court set the style for the entire nation. Moreover, the hierarchical view of the universe, inherited from the middle ages and exaggerated by political theorists, held that a similar coincidence of rank and enlightenment ought to typify every subordinate social organization. While this may be stating the obvious, it deserves to be recalled if only to prepare for the revolutionary reversal which took place within less than a century: by 1760 it was already a cliché that true enlightenment was to be found among the simple folk. There is no sign of such a belief in *Les Illustres Françoises* or *Gil Blas*.

Aristocracy does not imply total rigidity. Historically, there was considerable social movement under Louis XIV, with commoners rising to prominence and power, and even buying or marrying into the nobility with great frequency. Even for those born at the highest level, however, entry into society posed difficulties in a personal sense. The novelist thus describes the education of the hero for society. What he learns, and what he wants to learn, are the manners and customs of the group he aspires to join. Once again, this attitude was on the point of disappearing; by the mid-eighteenth century, the hero is more likely to be defending the integrity of his private vision against the demands of society.

The condition for entrance into society is the acquisition of a certain kind of wisdom, consisting largely of rather arbitrary rules of etiquette. The moral precepts derive from ordinary religious teaching, and in fact are secondary in importance. The key element is a sense of propriety and a willingness to live by it. This attitude implies that the opinion of others plays a large role in anyone's life, since propriety is more avoidance of scandal than governance by principle. By the same token, it implies that wisdom lies in resignation and acceptance; individual rights, and even justice, must be sacrificed to the tranquillity of the society. Both Challe and Lesage offer this kind of teaching in their novels.

A final element which unites *Gil Blas* and *Les Illustres Françoises* is structural awkwardness. The first-person narrator is ill situated to analyze or describe a whole society. Challe's effort to get around this problem merits admiration for its ingenuity, but must nonetheless be counted a failure. As he himself confessed in the foreword, the exposition is confusing. The frame story often lags, the conversations sometimes become boring, and the plot devices are implausible. Despite the apparent influence of the separate stories, no author tried to imitate the structural apparatus. With Lesage, the structure is equally awkward, although somewhat more familiar. In the first six books of *Gil Blas*, Lesage's dominant interest was to satirize society. Thus, *Gil Blas* hardly improved on the original version of *Le Diable boiteux*, which had no plot at all, but was merely a series of disconnected scenes and anecdotes. Lesage sends his heroes like sociologists through all the strata of society; when, belatedly, he develops a novelist's interest in the growth of the character, it is too late to make a tight structure.

While sharing those general characteristics each novel treats the theme in its own way. Challe concentrates on a society composed of the upper bourgeoisie, mainly financiers and magistrates, with some contacts among the nobility. The small groups who appear in the frame represent this society, and also constitute an enlightened élite. The laws which govern them, and which come into question, deal primarily with matters of caste and specifically with the propriety of various possible marriages. Although this is initially a social matter, both the religious and the civil laws support the caste system. As the author's introductory remarks make absolutely clear, he has no intention whatsoever of challenging the validity or even the wisdom of these laws or this system.

Every story, however, presents a couple in conflict with the law. In some cases, the match violates the accepted standards, and in others, the arbitrary opposition of a parent hinders the couple. All the couples manage to be married anyway: for Jussy and Terny, this requires an abduction; for Contamine a long secret engagement; for Des Prez and Des Frans, a secret marriage; for Des Ronais and Dupuis a long wait. For the first three, the experience entails some risk, but in the crisis they find society more tolerant than they had expected: Jussy is spared by the court, Terny forces the Church to recognize his marriage, and Contamine's mother gives her consent. The other four men undergo a more serious alienation, especially Des Frans and Dupuis, and they are the ones who are educated for society in the course of the novel. All of them, as well as Gallouïn, respond to the hypocrisies and injustices they see around them by espousing the injustice with exaggerated cynicism. For Des Ronais and Des Prez, this can be inferred from their having belonged to the little band which included Dupuis and Gallouïn, as well as from Des Ronais's infidelity to Manon Dupuis and from Des Prez's bullying of Mlle de l'Epine. Des Frans and Dupuis discuss it explicitly, from opposite poles—Des Frans as the man betrayed, and Dupuis as the seducer. They are ancestors of Versac, Meilcour, the comte de ***, and Valmont, but their revolt has not yet gone so far. Dupuis, like Meilcour and the comte de *** after him, is redeemed by a virtuous woman. Des Frans is brought back in large part by homesickness, which is to say that he aspires to rejoin the society he had renounced in his despair. His return is facilitated by the news that Silvie had not betrayed him as he thought; thus he can accept the obligation to marry Mme de Mongey. Even Des Prez and Des Frans find society more permissive than they had expected; Des Frans's mother recognizes Silvie, and apparently Des Prez's father regrets his fatal intervention, which had been based partly on ignorance of the facts. Their error, to the extent that they were wrong, was in mistrusting justice. When they finally bring their plea into the open, society proves reasonably flexible. Des Frans and Dupuis, however, jeopardize their chances for happiness by their intransigeant hostility to society.

None of the heroines ever adopts such a stance. All of them, in one way or another, demonstrate exceptional courage or initiative, which they must do in order to overcome tradition. In some cases, this struggle requires a very serious breach of propriety, or even law. The women never expect to remain outside the law, however. Mlle Fenoüil gets pregnant and arranges to be abducted, because she expects these misdeeds to force her marriage to Jussy. Angélique accepts the dubious arrangement Contamine proposes, only in the expectation that eventually he will acknowledge her and marry her. When by chance her reputation is compromised, she forces the issue immediately, preferring to give up her fiancé rather than forfeit all hope of normal social existence. The two women who reform Dupuis both preach patience and resignation; both endure loveless marriages and remain faithful. It is perhaps similar conduct on the part of Mme de Mongey that persuades Des Frans to risk another marriage. In any case it is obvious that all the women have faith in the ultimate justice of society—of *their* society. They will take risks, but they will not willingly abandon their chances to live within their society. Their heroism consists in knowing exactly the right dosage of obedience and resistance to maximize their chances for happiness.

Jussy undergoes the most dramatic confrontation with the law, as a result of Babet Fenoüil's insistence that he run away with her. Deloffre confirms that this was regarded as a capital offense.[7] On the face of it, Jussy has little hope; being a lawyer himself, he had explained to his fiancée that her youth, and his relatively lower social position and inferior wealth, would all be held against him, as presumptive evidence that he had acted out of self-interest. As he had predicted, the initial findings of the judges are unfavorable. Mlle Fenoüil herself saves him by appearing in court in person, by declaring that she had instigated the abduction, and furthermore by reiterating the threat of suicide which she had used to convince Jussy. Jussy remarks:

> les juges qui voyoient que je n'étois point si criminel qu'ils avoient cru, et qui peut-être étoient attendris par un spectacle si touchant, ou du moins bien convaincus qu'il y avoit beaucoup d'animosité dans mes parties, expliquérent en notre faveur la sévérité des loix. . . . Le Procureur du Roi lui-même . . . dit avec une intégrité de véritable magistrat: que le devoir de la charge l'avoit obligé de pancher vers la sévérité, mais que les circonstances qu'il venoit de voir l'obligeoient à réformer ses conclusions trop rudes; et il conclut plus favorablement pour moi (pp. 189-90).

Thus Challe, through Jussy, plainly expresses his trust in the ability of the judges to reach a just decision. Their office does not immunize them from human emotions and sympathy. I have commented already that the sentence seems, in

---

[7] Challe, *Œuvres*, p. 189n.

modern terms, very harsh indeed—Jussy is exiled for seven years and condemned to pay high expense and damage costs. The victims, however, accept the decision, and appear to agree that their previous action was wrong. Jussy, in fact, thought so all along. They then proceed to accomplish through laudable constancy what they had failed to gain by reckless impatience.

The most important court in *Les Illustres Françoises* is, however, the unofficial one composed of the storytellers and their friends. Mme de Contamine, by virtue of her condition as wife and mother, and her superior rank and wealth since her marriage, and perhaps also her heroic virtue before her marriage, holds the chief position. Her judgments have the greatest moral force. She pronounces the first opinion on Jussy's story, to wit: "Je sçai bon gré à Madame de Jussy; sa constance fait que je lui pardonne volontiers sa faute; en effet elle l'a lavée, et n'en est à présent que plus à estimer; quoiqu'on ne doive pas l'imiter" (p. 203). As the last reservation indicates, Mme de Contamine endorses the decision of the real court; they were right to condemn the act, but also right to allow the offenders the opportunity to redeem themselves. For the rest, Mme de Contamine demonstrates the surprising openness of this society. She had benefited from it herself when the princesse de Cologny suspected her of living a dishonorable life. Angélique's friend, Manon Dupuis, pleads with the princesse "de ne la point condamner sans l'avoir entenduë" (p. 109), and the princesse, despite the difference in rank and the weight of appearances, not only grants the hearing but takes some trouble to retract what she had already said.

To judge by his preface, Challe's main interest in writing was to teach a practical morality. Hence the real significance of the novel lies in the judgments of the group on the dissident members; for at the beginning, the bonds between them are weak and in danger of being destroyed. Des Frans has just returned from seven years' travels; Des Ronais has not spoken to his fiancée Manon Dupuis for months; Jussy has been in exile; Des Prez is blamed for the death of Mlle de

The Individual against Society

l'Epine. Des Frans threatens to break off his friendship with Des Ronais, unless the latter consents to hear Manon Dupuis's defense (p. 67); Des Ronais agrees, and later declares, "Je suis très persuadé de l'innocence de ma belle maîtresse" (p. 151). Jussy and Babet Fenoüil win admittance to the group. Des Frans learns of the extenuating circumstances in Silvie's infidelity, and accepts the proposed marriage with Mme de Mongey as a sign that he no longer distrusts all women.

Des Prez has been the victim of public gossip; Dupuis announces his story by rebuking Mme de Contamine: "Pour Mr. Des Prez, il est plus digne de pitié que de blame; et vous-même, Madame, qui lui faites son procès sur l'étiquete du sac, en conviendriez, si la vérité vous étoit connuë comme à moi" (p. 204). At the conclusion, Mme de Contamine does in fact retract; but her judgment contains a restriction, as it did with Mlle Fenoüil: "Je les plains aussi, mais je ne puis m'empêcher de dire, que presque toutes ces sortes de mariages faits à l'insçu ou malgré les parens ne sont jamais heureux" (p. 271). Challe himself moralized that the story of Des Prez "fait voir à quels malheurs une passion trop écoutée aboutit" (p. lx). In short, all of Challe's stories show a couple overcoming—if only temporarily—the obstacles that society raises against their love; all teach a morality that gives the individual the right to appeal from the superficial rules and prejudices of society; all insist at the same time on the basic soundness of society's rules and the means of their enforcement.

To any modern reader, Challe's optimism about his society seems excessive and ill-grounded. It would appear that in revising the common judgment, the characters apply a standard of constancy and sincerity, and for the most part their experiences suggest that society also will accept it. Yet there are exceptions. Des Prez's father never gives in, and his arbitrary power to intervene precipitates a disaster. Jussy and Terny were at the brink of a similar outcome. Angélique's reputation and Manon's marriage were jeopardized. The characters have survived with their integrity unharmed, but their faith in a system which so nearly destroyed them is unconvincing.

The characters are properly termed "illustrious" in the title; they owe their success to their heroism. They descend from the heroes of romance, whose actions provoke admiration but not imitation. Challe himself must have had doubts, and the interest of the novel lies partly in the tension between his expressed aims and his real feelings. I have suggested before that he had learned from Cervantes to profess a moderate wisdom even as he regretted the quixotic idealism of youth. In both the concluding stories, Des Frans's and Dupuis's, a relevant morality must find a pretext to tolerate inconstancy. Neither men nor women have it within their power to will themselves always to act as they think they should. This leads once again to a morality of resignation; one must not ask too perfect a happiness, but seize what conditions permit. Obviously, life will be easier if a person can avoid challenging the accepted ways of doing things. But this recommendation of conformity carries no implication that the conventional ways are good. Thus, in the experiences of Dupuis and Des Frans, Challe hints at a feeling which belies his stated credo. He can argue, with examples, in favor of society's ways; but his heart goes with the young men and women who are in revolt.

Gil Blas obviously differs from *Les Illustres Françoises* in several important respects. Lesage defines society more broadly than Challe and attempts to depict virtually all levels. Furthermore, Lesage writes as a satirist; even his most sympathetic portrayals often conceal a cutting edge of mockery. On the other hand, Lesage is generally acknowledged to have very little emotional power; one can hardly speak of his heart conflicting with his mind, because his heart plays so little part in his works. These differences are great enough so that on the surface the two novels appear to have almost nothing in common, but on a deeper level, the two authors share certain fundamental attitudes.

Gil Blas's Spain takes in a wide variety of characters from all sorts of professions. Gil Blas himself begins as the son of respectable but impoverished parents, in a small provincial town; he owes his escape from this situation to his intelligence, which manifested itself early and won him the protection of an uncle. After a brief contact with the highest—doña Mencia—and the lowest—highwaymen—elements of society, the young hero accepts a job as a servant and thus starts his long climb. He then moves from class to class, serving a canon, a doctor, members of the parasitic nobility, actors, two wealthy old nobles, a wealthy lady, and finally a worthy young nobleman, don Alphonse. The 1715 version of the novel ended at this stage, but Lesage clearly hoped that the novel's reception would invite an extension. The 1724 addition sends Gil Blas to serve an archbishop, several more noblemen, and finally the duc de Lerme; at this point he has become a secretary to the minister, has amassed a fortune, and possesses considerable power in his own right. Unfortunately, he has at the same time succumbed to the prevailing atmosphere of corruption, meant by Lesage as a satire on the Regency, which followed Louis XIV's death in 1715 and ended in 1723. Consequently, Gil Blas is disgraced at the moment when he seemed at the peak of success, and he returns to don Alphonse. In the final books, published in 1735, Gil Blas lives happily in retreat, marries, but loses his wife. He then returns to Madrid and regains his power as secretary to the comte d'Olivarès, this time conducting himself with honor. After twenty years, d'Olivarès falls from power, and Gil Blas again must retire, but in this case without punishment or regret. He returns to the country again, marries Dorothée, and has been living happily for three years as he writes.

With as complicated a society as this one, any generalization risks oversimplification. The enlightened élite are certainly more difficult to isolate and define in Lesage than they were in Challe. In the case of the duc de Lerme, it can fairly be said that the most powerful man in the kingdom exemplifies the worst morality. Many other "great" men turn out to be frauds, or villains, and many worthy men have difficulty getting their rightful rewards. Throughout much of the early part of the novel, before Gil Blas has completed his education, it appears that the forces of justice are unjust, the clergy are hypocritical, and the nobility are petty in all things. Their meanness contrasts with the candor and generosity of such insignificant people as Fabrice, Melchior Zapata, Scipion, even Laure and Raphaël. Lesage seems to regard this state of affairs as unnatural, however, although probably not uncommon. The evidence of numbers notwithstanding, don Alphonse emerges as the representative nobleman—humane, generous, just, and intelligent. His protection suffices to counteract the pressures of evil that Gil Blas has encountered elsewhere. Moreover, the duc de Lerme is eventually succeeded by the comte d'Olivarès, another worthy nobleman. Under d'Olivarès society recovers its equilibrium, and while one can not assume that evil and stupidity have disappeared, at least they are opposed by the forces of society. Over a period of time, then, if not at every moment, the enlightened élite tend to rise to the positions of power.

Challe's most interesting heroes oppose society because of some quixotic vision of their own; Gil Blas begins as a blank page. In some ways, he learns by a simple process of conditioning, rather than developing any deep understanding of moral problems. Sooner or later, his good deeds are rewarded and his bad deeds are punished; thus he learns to prefer good ones. Gil Blas himself oversimplifies in that manner, but of course he has to assign responsibilities somewhat arbitrarily. After his disgrace under the duc de Lerme, he concludes that the court itself is corrupting, and is actually pleased to be exiled from it.[8] Later Gil Blas tells don Alphonse: "Les biens ne sont propres qu'à corrompre mes mœurs. Je ne l'ai que trop éprouvé" (p. 1022). Further experience will show these lessons to be only partly true. Lesage has in fact made some effort to describe a genuine education, but Gil Blas lacks the introspective gift to bring it out. In Book One, the naive young man has wild dreams of wealth and glory, which make him an easy target for the deceptions of "Camille" and others. He actually gets what seems to him an enormous fortune, as a reward for saving doña Mencia, and just as promptly loses it. The implausible vicissitudes of the beginning serve to disillusion the dreamer, to

[8] *Romanciers du XVIIIe siècle*, Vol. 1, p. 1018.

teach him patience and caution. In Book Two, he has taken the first step down a more practical road, as a servant; and while he is still very innocent, he has learned at least to observe the world around him. The same process continues through Book Three, with the teachers becoming more and more elevated in society. In Book Four, Gil Blas finally returns to an active role. He makes some mistakes, such as believing that Aurore is in love with him, or that he can warn old Gonzale Pacheco, whose mistress is duping him. But these mistakes are neither shameful nor foolish, and Gil Blas recovers by his own initiative. At the end, he wins the friendship of don Alphonse by a spontaneous intervention. By Book Seven, he has acquired some sense of right and wrong, does good deeds as secretary to the archbishop, and is honest as Galiano's intendant. His basic nature, however, is still oriented toward wealth and ambition, as his service under the duc de Lerme soon proves. In the beginning, Gil Blas says: "Quoique ma droiture eût été si mal payée chez mon dernier maître, j'avais résolu de la conserver toujours" (p. 928). Gil Blas may think that he has made a moral decision, but in fact, as the concessive clause makes obvious, he expects to be rewarded. When the duc de Lerme offers him money for dishonest acts, the resolution is quickly forgotten, and all of Gil Blas's training in virtue is undone. Since Lesage is pulling the strings, vice does not hold sway forever; Gil Blas is disgraced, and in his fall he learns once again that his good deeds stand him in good stead—Tordesillas remembers an old favor, don Alphonse honors his obligations, and Scipion remains loyal since he has been well treated. Therefore Gil Blas sets out immediately after his release from jail to rectify his recent sins of ingratitude. The 1724 version closes with the hero on his way to his native village, where he plans to rescue his parents from poverty.

The last three books present the mature Gil Blas. The opening scene contains a surprise. Gil Blas retraces his steps, as he had planned, to his origins, ostensibly to help his parents, but his reception by his fellow villagers is hostile. Lesage suggests that Gil Blas has outgrown his origins and can not go back again. For a short time he and Scipion enjoy an idyllic life in retirement at Lirias, and they even take wives. But Gil Blas has to prove that he has acquired true wisdom, and this requires a return to the arena of his previous defeat. A change in the government brings the comte d'Olivarès to power, and Gil Blas goes back to Madrid, where he serves for twenty years as an exemplary public servant. All his mistakes from the first time are specifically corrected, for he regains the friendship of all those whom he mistreated before.

The lessons which *Gil Blas* teaches are the common virtues: honesty, gratitude, generosity, and patience. Lesage's conception of morality is so conventional that one may doubt whether he himself believed in it. The rewards which Gil Blas earns have no emotional content whatsoever; the love affair between Gil Blas and Antonia is surely one of literature's least interesting, and her death one of the least moving: "Que le lecteur conçoive, s'il est possible, la douleur dont je fus saisi! Je tombai dans un accablement stupide; à force de sentir la perte que je faisais, j'y paraissais comme insensible," writes the hero, ever alert for an antithesis, and by the end of the paragraph he is on the way to a recovery (p. 1112). The happy days at Lirias seem empty; Lesage plainly has nothing to say about them, although he reforms his estate along lines that could have prefigured Rousseau's Clarens, had Lesage been interested. Similarly, the concluding chapter presents the hero married a second time, and surrounded by his devoted family; but the best he says of his marriage is "Je n'eus pas sujet de m'en repentir," and of his wife, "Dorothée, en femme vertueuse, se fit un plaisir de son devoir" (p. 1197). Like many another moralist, Lesage found wickedness a more fruitful topic than goodness; and perhaps one ought not to regret his failure to invent the "style sensible" with its melodramatic displays of virtue triumphant.

Even though the well-schooled moralist in him remains dominant, Lesage quite evidently did feel the attraction of a less conventional view of morality, in which the outlaw is hero. Captain Rolando, chief of the band of thieves who capture Gil Blas in Book One, defends his style of life both in the

the cavern, and later in Madrid, where he has become an *alguazil*, or policeman. He tells Gil Blas, "Oh! je regrette mon premier métier. J'avoue qu'il y a plus de sûreté dans le nouveau; mais il y a plus d'agrément dans l'autre, et j'aime la liberté." He proposes to Gil Blas that they join another band together, and when Gil Blas refuses, Rolando leaves him, saying, "Je t'abandonne à la bassesse de tes inclinations." Although the hero chooses the safe life of conventionality, even he becomes a spokesman for the romance of the highwayman, telling Rolando: "Vous êtes né pour les entreprises hardies, et moi pour une vie douce et tranquille," as he declines the invitation (pp. 635-36).

If Rolando prefigures the Romantic outlaw hero, other characters point in equally promising new directions. The rascally Raphaël dupes Gil Blas in Book One, then turns up disguised as a hermit in Books Four and Five, the latter being entirely devoted to Raphaël's story. He claims to live by his wits, but since most of his exploits end in trouble for him, this pretension is hard to credit. What he does seem to have is inexhaustible charm and resiliency. Raphaël makes another fleeting appearance in Book Ten, as a *chartreux*, and finally in Book Twelve where Gil Blas happens to see him marching to his execution in an auto-da-fé. Raphaël's fate leaves no doubt about Lesage's opinion of his conduct, which Gil Blas confirms: "Le ciel, las des désordres de la vie de ces deux scélérats, les a donc livrés à la justice de l'Inquisition!" (p. 1157). Gil Blas also, however, feels a shudder of fear as he recalls how much he had in common with Raphaël and Ambroise, and the many adventures they had had together. Raphaël possesses none of Rolando's heroic qualities; rather he conveys a sort of human fallibility that is very appealing. His most immediate descendant would be Rameau's Nephew. His crimes seem unimportant because of his incompetence in committing them, and his criminal instincts are largely redeemed by his humanity.

Gil Blas accedes in his society's condemnation of both Rolando and Raphaël, and unequivocally prefers the ordinary way. His contacts with the criminals, and his lapses into crime, are unfortunate mistakes, for which he has paid by becoming better and where possible by righting his wrongs. Gil Blas runs afoul of the law twice himself. The first time, in Book One, he falls victim to a misunderstanding, and is imprisoned as a thief. Significantly, the prison is a much lower point in his still new career than his captivity in the thieves' cave. "Quand je songeais que je ne pouvais me tirer des griffes de la justice, bien que je n'eusse pas commis le moindre crime, cette pensée me mettait au désespoir. Je regrettais le souterrain," laments the prisoner. He is wrong, however; justice is eventually done after all, and he is released. There is a sharp irony in Gil Blas's account of his release: "Ils parlèrent en ma faveur au corrégidor, qui, ne doutant plus de mon innocence, surtout lorsque le chantre lui eut conté ce qu'il savait, vint *trois semaines après* dans ma prison. Gil Blas, me dit-il, *je ne veux pas traîner les choses en longueur.*" Furthermore, Gil Blas is set free with only an old sack to wear, but he says, "Je ne me plains pas de la justice; elle est très équitable; je voudrais seulement que tous ses officiers fussent d'honnêtes gens" (pp. 540-42; my italics). That seems to express Lesage's general attitude. The system of justice itself is equitable, but the men who administer it are subject to error and vice.

The second time Gil Blas finds himself in prison he has more or less deserved his punishment. The particular crime for which he is locked in the tower is not, however, his most serious offense. He has in fact been completely corrupted by the power and wealth he acquired under the duc de Lerme. His initial response is to fear for his treasure, and later he hopes to use the duc de Lerme's protection to be freed. The duc de Lerme replies cynically, but truthfully, that Gil Blas has been "justement châtié," whereupon Gil Blas takes sick, nearly dies, and does in fact learn the lesson (pp. 1014-15). Henceforth, he will have only contempt for wealth and glory. Once again, the system has served justice, even though the administrators were serving only their selfish ends.

Gil Blas's weakness as a novel stems to a great extent from the ambiguities of its point of view. Gil Blas, as a result of his own experiences, is an optimist. Insofar as Lesage manipulates his main character for the purpose of proving a point, one should assume that he too believes that more good than evil results from the system, that in the long run virtue succeeds, that the best men find their way to power in society. The subsidiary stories, however, often run counter to the central one. Raphaël especially parallels Gil Blas in many respects, but comes to a bad end; the difference seems to be a matter of luck. Laure is another whose ultimate unhappiness can be blamed as much on capricious fate as on her own doing, at least by comparison to Gil Blas; for in fact the two of them collaborate in making Lucrèce the king's mistress, not anticipating that the girl would die of shame. Yet the grief-stricken Laure retires to the convent "des Filles Pénitentes," while Gil Blas only makes practical application of the lesson:

> Je résolus d'abandonner pour jamais le caducée: je témoignai même au ministre la répugnance que j'avais à le porter, et je le priai de m'employer à toute autre chose. Santillane, me dit-il, ta délicatesse me charme; et, puisque tu es un si honnête garçon, je veux te donner une occupation plus convenable à ta sagesse (p. 1170).

The new task is to arrange for the minister to adopt his bastard son, the fruit of an old love.

Perhaps the narrator has a rosier view of society than the author. Lesage has not granted Gil Blas the intellectual or sentimental faculties to bring out the role good fortune has played in his life. Gil Blas persists in mouthing the platitude that virtue is charming, even when a minister detects it in one of his flunkeys; he apparently fails to see that it would have been far less charming if the minister had not had an immediate use for it. Consequently, the tragedies he sees leave no mark on him, not the death of his own wife and child, nor the death of Lucrèce, nor the execution of Raphaël, nor any other. They impress Gil Blas as acts of fate, and he never suspects that society itself might be corrupt. In giving up the career of royal pimp, he still prefaces his reform with "malgré la qualité de l'amant dont j'avais servi les amours," which is to say that he regards it as excusable for a king to debauch a virtuous girl and not even be moved by her death. Gil Blas's virtue goes no farther than to find that particular work distasteful and unrewarding. In many scenes, Lesage's satire strikes home, as he unmasks the pretense and hypocrisy of the great: in that sense, his reputation as moralist is fully deserved. Nonetheless, his weakness as a novelist is ultimately due to a failure as a moralist. His vision is too limited, and he never integrates his observations into a general moral pattern for society, nor does he ever challenge the fundamental morality of society itself.

Marivaux, Crébillon fils, Duclos: Disenchantment

Louis XIV died in 1715. For some thirty years France had been sinking into deeper and deeper gloom. The heyday of Classicism was long past, the power of the French armies had been checked, the treasury was strained to bankruptcy, austere piety and religious persecutions had replaced the festive court life of the 1660's, the common people were grumbling about the burdens of taxation and military conscription, and the old king spent his isolated last years in permanent mourning, for he outlived his entire family. The Regency released a lot of pent up energies; it was a period of turmoil, scandal, and excess, culminating in the financial, social, and moral disaster of the collapse of Law's Bank in 1719. When stability returned, a new Parisian society assumed a leadership which it maintained throughout the century. The old aristocracy remained at the top, of course; but outsiders from the world of finance and law had joined them, while men of letters and science mingled with them as well. In the 1730's Voltaire wrote, "Le paradis terrestre est à Paris," and for a time this opinion prevailed throughout France and most of Europe.[9]

The fourth decade of the century also witnessed one of the earliest flourishings of the novel. Major authors like Prévost and Marivaux produced their principal works then, while a

[9] This was the original last line of the well-known poem *Le Mondain*; Voltaire later replaced "à Paris" with "où je suis."

host of worthy minor novelists, of whom Crébillon and Duclos are the best known, were also active. Prévost's attitudes and themes have more in common with later writers, however, largely because of the influence he exercised on them. I have therefore preferred to postpone discussion of *Manon Lescaut*, in order to take up four other important works: Marivaux's *Le Paysan parvenu* (1734-35) and *La Vie de Marianne* (1731-42), Crébillon's *Les Egarements du cœur et de l'esprit* (1736-38), and Duclos's *Les Confessions du comte de **** (1741). All of them deal with the polite society of this era. Peter Brooks has written at length of these novels in *The Novel of Worldliness*. He defines "worldliness" as a system in which the primary value is an ordered social existence, and its literature is directed to man's self-conscious social behavior.[10] Brooks's description of the society itself, its historical and sociological roots, and his defense of the novel of manners, as opposed to nineteenth-century bourgeois realism, shed important light on the literature of the period. I believe, however, that he neglects the moral import of the novels; for despite their fascination with *le monde*, all the authors ultimately proclaim its emptiness.

In most respects, Marivaux, Crébillon, and Duclos understand much the same thing as Lesage and Challe by the term society. The same acceptance of structure and hierarchy obtains in all. In the novels of the 1730's, just as in the earlier ones, justice is eventually served, in spite of the obstacles. Thus the overall attitude can be called optimistic. The enlightened élite of the society, however, no longer seem to be at its centers of power. The risk runs high in every case that a selfish or bigoted person may abuse the rules for his own benefit, with an injustice as the result. The laws, too, seem more arbitrary and less flexible than previously. Most of the laws deal only with the preservation of the social order, which is to say with the propriety of marriages and social behavior. One mark of the élite is their willingness to abide by the spirit of the law, which is perceptibly different from the letter.

[10] Brooks, *The Novel of Worldliness*, p. 3.

Evolution of the French Novel

The earlier novelists described the hero's education, which fit him to belong to society. In the second group of novels, no education takes place in the proper sense. The heroes belong where they are by birthright, and they do no more than acquire the style of the society around them. Or, in the case of Marivaux, lacking the birthright the heroes demonstrate an innate nobility which leads them to act instinctively in accordance with society's rules. Both Challe and Lesage confront their characters with some moral choices about the values which they will adopt as their own; such choices play very little role in the later novels. The hero does not have to learn the correct choice; the sign of his nobility is that he makes the right choice without having to learn.

Brooks has outlined the value systems which constitute the wisdom of this society. Paramount are stability and order. The continuity of the bloodlines and the maintenance of status dictate the laws, and these values take precedence over individual rights. Within the system, the code emphasizes the art of living, especially one's public, social existence. The art consists primarily of symbolic interchange, through conversation and gesture; its goals are to keep one's own inner self as secret as possible, while discovering the secrets of others. Finally, the insistence on form and style itself becomes a force for stability, in that it enables the practitioner to escape the problems that beset others. This evasion holds good not only for the trivial and sordid details, but perhaps more importantly for the profound questions regarding man's fate—good, evil, happiness, pain, responsibility.

All of the major novels of this period use the memoir technique. The narrator is an old, experienced person, looking back at his youth. He is presumably an expert authority in the manners of society, but in most cases, as Brooks observes, the author simply assumes that the reader will understand the code of worldliness. All the novels relate the young person's progress through society, in the course of which there are many occasions for society to make a judgment. Marivaux utilizes very formal pseudo-courtroom scenes, while the others rely more on the informed narrator's analysis of a typical social situation. Since the plot leads to the hero's acceptance into society, or triumph within it, one can very easily take these social judgments for the moral emphasis of the book. Some account must be taken, however, of the persistent tendency of the old narrator to deprecate his past, to condemn the society, and to recommend withdrawal from it. The worldly heroes of the 1730's are a disenchanted lot. Moreover, they address themselves to an audience which they suppose to be disenchanted as well. Indeed, this disenchantment with the ways of society can be taken as the definition of the élite.

Marivaux published two parts of *Marianne* before beginning *Le Paysan parvenu*, then wrote all five authentic parts of the *Paysan* before returning to *Marianne*. It is thus somewhat debatable which one is first chronologically. I have chosen to speak first of *Le Paysan parvenu* for two reasons. First, it does precede the largest part of *Marianne*, which ran to eleven parts before Marivaux abandoned it, and furthermore *Marianne* borrows several episodes from the *Paysan*, which seems to have served as a kind of testing ground. Second, *Le Paysan parvenu*, of the four from this decade, also seems to me to be closest in conception to the earlier novels. Thus it permits the greatest continuity in the analysis.

The society through which Jacob moves has more range than Marianne's, although far less than Gil Blas's. Jacob starts as a prosperous peasant, meets at various times wealthy financiers, petty bourgeois, and nobility. The movement is always upward, and in the final scene of Book Five, he is on the stage of the Comédie Française, among the dashing young nobles who disported themselves there under the gaze of the elegant spectators. Even before that, however, he had been favorably received by attractive, though older, ladies from this worldly society. By and large, the powerful members of the society perceive Jacob's good qualities and reward them by ignoring his peasant origins. If M. de Fécour greets Jacob's generosity with a crude rebuff, the equally wealthy M. Bono stands ready to pay a proper, practical tribute to virtue. In Book Five, Jacob's impulsive courage brings him to the aid of the comte d'Orsan, who is not only the nephew of the prime minister, but "un des plus honnêtes hommes du monde."[11] He therefore feels no contempt for his rescuer's lowly birth, but, like the readers to whom the book is addressed, he appreciates Jacob at his true worth. He is thus distinguished from the "nombre de sots qui n'avaient et ne connaissaient point d'autre mérite dans le monde, que celui d'être nés nobles, ou dans un rang distingué" (p. 5). They belong to the same society, however, and abide by the same code, which normally would exclude Jacob from marrying at their rank, if not altogether from associating with them.

Jacob has a natural vocation to succeed in this society. At his first sight of it, he remarks: "Ce qu'on appelle le grand monde me paraissait plaisant" (p. 9). His actions from then on are primarily intuitive. As he expresses it, "Je n'étais pas honteux des bêtises que je disais, pourvu qu'elles fussent plaisantes; car à travers l'épaisseur de mon ignorance, je voyais qu'elles ne nuisaient jamais à un homme qui n'était pas obligé d'en savoir davantage. . . ." (p. 11). In just the same way, he senses that he stands to gain from telling his story to Mlle Habert (p. 44), and much later, when he helps the comte d'Orsan, it is "sans hésiter et sans aucune réflexion" (p. 251). His education consists entirely of testing and confirming his guesses: "Je l'épiai pour voir si je pensais juste," he says of his first compliment to Geneviève, and it is his standard procedure throughout the novel (p. 12).

The place he earns in the society belongs to him, if not by the title of his ancestors, at least by the good qualities he inherited. He does not rise as high as Marianne, for example, who writes as a comtesse; but her birth was mysterious, with a high probability of being noble. Jacob knows that he is a peasant, but, as he argues before the président, that is no dishonor. The only wisdom he claims to have acquired as a result of his experience is that of honesty. The opening remarks to the reader announce this as the moral of the story, and the

[11] Marivaux, *Le Paysan parvenu*, p. 257.

incident of his nephews, in which Jacob scolds them for their pretension, reinforces it (pp. 8-9). Although Jacob's candid confession of his lowly rank is repeated several times—when he meets Mlle Habert, for example, and with some reservations when he meets d'Orsan— Marivaux makes it the crucial element chiefly by means of the famous hearing before the président in Book Three. Jacob says in the beginning, of this frank confession, "[Les hommes] . . . trouvent qu'il est beau d'affronter leurs mépris injustes; cela les rend à la raison. Ils sentent dans ce courage-là une noblesse qui les fait taire" (p. 6). The application of the principle can be seen in his plea, for rather than deny the charges against him, Jacob admits everything: "J'allais être mendiant sans elle; hélas! non pas le même jour, mais un peu plus tard, il aurait bien fallu en venir là ou s'en retourner à la ferme; je le confesse franchement, car je n'y entends point finesse" (p. 132). To be sure, he counts on the impression his looks make, but his real defense is the truth. As he explains in the preface, his enemies are disarmed, and in particular, the jealousy and bitterness of the elder Mlle Habert are exposed. In the terms of the game of worldliness, Jacob has successfully pierced the mask of his adversary, by the somewhat unusual gambit of unmasking himself. Her motives are shown to be even baser than the ones she imputed to him, so that the président, "magistrat plein de raison et d'équité" (p. 123), must conclude: "Si tout ce qu'il dit est vrai, il ne serait ni juste ni possible de s'opposer à [son] mariage" (p. 133).

Jacob has to pass a sterner test immediately afterwards, when he picks up an épée in an alleyway, and finds himself charged with murder. Appearances seem to be against him, and the truth seems so preposterous that his lawyer fears for his life. Jacob's candor does not suffice in this case, but the real murderer confesses in time to save Jacob. The incident is not only quite implausible, it has little relation to the rest of the plot. Nothing depends on it once Jacob is released. One can only infer that Marivaux's basic faith in his society's justice prompted him to insert this test. In *Marianne*, a similar imprisonment will be used, but more logically it will be the consequence of her enemies' intervention. It will be followed by an unofficial hearing, like Jacob's, but one decision will encompass both justices, the personal and the public. Marivaux's conception of his society as ultimately good is responsible not only for the development of the plot, but also explains some of the troubling aspects in Jacob's character. The man who narrates has every reason to applaud the system that allowed him to succeed, and he quite naturally takes a tolerant view of his own sins. The incident he recounts in the beginning, where he berates his nephews for their pretensions and ingratitude, foreshadows the rising tide of *sensibilité*; the scene would fit perfectly into a *drame* by Diderot or a genre painting by Greuze. All seem repugnant today for their self-righteousness. No one would want to condemn an unsophisticated peasant for seizing every opportunity, even at the expense of others, like Geneviève, whom he exploits and abandons hypocritically, or like Mlle Habert, whom he betrays on the first day of their married life. Yet one is entitled to expect a bit more sensitivity from the older man than this remark on the money he took from Geneviève's prostitution: "Il y a apparence que Dieu me pardonna ce gain, car j'en fis un très bon usage" (p. 23). In other words, since it worked well for Jacob, it must have been right. A more complacent egotism is hard to imagine.

Jacob ignores the role that fate has had in his rise. Deloffre is justified in giving Jacob full credit for the bold and spontaneous gesture of coming to d'Orsan's aid; fate gave him the chance, but he recognized and took it. On how many other occasions, however, fate gets him out of difficulties of his own making! For his first master had given him the choice of marrying Geneviève or going to prison, and he is rescued from that terrible dilemma only by the timely arrival of his master's creditors. Similarly, Jacob had made an immoral bargain in accepting the assistance of Mme de Ferval and Mme de Fécour. Mme de Fécour falls ill opportunely, and Jacob's rendezvous with Mme de Ferval is embarrassingly, but fortunately, interrupted by a chevalier who knows them both. Marivaux never completed the story, but plainly indicated his intention of extricating Jacob from another dubious arrangement—his profitable marriage to the fiftyish Mlle Habert—by having the bride die conveniently. Even the moral lesson which Jacob presents most proudly as his own does not stand up. "Le titre que je donne à mes Mémoires annonce ma naissance; je ne l'ai jamais dissimulée à qui me l'a demandée, et il semble qu'en tout temps Dieu ait récompensé ma franchise là-dessus" (p. 5), writes the narrator as his first words; yet what sort of frankness is it, if he conceals his identity? "Pour mon nom, je ne le dis point: on peut s'en passer; si je le disais, cela me gênerait dans mes récits" (p. 7). It is only as a literary type that this peasant asks or obtains indulgence; amid all the memoirs of counts and marquises, the autobiography of a commoner might well meet some prejudice.

Jacob is a more puzzling figure than Marianne; her self-awareness is integral and her sense of identity unchanged almost from the beginning, whereas Jacob seems to be born out of each occasion, and never achieves much self-consciousness. Marivaux had given a brilliant first demonstration of how the narrator could be contrasted to her former self in the first two parts of *Marianne*; alas, this aspect of the work was little understood, and Marivaux gave it diminishing attention. It is lacking badly in *Le Paysan parvenu*. The young Jacob is an interesting character because he is disturbing, in his amorality, in his spontaneity, in his somewhat perverse sexuality. The conventional narrative device permits the reader to accept the account as authentic, but it is an unmediated version. The narrator brings no depth to the events, but effectively prevents Marivaux from offering his commentary. What Marivaux hoped to convey appears to have been the immediacy of the young man's experience, rather than the old man's nostalgia. He is on the whole very successful in portraying Jacob's battle to make his way upwards in society. The narrative technique imposes a second perspective, however, and Marivaux was surely aware of it. Of all the difficulties he had to face, this was undoubtedly the hardest to resolve—how to prevent the old man's wisdom from under-mining and dissipating the young man's verve, or conversely, how to prevent his uncritical complacency from distorting the moral tone. The latter is what in fact happens. Among the possible reasons why Marivaux abandoned the novel after the fifth part, his realization of this inevitable bad faith seems highly probable.

The composition and publication of *La Vie de Marianne* stretches over a full decade, and the last three parts—the long-awaited story of the nun—really form a separate novel. In my judgment, there is also a perceptible change in feeling within the story of Marianne; the first two parts, published in 1731 and 1734, display the same sort of gaiety as *Le Paysan parvenu*, while parts three through eight, dated from 1735 to 1737, are marked by a growing world-weariness, which the nun's story makes dominant. The comtesse de ***, the grown-up Marianne who narrates, is a sufficiently vivid personality so that the change in mood seems to indicate a subtle change in her opinion of the events; it is as if she understood, in retelling, how much her success had cost her.

The world in which she moves is a very closed society. The apparent diversity of "cette grande ville, et son fracas, et son peuple, et ses rues,"[12] which struck her at first, in fact hides a kind of public visibility and inevitable exposure as intense and oppressive as the court in *La Princesse de Clèves*. Marianne's first protector, M. de Climal, turns out to be the uncle of her first suitor, Valville, and the latter then turns out to be the son of her second protector, Mme de Miran. Despite the implausibility of this chain of coincidental meetings, the impact is felt; Marianne's instinct has led her into the most exclusive circles of her society. Even the lower-class characters contribute to this impression. Mme Dutour is a shopkeeper, but she seems to have as clients only the members of this same circle; for M. de Climal places Marianne with her, but Valville also knows her, and it is she who betrays Marianne at Mme de Fare's country house.

Within the circle there are important distinctions, however.

[12] Marivaux, *La Vie de Marianne*, p. 17.

The Individual against Society

Mme de Miran, Mme Dorsin, the minister and his wife, and Mlle de Fare demonstrate by words and actions the elevation of their souls. They belong to the élite which is capable of appreciating similar nobility in others and, what is perhaps more important, of detecting it when circumstances are misleading. On the other hand, the talkative and indiscreet Mme de Fare, the relative who instigates the opposition to Marianne's marriage, and Mlle Varthon, although they belong by birthright to the same society, show themselves incapable of real grandeur. The dissension takes on a far more serious aspect here than in *Le Paysan parvenu*. The elder Habert sister was moved by obvious personal motives, primarily jealousy. The relatives who attack Marianne do so on principle, although their fervor grows out of false pride. Yet pride is the unifying force of the society—Marianne has it to an extraordinary degree. The laws that the hostile relatives invoke and the power that they wield exist to maintain the purity and superiority of their élite. The injustice they almost perpetrate suggests a fundamental flaw, which Marivaux himself could not evade despite the timely arrival of Mme de Miran and Marianne's eventual triumph.

To an even greater extent than Jacob, Marianne knows the rules of behavior without having to be taught. In a famous passage on her first impressions of Paris, Marianne states: "Il y avait une douce sympathie entre mon imagination et les objets que je voyais. . . . Voyez si ce n'était pas là un vrai instinct de femme" (p. 17). Her first triumph occurs at the beginning of Part Two, when she wears her new finery to church; again, she says, "Et moi, je devinais la pensée de toutes ces personnes-là sans aucun effort; mon instinct ne voyait rien là qui ne fût de sa connaissance. . . ." (p. 59). According to Deloffre, Marivaux had not even included the church scene in the original version of Part Two. Marianne learns very little about others in the course of her adventures; rather she becomes aware of herself. The instinct to which she refers so often is not merely feminine but aristocratic. Mme Dutour and Toinette have none of it, although neither is a bad person. Marianne's place among the élite is deserved by her noble manner, but to her friends, this is just a sign of her noble birth. As Mme de Miran puts it "Il faut que cela soit dans le sang" (p. 329). Marianne does not win the right to her high station, for it should have been hers by birthright. By the same token, however, the narrowness of her escape from injustice indicts the arbitrary laws of society. If Marianne with all her qualities might have been sacrificed to a boorish Villot or locked up in a convent, the essential trait of nobility has plainly ceased to have substance, and has been reduced to mere form.

Marianne does avoid disgrace, and indeed she must actively prove her nobility on several occasions. Much of her manner depends on her tact and subtlety. The immediate communion between her and Mme de Miran is created by a mutual appreciation of what Marianne terms "secrètes politesses de sentiment," but among equals this secrecy is meant to be seen through: "Les gens qui ont eux-mêmes un peu de noblesse de cœur se connaissent en égards de cette espèce, et remarquent bien ce qu'on fait pour eux" (pp. 154-55). This is a classic example of the worldliness that Brooks describes, but on certain levels the player is pleased to lose. Marianne's ability to pierce Mme de Miran's mask signifies her acceptability in Mme de Miran's exalted society. It is not merely that Marianne and Mme de Miran are both women, either; a similar feeling marks the first meeting of Marianne and Valville. Marivaux admires the art of worldliness perhaps more than any other French novelist. The inference one would draw from the first parts of *Marianne* is that worldly manners function most effectively to enable the natural élite to know one another and to bar outsiders from their privileged communications. A great deal of Marianne's, or the comtesse's, chattery narration is devoted to analyzing the science of coquetry, which is the woman's role in the game. In Part One, she jokes about the science of placing a ribbon and picking the right color, saying, "Cela ferait peur, cela humilierait les plus forts esprits, et Aristote ne paraîtrait plus qu'un petit garçon" (p. 50). It is not only a joke, however. As Marivaux argues in *Le Cabinet du philosophe*, women have been prevented by men from exercising their intelligence and their strength in any more worthwhile enterprise; consequently they have devoted all their efforts to this more devious route to power, and the results might well astound the most brilliant male mind.

Marianne's greatest accomplishments depend on a different art, however, which is her intuitive knowledge of when to be sincere. Jacob employs a similar tactic, confessing the truth about his peasant origins to disarm his adversaries. Marianne carries the device a large step farther, in always confessing the truth when it appears most damaging to her hopes. Thus she has to tell Valville that she lives in Mme Dutour's shop; she has to tell the père Saint-Vincent that Climal is a tartuffe; she has to tell Mme de Miran that Valville loves her; and she has to tell the minister that she would rather stay unmarried than marry anyone except Valville. Her confessions always risk plunging her back into obscurity, but the group in which she moves comprehends the nobility of her gesture, and never actually requires the sacrifice. This willingness to forgo anything, where honor or loyalty demands it, becomes the sign of true nobility in *Marianne.*

The comtesse de *** differs from the mature Jacob in her reluctance to preach. As an authority, she reserves her commentary for the area of her expertise, namely, the arts of coquetry and the subtle analysis of the heart. Where moral questions are raised, she tends to undercut her own righteousness, by hinting that she might have acted from more than one motive, or that she half counted on the favorable outcome. Thus she appears to the reader very much as she claims to have done to her friends, charming, amusing, and agreeable. The moral lessons are implied by the events of the plot, and in particular by the two occasions when Marianne is put on trial by her society.

The first regards her arrangement with M. de Climal. Despite her rationalizations, to accept his largesse with full knowledge of his lustful intentions casts grave doubts on her virtue. Mme Dutour's suspicions in Part Two are justified; so is Valville's scorn when he finds Climal at her knees (pp. 45-

46, 129). The latter incident finally settles her resolve, and she proceeds to extricate herself from the relationship, not without risk, for Climal is her only resource. The père Saint-Vincent, a good but simple man, submits her to an interrogation before believing her story. Even then it is only the circumstantial details which convince him. By contrast, Mme de Miran is immediately disposed to lend credence to the story. In this first instance, Marianne's proud virtue is ultimately recognized by the enlightened persons of society, largely because of her tears, but partly because of her courage and candor.

The second trial, an obvious reworking of the trial scene in *Le Paysan parvenu*, poses more menacing obstacles. Under a strict construction, the code of society would not permit a foundling to marry a wealthy nobleman like Valville. Once again the climax builds from an embarrassing exposure: this time, Mme Dutour unwittingly betrays Marianne when she is visiting the De Fares. Mme de Miran pleads that the mystery of Marianne's birth, and her nobility of heart, justify treating her as an equal. The minister does not disagree, but he nevertheless follows a conventional wisdom in proposing to Marianne that she marry Villot or retire into a convent. Such a step would not dishonor her, but would avoid the financial misalliance. Marianne's own speech, in substance, merely consents to obey the minister; but Marianne paints her earlier resistance in such colors that it becomes an act of gratitude toward Valville, and she accedes to the minister's request of her own free will, as another expression of gratitude, to Mme de Miran. Her dilemma is a cruel one: the sole proof of her nobility consists in renouncing any benefit she might gain from it: "Il ne serait pas vrai que j'aurais le caractère que vous me croyez; et je n'ai que le parti que je prends pour montrer que vous n'avez pas eu tort de le croire." The minister then displays his genuine sense of justice, and rules: "La noblesse de vos parents est incertaine, mais celle de votre cœur est incontestable, et je la préférerais, s'il fallait opter" (pp. 336-37). The other relatives, except for the skinny lady who started the whole affair, concur in the judgment.

Up to this point, one could regard the whole work as a sympathetic portrait of society. Marianne's peculiar situation has entailed some dangers, but in the end the basic sense of justice has prevailed through the regular institutions. The plot, however, suddenly takes a surprising turn—Valville is unfaithful. The development forces one to reconsider the implications of what has gone before. The comtesse has known all along that Valville would be fickle; from the clues Marivaux has given, it appears that Marianne never marries him. She has dwelt on this futureless love story purely for its sentimental value, not because it led to anything. The pretext for her writing, to be sure, is the request of a friend; but the emphasis is all her own. It is evident, not only from the ultimate futility of this first love, but still more from the vividness of the memories and the fondness in the tone, that the comtesse is reliving a lost past. The result of her life in society has been the fragmentation of her identity and the impossibility of true feeling.

Valville's infidelity surprised and shocked the readers of Marivaux's day; it is true that the narrator has given little hint of it. The cooling of his ardor surely has its source in the very instrument of Marianne's triumph, however. Valville discovered Marianne as a stranger, a pretty face in a crowded church, a shopgirl with her first fine dress. The happy accident of her twisted ankle furnished him the chance to act, and he carried out his part admirably, by inviting Marianne home and later by tracking her to the convent where she had fled. Valville is manifestly a romantic type, for whom the mystery and uncertainty add charms. The very hopelessness of his love may have embellished it in his eyes. To have it sanctioned by his mother and the minister would be reason enough to reduce it to the humdrum and monotonous. How much more disillusioning would it be to hear Marianne's repeated affirmations that she will sacrifice him: ". . . le mariage qu'ils appréhendent entre M. de Valville et moi; c'est que jamais il ne se fera; je le garantis, j'en donne ma parole et on peut s'en fier à moi . . . "; "Peut-être est-ce ici la dernière fois que je le verrai, et j'en profite pour m'acquitter de ce que je lui dois . . . "; " . . . il n'y a qu'à donner ordre que je ne voie personne, à l'exception de madame, qui est comme ma mère, et dont je supplie qu'on ne me prive pas tout d'un coup, si elle veut me voir quelquefois. . . ." (pp. 335-37).

In short, although the minister and the assembled kinfolk nullified Marianne's promise and ostensibly gave her back her freedom, they had already forced her to accomplish the sacrifice. The spontaneous emotion that she and Valville felt for each other the day they met has no place in a society as prudent and proper as theirs.

Marianne says in the last part of the novel devoted to her own story that Valville's love for her would return. But winning him back has its own price, and it is the same as the price she paid before the minister: self-transcendence. Marianne refuses to acknowledge the blow her pride has suffered, but draws on all her dignity to become a new person: "Ce ne sera plus la même Marianne," she says (p. 377). That, however, is not just the necessary tactic to recapture a wandering fiancé; it becomes the very condition of Marianne's existence. She lives for others. As she remarks in the beginning, "Je savais être plusieurs femmes en une" (p. 51). What she does not know how to be is sincere, with herself even. The élite of souls like Mme de Miran and Mme Dorsin, for whom one's secrets are open, because they read your heart as well as you read theirs, is too small to fill a life. With growing anxiety, the comtesse realizes that in telling the first steps she has told the best of her life. The rest is all superficial, but destructive. There seems to be no way for that society to fulfill the promises of a tenderness like Marianne's and Valville's.

Marianne sets out to celebrate her joyous conquest of society, but in the course of her story she comes to realize that society has conquered her. Having reached this impasse, Marivaux launches an entirely new story, that of the nun Tervire. Although the story never reaches Tervire's taking of vows, what it does relate is the fate of a less fortunate Marianne.

Tervire's parents were noble, but her father died and her mother remarried. She ought therefore to have an easier time of it than Marianne, but her pride and magnanimity always go unrewarded, if indeed they do not get her into trouble. For example, the baron de Sercour offers to conclude their marriage, after a scandal has been exposed as a deliberately staged attempt to blacken Tervire's reputation. Tervire refuses him: "Je ne pus plus m'y résoudre. Il m'avait trop peu ménagée" (p. 483). Certainly no one could blame her for her feelings, although her decision leaves her once again without protection or resources. When Marianne made a similar decision in refusing to marry Villot, her proud choice of solitude contributed to the good opinion that the minister formed of her. No one, however, takes any notice of Tervire's pride. A still more striking case concerns the rehabilitation of Mme Dursan's disinherited son. Through an act of pure generosity, Mlle de Tervire persuades Mme Dursan to recognize him and his wife, thereby eliminating herself as Mme Dursan's principal heir. When Mme Dursan dies shortly thereafter, the newly acknowledged Mme Dursan the younger wastes no time in trying to revoke the provision of the will that left part of the estate to Tervire. The young grandson, who loves Tervire, has not got enough courage to contradict his mother. Tervire thus loses everything, at least temporarily, as the recompense of her generosity. In the final scene of the book, Tervire is trying to help her mother out of a similar difficulty —her daughter-in-law no longer wishes to recognize her; the mother had herself once abandoned Tervire for similar causes. One can only speculate about what further misfortunes would befall her, leading to the decision to bury herself in a convent. One thing at least is clear: in Tervire's story, Marivaux no longer trusts society to recognize merit and carry out justice.

Both Crébillon's *Les Egarements du cœur et de l'esprit* and Duclos's *Les Confessions du comte de **** are set entirely within the highest circles of society. Duclos, who writes as a self-conscious moralist, sends his hero on a tour of Parisian and European bedrooms, so as to present a picture of all levels of society. Crébillon writes more probingly, while limiting his scope to the rather small society that the hero Meilcour might have known. Except for the range of characters, this society, which Meilcour calls *le monde*, differs very little from that of Marivaux's novels, or even Challe's. The male hero is free to pursue conquests in circumstances that would dishonor a woman, but Valville assumes this same liberty. It is a society whose only function seems to be to amuse itself. The days are filled with visits, promenades, tête-à-têtes, rendezvous, theatre-going, and excursions to the country. It is the realm of pure worldliness.

Since both Meilcour and the comte are destined by birth and wealth to enter this world, neither novel has occasion to explore the sort of protective rules which Marianne and Jacob challenge. Instead, they portray the society in operation, analyzing in meticulous detail the methods of success and the implications of such a life. Both narrators are masters of the worldly arts, and have full authority to offer such a general description. Crébillon, however, also introduces the prestigious figure of Versac, who delivers a lengthy discourse on the techniques of success in *le monde*. Generally speaking, Versac's rules are ways of maintaining the mask, as Brooks has said. Everything depends on absolute control of appearances.

Nevertheless, both novels address their message to a different group from the active members of society. The moral élite is not made up of Versac's disciples, but rather of virtuous and even solitary people. Meilcour's story is one of *égarements*, after all, and it is clear that Versac is responsible for many of them. The preface speaks of the hero as "un homme plein de fausses idées, et pétri de ridicules, et qui y est moins entraîné encore par lui-même, que par des personnes intéressées à lui corrompre le cœur, et l'esprit."[13] As Meilcour repeats Versac's long discourse on society, he calls

[13] *Romanciers du XVIIIe siècle*, Vol. 2, p. 11.

it "une conversation qui n'a que trop influé sur les actions de ma vie" (p. 150). The preface promises that the conclusion will show Meilcour "rendu à lui-même" by an estimable woman, and while this ending was never written, the most estimable women in the novel—Mme de Meilcour, Mme de Théville and Mlle de Théville—all condemn Versac. *Les Confessions du comte de **** does describe the comte's reform under the influence of the virtuous Mme de Selve, and the narrator begins by denouncing *le monde* in comparison to his retreat: "Cette tranquillité, ou, si vous voulez, pour m'accommoder à vos idées, cette espèce d'insensibilité est un dédommagement bien avantageux, et peut-être l'unique bonheur qui soit à la portée de l'homme" (p. 199). A few individuals have attained a state of enlightenment which not only exceeds the wisdom of society but in fact contradicts it.

Vivienne Mylne has accurately observed that the stated moral of *Les Egarements* is belied by the stress that the narrator lays on the supposedly ridiculous behavior.[14] In the same way, the comte's voluminous reminiscences about his mistresses subvert his stance of finding that career odious. This does not necessarily mean that the authors are insincere; it suggests that they had imperfectly understood the effect of their techniques. The reader tends to identify with the point of view of the narrator, and develops sympathy for Meilcour and the comte no matter how foolish or callous their behavior. They have unfortunately reconstructed their pasts, so that the reader shares their pleasure in becoming "un homme à la mode," a rival to Versac. While this is informative about the workings of society, and is not formally implausible, it works contrary to the conclusion. The sort of disillusionment Duclos and Crébillon sought to describe will be greatly facilitated by the revival of third-person narration, so that the study of society can be made from a different point of view from that of the hero, namely the omniscient author's. It requires an extraordinarily complex—Proustian—manipulation of narrator and narrative to fit such a story into the memoir form.

[14] Mylne, *The Eighteenth-Century French Novel*, ch. 7.

The novels of the 1730's led more immediately to a better usage of the simple first-person technique. The disenchantment of the narrators, including Marivaux's nun and even Marianne, prepared the way for the next step, in which the hero or heroine is genuinely alienated from society. Duclos's comte, even as he praised the provincial life, understood why the younger man to whom he addressed his confessions should still find pleasure in society. Certainly none of these characters would have challenged the concept of society in the beginning; Meilcour and the comte accepted it as their destiny, Marianne, Jacob, and the nun aspired to it as the sign of their nobility. When they had been through it, they had a sense of emptiness, and a thirst particularly for authenticity. Real passion, real danger, real virtue, and even real vice grew in appeal. The next wave of fictional heroes did not wait until old age to discover what had been missed. They demanded their rights to their personal vision of happiness from the very start, and in so doing challenged the very bases of society.

Prévost, Voltaire, Rousseau, Diderot: Criticism

It was obvious to many people long before mid-century that the glories of French civilization rested on a precarious foundation. The luxurious life of the Parisian high society contrasted too brutally with the misery of both peasants and the urban poor. Discontent was widespread, and occasionally erupted into violent disturbances. All was not well at the top, either. Unscrupulous financiers and prostitutes acquired immense fortunes, and they, along with many members of the old nobility, abused the privileges of their position by giving free rein to their worst appetites. The ethical principles which had formerly sustained the aristocracy disintegrated. More and more, the polite manners and discreet language masked vulgar tastes and crude actions.

The interest in high society that had marked the novels of the 1730's flickered out around 1740. One major reason was surely the ban on the publication of fiction, promulgated in 1737; the respectable novelists were more affected than the pornographers and hacks. The 1740's and 1750's were, more-over, relatively barren decades for French fiction. The new generation of authors who came to prominence in those years brought a new orientation to literature, and they dominate the eighteenth century. Diderot and Rousseau both achieved success around 1750. Voltaire had been famous for thirty years, but his writing shifted around 1750 from an emphasis on poetry and tragedy to a concern for social, political, economic, and moral problems—what the eighteenth century summed up under the term "philosophie." These men were all primarily critics of society. They took themselves very seriously, and all of them expressed contempt for the novel, still widely regarded as a frivolous genre. Nonetheless they all eventually wrote at least one novel; and I will consider as a third group Diderot's *La Religieuse* (ca. 1760), Rousseau's *Julie, ou la Nouvelle Héloïse* (1761), Voltaire's *L'Ingénu* (1767) and Prévost's *Manon Lescaut* (1731).

No one will be surprised to see Voltaire, Diderot, and Rousseau grouped together. The addition of the abbé Prévost requires some explanation. His major fiction was written during the 1730's, and from 1740 to 1760 his chief occupation was translating. Moreover, he died in 1763, at the moment when the *philosophes* were just beginning to utilize the novel. Chronologically, he is a precursor, and in fact his influence on the *philosophes* was very strong, although this fact has been little recognized. Jean Sgard's recently published *Prévost romancier* goes a long way toward restoring some historical perspective on Prévost's importance in his own time. Rousseau was particularly indebted to him. *Les Confessions* relate his intense reaction to *Cleveland*, and his later friendship with Prévost, whose works he calls "dignes de l'immortalité."[15] *Cleveland* was in fact one of the first truly philosophical novels, dealing with the hero's spiritual quest, and Sgard has also illuminated the similarities between Pré-

---

[15] Jean-Jacques Rousseau, *Les Confessions et autres textes auto-biographiques*, ed. Bernard Gagnebin and Marcel Raymond, in *Œuvres complètes*, Vol. 1, Bibliothèque de la Pléiade (Paris: Editions Gallimard, 1959), pp. 220, 374. Hereafter cited as Rousseau, *Confessions*.

vost's painful solution of his own spiritual crises and Rousseau's solution as he presents it in *La Profession de foi d'un vicaire savoyard*, for example, one of the major documents of eighteenth-century deism. Before Rousseau, Voltaire had been a friend of Prévost's; in 1740 the abbé had to flee from Paris to Brussels, and Voltaire was one of those who helped him. Voltaire would not have attached much value to Prévost's novels, but the parody of them in *Candide* makes it plain that he read them. What Voltaire, and also Diderot, could appreciate in Prévost was his reporting on English affairs in *Le Pour et contre* during the 1730's, and his editing of the *Histoire générale des voyages*, an encyclopedic compilation of travel accounts from which the *philosophes* drew freely. Diderot likewise never admitted any liking for Prévost's fiction and accused him of ruining Richardson's novels in translating them; but Diderot had read them enough to parody them in *Jacques le fataliste*.

In short, Prévost was considered the major French novelist of the eighteenth century by his contemporaries. Despite a growing scholarly interest in him, his works do not appear likely to regain much favor with the general public today. Only the one acknowledged masterpiece, *Manon Lescaut,* has kept its audience. I have therefore limited most of my remarks to it, but the general tendencies of this third group of novelists characterize many more of Prévost's works. He really initiated the theme of the individual in open conflict with his society. In all the novels examined until now, the hero or heroine was working to enter society. Prévost's heroes usually belong to society by birth, as do Crébillon's or Duclos's; but they find their personal vision of happiness incompatible with the behavior that society demands of them.

Society, still defined basically as the uppermost levels of the Parisian aristocracy, appears in this group of works as corrupt, unjust, and destructive. The close inspection of conversation and manners gives way to anger and bitterness about the broader implications of the system that fosters such triviality. The official institutions of society are explicitly called to account, notably the Church and the various branches of the police. The freedom enjoyed by the comtes de ***, the Meilcours, the Mariannes, even the Jacobs, is bought by the sacrifices of others, whom the novelists had complacently ignored—at least until Marivaux brought Tervire into the story. The novels of the later period focus on the repressive laws that protect the freedom of the aristocracy and maintain its stability. These laws have the sanction of opinion within the society; an authority figure, usually a parent, actively solicits enforcement, while the rest of society tolerates it by silence. The actual enforcement, however, is carried out by social institutions, the police and the Church, which ought to serve all people equally, but which in reality protect the few by oppressing the many. Such, at least, is the picture that emerges from these novels. The laws are made to seem extraordinarily arbitrary, with little or no relation to any humane function. They are brutal instruments of power. Enforcement seems harsh and rigid. The flexibility which Challe attributed to the court in Jussy's story disappears altogether; the authorities in these novels are rather more disposed to seize on technicalities and give the benefit of any doubt to the prosecution, than to exercise restraint or show mercy. Needless to say, the general coincidence of high rank and enlightenment that prevailed previously has gone as well. The élite who share the hero's point of view are now dispersed and powerless. One can almost say that the author's sympathy for a character increases in proportion to the character's distance from Paris—Prévost's American savages, Rousseau's Swiss, Voltaire's Bretons and Huron, Diderot's sequestered nuns.

All of the novels considered heretofore have centered around some form of education; the story ends, or would end, when the hero attains sufficient wisdom to settle into his proper place in society. The plots of the third group are more pessimistic. The hero believes that reason, if not custom, ought to make the place he wants available; and on the whole the reader must share his point of view. Custom and the law oppose the hero, however, and he struggles vainly to overcome them. The authors view the outcome with varying degrees of sadness, but the one result that seems impossible is a happy ending. In every case, the heroine dies, and only this tragic emancipation can permit the hero to contemplate his experience with some detachment and reconcile himself to failure.

As in many eighteenth-century novels, the moral position of the author is not clear in the four I am treating as attacks on society. The Man of Quality, who introduces *Manon*, and even Des Grieux at the end of his story, affirm their allegiance to a fairly conventional sort of moral code. Yet Des Grieux tells his tale without hindsight, investing his criminal love with all its original seduction; despite his return to his senses, his indulgence for his past sins is virtually limitless. Similarly, Rousseau's conscientious rehabilitation of Saint-Preux and Julie has never impressed readers as strongly as the lyrical opening, when they fall in love, and the following two parts, where they fight to hold each other in the face of the baron d'Etange's opposition. Voltaire's *L'Ingénu* is ambiguous because of the characters' being caricatured at the start; the somber tone of the ending comes as a shock. Diderot's identification with Suzanne's point of view is almost complete, although of course he did not personally espouse her piety. In all four cases, however, the author's sympathy plainly does not go to the representatives of conventional morality. Where the author shades his moral lesson away from the hero's beliefs, it is always in the direction of some intermediate, often idealized character, such as Tiberge or Wolmar.

Each individual speaks for a different moral cause, but they all share a common orientation. For all of them freedom becomes a desperate need, in both a physical and moral sense. Three of the four are actually confined, two are exiled. Self-discipline and self-denial, which Marianne practiced instinctively, offer no salvation to these later heroes. What Marianne accepted as an ennobling sacrifice seems now to be an intolerable punishment; and what Marianne appreciated as an art of living seems now to be a stifling regimentation. The specific elements of the free existence follow the same pattern. Except for Suzanne, all of the major characters find passion a positive force. It causes great disorders, but its very strength is a sign of their nobility. All of the characters respond favorably to sincerity, indicating their general weariness with the artificial politeness and highly formalized structure of society. For Rousseau this need ran deeper perhaps than any other, and led him to doubt all the symbolic structures of civilization including languages. Obviously, the aspirations of these heroes reflect the growing vogue of *sensibilité*, and look forward to the eventual explosion of Romanticism.

Des Grieux and Suzanne continue the tradition of pure first-person narration. In both cases they tell their story in part as a plea—in Suzanne's case, it has even been suggested that Diderot consciously modeled his style after the legal rhetoric of the day. Rousseau adopted the epistolary form, an extension of first-person narration, which permits multiple points of view and suspenseful plotting. There is actually rather little contrast between the points of view of the letter-writers. The baron d'Etange, who plays the role of obstacle, writes only one letter, of less than a page; Julie's mother never writes at all. These three novels thus make their point through direct subjective involvement. Voltaire seems to have begun *L'Ingénu* with designs like those behind *Candide*—the similarity of the titles is no accident. He thus employed the third-person omniscient narration to which he was accustomed, and of which he was master, selecting points of view with subtle malice so as to bring out the humor in the situation. In the last third of the work, however, his tone became more serious, and the narrator's identification with one point of view—Mlle de St. Yves's—became more consistent. Furthermore, Voltaire made extensive use of quoted dialog, so that both the hero and Mlle de St. Yves speak quite lengthily for themselves. Voltaire, however, has already moved in the direction which Diderot was to take. As I will show in the final group of novels, the criticism began to exceed the confines of plausibility and discretion, so long as a rationalized first-person narrator had to be provided. In *L'Ingénu*, it is already evident that Mlle de St. Yves would never, under any circumstances, relate the details of her rape by St. Pouange. In order to reveal such private tragedies, novelists had to return to third-person omniscient narration.

By contrast to the ever-present and articulate hero's voice, the spokesmen for conventional morality appear foolish, when they are not brazenly cynical or hypocritical. Furthermore, their moral authority is regularly undermined by their conduct. M. de G . . . M . . . is an excellent example of this; his rage at Manon's thefts and trickery rings hollow from a man who was luring her into whoredom. Voltaire delights in placing absurd reasoning in the mouths of his enemies. Even Rousseau adopts this technique, inasmuch as the one letter from the baron d'Etange is offensive in tone and quite lacking in reason. A last refinement consists in having the persecuted hero defend the system that causes his suffering; all the characters do this to some extent. Besides the sympathy they gain for moderation, their interpretation of convention is certain to include some criticism.

Once again, the conflict between individuals and society appears in sharpest focus when the hero or heroine is judged by the "proper" authorities. In some form or other, a judgment is rendered in all four of these conflict novels. The technique remains essentially unchanged from previous uses, but now the verdict is always guilty. Furthermore, the courts make no effort to justify their decision, other than to refer to the law; the kind of interpretation which Jussy described is absent, and leniency of course is out of the question.

By every standard, the chevalier des Grieux belongs to the highest ranks of society. His appearance immediately impresses the marquis de Renoncour, who thereby certifies his nobility to the reader. His manner further ingratiates him, and ultimately he tells Renoncour that "mes parents . . . sont d'une des meilleures maisons de P."[16] Des Grieux goes so far as to remind G . . . M . . . of the difference in blood between them: "Apprends que je suis d'un sang plus noble et plus pur que le tien" (p. 153), retorts Des Grieux, caught in several acts at once and threatened with hanging: he means that he

[16] Prévost, *Manon Lescaut*, p. 17.

will have the honor of decapitation instead of the noose. Although Des Grieux belongs to an élite group outside of this society, in most respects his attitude resembles that of everyone in it. By and large, everyone Des Grieux meets is bebauched, power-mad, and unscrupulous. Old G . . . M . . . is the worst; his own lechery drives him into the deal he makes with Manon, and from that point on none of his moral indignation has much weight. Old G . . . M . . . , however, learns no more lessons about himself than Des Grieux does; far from accepting the loss of his money and the blow to his pride as a chastisement of his lust, he abuses his power to get revenge on Des Grieux and Manon. He has them arrested as "fieffés libertins," not criminals, surely as bold an instance of hypocrisy as one could wish for (p. 78).

Old G . . . M . . . is presented in the worst light; not only is he corrupt and hypocritical, he is also inept and credulous. For all that, he does not differ greatly from any of his contemporaries—Monsieur de B . . . , the governor of New Orleans, or Des Grieux's own father. All of them are very tolerant of peccadillos. Des Grieux's father even proposes to supply his son with a mistress as a consolation for the loss of Manon, following his first escapade: "Tu aimes les jolies femmes. Je suis d'avis de t'en chercher une qui te plaise. . . . Je t'en chercherai une, qui ressemblera à Manon, et qui sera plus fidèle" (p. 37). As this passage indicates, and as the governor's crude intervention shows of him, all men of this generation use arbitrary power without compunction, in order to have their will done. The younger men, Synnelet, young G . . . M . . . , M. de T . . . , and Des Grieux himself, are described with much greater sympathy; but it should be recognized that they behave no differently from their fathers. Their disregard for law is virtually complete; their egotism is unmarred by any sense of the rights of others. Toward the end, Des Grieux argues to his father that he has done no worse than "les deux tiers des honnêtes gens de France," and he is right (p. 163). In recognizing his moral kinship to this corrupt society, however, he does himself no credit, and indeed weakens his claim to a separate moral status.

Des Grieux's father seems to be disturbed by only one element in Des Grieux's conduct: the possibility that he might marry Manon and dishonor his family; and the rest of society agrees with him. All the other crimes, not excepting the murder of the porter at Saint-Lazare, are forgivable. Consequently Des Grieux's father and old G ... M ... agree on Des Grieux's release and Manon's shipment to New Orleans. Compared to Des Grieux, Manon is relatively innocent, moreover; had she committed his crimes—stealing, cheating, and the like —she would have been dealt with much more harshly. A bizarre inversion of values has occurred, so that the only significant moral law of this aristocracy commands that it preserve its exclusivity. Des Grieux's casuistry reflects the moral confusion of the times; he is not the only one who considers the satisfaction of his ego an absolute moral good. That is in fact the ethic of his class.

Des Grieux, however, claims to belong to an élite distinct from the social élite. He does not escape from their sin of pride, but he does pay allegiance to a still higher principle: love. Des Grieux plays the sophist with his pride and honor, claims his privileges when it seems convenient and dispenses with his obligations. With his love, on the other hand, he maintains absolute integrity. His own safety does not concern him when Manon is in prison. He refuses to share Manon's favors, or to take another woman as a temporary substitute, although this arrangement could solve their financial difficulties. He willfully refuses a chance to escape from destiny's trap when he persists in freeing Manon or following her to America. As late as that, none of his actions was irremediable, on the sole condition that he renounce Manon. His constancy in this illicit passion wins him the sympathy of the marquis de Renoncour, the hero-narrator of the *Mémoires et Avantures d'un homme de qualité qui s'est retiré du monde.* Renoncour has known passion himself; without condoning Des Grieux's misdeeds, he nonetheless accepts Des Grieux's belief that only the elect feel such passions. As he prepares to sail to the New World, Des Grieux imagines that the savages will share his respect for love: "Ils suivent les lois de la nature. Ils ne connaissent ni les fureurs de l'avarice, qui possèdent G . . . M . . . , ni les idées fantastiques de l'honneur, qui m'ont fait un ennemi de mon père. Ils ne troubleront point deux amants qu'ils verront vivre avec autant de simplicité qu'eux" (p. 180-81). This fantasy never meets the test of reality, but serves to show the sources of Prévost's thinking.

One other character earns inclusion in the special class of men of feeling: Tiberge. His pursuit of Des Grieux is as relentless as Des Grieux's attachment to Manon, and for most of the book seems to be as hopeless. It appears from the vignette at the head of the 1753 edition, that Prévost intended the novel to show a battle between sacred and profane love. That is to say, for Prévost the moral of the story lay in Tiberge's eleventh-hour victory, since it is he who gets credit for Des Grieux's return to the path of virtue: "Je lui déclarai que les semences de vertu qu'il avait jetées autrefois dans mon cœur commençaient à produire des fruits dont il allait être satisfait" (p. 204). Many critics have observed that the long descriptions of his profane passion make much the stronger impression on the reader, notwithstanding the author's purposes. Even within his concept, however, the parallel between Tiberge and Des Grieux proves how unorthodox his moral idea was. Des Grieux's persistence of course is rewarded too; in the end his devotion wrests a kind of repentance from Manon. Perhaps Prévost did not mean to go so far as to suggest an equivalence between Nature, Tiberge's God, and human passions, in spite of Des Grieux's habit of attributing his actions to "le Ciel." It seems beyond question, though, that he regarded the purity and tenacity of their sentiments as a bond between Des Grieux and Tiberge, as one of the reasons by which Tiberge knows Des Grieux can be saved and is worth saving, or, in short, as a sign of election for both.

Des Grieux differs from other heroes in that his announced goal in life is to enter the priesthood. Before that, his family had destined him for the Knights of Malta. As a younger son, Des Grieux is less privileged than Meilcour or the comte de * * *, but obviously better placed than Jacob or Gil Blas or Marianne. He does not complain of his family's plans, however, and after his first flight with Manon his father, as I have noted, offers to procure him a girl. Des Grieux appears to have appreciated the power and distinction that an intelligent man could obtain within the Church. When he leaves for Paris to study at Saint-Sulpice, he believes that his vocation is sincere and that his personal ambitions will be amply fulfilled. Certainly every evidence suggests that his natural ability would have smoothed any path for him. His diligence and brilliance win him a wide reputation within a year at the seminary. In short, Des Grieux possesses the personal qualities necessary for success in any of several areas, and chooses the priesthood: his family possesses the rank and means to support any of several choices, and his father lets him choose freely. Des Grieux has no problems about entering society.

He runs afoul of social convention, however, as soon as he makes his love for Manon more important than his duties. These duties are few enough and easy enough; he could even have Manon, if she would be content to follow him. Des Grieux takes the language of fatal love literally, and thereby alienates himself from his contemporaries. Des Grieux commits the unpardonable sin of comparing his feelings for Manon to his father's feelings for his mother. One can hardly disagree with Des Grieux's father in his outrage, or with readers like Montesquieu who dismissed Manon as a whore. By every normal standard, Manon is unworthy of the fidelity Des Grieux vows to her and keeps. She betrays him repeatedly, and exposes the vulgarity of her upbringing in many other things. Des Grieux has to fight two battles at once: on one side he endeavors by persistence to overcome Manon's amorality, and on the other he struggles by hook and crook to survive long enough in society to save Manon.

He wins the first battle, but loses the second. Manon finally responds to his dogged loyalty, and in New Orleans she is purified. Humility forbids her to ask Des Grieux to marry her in a legal ceremony, but she gladly consents when he suggests it. After the governor's refusal, she insists on sharing Des Grieux's fate, as he had shared hers. This last gesture leads to her death. There can be no doubt in those final moments that her motives are honest; she has nothing material to gain from following Des Grieux into the wilderness, but it is her decision. The second battle seemed to have been won when Des Grieux went with Manon to America. The conditions in the colonies abolished the false pride that kept them from marrying in Paris; the men in New Orleans were apparently only too happy to have prostitutes to marry. Yet the remnant of society represented by the governor and the chaplain suffices to destroy them. It is not pride or avarice, but simple egotism that brings on the disaster. Synnelet never thinks to consult Manon, and the governor consults neither justice nor the people involved, before his authoritarian order to Manon to marry Synnelet. The net effect of the plot is to justify Des Grieux's obstinacy and to condemn society's intolerance. A wiser and more virtuous society would appreciate the moral excellence of such a passion.

Yet society repeatedly calls Des Grieux before the bar of justice, hears his plea, and condemns him. Prévost conditions the reader's reaction to this in the first scene, where Des Grieux and Manon are already in the hands of the archers. Nevertheless, the populace is favorably disposed toward them, and the marquis de Renoncour confirms their good opinion. The archers, whom society has charged to carry out its sentence, reveal their greed and churlishness. Thus the prevalent mood is favorable to the outsiders and hostile to the established authorities.

Des Grieux's first real conflict with the law arises from his duping old G . . . M . . . . As was often the case in reality, Des Grieux and Manon spend two months in prison on the mere complaint of G . . . M . . . ; no trial or hearing takes place. Des Grieux hypocritically pretends to be penitent, thereby winning the good will of his jailor, the superior at Saint-Lazare. This kindly father might with some justice be cited among the élite who are responsive to Des Grieux's passionate nature. In any case, the superior tells Des Grieux that his release depends upon the consent of old G . . . M . . . , and the young prisoner, under the misapprehension that G . . . M . . . has locked him up only to possess Manon undisturbed, listens respectfully to a sermon from the old lecher—until he learns that Manon is in prison too. Subsequently, having assaulted old G . . . M . . . , Des Grieux tells the superior his own side of the story, with the result that the jailor intercedes for him with the lieutenant general of police. His efforts produce this outcome: "Cependant, lorsque je lui ai appris le fond de vos affaires, il a paru s'adoucir beaucoup, et riant un peu de l'incontinence du vieux M. de G . . . M . . . , il m'a dit qu'il fallait vous laisser ici six mois pour le satisfaire" (p. 88).

The situation resembles the verdict against M. de Jussy in *Les Illustres Françoises*; but the hero's attitude has changed greatly. Jussy gratefully welcomes the opportunity to gain by patience what he had failed to get by vigorous action. Des Grieux is reduced to despair by the thought that Manon may languish in her cell for another six months and he resolves to execute his escape plan. Des Grieux's resentment is related to a second important difference; Jussy's adversaries were moved by greed, perhaps, but they were neither criminal nor hypocritical like old G . . . M . . . . It is very difficult to see why justice requires that G . . . M . . . be satisfied. Des Grieux really analyzes the entire situation when he tells the superior: "Il a eu le crédit de me faire ici renfermer, par un pur motif de vengeance" (p. 86). "Crédit," or arbitrary power, is the only effective force in society.

After Des Grieux's second arrest, again at the hands of old G . . . M . . . , the lieutenant-general of police more or less says the same thing: "Il me dit . . . que j'avais manqué de sagesse en me faisant un ennemi tel que M. de G . . . M . . . ." The judge indeed strikes Des Grieux as another very reasonable man, and once again he feigns humble regret for his crimes in the hope of shortening his punishment. The magistrate responds by assuring Des Grieux that "il était disposé à me rendre service, en faveur de ma naissance et de ma jeunesse." As Deloffre remarks, "On voit assez l'indulgence de l'époque à l'égard des jeunes gens de famille" (p. 160). But for all his indulgence, the magistrate turns a deaf ear to Des Grieux's plea on Manon's behalf. He, Des Grieux's father, and old G . . . M . . . reach an accord, as Deloffre puts it, "sur le dos de Manon," who will pay by imprisonment or deportation for the assorted crimes of actual or would-be lovers. The legal system is evidently at the service of power, and has no regard for justice or morality. The egotistical morality which Des Grieux founds on passion does not arise to challenge the traditional Christian code, or even the more worldly aristocratic code, but rather it is born into a moral vacuum.

Even in the New World Des Grieux comes into conflict with the law. There the basis of the social order is exposed even more nakedly. When Des Grieux goes to plead his case before the governor, the old man repeats the same two answers over and over: "Manon, me dit-il, dépendait de lui; il avait donné sa parole à son neveu" (p. 194). The final irony is that the society which has persecuted the couple for two years, and driven Manon to her death, then accuses Des Grieux of murder and puts him on trial for it. Despite his innocence, it appears that only Synnelet's generous solicitation of grace prevents Des Grieux from being convicted.

Prévost thus consistently presents the legal system in a bad light. Officials openly admit that justice belongs to the most powerful, and that different standards of conduct are applied to different people, Manon bearing the heaviest burden. The presence within this system of several good administrators—the superior, the lieutenant-general, and to a certain degree, Des Grieux's father, M. de T . . . , and Synnelet—only makes its corruptness the more appalling. These sensible men are powerless to halt the ruthless exploitation of the courts and the police for selfish ends. In this context, much can be forgiven Des Grieux. To be sure, his own moral code is replete with egotism, hypocrisy, and inconsistency. Still he makes some effort to accept responsibility for another, be it only Manon. His egocentrism does not extend to letting her expiate for his sins. Rather, he presents his passion as the anguished struggle of a human soul to be true to itself in an environment where only appearances count.

Virtually all of Prévost's novels deal with the individual trying to live his own truth against society's opposition. To an alarming extent, their vehement pleas for sincerity ring as false and as hypocritical as the badinage of the best society. In many cases this can be blamed on one central misunderstanding: Prévost's heroes (and no doubt Prévost himself) try to analyze their feelings in society's terms. Des Grieux, like Des Frans with Silvie, genuinely loves Manon, to the point of accepting all her faults, including those which hurt him—her infidelities, especially. Yet Des Grieux is the dupe of his own rhetoric; he expects happiness to follow from his constancy. Manon herself fails to comprehend his literal faith in love until the very end. After her third betrayal, she claims that she thought he was angry at being mocked, not at being betrayed. Manon's attitude is much more conventional than Des Grieux's. No one else in the novel places such importance on physical fidelity; it is amusing to note that Manon sends a replacement for herself when she goes to young G ... M ..., just as Des Grieux's father had proposed the first time. No one else interprets fidelity as such an integral commitment of the self to the other. No one else prizes constancy so highly. Des Grieux's understanding of his emotions is based on these romantic, novelistic qualities. By a heroic persistence, he compels a small part of reality to fit his quixotic vision. Manon's death, however, intervenes soon enough to make his victory a brief and ambiguous one. Other Prévostian heroes emerge from their experiences more deeply confused.

The clearest example is no doubt *L'Histoire d'une Grecque moderne* (1740). The narrator-hero has bought a slave-girl, whom he frees and educates, only to fall in love with her without her reciprocating his feeling. One can easily see the possibilities for irony and pathos in this situation. A modern reader is likely to be staggered, however, by the blatant bad faith of the narrator, who at the same time applauds himself for instilling virtue in Théophé and plots by guile and force to deprive her of it. In his moments of keen desire, the hero thinks of love as the language and practice of his time defined it: conquest and possession. Yet the desire itself was stimulated by her autonomy. The social solution to this age-old dilemma of passionate love, under the code of Prévost's time, consisted in preventing these passionate matches from becoming permanent. Men were free to pursue their conquests and enjoy the fruits of victory, but only outside marriage. Although there were numerous celebrated cases of courtesans who ruined wealthy men, to do so entailed some risk, as *Manon* indicates. For the most part, the elevated language of love masked a game whose consequences, all emotional, were treated as trivial by the eighteenth century. Prévost's characters seek the right to take the language of love seriously, and to follow the dictates of passion as far as human capacity allows, either to self-annihilation or to self-transcendence. The concepts of this courtly style of love fit badly into the real exigencies of life in many cases. The financial problems which beset Des Grieux and Manon from the outset symbolize this underlying conflict between an inherited ideal and a practical possibility. The sort of love that Prévost's heroes dream about can not be realized without some further exploration of its context; more provision must be made for the vagaries of the other; human propensities to change must be acknowledged; and the physical conditions of existence must be accounted for.

In *Cleveland* Prévost raises the problem to its highest level, and poses the philosophical question of what happiness man can find on earth. Cleveland adopts and rejects virtually all the intellectual systems man has devised to help him be happy. The conclusion is an ambiguous return to religion. Cleveland meets the same problems in love that other heroes do; he demands a fidelity he can scarcely practice himself, and discovers his happiness slipping away from him as the circumstances change imperceptibly. Prévost is of two minds: his intellect continues to scan the systems and dictate conformity to the traditional wisdom of resignation, while his heart revolts and demands the freedom to find its individual happiness. Vacillations between the head and the heart give many of Prévost's characters the appearance of bad faith, but it is probably more accurate to say that they try to do the impossible, and explain their entire past in the terms of their present perceptions, admitting no alterations.

Des Grieux is an exceptional instance of perseverance, at

least where his main object is concerned. In all situations and to the bitter end, he never betrays Manon. One could not recommend his beliefs, nor even his method of searching. It is not clear, either, that Prévost had a fine sense of the moral import of all that he wrote. What Prévost has provided is a painfully honest portrait of a man with a conscience in a society without one. As often happens when the moral structure of a society collapses, the first stirrings of a new morality occur among the outcasts, and the first voices to speak out sound subversive and are suppressed.

Rousseau experienced life much as did Prévost's heroes. His mind and also something deeper and more emotional, a kind of cultural memory, were haunted by notions of permanence, unity, and stability, while his senses told him that everything changed and his heart delighted in the most absolute freedom. In all his autobiographical works, the anguished contemplation of his own modifications and the desperate affirmation of an underlying coherence preoccupy him. "Le bonheur est un état permanent. . . . Tout change autour de nous," he writes in the beginning of the ninth *Promenade*, summing up the inevitable paradox of existence which seemed to many men of his time to render happiness impossible. In *Les Confessions* he notes, " . . . pour me connoitre dans mon age avancé, il faut m'avoir bien connu dans ma jeunesse," expressing the faith in his own integrity which all the autobiographical works attempt to communicate to the world at large.[17]

Rousseau's novel, *Julie*, treats the same theme. In an even more lapidary formula than the one just quoted from the *Confessions*, Saint-Preux writes to Milord Edouard, "Je sens qu'il faut avoir été ce que je fus pour devenir ce que je veux être."[18] Rousseau approaches the problem with more philosophical method than Prévost, whose fictional heroes most often draw up the sorrowful and confused balance sheet of

---

[17] Rousseau, *Confessions*, pp. 1086, 174.

[18] Jean-Jacques Rousseau, *La Nouvelle Héloïse*, ed. Henri Coulet and Bernard Guyon, in *Œuvres complètes*, Vol. 2, Bibliothèque de la Pléiade (Paris: Editions Gallimard, 1964), Part 5, Letter 3, p. 557.

The Individual against Society

a life that failed. Rousseau conscientiously designs a plan of rehabilitation for Saint-Preux, by which the passions of youth become the virtues of maturity. At its most profound, then, *La Nouvelle Héloïse* is a conflict of cosmic dimensions, man against time. As in any novel, however, the conflict is played out in a real context, and here the more banal theme of man against society appears again: the first obstacle to Saint-Preux's imposition of his selfhood arises from the arbitrary class distinction between Julie and her lover. Moreover, like most of the eighteenth-century thinkers, Rousseau's philosophy dealt with practical reforms: political, economic, and social. The rehabilitation of Saint-Preux occurs within a specially structured social environment, created by M. de Wolmar and Julie in the utopian estate of Clarens. Saint-Preux's conflict with society is terminated by his entry into a new society.

Parisian society is relegated to a secondary position by Rousseau; all the important action takes place in Switzerland. Nonetheless Saint-Preux visits Paris, and his first line to Julie offers an instructive contrast to the first impressions of Marianne and Jacob: "J'entre avec une secrètte horreur dans ce vaste desert du monde."[19] He observes the principal elements of social life, dinners, salons, the theatres, and succumbs to the pressures of a perverse public opinion in going to a house of ill repute. His celebrated criticisms of all that he sees make up the greater part of his correspondence to Julie in Book Two. Needless to say, he leaves with his worst premonitions confirmed.

It would appear, however, that Saint-Preux is defeated not by Parisian society, but by the anachronistic pride of the Swiss nobility, represented by Julie's father, the baron d'Etange. Everyone else in this privileged corner of the world, from the noble Englishman Lord Bomston to the baron's hand-picked son-in-law Wolmar, including Julie's mother and cousin, deems Saint-Preux a suitable husband for Julie. Why then should the baron alone hold such bizarre prejudices? Julie provides the answer: "Mon Pere, qui a passé

[19] ibid., Part 2, Letter 14, p. 231.

sa vie en France ne parle qu'avec transport de ce bon et aimable peuple."[20] Even the baron is a fine person except for his corrupt French manner of thinking; in the later part of the novel, with the threat of a misalliance gone, he is sincerely reconciled with Saint-Preux, who becomes his preferred hunting companion.

Despite his moral isolation, the baron can call on terrible powers of enforcement, for he commands absolute obedience under the very code of virtue which Julie and Saint-Preux profess to abide by. More compelling still, he has the natural right to Julie's filial respect and love. No one contests his authority to decide on Julie's husband, which was a matter of legal prescription: thus he had no need of police, like Des Grieux's father or Valville's family. Faced with some dissent, the baron resorts to brute force and beats his daughter, but Julie's natural virtue is such that she marvels at her father's touching embarrassment when he calms down, feels guilty, but is too proud to ask her forgiveness. In like manner, he threatens Saint-Preux with a beating, if he does not leave. Yet for all his physical superiority and legal authority, the baron is capable only of preventing what he does not want: he can not force Julie to marry against her will. In the crucial confrontation, she protests against his tyranny for the first time in her life, saying that he was "maitre de ma vie, mais non pas de mon cœur."[21] The baron responds typically with anger and mistreatment, to no avail. At last, however, he weeps and falls to his knees, and thus obtains from Julie's virtuous affection what he could not from his exercise of authority. It is the same social pressure, nonetheless. Julie's soft heart is not so moved by many others—beggars, for example, or Lauretta Pisana—even though they have good claims on her charity and have never brutalized her. Julie—and Saint-Preux as well —believes in an authoritarian society and considers herself duty-bound to obey. Her father's desperate appeal by tears, seemingly to her free generosity, in fact serves to remind her that authority is benevolent and that obedience is good.

[20] ibid., Part 2, Letter 18, p. 259.
[21] ibid., Part 3, Letter 18, p. 348.

The Individual against Society

Saint-Preux's entrance into Julie's society is not recounted. He was of lower birth, and came as a tutor; but his merit wins him the right to equality. Julie transforms this equality from a tacit recognition to a source of inescapable conflict, by her vow to marry no one but Saint-Preux. This personal commitment resembles Des Grieux's in many ways, although Julie's is incomparably riskier in such a society. The first half of the novel tells in three stages how the conflict arises, how it bursts into the open, and finally how society conquers the lovers.

As I have already said, Rousseau sought to discover a transcending solution. After the defeat, with Saint-Preux sailing around the world and Julie married to another, the couple is reunited under new circumstances, and a way is found to divert their passionate and egotistical energy so as to make them and society better. The mechanism for this terrestrial salvation lies in a peculiar form of self-denial. When it can be accomplished in pure freedom, it exalts the person who denies himself, so that in the end more is gained than is lost. The same mechanism underlies the political theory of the *Social Contract*: when the individual will submerges itself in the general will, a new entity is created greater than the sum of its parts, and every individual feels magnified by the new spirit, be it patriotic fervor, *esprit de corps*, or mob hysteria. Just so, Julie and Saint-Preux gain a sense of enlarged purpose by submitting to the will of the baron d'Etange and then of Wolmar. The secret of making this mechanism work is in affording the individual that precious instant of pure freedom to make the right choice without coercion. As Rousseau remarked of himself, " . . . Pour bien faire avec plaisir, il falloit que j'agisse librement. . . ."[22] Wolmar's trick for rehabilitating Saint-Preux consists of giving him these moments of freedom—some might say temptation—so that he may experience the uplifting emotion of his own virtue.

Wolmar's and Julie's social organization encompasses a great many people, including servants and children. The structure is undeniably authoritarian; the master and mistress

[22] Rousseau, *Confessions*, p. 1052.

regulate everything, sometimes in such a devious manner that they seem not to. What justifies this is that they have the best interests of everyone at heart, and that by and large they obey their own regulations, thereby setting a good example. The unblemished perfection of the operation marks it as a utopian vision, although it has substantial contacts with reality. One must note, however, the basically static nature of Rousseau's plan. Even the staff of servants almost never changes. The dream of the little group is a self-sufficient isolation; they are reluctant to extend their happiness to the world outside, and have no need of what the outside might furnish them. This equilibrium is obviously precarious, and Rousseau himself sensed it. The charm of passion derives partly from its movement; it promises exhilarating change. For a time, perhaps a very long time, the new exhilaration of virtue could serve the same purpose, but the old temptation would never disappear completely. Julie's last letter confesses that her virtue depended on a daily reassertion of control, and that she was not sure she could have continued forever. As has been pointed out before, the novel gains in stature what the system loses in persuasiveness. The artist Rousseau could not eliminate what he perceived or felt to be the truth, even if it undermined the moral lesson he was preaching.

Because of the nature of the Swiss society Rousseau describes, and because of the lesson he hoped to teach, no actual trial scenes occur. Instead, all the various members of the élite continually pass judgment on each other. Only Julie, after her marriage, attains a position of unquestionable rectitude. In their relationships, her say is final, just as she may overrule Wolmar's firing a servant, while her own dismissals are irrevocable. Wolmar ranks second in the hierarchy; his one flaw is a lack of religious faith. He brings a sense of order and reason to complement Julie's sentiment and spontaneity. Wolmar becomes the chief judge of Saint-Preux's conduct after his return from exile, and arranges the test situations where Saint-Preux discovers the pleasures of virtue. Claire and Bomston participate in the discussions, although Bomston in particular has had his own difficulties. It is Claire who bestows the glorious pseudonym "Saint-Preux" on the otherwise nameless hero, and Bomston who guides him through his exile. Near the end, Saint-Preux himself assumes the role of authority, and sends Lauretta Pisana into a convent to prevent her marriage to Bomston—a bit of benevolent despotism applauded by all, even Bomston.

These self-congratulatory displays of virtue belong to the utopian side of the novel, however. The truth of how justice was administered is contained in the baron d'Etange's angry reactions to every effort made on behalf of justice and reason. His speech to Julie following the beating he gave her makes it clear that the ordinary application of the law was based on the whims of authority, not justice:

> Vous savez à qui je vous destine; je vous l'ai déclaré dès mon arrivée, et ne changerai jamais d'intention sur ce point. Quant à l'homme dont m'a parlé Milord Edouard, quoique je ne lui dispute point le mérite que tout le monde lui trouve, je ne sais s'il a conçu lui-même le ridicule espoir de s'allier à moi, ou si quelqu'un a pu le lui inspirer; mais, quand je n'aurois personne en vue, et qu'il aurait toutes les guinées de l'Angleterre, soyez sûre que je n'accepterois jamais un tel gendre. Je vous défends de le voir et de lui parler de votre vie, et cela, autant pour la sûreté de la sienne que pour votre honneur. Quoique je me sois toujours senti peu d'inclination pour lui, je le hais sur tout à présent pour les excès qu'il m'a fait commettre, et *ne lui pardonnerai jamais ma brutalité.*[23]

Rousseau's description of the authoritarian mind still rings true; its own failures and deviations from principle can somehow be blamed on its recalcitrant subjects.

Unlike *Manon*, where justice is equally absolutist, irrational, violent, and partial to rank, *La Nouvelle Héloïse* has its characters submit to authority. Nevertheless Rousseau's novel is as thoroughgoing an attack on society as Prévost's. As all readers have sensed from the beginning, the author's sym-

---

[23] Rousseau, *La Nouvelle Héloïse*, Part 1, Letter 63, p. 177. My italics.

pathy plainly goes to the lovers, not to the father. As I pointed out before, the father is allowed only one letter in the collection, and a notoriously offensive letter at that. Even in announcing their reconciliation, Saint-Preux objects to the baron's prejudices. By contrast, the growth and consummation of the love affair is detailed in some fifty letters in the first part alone, to be followed by the pathetic separation and eventual heroic renunciation of the two lovers. Finally, as noted before, Julie admits in the end that, in spite of virtue and in spite of her experience, the flames of passion still burned within her; and her last letter is for Saint-Preux. Not to belabor the obvious, the novel clearly makes illicit love seem justified in this case, and makes society's laws forbidding it seem capricious, anachronistic, and unjust.

Furthermore, the solution proposed by Rousseau involves a radical reconstruction of society. Saint-Preux discovers the rewards of virtue only because the godlike Wolmar arranges the proper choices for him. In reality, as Rousseau well knew, the tendency was exactly the opposite; all the constraints of civilization worked to deprave the character and make virtue disagreeable. In the same *Promenade* where he confessed that he could not enjoy doing good except in freedom, he states in conclusion: "Je n'ai jamais été vraiment propre à la societé civile."[24] That describes the author in real society; in the fantasy world of the novel, the hero finds a society to his own liking. For pages and pages he describes the minutest details of life at Clarens—the house, the furniture, meals, gardens, crops, servants and all their problems, children and all their problems, holidays, amusements—the list is endless, and every item carries a reproach to the existent society of Paris. Like Prévost and like the other *philosophes*, Rousseau holds to an idea of reason and virtue that conflicts with society's. In the first half of his novel, the hero battles with society, and is defeated; but the defeat signifies the intensity of the author's condemnation, not the outcome he advocates. The concluding half of *Julie* is the wish-fulfilling daydream of a brilliant philosopher, not a novelist's depiction of society.

[24] Rousseau, *Confessions*, p. 1059.

The Individual against Society

La Religieuse was probably Diderot's initial work of serious fiction, although precise dates can not be established for most of his works. It is generally thought, however, that *La Religieuse* began as a hoax, invented to lure the marquis de Croismare back to Paris from Caen, in 1760. Furthermore, allusions to the work in progress appear in Diderot's letters at about this time. And finally, it was about this date that he read Richardson's *Clarissa* in the original, and became a convert to the genre, an event signaled by the *Eloge de Richardson*, published in 1762.

Diderot's ambitions contrast somewhat with those of Prévost and Rousseau. In particular, Diderot undertook to eliminate what many regarded as the very soul of a novel, namely the love story. The heroine, Suzanne, modeled after a real person, is seeking nothing more than the right to decide her own fate, in a society which offered a girl the choice between *le monde* and a convent. Suzanne, for reasons that are obscure, but probably because she is the offspring of an adulterous affair, is denied even that much choice, and is forced to take vows. This is still Parisian society, but one of its dark corners. One of Diderot's objectives was to show that the convent was not the retreat it should be; too many frustrated women had no other place in which to satisfy their cravings for power, wealth, celebrity—all the ambitions one might find in *le monde*, in other words. Moreover, since the convent society was so closed and unnatural, the manifestations of these drives tended to be more extreme than in the world. The evils of society are magnified by claustration. The possessors of power and authority differ only slightly from those in the outside world; the mother superior has an immediate position similar to a father in the family. Beyond the walls, the Church hierarchy and the state support the mother superior's autocracy, as they do the father's—and indeed, since it is ultimately Suzanne's family who demand that she be a nun and who oppose the dissolution of her vows, her situation in society is no different from Des Grieux's or Julie's. In all cases the laws serve power, not justice; the reasonable pleas of the individual have no force.

Suzanne's allies against the tyranny of society share the ideals of the Encyclopedists, principally their faith in reason. Diderot deliberately refrains from appealing to the sentiments, as Prévost and Rousseau did. Suzanne grounds her case on her basic human rights. Unfortunately, only a select few in her society are sufficiently enlightened to recognize these rights, or at least to defend them. The most important of these few is the lawyer Manouri, but again Diderot has carefully placed some of them within the Church, so as not to expose his bias. Several nuns, including a mother superior, sympathize with Suzanne, and the vicar's staff order that she be treated more justly. None of them goes so far as to attack the system itself, to be sure, nor for that matter does anyone but Manouri actually support Suzanne's attack. The novel purports to be a memoir addressed to the marquis de Croismare, and there is an open appeal to men of reason outside the novel.

As has been observed several times before, in *Marianne* and in *Les Illustres Françoises*, a girl trying to make her way into society had a far more difficult task than a man. Although the legal rights of men were severely limited until their maturity at age twenty-five, at least society put some value on their initiative and audacity, and tolerated their misdeeds. Girls were supposed only to obey their parents, especially their fathers, because wives were supposed to obey their husbands, too. For a girl of good family, marriage to a proper husband or the convent were really the only options. Men had the army and the priesthood as well as the monastery, and for the typical fictional hero, finance and business were possibilities. One might also include adventure overseas. Since Suzanne's parents do not wish to marry her, society has little place for her outside the convent. Consequently, her refusal to take vows, and her desire to have them resiliated when she has been cowed into taking them, place her in very sharp conflict with society, even though she poses no threat of misalliance, like Des Grieux or Julie. To a society as authoritarian as that of eighteenth-century France, any staunch insistence on individual rights constituted a minor menace, by disturbing the prevailing order and setting an undesirable precedent. Suzanne's specific request would further endanger the existing order by granting her a special status outside the normal categories.

In spite of Diderot's precautions, like creating sympathetic churchmen and insisting on Suzanne's piety, the moral thrust of *La Religieuse* has been commonly misunderstood. It does not attack religion, nor even the eighteenth-century French Catholic Church. Georges May has conclusively argued this point in *Diderot et la Religieuse,* and I need not dwell on it now. Suzanne asks for the freedom to choose her own way of life. Society denies her that right. The Church is implicated to the extent that it collaborates with her family and the state in holding her a prisoner and in coercing a decision from her. As Diderot is at pains to show, however, this is the work of misguided individuals within the Church and is opposed by other spokesmen for the Church. The situation can be compared to that in *Manon Lescaut,* where the jailors and magistrates were, on the whole, men of good will and even feeling; but that could not stop the implacable machinery of society from crushing Des Grieux and Manon. The same thing happens to Suzanne; although she finds eloquent defenders and sympathizers even among her adversaries, they can not deter the application of the general social law. Diderot obviously wrote *La Religieuse* to plead the cause of individual rights against society's demands.

Since Suzanne relates her story as part of a request for aid, her side of the case is everywhere in evidence. She is a model defendant, in that she has no selfish motives (such as an inheritance or a lover), seeks to harm no one (such as her more favored sisters), and does not even accuse her tormentors. Her whole complaint is that she can not force herself to do what is required of her: "Ah! quel sort! être religieuse à jamais, et sentir qu'on ne sera jamais que mauvaise religieuse!" she confides to her lawyer, and she continues: "J'ai envié, j'ai demandé à Dieu l'heureuse imbécillité d'esprit de mes compagnes: je ne l'ai point obtenue, il ne me l'accordera pas."[25] She is the victim of a sort of alienation, and while the causes are social, Diderot focuses on the person suffering. The arguments of her oppressors are never articulated. Being a prisoner, Suzanne never confronts her sisters, and in fact she usually does not know whether her defense is being pushed or not. The only representative of the other side to whom Suzanne speaks directly is the sadistic superior, Sister Sainte-Christine, at the beginning of her suit. Suzanne explains with lucidity her reasons for the suit, but the only response she gets is, "Que dira le monde! Que diront nos sœurs!" (pp. 288-89). Obviously the fear of scandal is the superior's only consideration. Suzanne comments on the failure of Manouri's first *Mémoire* to suggest that similar qualms prevail within the courts "où les contestations de la nature de la mienne sont toujours regardées d'un œil défavorable par l'homme politique, qui craint que, sur le succès d'une religieuse réclamant contre ses vœux, une infinité d'autres ne soient engagées dans la même démarche." Suzanne summarizes the *Mémoire*, which was a long tirade against convents and forced vocations; but when the decision is finally reached, she says only: "Mon affaire fut plaidée à l'audience et perdue" (pp. 310-12).

The Archdeacon Hébert serves as judge in the series of interrogations about the administration of her convent. As Suzanne describes him, he is an "homme d'âge et d'expérience, brusque, mais juste, mais éclairé" (p. 296). His questioning is simple and to the point; Suzanne's answers are humble and honest. The guilty mother superior attempts to interrupt, but Hébert imposes silence. Before the evidence of her guilt—Suzanne's stripped cell—she claims to have been unaware of the persecutions, but Hébert is not fooled. His final judgment is: "Vous êtes indigne de vos fonctions; vous mériteriez d'être déposée. . . . Cela est horrible" (p. 309). Hébert does not express an opinion regarding Suzanne's lack of vocation, although the subject comes up during her interrogation; his attitude is: "C'est aux lois à décider cette affaire; et de

[25] Diderot, *Œuvres romanesques*, p. 316.

326

quelque manière qu'elles prononcent, il faut, en attendant, que vous remplissiez les devoirs de la vie religieuse" (p. 307). Suzanne agrees, and the presumption of individual responsibility to accept the penalty until the court decides otherwise probably reflects a fairly enlightened view of justice. In the convent, however, Hébert's verdict may be ignored; he has to return later to re-interrogate Suzanne, and in the interval she has not been well treated.

Against her will, Suzanne goes to court once more, at the insistence of her friends at Saint-Eutrope, to reclaim her dowry from Longchamp. This decision, significantly, marks the end of her happy days in the new convent. The contestation requires that new *Mémoires* be published; those on the other side calumniate Suzanne. The cordial relations she has had with most of her companions begin to deteriorate, as the rumors spread about her past. There is no actual link between this event and the superior's breakdown, but just as she had said, on leaving Longchamp, "Un bonheur ne vient point sans un autre," now she says "Mais une peine ne vient jamais seule" (pp. 327, 364). Her new superior is a lesbian, and at the behest of her director, Suzanne refuses to associate with her. The superior slowly loses her mind, the mood in the convent fluctuates wildly, until at last the superior tells her confessor, "Mon père, je suis damnée. . . ." (p. 383).

All the nuns are damned in Diderot's opinion, even those who chose the veil of their own free will; the oppression of some contaminates the entire society. Thus Suzanne tells the story of a girl who was obliged to wait six years before being allowed to take her vows; yet her director abused her docility by asking her to spy on her superior, who found out and drove the poor nun insane. The spying, the persecution, the jealousy, the hatred, and the insanity are fostered by the atmosphere of repression. Suzanne shows remarkable tenacity in maintaining her sanity, but she is the innocent cause of disorders in others. The lesbian superior is the most obvious example; tormented by guilt and by lust, she loses all control of herself. Before Suzanne's arrival, the convent had been happy under her, because her passion was reciprocated by another nun. Suzanne's innocence frustrates the superior, who can not avoid the temptation; and Suzanne naively informs her director, whose instructions only aggravate the evil. The superior comes to be treated as Suzanne had been at Longchamp: the director orders Suzanne to regard her superior as Satan. Ultimately the woman is convinced of her own irreparable guilt, and passes through madness, sickness, to death. The evil does not die with her, however; Suzanne is accused of her death under the next superior, and the director, dom Morel, finds himself persecuted by his superiors as well. The unintentional pain which resulted from their virtuous reaction to the superior's homosexuality produces a second effect: dom Morel and Suzanne flee together in desperation, and he turns out to have sinful designs on her. Suzanne's innocence is a maddening temptation, not only for those with wicked intentions, but for the virtuous too. The first superior, Mme de Moni, has genuine affection for Suzanne in the most honorable sense. She undertakes to awaken a calling in Suzanne, but instead, Suzanne destroys Mme de Moni's faith. Her fate is hardly better than Suzanne's; she tells Suzanne, "Je suis lasse de vivre, je souhaite de mourir, j'ai demandé à Dieu de ne point voir ce jour, mais ce n'est pas sa volonté" (p. 260), and she tries by brutal self-maceration to win God's intercession for Suzanne, to no avail of course. Shortly after Suzanne takes her vows, Mme de Moni dies, having spent her last days in a state of agitation and doubt.

It would appear, then, that the monastic system and the social order behind it are absolutely corrupting. Even the virtuous Mme de Moni is destroyed by participating in it, when her conscience encounters the innocent victim, Suzanne Simonin. The attack on the society suffers, however, from the limitations in Suzanne's point of view, for her personal experience must necessarily be singular. The series of convents and superiors has struck most readers as implausible; clearly, Diderot hoped it would give more panoramic scope to his study of the convents. The criticism which Diderot wished to make could not be put in the mouth of Suzanne; she was not sophisticated enough, and moreover appears too modest to draw the general conclusions, which Diderot contrived to have her quote from Manouri's *Mémoire*. Suzanne's innocence made it hard to tell everything; her belated comprehension made it implausible to build suspense. The odd postscriptum seems to betray in part Diderot's worry that he had allowed Suzanne's subjectivity to taint the objective truths he wished to dramatize. Suzanne writes after rereading her *Mémoire*: "Je me suis aperçue que sans en avoir le moindre projet, je m'étais montrée à chaque ligne aussi malheureuse à la vérité que je l'étais, mais beaucoup plus aimable que je ne le suis" (p. 392). The novel's power to interest readers in a character had seemed to Diderot the most impressive of Richardson's qualities, and Diderot follows Richardson in using a first-person narrative, which invariably puts the character at the center. Diderot's uneasiness about *La Religieuse* was well founded, however. To a very large extent, the identification of readers with Suzanne accomplishes the goal of exposing the vices of convents; but at the same time, her perspective usurps the broader perspective, and defeats the goal of a general attack on the system. Since Diderot was by nature more drawn to the general analysis, it may be fairly supposed that he felt dissatisfied with the narrow first-person narration, and in his later works, examined ways of reintroducing the author's perspective alongside the character's.

Voltaire never admitted to any esteem for the novel as a genre. His own practice of fiction was entirely utilitarian; he needed to reach a wide audience. Inasmuch as his primary purpose was always to effect social changes, the non-fictional elements often overshadow the fiction in a Voltairean tale. Even in the best balanced, moreover, the author gives little evidence of trying to win strong sympathy or identification for his characters. The hero of a Voltairean tale is Voltaire; Candide, Micromegas, Zadig, and Hercule the Ingénu come under his satirical scrutiny as much as anyone else. To the extent that Diderot's definition of what he calls the "conteur historique" applies to the novelist, Voltaire is not a novelist, but a "conteur plaisant," like La Fontaine. The "conteur historique" descends from Scarron and Cervantes (as writers of *nouvelles,* not *romans comiques*), and "il veut être cru: il veut intéresser, toucher, entraîner, émouvoir, faire frissonner la peau et couler les larmes" (p. 791). Voltaire is more concerned to get a laugh. *L'Ingénu,* however, constitutes a partial exception to that description. It begins very much like *Candide* or *Zadig,* with the narrator standing well above the action and exercising full freedom of omniscience, and, one might add, omnipotence. At the end, though, Voltaire apparently wishes to build some genuine sympathy for Mlle de St. Yves, who allows herself to be raped by St. Pouange to save the Ingénu's life. The shift in style is very noticeable; the short, action-filled sentences give way to long, abstract, and sentiment-filled sentences. The ironic undercutting disappears. Thus, at least in this one work, Voltaire's fiction can be compared to that of other novelists.

Although the action is set in late seventeenth-century France, the society of *L'Ingénu* is obviously of Voltaire's own day, just as it is in *Zadig.* Voltaire concentrates on two institutions, the Church and the state, which possess all the power. As in the other cases, this power is abused; real merit, like the Ingénu's military service, is ignored, while the demands of the Jesuits and bureaucrats are met. When the Ingénu goes to Versailles to seek some recompense for his service, he can not even see the king, and his reward is to be allowed to purchase a rank in the army. He is imprisoned in the Bastille for having sympathized with the persecuted Huguenots and for having annoyed the bailiff, whose son hoped to marry Mlle de St. Yves. The Ingénu's unexpected reception is basically comic, however, because Voltaire underscores the absurdity by such statements as this protest of the Ingénu's: "Moi! que je donne de l'argent pour avoir repoussé les Anglais? Que je paie le droit de me faire tuer pour vous, pendant que vous donnez ici vos audiances tranquillement? Je crois que vous voulez rire."[26]

[26] Voltaire, *L'Ingénu,* ed. William R. Jones, Textes Littéraires Français (Genève: Librairie Droz and Paris: Librairie Minard, 1957), p. 119.

The Individual against Society

Mlle de St. Yves is received no more favorably at Versailles, when she comes to plead for the Ingénu's release. M. de St. Pouange offers to free her fiancé "si elle commençait par lui donner les prémices de ce qu'elle réservait à son amant" (p. 151). Society, represented by a Jesuit confessor and one of his penitents, advises Mlle de St. Yves to accept the bargain. To Voltaire, sexual fidelity was a rather ridiculous virtue, and in *Cosi-Sancta*, the heroine does three times what Mlle de St. Yves refuses to do, and is none the worse for it. It was not therefore the act itself, but the abuse of authority that outraged Voltaire. The society was full of men who exploited their positions and the powers entrusted to them for the basest of motives. In relating the Ingénu's troubles, Voltaire provoked amused scorn; with Mlle de St. Yves, he hoped to arouse some anger.

As was often the case, Voltaire singled out the most absurd laws and abuses. The Church, his favorite target, bears the blame for the rule by which a godmother may not marry her godson; lack of foresight and ignorance led Mlle de St. Yves to serve as the Ingénu's godmother, and thus their marriage is blocked. This incident furnishes a pretext for the plot. The laws against the Huguenots, the use of police spies, the venality of offices—all these quasi-legal abuses crop up. It is clear that Voltaire accumulates for effect. On the other side, it is not easy to identify an enlightened group. The Ingénu represents common sense, but in the beginning he lacks the discipline of sound law. Mlle de St. Yves is simple and virtuous, but her naiveté is not a positive quality. The people of Basse-Bretagne as a whole are kindly, but ignorant and superstitious. In prison with Gordon, the Jansenist, the Ingénu acquires an education in the European sense, and emerges as a truly reasonable man—not only in tune with nature's laws, but aware of man's, and willing to settle for the possible short of perfection. In *L'Ingénu* as in *Candide*, although there is little doubt what Voltaire disapproves, there is considerable doubt about what he advocates. Rousseau, Diderot, and even Prévost have a sharper vision of the better society than Voltaire, who seeks mainly to eliminate one by one the imperfections he sees in the existing society.

The conflict between the Ingénu and society grows out of the ban on his marriage. Voltaire then amuses himself by adding obstruction on obstruction. By the time Mlle de St. Yves enters the battle, the subject of dispute has advanced far beyond the original pretext. On all the substantive points, the Ingénu speaks for nature and reason, while society operates by foolish or corrupt customs and laws. The Ingénu is an ambiguous figure, however, and he does receive an education. He thereby resembles Gil Blas and the older traditions in fiction. Mlle de St. Yves, on the other hand, is a simple victim. The Ingénu is frustrated in his ambitions and disappointed in his expectations, but the integrity of his inner self remains unmolested. St. Pouange violates this most sacred part of Mlle de St. Yves's being, forcing her to be untrue to herself. Diderot had dramatized the same conflict in *La Religieuse*. Frustrations and even confinement are not the real evil, but only the means by which the human soul can be destroyed.

The Ingénu, of course, runs afoul of justice and is imprisoned. He had no trial; but Voltaire's omniscience enables him to lay bare the mechanisms of justice anyway. Thus in one paragraph, Voltaire says that Louis XIV's confessor received a letter from his spy, while Louvois received one from the bailiff. In the next paragraph, the police burst into the Ingénu's room and haul him away to the Bastille. Much later, St. Pouange shows the accusing letters to Mlle de St. Yves, who exclaims, " . . . et c'est sur de pareils avis qu'on décide ici de la destinée des citoiens." She reacts in the same way to St. Pouange's offer to issue a *lettre de cachet* against her brother: "On est donc bien libéral de Lettres de cachet dans vos bureaux. . . ." (p. 151). Voltaire's selective use of detail and point of view heighten the impression that the administration of justice is purely arbitrary.

Voltaire's third-person narration is thus a great advantage in the presentation of his theme. As the need arises, the reader is transported into the prison cell, the confessional, and the seducer's bedroom. No piece of cynicism or hypocrisy, no machination or ulterior motive can elude the narrator. Where he deems it necessary, he can instruct about the deeper causes: "St. Pouange n'était point né méchant; le torrent des affaires et des amusements avaient emporté son ame qui ne se connaissait pas encor" (p. 178), he writes of the villain near the conclusion. Thus he attributes more responsibility to society than one could demonstrate from the evidence of the novel. There is a decided loss of personal involvement with the hero and heroine, yet even that is not necessary. The most original element in *L'Ingénu* is not the wide-ranging omniscient narrator, but the self-limiting narrator who tries to involve the reader in Mlle de St. Yves's humiliation. To do so, he has to put aside his scorn for chastity, his own masculine concupiscence, his sophistication, and his detached wit, and he has to adopt Mlle de St. Yves's attitudes and some of her style. The point of view stays close to Mlle de St. Yves's; the language becomes evasive out of shame.

Voltaire did not care enough for the novel to consider this discovery worth pursuing. Other novelists did, including Diderot. The ambitions of writers were outgrowing the possibilities they recognized in the first-person devices. First-person narration had provided them with the necessary reader involvement, and it had made possible great progress in realistic representation. It did not offer much opportunity for the exploration of the outside world, or to explore the private experience of the hero's opposition, whether it be an impersonal society or a diabolical individual.

The older technique had served adequately, even brilliantly, so long as the society in question was viewed with admiration. Then the hero could speak from within it, possessing the expert knowledge of an initiate, reflecting on his or another's experiences as a neophyte. With increasing criticism of society, this technique grew less and less manageable. The four novels just examined all take a reformist but not revolutionary stance in the end; Des Grieux returns from America resolving to do better, Suzanne Simonin remains pious after her escape, *La Nouvelle Héloïse* proposes a method of personal reform, St. Pouange repents and the Ingénu becomes a useful citizen after the tragedy. This no doubt has some connection to the tendency for the victims to be the heroines. The deaths of Manon, Julie, and Mlle de St. Yves, and the imminent threat to Suzanne Simonin, call for pity, not revenge. The last stage will bring forth a more desperate group of works. The picture of society leaves no hope of reform, and while there is no explicit suggestion of a revolutionary change, the state of corruption is such that this would seem to be the only possibility.

Diderot's Tales, Laclos: Revolt

The last years before the French Revolution produced no stunning new developments, only a growing sense of lassitude and discontent. France's political and economic troubles grew more and more severe, but the entrenched order resisted most efforts at readjustment. Thus the structure of society in 1780 was essentially the same as it had been in 1730. In the meantime, the abuses of power had deepened the resentment of the less privileged classes, and the uppermost classes had lost all sense of responsibility for the general welfare of the nation. In the 1760's, several incidents signaled the victory of the *philosophes*: after having been banned, the *Encyclopédie* was completed; the Jesuits were expelled from France by the Parlements; Calas was rehabilitated legally, after a vigorous publicity campaign by Voltaire. The conquest of public opinion did not mean immediate reforms, however, so that the little group of immensely rich, irresponsible, powerful nobles and parasites stayed on top, in ever greater isolation from the rest of the population.

It has often been said that Rousseau's *La Nouvelle Héloïse* conferred letters of nobility on the novel, theretofore disdained as a frivolous genre. *La Nouvelle Héloïse* was indisputably popular, and reached a new public. Furthermore, it was imitated widely for several decades. On the other hand, almost none of the imitations has survived until today. The most interesting fiction of these waning years was written in reaction against Rousseau's influence. The hack writers and the general public, cheapening Rousseau's ideas, seemed to think that copious displays of sentimentality would reconcile man and society. A new anti-realism took over, typified by such writers as Marmontel, Baculard d'Arnaud, and Bernardin de St.-Pierre, who valued fiction only for its edifying ability. Morality was interpreted as a simplistic application of poetic justice—the good were rewarded and the wicked punished. Providence ruled over the affairs of their fictional worlds, although, in setting up the twists of plot, they unwittingly implied as perverse a providence as the marquis de Sade himself could have wished. One novel stands out in this period for its icy clarity of vision: Laclos's *Les Liaisons dangereuses* (1782). Some of Diderot's tales, written during the 1770's for the most part, bear strong resemblance to Laclos's novel. These will serve as the major documents of the final phase in the eighteenth-century novel's examination of man in relation to his society.

Since historically there had been little change, it is not surprising that the fictional societies of Diderot and Laclos are much the same as those of earlier periods—the wealthy upper-class Parisians. If there has been any change, it is that the laws and customs are more arbitrary, and the exercise of power more naked. The élite has almost disappeared. The representatives of virtue and reason who figure in the stories are usually crushed; within the novel, they find no allies inside the circles of power. As a consequence, the author's interest in the hero has diminished—or perhaps it is more accurate to say that the notion of hero has altered. The prestigious characters in these works tend to be villainous—Mme de Merteuil, Valmont, La Reymer, Mme de la Carlière, Mme de la Pommeraye. They have defeated society by completely mastering its rules and cynically exploiting them to satisfy their personal ambitions. Even when the author sees fit to destroy such characters at the end, they die unrepentant.

The moral import of these works is negative; they expose evil, but they stop short of recommending any particular virtue. Laclos states very directly that his moral purpose is to open the eyes of his readers, and his title carries the message: danger!

For both Diderot and Laclos, society itself is an active force in the story, and they thus make it clear that they hold society responsible.

The simple first-person narration was not adequate for this kind of theme. The subject has grown more complex, since it is the society rather than the individual; therefore no single figure can have the necessary breadth and depth of knowledge. Laclos overcomes this problem by his use of the epistolary form; *Les Liaisons dangereuses* is in fact the only epistolary novel where the advantages of the form are fully utilized and the disadvantages completely avoided. The multiplicity of opinions and impressions is perfectly rendered by the various letters; but more important for the novel's success, the letters themselves constitute a significant action within the fictional society. They are documents from that society, not a narrative device. Diderot prefers to use a third-person narrative form. The principal narrator has extensive privileged information, a wide knowledge of society, and objectivity. Often the narrator seems to be Diderot himself. For both authors, the need to have such various inside views arose from the nature of their characters. They are now secretive, exceptional; the classical psychological analysis does not apply to them, and they would not under normal circumstances willingly publish their memoirs. In his preface to Diderot's tales Jacques Proust quotes the marquis d'Argens, asking that novelists seek out the "causes cachées des actions";[27] that is just what Diderot and Laclos attempt, but they must find a new device to pry into those secrets and a new pretext to bring their results to light.

Among Diderot's tales, the three which best illustrate the mood of this period are *Ceci n'est pas un conte* (ca. 1772), *Madame de la Carlière* (ca. 1772), and the tale of Mme de la Pommeraye, which is told by the hostess in *Jacques le fataliste* (1773-74?). *Les Deux Amis de Bourbonne* (1770) has more in common with earlier works; I will mention it, but most of my remarks refer only to the first three. All of them

[27] Diderot, *Quatre Contes*, ed. Jacques Proust, Textes Littéraires Français (Genève: Librairie Droz, 1964), p. xxvi.

use the typical Parisian society characters, although *Ceci n'est pas un conte* descends into the bohemian circles for the true story of Gardeil and Mlle de la Chaux. Even this anecdote is related to the others, however, by its theme, which is the unnatural constraint on human freedom posed by vows of fidelity, especially in marriage. Obviously, *La Religieuse* touched on the same question indirectly. In each of the three tales— twice in *Ceci n'est pas un conte*—a couple forms out of mutual attraction; they swear the conventional vows of fidelity; one partner gradually ceases to love as he or she had at the start, and the other must respond somehow to this betrayal.

It is not immediately evident from the plot summary that society is implicated, but Diderot emphasizes the social element in the details. The pathos of Mlle de la Chaux's predicament derives from the fact that she had sacrificed her reputation and even her freedom to Gardeil:

> Mais j'oublie un de ses premiers malheurs; c'est la persécution qu'elle eut à souffrir d'une famille indignée d'un attachement public et scandaleux. On employa et la vérité et le mensonge pour disposer de sa liberté d'une manière infamante. Ses parents et les prêtres la poursuivirent de quartier en quartier, de maison en maison, et la réduisirent plusieurs années à vivre seule et cachée.[28]

Mme de la Carlière and Desroches swear their vows before "un cercle nombreux, composé des deux familles et d'un certain nombre d'amis" (p. 818), and she reassembles the same group to announce the termination of their marriage. Mme de la Pommeraye obtains a suitable revenge on Des Arcis by tricking him into marriage with a former prostitute —that is, by disgracing him socially.

In Diderot's opinion, as explained in the *Supplément au Voyage de Bougainville*, also written in the early 1770's, the social conditions surrounding relations between the sexes were contrary to nature. The hypothetical society of Tahiti provides a sharp contrast; sexual unions there are temporary, with mutual pleasure the only object, and reproduction a de-

[28] Diderot, *Œuvres romanesques*, p. 802.

sirable fringe benefit. Mme de la Carlière's gesture, of surrounding herself with witnesses to the ceremonial vows, most clearly illustrates society's hurtful intrusion into this private realm. Tanié, although he labors hardest perhaps and is most callously deceived by La Reymer, is probably the happiest of these characters, because he never knows the truth. That is to say that the needs of love can be more easily gratified than those of pride, and society has entangled the two emotions. Again, it is Mme de la Carlière who best demonstrates this. Desroches did make love to another woman; yet there were extenuating circumstances, and he continued to love his wife. Mme de la Carlière pushes her resentment too far, even in the opinion of her friends; but in the beginning they had enthusiastically joined in witnessing her oath: " . . . permettez que s'il arrive que vous me donniez quelques sujets légitimes de me plaindre, je vous dénonce à ce tribunal et vous livre à son indignation. Consentez qu'ils se rassemblent à ma voix et qu'ils vous appellent traître, ingrat, perfide, homme faux, homme méchant. . . ." (p. 821). Their error lies not in tolerating violations, but in encouraging the delusion that such absolute standards were possible in human conduct. The same excessive pride prompts Mme de la Pommeraye in her cold-blooded plot.

To be sure, the rights and wrongs are hard to assess. For every good Tanié and heartless Reymer, there is an ungrateful Gardeil and a desolate Mlle de la Chaux. Mme de la Carlière's pride brings her no satisfaction; eventually she dies, after a series of misfortunes. Mme de la Pommeraye, on the other hand, seems to come through her humiliation and her revenge unscathed. Desroches suffers deeply as a result of Mme de la Carlière's refusal to see him, while Des Arcis thwarts Mme de la Pommeraye's revenge by overcoming his own pride and accepting Mlle d'Aisnon as his beloved wife. To Diderot this confusion of rights and wrongs suggests that the system itself is at fault. The laws and codes by which emotions like love are judged do not allow for the ambiguity of human beings. Mlle de la Chaux was no doubt ill-advised to be seduced by Gardeil and foolish to go on loving an ingrate, and Gardeil was certainly ungrateful and heartless to abandon her; but the worst of the situation is that society insists on the relationship's being permanent and ostracizes the woman who is deceived. To this extent, the revenges of Mme de la Carlière and Mme de la Pommeraye are justifiable as defenses of the oppressed sex. Still, Diderot deplores the fate of Mlle de la Chaux, but he does not advocate turning the tables. A wiser solution would discourage either partner from expecting total possession of the other. If women were less penalized and handicapped, if men were less burdened with obligations, freer and happier couples might result.

The story of Mme de la Carlière is so obviously directed at society rather than at either of the main characters, that Diderot's friend Naigeon gave it the title *Sur l'inconséquence du jugement public de nos actions particulières*. The crowd of friends egg Mme de la Carlière on when she and Desroches make their rash vows, and they fail to set things right when she calls on them to carry out their pledge. Their failure to grasp the human complexities continues to aggravate the situation. At first they console Desroches, and blame themselves for having been taken in by Mme de la Carlière's "sublime momerie." For a time, public opinion decrees Mme de la Carlière "une folle à enfermer," but then as her melancholy progresses, she becomes "La pauvre Madame de la Carlière!" Desroches's discretion in all his gestures and efforts at reconciliation is taken as a sign of indifference; all his wife's misfortunes are blamed on him, including her death. At the moment when the story is narrated, the public regards Desroches as "un barbare, un inhumain . . . une bête féroce." The narrator, however, knows the truth; he foresees in the near future that "la chose sera vue telle qu'elle est, Mme de la Carlière accusée et Desroches absous." Finally, the narrator appraises Desroches's character according to the events of the story and finds him a good man. Then he concludes: "Et puis j'ai mes idées, peut être justes, à coup sûr bizarres, sur certaines actions que je regarde moins comme des vices de l'homme que comme des conséquences de nos législations absurdes, sources de mœurs aussi absurdes qu'elles et d'une dépravation que j'appellerais volontiers artificielle" (p. 828-35). The explanation of this enigmatic sentence can be found in the *Supplément au Voyage de Bougainville*.

Thus the narrator's superior knowledge and detachment permit him to revise the false judgment of those who were there and fix the causes of the trouble on society, the very group so busily occupied in blaming Desroches. The story of Mme de la Pommeraye calls for less running analysis, since the plot hangs on suspense, not irony. At the end, however, the Hostess, Jacques, and the Master discuss the characters, blaming Mme de la Pommeraye. The main narrator of *Jacques* intervenes then to speak directly to the reader in Mme de la Pommeraye's defense. As in the case of Mme de la Carlière, he emphasizes the social considerations. Mme de la Pommeraye's bitterness was intensified by the affront to her vanity: "Elle avait remarqué autour d'elle les souris ironiques; elle avait entendu les plaisanteries, et souvent elle en avait rougi et baissé les yeux." Thus again Diderot seems to blame society for the monstrous actions of individuals. In order to make such an accusation, the narrator must have total knowledge of Mme de la Pommeraye's soul, and he does not hesitate to claim it: "Sa vengeance est atroce; mais elle n'est souillée d'aucun motif d'intéret. On ne vous a pas dit qu'elle avait jeté au nez du marquis le beau diamant dont il lui avait fait présent; mais elle le fit: je le sais par les voies les plus sûres" (pp. 651-52). He explains no farther how he knew, and no one asks. The imagination of the author can now go to war against society on behalf of all the inarticulate, confused, and reticent victims.

The society of *Les Liaisons dangereuses* descends directly from that of Duclos, Crébillon, and Challe. The dandified young rakes dominate at first glance, by their flamboyant style; but the flirtatious and impenetrable women have their own strength, based on their greater skill at the arts of self-control and deception. Appearances count for everything among the followers of fashion. One's reputation is a priceless factor in success, and any competitor for the leading roles must be proficient at advertising himself. Valmont is of course the master, a disciple of Versac who has surpassed his teacher. Valmont, however, for all his prestige, is already a literary type. Laclos tears the mask off an almost entirely new creation in Mme de Merteuil, who plays the same game as Valmont, but with the disadvantages inherent in a woman's role in society. Valmont displays himself, if not on the stage at the Comédie (spectators had been banned in 1759) like Jacob and d'Orsan, at least in the loges. Mme de Merteuil has to insure silence around her exploits, and indeed, she acts the role of a *dévote* while living clandestinely the life of a libertine. Whether the reputation be false or true, however, is ultimately less significant than the fact that public opinion counts for so much.

Alongside this artificial society there persists a small élite, believers in virtue and sentiment. Mme de Tourvel not only preaches but practices this Rousseauistic form of morality. Her devotion to chastity is sincere, but so too is her confidence in the voice of nature, speaking through the senses. The other members of the society pay lip-service to this virtuous way of life, but do not follow their own advice. Crébillon had felt it necessary to explain why a reasonable woman like Mme de Meilcour continued to receive a vapid fop like Versac; his reasons still apply to Mme de Volanges. If Mme de Volanges mistrusts the notorious Valmont, she sees nothing wrong in delivering her innocent daughter to Gercourt, who at one time frequented the same ladies as Valmont. The supposedly virtuous leaders of society do more than tolerate the Valmonts, they contribute to their prestige and success.

Laclos demonstrates brilliantly, moreover, that even their apparent nostalgia for virtue is a fraud. They want only the superficial appearances of virtue. One can not be too critical of Mme de Volanges for failing to detect the hypocrisy of Mme de Merteuil, a master of the art. Her conventional education of Cécile, however—that is, to lock her in a convent for fifteen years—leaves the girl unprepared for the ruses even of the infamous Valmont. Mme de Tourvel is the most gullible of all; Valmont toys with her notions of sincerity by writing a love letter which is an extended double entendre, and subverts her judgment entirely by feigning a single act of charity. Rousseau had complacently imagined that a passionate style like Julie's was beyond the talents of a Parisian fop; Valmont's letter seems to be a deliberate refutation. Mme de Tourvel relates the story of Valmont's almsgiving in the commonplace language of the moralists of that time: "Quoi! les méchants partageraient-ils avec les bons le plaisir sacré de la bienfaisance? Dieu permettrait-il qu'une famille vertueuse reçût, de la main d'un scélérat, des secours dont elle rendrait grace à sa divine Providence? et pourrait-il se plaire à entendre des bouches pures répandre leurs bénédictions sur un réprouvé?"[29] The answer to all these questions is apparently affirmative. Whatever the role of Providence and God in human affairs, when humans attempt to judge the feelings and virtue of others—the poor family as well as Valmont—they risk errors. The new vogue of virtue had not deviated from the old worldly principle of judging on appearances. In such a society, whether one applauds virtue or vice, the greatest figures will be the greatest actors—Valmont and Mme de Merteuil.

The innocent victims—Cécile, Mme de Tourvel, Danceny —play a very secondary role in the novel. Cécile and Danceny can be compared to Marianne and Meilcour, as young people making their entry into the world. Instead of being educated, they are corrupted, seduced, debauched, finally depraved. Their naive conceptions of love and virtue prove to have no power over their adversaries on either side; Cécile can neither avoid Valmont nor reduce her mother's hostility to Danceny. Danceny succumbs to Mme de Merteuil and fails to win Cécile. The easy ruin of this young couple can be attributed to their wholly false beliefs about their society. They believe in Mme de Volanges's prattle about virtue; they believe that most members of their society practice it and respect it. They think, correctly, that they are ignorant, and they are eager to accept guidance; but they have been misled into thinking that this ignorance will protect them. The guidance they receive from the supposed defenders of virtue,

[29] Laclos, *Les Liaisons dangereuses*, p. 47.

such as Mme de Volanges, consists primarily of prolonging their ignorance and dependency. Into this vacuum of real guidance, Valmont and Mme de Merteuil bring superior knowledge and prestige. They meet no serious opposition with Cécile and Danceny. Valmont spends more time and energy on Mme de Tourvel, because she is more experienced and aware. Nonetheless his conquest takes only three months, and could have been faster had he not waited for total capitulation. Mme de Tourvel is caught in the trap of her own virtue. Valmont understands how much her virtue is a gratification of her pride; he therefore pretends to be one of her converts, and in a fine stroke of irony, summons Mme de Tourvel to the fatal rendezvous through the intermediary of a priest. None of the victims, in short, has been told the truth about society, especially about the nature of virtue. They have been trained to indulge their egos, just as Mme de Merteuil and Valmont do, but they have not been given the means. Instead, they have been taught to trust Providence.

If Marianne were to appear in Laclos's society, she too would probably be destroyed; her virtue, which makes such a strong impression on Marivaux's characters, would pass unnoticed by Laclos's. Marianne would in fact be overshadowed in the practice of virtue by her worst enemy, Mme de Merteuil. Marivaux depicts society as fundamentally desirous of welcoming the Mariannes into its midst. A Climal or a hostile cousin are exceptional, and they expose their purposes too brazenly. Marianne does not really struggle against society, but against a few members of it who do not represent the general attitudes. The evolving picture of society suggests that the struggles grew more and more intense, as the social codes grew more rigid. In any event, the real parallel to Marianne in *Les Liaisons dangereuses* is not Cécile, but Mme de Merteuil. The long letter 81 where Mme de Merteuil recounts her entry into the world recalls many of Marianne's comments. "Je me jouais de toutes les façons de plaire, je savais être plusieurs femmes en une," wrote Marianne; "Je m'amusais à me montrer sous des formes différentes," writes Mme de Merteuil.[30] Both women know by intuition that their

[30] ibid., p. 175; and Marivaux, *La Vie de Marianne*, p. 51.

only protection is to have complete control of their own appearance while seeing through the defensive poses of others. "Et moi, je devinais la pensée de toutes ces personnes-là sans aucun effort," noted Marianne at her first triumph, in the church; "Ce travail sur moi-même avait fixé mon attention sur l'expression des figures et le caractère des physionomies; et j'y gagnai ce coup d'œil pénétrant,"[31] explains Mme de Merteuil. Marianne would have the arms with which to defend herself; one can only speculate about whether her instinct for virtue would prevail over her ambition, or vice versa. Laclos's portrait of the heroine in society hardly differs from Marivaux's but Laclos has a different view of the society. The vague sense of emptiness which troubles the comtesse de *** has expanded into a fascinated horror. The intricate and graceful games of society now are revealed to cover over, but not to abolish, real anguish. Mme de Merteuil is no more a monster than Marianne; she is the perfect product of her society, the best fitted to survive under the laws she is forced to live by. These laws are all the natural laws of savage conflict; survival depends on eliminating the rival and devouring the victim. It was a subject calculated to appeal to General Laclos.

Laclos's moral has been debated ever since the book appeared. In the preface, a conventional aim of edification is professed, but this may be just a ritual disclaimer designed to disarm the censors. Readers have always been intrigued and to that extent seduced by the evil heroes; in Laclos's own time, he was accused of being a Valmont, and seeking to corrupt. Biographers have found little to support such a charge, and in fact all the biographical evidence would support taking the preface at face value. Laclos was a rather conventional person in his morals, and lived a more exemplary life as husband than the majority of his contemporaries. Within the work, the conclusion brings about the death of Valmont and the exile of Mme de Merteuil; evil is thus punished. One could counter by pointing out that Mme de Tourvel also dies,

---

[31] ibid., p. 175; and Marivaux, op. cit., p. 59.

and that Cécile and Danceny also suffer a kind of exile, so that the distribution of rewards and punishments hardly encourages virtue. Still worse, the fates of the innocent victims seem plausible, while the death of Valmont at Danceny's hands strikes one as unlikely, and Mme de Merteuil's sickness and lost lawsuit are coincidental. No simple answer can be given to the question of the moral lesson implied, but it would appear most satisfactory to assume that Laclos sincerely meant to expose the real corruption, and that part of his righteous indignation arose from the fact that in real life the villains were seldom punished.

If one looks closely at the conclusion, it is obvious that the unmasking of Valmont and Merteuil has had no effect on the society at all. The principal event in Mme de Merteuil's disgrace takes place on the most public of society's stages, the Comédie Italienne. The incident deserves to be quoted in full:

> Pour que rien ne manquât à son humiliation, son malheur voulut que M. de Prévan, qui ne s'était montré nulle part depuis son aventure, entrât dans le même moment dans le petit salon. Dès qu'on l'aperçut, tout le monde, hommes et femmes, l'entoura et l'applaudit; et il se trouva, pour ainsi dire, porté devant Mme de Merteuil, par le public qui faisait cercle autour d'eux. . . . M. de Prévan a été, le même soir, fort accueilli de tous ceux des officiers de son corps qui se trouvaient là, et on ne doute pas qu'on ne lui rende bientôt son emploi et son rang (p. 391).

Society adores the victor, and Laclos would surely endorse Diderot's contempt for public opinion. Prévan had been disgraced for a crime he did not commit, it is true; but he was in the process of trying to commit an equally heinous crime, the seduction of a virtuous woman. Before Mme de Merteuil beat him with his own weapons, he had been Valmont's principal rival as a formidable seducer. By reinstating Prévan, the public has guaranteed that Valmont's death was for nothing; a new Valmont is already flourishing before the novel ends, like the old one, with the enthusiastic applause of the silly crowd which condemns Mme de Merteuil. And who knows what innocent face and modest manner in that very crowd disguises another Mme de Merteuil?

Thus Laclos brings the crowd itself into the novel to express its judgment. In the last letter of the collection, Mme de Volanges proves that the evil survives. She relates to Mme de Rosemonde the witticisms of the marquis de *** on Mme de Merteuil's disgrace. She observes that the greatest scandal of all has been Mme de Merteuil's bankruptcy. And she laments the sacrifice she is making, in allowing her daughter to go into a convent as she desires, instead of into the arranged marriage with Gercourt. The same greed still drives Mme de Volanges, and she has learned no better ways for judging other people.

The final touch of irony in Laclos's picture of society comes from the courts. Mme de Merteuil has a lawsuit pending, which she describes in letter 113: "D'abord j'ai raison, tous mes avocats me l'assurent. Et quand je ne l'aurais pas, je serais donc bien maladroite, si je ne savais pas gagner un procès, où je n'ai pour adversaires que des mineures encore en bas âge, et leur vieux tuteur!" (p. 268). Justice itself belongs to the mighty. Of course, after her own disgrace, Mme de Merteuil loses her case, even though she was in the right: "Son procès a été jugé avant-hier, et elle l'a perdu tout d'une voix. Dépens, dommages et intérêts, restitution des fruits, tout a été adjugé aux mineurs" (p. 394). The court itself sways with the fickle moods of the public. The institution which ought in the last instance to uncover the truth and apply the most rigorous standards of morality has become venal and therefore as corrupt as the rest of society.

Laclos's pessimism goes beyond social criticism. When he quotes Rousseau's prefatory line, "J'ai vu les mœurs de ce siècle et j'ai publié ces lettres," as his own epigraph, Laclos invites comparison between the two works, and they are opposite in almost every respect. Most significantly, though, Rousseau believed that reforms could be made in society which would regenerate the citizens. *La Nouvelle Héloïse* illustrates some of the reforms in action at Clarens. Laclos nowhere gives any hint that either the individuals or the society might be modified. The best that a moralist could do was to warn the unwary. Perhaps Laclos did not conceive of this despair as a revolutionary analysis; yet it leaves no hope except the complete overthrow of the existing order.

— VI —

The Emergence of the Novel

From Scudéry's *Ibrahim* to Laclos's *Les Liaisons dangereuses* appears a very large span, not only because a century and a half separate the two works, but also because the works differ so radically from each other. Yet there is no moment within that span when a radical change occurs, to produce a permanent difference between the old fictions, now called romances, and the new, now called novels. Instead there is evolution, continuous, albeit at varying rates, throughout the period. If it seems that something entirely new arose, it is because the evolution at several times had the rapidity characteristic of literary golden ages. One such period occurred in the 1660's, when the *nouvelle* suddenly blossomed and replaced the long *roman*; another occurred in the 1730's, when the first-person forms of narration reached their peak. The literary forms and techniques were not new in either case, but individual authors of exceptional ability exploited the existing materials so as to realize their full potential.

In the particular historical period from 1641 to 1782, the general course of the evolution can be described as the application of a romance vision to wider and wider areas of contemporary reality. This will obviously create some correlation between advances in fictional techniques and social changes. It is not accurate, however, to state that the novel begins when authors attempt to describe "reality," and that it progresses as they try to describe more and more ordinary "realities." Every evidence indicates that, first, romance writers thought they were describing a type of reality not far distant from that of the novel, and second, writers of the earliest novels described (and perhaps saw) reality through the conventions of romance.

Social, intellectual, and political changes surely encouraged experimentation and exploration, but such factors give no ac-

348

count of the specific forms and contents of the "new" fictions. These depend almost entirely on the literary traditions, plus the occasional innovations of the genuinely exceptional authors. The literary traditions can be traced quite easily; the innovations are harder to pin down at the point of origin, but they survive and become part of the tradition whenever they succeed in pleasing readers. The emergence of the novel depended on readers' enjoying a persuasive portrayal of contemporary life. They did enjoy it in the late seventeenth century, and so responded favorably to the devices that constitute what we now term Realism. Readers of that age enjoyed many other things in fiction, too, and since the realistic novel had not been clearly defined as a special genre destined for future greatness, readers did not apparently mind having fantasy and adventure mixed in with realism on occasion. A clearcut distinction between novel and romance came about ultimately because the novel's unique power of illusion functions best when its realism is undisturbed by other elements.

The early theorists of "realism" in the seventeenth and eighteenth centuries seem to have approached the problem of describing reality in an abstract, rationalistic manner. Their arguments were always based on the idea that to be credible, a work of fiction must be able to exist in the same dimensions of reality as the reader. At first this took the form of Scudéry's historical romance, where real battles and important events provided a framework within which the novelist's imagination could work freely, so long as it did not contradict history. The readers' and authors' perceptions of plausibility were consistently ahead of the theories, however, and it was quickly obvious that Scudéry's theory did not suffice to guarantee a realistic fiction. Later theorists refined and modified Scudéry's precepts, but without abandoning his fundamental rationalism. Critics and authors isolated many specific technical problems and achieved progress in most, but the narrator proved to be an insuperable obstacle and eventually monopolized everyone's attention. Thus, the efforts of authors to apply the literal prescriptions of the theorists led to an impasse, which explains in some measure the generally declining trend in quality during the late eighteenth century.

The technical flaws in the best eighteenth-century novels occur most often not because the author was clumsy, nor even because he was unaware of other ways of treating his subject, but because some artistic principle restricted his freedom to use all the available resources. Obviously, I do not mean to suggest that if no theories had been present, all eighteenth-century novels would have been perfect. But I think it is true that most writers, even rather poor ones, set out to write about their theme, not to illustrate the perfection of some abstract literary form. In many cases, the themes simply did not fit very well into the forms allowed the eighteenth-century novelist, and the authors made do as best they could, sometimes with comically awkward results.

At the same time, talented authors whose themes fit well within the forms produced good novels, despite minor incidental lapses. Perfect congruences of theme and form are rare; I myself would cite only *Manon Lescaut* and *Les Liaisons dangereuses* among eighteenth-century French novels as being nearly perfect in this respect. The reason for this poverty is obvious: the novel, like other genres, was severely limited by its rules, while the ambitions of the serious authors ranged widely.

Literary forms may then exercise a limiting influence on the themes and subjects of a given era, but I doubt that they exercise much creative force. Periods of creativity seem to occur when the themes exceed the capacities of the forms; such was the case in the 1660's, when the long epic form failed to provide a vehicle for realism or for intense analysis of emotions; such was the case again in the 1730's, when the desire for realism conflicted with the rules of propriety; and such was the case in the early nineteenth century, after the first-person narrative failed to allow the probing of isolated and eccentric characters and the bold reconstruction of society. On the other hand, the availability of most of Realism's techniques and theories did not inspire much good work in the first two decades of the eighteenth century.

Although the forms and the themes obey laws that are to some degree independent of each other, there will undeniably be some mutual influence as well. The intellectual movements that subtend realism in art, such as empiricism, individualism, and rejection of authority, pervade all areas of eighteenth-century history. The novel absorbed as much of the current as it could bear, and it was quite a lot, more than the tradition-bound genres like poetry and drama, at least. The pressure to include more must have exerted some force for change; that is surely a reasonable inference from the last part of this study. Rousseau, Voltaire, Diderot, and Laclos were determined first and foremost to communicate their ideas; it happened that the existing forms of the novel could not quite accommodate them, and so as novelists they went just a bit beyond the common practice. In so doing, they were preparing for a dramatic change, albeit unintentionally. To that extent, I believe that the historical and sociological approach may be valid as an explanation of literary evolution.

On another level of interaction, a work of literature is in some sense a piece of knowledge, a statement of a discovered truth. The fundamental assumptions of an age with a regard to truth and reality will no doubt affect its attitudes toward the forms of its art. The crisis of self-doubt in the late seventeenth century carried over into the novel through the assumed kinship between fiction and history. It is not therefore purely a matter of coincidence that the novel becomes an instrument ideally suited for a subversive critique of the individual's place in society. The same intellectual biases that presided over the rules for the novel informed the thought of most of the century; and novels like *Cleveland* and *Clarissa* surely contributed to the formation of thinkers like Rousseau and Diderot. Here again, I recognize a real influence of society on the genre.

Neither sort of influence justifies attributing the dominant role to social factors, however, and it is particularly misleading to suppose that a new aesthetic appetite called a new genre into existence. The genre existed before the influence was exerted upon it, and the social influences applied to Scudéry in 1641 as well as to Richardson in 1740. I have tried in the preceding pages to show that, in the literary sense at least, there was great continuity throughout the period. This particular evolutionary trail does not, to be sure, explain the whole history of the novel. It does provide at least a basis for it, by establishing a coherent pattern that links not only technique to technique and theme to theme, but also connects the pedantic rules of Scudéry to the revolutionary themes of Laclos.

Index

353

Index

Index

Index

Index

Index

Index

Index

Index

Index

Index

Index

Index

Index

Index

Index

comic novel, 33, 82; criticism of Cervantes, 91, 93; geography, 149; illusion, 83; in *Manon*, 156; in Marivaux, 142; in Prévost, 147-48; money, 158, 161; names, 168; serious fiction, 125; techniques, 192; theory of Congreve, 21-22; theory of Clara Reeve, 24

Romanciers du XVIIe siècle, 46n; Adam's introduction quoted, 86, 113-14; novels quoted from, 46, 94, 95, 99-101, 103-104, 106-107, 112-17

Romanciers du XVIIIe siècle, 18n; novels quoted from, 18, 41, 50, 141, 276-81, 298-99

romanesque, 33, 55, 64, 84, 149, 174

Romans, see Marivaux

Romanticism, 137-38, 173, 279, 305

Rougemont, Denis de, 236

Rousseau, Jean-Jacques, 9, 62, 351; and Challe, 259-60; and Diderot, 121, 323-24; and Laclos, 341-42, 346; and Lesage, 278; and Prévost, 138; and Voltaire, 331-32; as reader, 71, 351; theme of the individual and society, 265, 300-306
  Les Confessions: 301, 316, 319, 322n
  Discours sur l'inégalité: 71
  Du contrat social: 319
  Emile: 9
  Nouvelle Héloïse: 38-39, 69n, 71, 316n, 334-35; and *Gil Blas*, 278; and *Illustres Françoises*, 259-60; and *Ingénu*, 333-34; and *Liaisons dangereuses*, 342, 346; authority figures, 266; chronology, 144-45; geography, 152; illusion, 59, 80; names, 168; narrator, 169, 189; techniques,

65; theme of the individual and society, 301-306, 316-22
  Profession de foi d'un vicaire savoyard: 302
  Rêveries d'un promeneur solitaire: 316, 322

Rousset, Jean, 87, 171-75, 179-80, 188, 192

rules, 27, 29, 126, 174, 350; in Challe's sequel to *Don Quixote*, 119; in *Effets suprenans de la sympathie*, 117; in *Jacques le fataliste*, 123; in *Roman bourgeois*, 114-15; in *Roman comique*, 85; theory of Scudéry, 127

Rustaing de Saint-Jory, Louis, 41, 60

Rustin, J., 37

Sacy, de, 26, 62

Sade, 335

Saint-Evremond, 162, 203

Sand, George, 4

Sartre, 171

satire, 39, 41, 106-107, 162, 269

Scarron, Paul, 4, 82, 126; and Challe, 120; and Diderot, 90, 104; and Furetière, 104, 113-15; and Marivaux, 96; *nouvelle*, 33, 123, 329-30
  Roman comique: 5, 33, 46n, 86; and Challe, 202; and *Jacques le fataliste*, 122; and *Roman bourgeois*, 113-14; chronology, 94-95, 98, 131-32; comic novel, 85; geography, 100; names, 103, 164; narrator, 80, 112-13, 117; realism, 82, 85; *roman*, 13
  Suite d'Offray: 86, 94, 164
  Virgile travesti: 82

Scherer, Jacques, 174

Scudéry, Georges de, 30, 133, 348-49, 352; *Ibrahim ou l'illustre Bassa*, 14, 22, 129, 348; preface to

Index

Index

Index